Liberalism as U

Liberalism as Utopia challenges widespread perceptio̶ ̶ ̶ ̶ ̶ ̶̶ ̶ ̶u̶s̶ ̶o̶f̶ ̶M̶e̶x̶i̶c̶o̶'s̶ nineteenth-century state. Schaefer argues that after the War of Independence non-elite Mexicans – peasants, day laborers, artisans, local merchants – pioneered an egalitarian form of legal rule by serving in the town governments and civic militias that became the local faces of the state's coercive authority. These institutions were effective because they embodied patriarchal norms of labor and care for the family that were premised on the legal equality of adult, male citizens. The book also examines the emergence of new, illiberal norms that challenged the egalitarianism of the early republican period and, at the end of the century, overwhelmed it. By comparing the legal cultures of agricultural estates, mestizo towns, and indigenous towns, *Liberalism as Utopia* proposes a new way of understanding the social foundations of liberal and authoritarian pathways to state formation in the nineteenth century.

Timo H. Schaefer received his PhD in history from Indiana University. Between 2015 and 2017, he was a postdoctoral fellow at the University of British Columbia.

Liberalism as Utopia

The Rise and Fall of Legal Rule in Post-Colonial
Mexico, 1820–1900

TIMO H. SCHAEFER

CAMBRIDGE
UNIVERSITY PRESS

CAMBRIDGE
UNIVERSITY PRESS

University Printing House, Cambridge CB2 8BS, United Kingdom

One Liberty Plaza, 20th Floor, New York, NY 10006, USA

477 Williamstown Road, Port Melbourne, VIC 3207, Australia

314-321, 3rd Floor, Plot 3, Splendor Forum, Jasola District Centre, New Delhi - 110025, India

79 Anson Road, #06-04/06, Singapore 079906

Cambridge University Press is part of the University of Cambridge.

It furthers the University's mission by disseminating knowledge in the pursuit of
education, learning and research at the highest international levels of excellence.

www.cambridge.org
Information on this title: www.cambridge.org/9781316640784
DOI: 10.1017/9781108116145

First published 2017
First paperback edition 2019

A catalogue record for this publication is available from the British Library

ISBN 978-1-107-19073-3 Hardback
ISBN 978-1-316-64078-4 Paperback

For Allison. For our little history.

Contents

Acknowledgments

If historical research were financed on the expectation that it turn a profit, we would know little about the past. The research and writing of this book have been supported by an International Dissertation Research Fellowship from the Social Sciences Research Council (USA); a Dissertation Completion Fellowship from the Indiana University College of Arts and Sciences; a Summer Field Research Grant from the Indiana University Center for Latin American and Caribbean Studies; and Doctoral and Postdoctoral Fellowships from the Social Sciences and Humanities Research Council (Canada). I am grateful to those institutions and to the publics behind them. I must emphasize the indispensability of the support I received from the Social Sciences and Humanities Research Council, which partly funded my doctoral studies and rescued me from academic homelessness in the two years afterward, allowing me to both begin and complete the work on this book.

In writing this book I have depended on documentation safeguarded in Mexican historical archives. The Archivo General del Estado de Guanajuato, Archivo Municipal de Guanajuato, Archivo Histórico Municipal de León, Archivo Histórico del Estado de San Luis Potosí, Archivo Municipal de Ciudad Fernández, Archivo Municipal de Rioverde, Casa de la Cultura Jurídica de San Luis Potosí, Archivo Histórico Judicial de Querétaro, Archivo General de la Nación, Archivo Histórico Judicial (de Oaxaca), and Archivo Municipal de Teposcolula are documentary conservatories that must be the envy of scholars of other post-colonial nations. I am grateful to the staff of those archives, who have been welcoming and professional in equal measure. I must also thank Inocencio Noyola, director of the Casa de la Cultura Jurídica of San Luis Potosí, for introducing me to the Casa's archival holdings, and to María de la Luz Carregha Lamadrid for giving me access to the municipal archives-in-construction of Rioverde and Ciudad Fernández, then under her care.

I would like to thank friends and colleagues who aided me while I conducted my research. Sergio Cañedo Gamboa and Flor de María Salazar Mendoza,

Amorita and Abraham Rasgado, and Chris and Sarah Woolley offered me hospitality in San Luis Potosí and Mexico City. Flor and Sergio also oriented me in the archives and the historiography of San Luis Potosí and gave me personal copies of valuable, hard-to-find studies. José Alfredo Rangel Silva, by lending me his photocopies of historical documents that had disappeared from view during an archival reorganization, helped me assemble the evidentiary base of Chapter 3 of this book.

This book has benefited from the insights of early discussants and readers. I owe thanks to Raúl Gatica for years of argument about the ideas I grapple with in the pages that follow; to Max Cameron, Agustín Goenaga, Chris Moore, Anjali Vithayathil, and Chris Woolley for commenting on parts of the manuscript-in-progress; and to Marc Antone and Eddie Brudney for reading several versions of several chapters, improving them little by little. A few people have commented on all of the manuscript: Bill French, Allison Schaefer, and the extraordinary members of my dissertation committee at Indiana University: Jeff Gould, Danny James, Jason McGraw, and Rebecca Spang. At Cambridge University Press I could count on the support of Debbie Gershenowitz, Matthew Restall, and Kris Lane, on the forceful interventions of James Sanders and a second reviewer, and on the sharp-eyed suggestions of my copy-editor, Jay Boggis. I am thankful to all those readers. For the weaknesses of this book they are not to blame, but for any strengths they are partly responsible.

I owe the largest thanks to my mentor and dissertation supervisor, Peter Guardino, whose doubts and suggestions have improved all parts of this book many times over and whose intellectual rigor I have done my best to emulate. My interest in nineteenth-century Mexico was first kindled by reading Peter's own research. Working with him has been one of the great pleasures and privileges of my professional life.

Introduction

I   Liberalism as Utopia

The nineteenth century began with the Declaration of the Rights of Man and ended with the triumph of new class- and race-based hierarchies. Across Europe and Latin America, wherever new, liberal ideals contended with entrenched structures of privilege, the equalizing experiments of the age of revolution eventually gave way to a reactionary resurgence. At the end of the century, new structures of exclusion had taken the place of the old. Though this is not, of course, the only way to tell a story about the nineteenth century, it may be the one that does most to acknowledge the weight of its historical legacy: it assesses the century by the light of a utopia – of the equality of men – that animated challenges to old-regime structures at the time and in many places continues to do so today.

Most historians now agree that the societies of Europe and Latin America emerged transformed from the decades of warfare and political experimentation first set in motion by the French Revolution. Legal privilege had been abolished or greatly diminished; absolute rule gave way to constitutional rule; governments, to count themselves legitimate, henceforth needed to serve the glory not of God but the people. Politics had acquired a social depth that made it strange to itself. How the post-revolutionary societies of Europe and Latin America grappled with the meanings of their new realities differed between countries and, within countries, between regions and localities. The rhythm of Europe's nineteenth-century history was marked by the fissure of the 1848 revolutions, which replaced the social fluidity and political instability of previous decades with a more stringent social hierarchy, policed by a state with growing repressive capacities. Differences remain not only in the temporal frameworks in which stories of utopian failure played out but also in the degrees to which alternative storylines suggest themselves. Take France and England, the countries that would become paradigmatic of a liberal-democratic historical trajectory.[1]

---

1   Some scholars of European history have described a strong division between countries developing in a liberal or democratic direction and those consolidating into modern autocracies; where the

Following more than a half-century of successive waves of political mobilization, France after 1851 achieved stability under the aggressively illiberal regime of the Second Empire, ushered in by a four-month state of exception that witnessed the harshest and most systematic country-wide crackdown on political dissent of the century.[2] In nineteenth-century Britain, history followed a gentler course. There, as Gareth Stedman Jones has famously argued, social mobilization was driven by a critique of political monopoly-power that faltered once governments proved themselves capable of incorporating popular demands into an elite-led national project.[3] A whiggish interpretation of history, positing a steady, gradual ascent toward freedom, has always seemed most at home in the British context. Yet in Britain, too, the second half of the century saw a renewed insistence on social hierarchy as elites stepped up efforts at suppressing the "rowdy" elements in working-class culture.[4] In both France and Britain, politics remained exclusionary until the final decades of the century,

Russian, Habsburg, and German Empires remained firmly under the grip of autocratic rulers at the end of the century, France had turned into a republic with full manhood suffrage and Britain was well on the way to including its entire adult population in the political process as well. The classic statement of that view is Barrington Moore, Jr., *Social Origins of Dictatorship and Democracy: Lord and Peasant in the Making of the Modern World* (Boston: Beacon Press, 1966). Other historians stress areas of similarity that existed in spite of such seemingly divergent experiences. Arno Mayer has argued that all of Europe by the outbreak of the First World War remained heavily dominated by landed, aristocratic interests and mentalities. Geoff Eley and Robin Blackbourn have also called attention to the areas of similarity between German and English paths to nineteenth-century state formation. See Arno J. Mayer, *The Persistence of the Old Regime: Europe to the Great War* (New York: Pantheon Books, 1981); and David Blackbourn and Geoff Eley, *The Peculiarities of German History: Bourgeois Society and Politics in Nineteenth-Century Germany* (New York: Oxford University Press, 1984).

2 On the provincial insurrection and its repression by Louis Napoleon's post-coup government, see Ted Margadant, *French Peasants in Revolt: The Insurrection of 1851* (Princeton: Princeton University Press, 1979); and Peter McPhee, *The Politics of Rural Life: Political Mobilization in the French Countryside, 1846–1852* (New York: Oxford University Press, 1992). On the consolidation of the Second Empire as a police state see also Howard C. Payne, *The Police State of Louis Napoleon Bonaparte 1851–1860* (Seattle: University of Washington Press, 1966); and Miranda Spieler, *Empire and Underworld: Captivity in French Guiana* (Harvard: Harvard University Press, 2012), 104–108.

3 Gareth Stedman Jones, *Languages of Class: Studies in English Working Class History 1832–1982* (Cambridge: Cambridge University Press, 1983), 106. The argument about the differential incorporation of popular demands is based on the work of Stedman Jones and comes from Ernesto Laclau, *On Populist Reason* (New York: Verso, 2005), 89–93. For a similar argument, based on a study of Chartism in the cotton town Ashton-under-Lyne near Manchester, see Robert Hall, *Voices of the People: Democracy and Chartist Political Identity, 1830–1870* (Monmouth: Merlin Press, 2007), chapter 5.

4 Richard Price, *British Society 1680–1880: Dynamism, Containment, Change* (New York: Cambridge University Press, 1999), 307–308; and Robert Storch, "The Policeman as Domestic Missionary: Urban Discipline and Popular Culture in Northern England, 1850–1880," *Journal of Social History* 9/4 (1976).

at which time race-based forms of labor coercion appeared in their new colonies.[5]

In Latin America's post-colonial republics, liberalizing efforts of varying strength were similarly followed by a turn toward autocratic consolidation. For example, in the ethnically divided republics of Bolivia, Ecuador, and Peru, revolutionary utopias of progress and social harmony that animated creole independence leaders – who in the Andean nations imposed independence at the head of occupying armies – left their mark on popular culture but were not widely shared in elite circles.[6] Measures like the abolition of indigenous tribute were quickly undone, and any vestige of the liberal ideal collapsed in the second half of the century under the pressure of economic modernization schemes premised on elite control over indigenous land and labor.[7] In Colombia, a more resolute liberalism drew strength from the mobilization of poor and dark-skinned laborers in the middle decades of the century, yet after 1879 was cut short by a conservative regime that proscribed popular political associations, employed harsh vagrancy laws, and in some Caribbean towns prohibited the mingling of plebeian and elite Colombians in public spaces.[8]

---

5   In spite of some setbacks in the 1870s, France can probably be said to have become an inclusive and liberal polity for its male adult population after the fall of the Paris Commune in 1871, albeit within limits most strongly suggested by the Dreyfus affair. For an overview of the early history of the third republic, see Robert Tombs, *France 1814–1914* (New York: Longman, 1996), chapter 21. Although Britain did not establish full manhood suffrage until 1918, Richard Price argues that with the electoral reform bill of 1867 "[t]he bias of the definition of the political nation had shifted from how people were to be excluded to how they were to be included." Price, *British Society*, 290. For discussions of global forms of labor coercion in the nineteenth century, see C. A. Bayly, *The Birth of the Modern World 1780–1914: Global Connections and Comparisons* (Malden, MA: Blackwell Publishing, 2004), 407–409; and Jürgen Osterhammel, *The Transformation of the World: A Global History of the Nineteenth Century*, trans. Patrick Camiller (Princeton: Princeton University Press), 682–683. For a case study of the particularly brutal labor regime that held sway in the mining industry of the British protectorate of Southern Rhodesia – where natives were forced to work under conditions leading to annual death rates by illness and accident that, in 1906, reached as high as 7.6 percent – see Charles van Onselen, *Chibaro: African Mine Labour in Southern Rhodesia 1900–1933* (Johannesburg: Ravan Press, 2001), chapters 2 and 3.

6   On popular appropriations of republican ideals in Peru, see Charles Walker, *Smoldering Ashes: Cuzco and the Creation of Republican Peru, 1780–1840* (Durham, NC: Duke University Press, 1999), chapters 5–7; Cecilia Méndez, *The Plebeian Republic: The Huanta Rebellion and the Making of the Peruvian State, 1820–1850* (Durham, NC: Duke University Press, 2005); and Sarah Chambers, *From Subjects to Citizens: Honor, Gender, and Politics in Arequipa, Peru, 1780–1854* (University Park: The Pennsylvania State University Press, 1999).

7   Brooke Larson, *Trials of Nation Making: Liberalism, Race, and Ethnicity in the Andes, 1810–1910* (New York: Cambridge University Press, 2004), 45–50, 68–69, 117–122, 155–156, 166–176, 216–217.

8   James Sanders, *Contentious Republicans: Popular Politics, Race, and Class in Nineteenth-Century Colombia* (Durham, NC: Duke University Press, 2004); Jason McGraw, *The Work of Recognition: Caribbean*

In all of these instances, high-minded ideals did not simply run up against the limits of the possible and settle into compromises that seemed stale to their adherents. Rather, a trend toward a partial and, necessarily, compromised institutionalization of liberal principles in the second half of the century gave way to new forms of hierarchy and exclusion. These forms found justification in dominant strands of nineteenth-century thought. Social-Darwinist ideas underwrote race-based systems of domination in Europe's colonies and fueled debates about the inferiority of the lower classes at home.[9] In Latin America, late-century positivism united national elites, after fifty years of political divisions, around a shared commitment to forms of progress that integrated the categories of scientific racism into national political projects.[10] For example, in the Andean republics the consolidation of autocracy and exclusion at the end of the century was accompanied by what one scholar calls "a redefinition of Indianness . . . to an inferior 'race' sentenced to the margins of nation and civilization."[11]

Among post-revolutionary nations in Europe and Latin America, Mexico stands out both for the profundity of its liberal experiment and the oppressiveness – indeed, the pervasive indecency – of the regime that came to power in the final quarter of the nineteenth century.[12] The Mexican War of Independence (1810–1821) was from its beginning accompanied by a social revolution that overturned colonial hierarchies and established popular actors as active participants in the country's political affairs. After achieving freedom from colonial rule, Mexicans inaugurated a national community premised on the equality of citizens. They abolished slavery in 1829, five years before owning slaves became illegal in the British

    Colombia and the Postemancipation Struggle for Citizenship (Chapel Hill: University of North Carolina Press, 2014), esp. p. 170 on the prohibition against the mixing of social classes.

9   Greta Jones, *Social Darwinism and English Thought: The Interaction between Biological and Social Theory* (Atlantic Highlands, NJ: Humanities Press, 1980), esp. chapter 8; Thomas Holt, *The Problem of Freedom: Race, Labor, and Politics in Jamaica and Britain, 1832–1938* (Baltimore: John Hopkins University Press, 1992).

10 Charles Hale, "Political and Social Ideas in Latin America, 1870–1930," in *The Cambridge History of Latin America*, vol. 4. (Cambridge: Cambridge University Press, 1986).

11 Larson, *Trials of Nation Making*, 246. On Peru, see also Mark Thurner, *From Two Republics to One Divided: Contradictions of Postcolonial Nationmaking in Andean Peru* (Durham, NC: Duke University Press, 1997).

12 The steepness of this arc in the cases of both Mexico and Colombia is stressed in James Sanders, *The Vanguard of the Atlantic World: Creating Modernity, Nation, and Democracy in Nineteenth-Century Latin America* (Durham, NC: Duke University Press, 2014). For a useful comparative study of indigenous society in Mexico and Peru in the independence era, stressing the relatively significant adoption of new, republican norms in the former country as against the latter, see Claudia Guarisco, *La reconstitución del espacio político indígena: Lima y el Valle de México durante la crisis de la monarquía española* (Castelló de la Plana: Universitat Jaume I, 2011).

Empire. Between 1824 and 1835, and during various briefer periods thereafter, they elected their politicians by near-universal male suffrage and participated widely in the government of their municipalities.[13] In the final decades of the century, these achievements were reversed. The same politicians who during the War of the French Intervention (1862–1867) had led the republic to victory against foreign occupation and domestic monarchy proceeded to build an illiberal political system that culminated in the long dictatorship of Porfirio Díaz, one of the heroes of the war against the French. Under the Díaz regime (1876–1911) perceptions of race and class organized central aspects of social life, nominally-upheld personal rights became a sham, private interests hijacked the legislative process, and ethnically-inflected systems of labor coercion reappeared in parts of the country.[14] In this post-colonial and post-revolutionary society, the nineteenth-century trajectory of utopian failure presents itself with exemplary clarity.

The case of Mexico, then, provides a vantage point from which to explore the fate of revolutionary liberalism in the nineteenth-century world. What I call "revolutionary liberalism" is not the same as "popular liberalism,"

---

13   Peter Guardino, *Peasants, Politics, and the Formation of Mexico's National State: Guerrero, 1800–1857* (Stanford: Stanford University Press, 1996), and *The Time of Liberty: Popular Political Culture in Oaxaca, 1750–1850* (Durham, NC: Duke University Press, 2005); Terry Rugeley, *Yucatán's Maya Peasantry and the Origins of the Caste War* (Austin: University of Texas Press, 1996); Timothy E. Anna, *Forging Mexico: 1821–1835* (Lincoln: University of Nebraska Press, 1998); José Antonio Serrano Ortega, *Jerarquía territorial y transición política: Guanajuato, 1790–1836* (Zamora: El Colegio de Michoacán; Mexico City: Instituto Mora, 2001); Richard Warren, *Vagrants and Citizens: Politics and the Masses in Mexico City from Colony to Republic* (Wilmington, DE: SR Books, 2001); Claudia Guarisco, *Los indios del valle de México y la construcción de una nueva sociabilidad política, 1770–1835* (Zincantepec: El Colegio Mexiquense, 2003); Michael Ducey, *A Nation of Villages: Riot and Rebellion in the Mexican Huasteca, 1750–1850* (Tucson: University of Arizona Press, 2004); Rosalina Ríos Zúñiga, *Formar ciudadanos: Sociedad civil y movilización popular en Zacatecas, 1821–1853* (Mexico City: Universidad Nacional Autónoma de México, 2005); Karen Caplan, *Indigenous Citizens: Local Liberalism in Early National Oaxaca and Yucatán* (Stanford: Stanford University Press, 2010).

14   For different perspectives on the illiberalism of the Díaz regime, see John Womack, Jr., *Zapata and the Mexican Revolution* (New York: Vintage Books, 1968), chapters 1–2; Laurens Ballard Perry, *Juárez and Díaz: Machine Politics in Mexico* (DeKalb: Northern Illinois University Press, 1978); Alan Knight, *The Mexican Revolution*, vol. 1, "Porfirians, Liberals, and Peasants" (Cambridge: Cambridge University Press, 1986), chapter 1; François-Xavier Guerra, *México: Del Antiguo Régimen a la Revolución*, 2 vol., trans. Sergio Fernández Bravo (Mexico City: Fondo de Cultura Económica, 1988); Friedrich Katz, "Mexico: Restored Republic and Porfiriato," in *Cambridge History of Latin America*, vol. 5 ed. Bethell; Charles A. Hale, *The Transformation of Liberalism in Late Nineteenth-Century Mexico* (Princeton: Princeton University Press, 1989); Stephen Haber, *Industry and Underdevelopment: The Industrialization of Mexico, 1890–1940* (Stanford: Stanford University Press, 1989); Armando Razo, *Social Foundations of Limited Dictatorship: Networks and Private Protection during Mexico's Early Industrialization* (Stanford: Stanford University Press, 2008).

in spite of considerable overlap between the two concepts. Historians of Mexico have used the term "popular liberalism" to denote popular actors' participation on the liberal side in the country's political conflicts as well as their appropriation, for purposes often at odds with those of elite liberals, of a rights-based and anti-colonial political idiom.[15] My definition of revolutionary liberalism is more restrictive. I understand revolutionary liberalism as the project, at once minimal and utopian, to assure the equal treatment of all men (in those years, not yet women) before the law.[16] The project was minimal because it was based on a general principle and did not distinguish between the justice or injustice of any particular laws. It was utopian because the principle of legal equality nevertheless defied the norms governing social relations not only at the time but in any known prior period of history.

Strictly speaking, the goal of legal equality may also be utopian in the stronger sense that, in Martin Amis's phrase, "reality cannot be expected to support it."[17] For no one has yet been able to devise a system of law that does not favor those with greater access to the resources of time, money, and expertise.[18] To ask about the failure of revolutionary liberalism is nevertheless to frame a meaningful research program. Revolutionary liberalism failed not in the sense that it did not bring about a state of perfection but in the sense that legal equality was repudiated as an institutional aspiration. Countries that, at the beginning of the century, had sought ways to increase popular rights to legal protection, at the end of the century sought ways to curtail them. In exploring this reversal in the particular case of post-colonial Mexico, this book seeks to answer two central questions:

---

15   Prominent works on popular liberalism in nineteenth-century Mexico include Alan Knight, "El liberalismo mexicano desde la Reforma hasta la Revolución (una interpretación)," *Historia Mexicana* 35/1 (1985); Guy Thomson, "Bulwarks of Patriotic Liberalism: The National Guard, Philharmonic Corps, and Patriotic Juntas in Mexico, 1847–1888," *Journal of Latin American Studies* 22/1 (1990); Florencia Mallon, *Peasant and Nation: The Making of Postcolonial Mexico and Peru* (Berkeley: University of California Press, 1995); and Guardino, *Peasants, Politics, and the Formation of Mexico's National State*.

16   To most writers – both legalists and utopian scholars – law and utopia have more often seemed like opposites than complementarities. For a recent collection of essays that attempt to "entertain a more constructive relationship between law and utopia," see Austin Sarat, Lawrence Douglas, and Martha Merill Umphrey (eds.), *Law and the Utopian Imagination* (Stanford: Stanford University Press, 2014). The quote is from Sarat, Douglas, and Umphrey's chapter "Law and the Utopian Imagination: An Introduction," 10. For a definition of liberalism that emphasizes the equality of rights and protections it affords to all citizens, see Brian Tamanaha, *On the Rule of Law: History, Politics, Theory* (Cambridge: Cambridge University Press, 2004), 32–33.

17   Martin Amis, *The War against Cliché: Essays and Reviews, 1971–2000* (London: Jonathan Cape, 2001), xiii.

18   The aspirational character of the liberal concept of "the rule of law" is stressed in Jeremy Waldron, *The Law* (New York: Routledge, 1990), chapter 3; and Guillermo O'Donnell, *Democracy, Agency, and the State: Theory with Comparative Intent* (New York: Oxford University Press, 2010), chapter 5.

why did liberalism fail in nineteenth-century Mexico? And what stayed behind of the egalitarianism of the age of revolution: what lasting impact, cultural or institutional, did it have on the development of a modern Mexican state?

II Peasant and Nation

This study asks questions that put it in conversation with a distinguished literature about the social conditions leading countries to follow liberal or authoritarian pathways to modern state formation. Yet being able to write about Mexico as an exemplar in the history of liberal politics – even an exemplar of eventual failure – is not a matter of course. Historians used to assume that Latin America's nineteenth-century republics had been rendered unreceptive to egalitarian ideas and institutions by the social legacies of three centuries of colonial rule.[19] They assumed that in nineteenth-century Latin America liberalism was at best a pretense and at worst another ideology of conquest, that beneath a veneer of articulated politics the region was dominated by regional warlords, or *caudillos*, who mobilized dependents, and sometimes raised popular armies, to fight each other for access to economic and political spoils.[20] In the comparative study of modern state formation, this version of Latin American history has been used to support an interpretation of liberalism as a bourgeois ideology and of the rise of the liberal state as the achievement mostly of a class of property owners: the "merchants and businessmen" whose social ascendancy, according to James Robinson and Daron Acemoglu, in seventeenth-century England and eighteenth- and nineteenth-century France, prepared the way for "the emergence of more inclusive political institutions" in the

---

19 The assumption that Latin America's colonial past inevitably set it on an authoritarian post-colonial trajectory is shared by scholars from a variety of fields and perspectives. See, e.g., Stanley and Barbara Stein, *The Colonial Heritage of Latin America: Essays on Economic Dependence in Perspective* (New York: Oxford University Press, 1970); Eduardo Galeano, *Open Veins of Latin America: Five Centuries of the Pillage of a Continent*, trans. Cedric Belfrage (New York: Monthly Review Press, 1973); John Lynch, *The Spanish American Revolutions 1808–1826* (London: Weidenfeld and Nicolson, 1973); François-Xavier Guerra, *Modernidad e Independencias: Ensayos sobre las revoluciones hispánicas* (Madrid: Editorial MAPFRE, 1992); Lester Langley, *The Americas in the Age of Revolution 1750–1850* (New Haven: Yale University Press, 1996); and Howard Wiarda, *The Soul of Latin America: The Cultural and Political Tradition* (New Haven: Yale University Press, 2001).

20 Miguel Angel Centeno, *Blood and Debt: War and the Nation-State in Latin America* (University Park: Pennsylvania State University Press, 2002); Daron Acemoglu and James Robinson, *Why Nations Fail: The Origins of Power, Prosperity, and Poverty* (New York: Crown Publishing Group, 2012), 28–37; Paul Drake, *Between Tyranny and Anarchy: A History of Democracy in Latin America, 1800–2006* (Stanford: Stanford University Press, 2009); Jorge Castañeda, *Mañana Forever? Mexico and the Mexicans* (New York: Alfred A. Knopf, 2011); Hillel David Soifer, *State Building in Latin America* (New York: Cambridge University Press, 2015), chapter 3.

aftermath of successful political revolutions.[21] In Latin America, scholars often suggest, liberalism atrophied because an independent middle class either did not exist or was no match for colonial-era oligarchs and their capacity for clientelistic social mobilization.

Such views have now been challenged by a generation of empirical research. Recent scholarship has emphasized the seriousness and creativity with which both elite and popular actors in Latin America responded to the ideological innovations of the revolutionary era. Where historians used to describe societies dominated by rent-seeking warlords, they now point to the development of practices and imaginaries capable of drawing wide and disparate social sectors into shared political projects.[22] But if it is no longer feasible to describe the period simply as one of military chaos, or else as a neo-colonial continuation of what came before, it has also become harder to explain the consolidation of authoritarian regimes, often dominated by strongmen such as Rafael Núñez in Colombia, Justo Rufino Barrios in Guatemala, and Porfirio Díaz in Mexico, in the second half of the century.[23] Indeed, it is a notable feature of the new political scholarship, and perhaps one corresponding to a broader trend in academic history, that it complicates rather than clarifies our understanding of the era it investigates: we now know a good deal more than we did and

---

21 Acemoglu and Robinson, *Why Nations Fail*, 362. Arguments about the central role of the bourgeoisie in the rise of liberalism go back at least to Barrington Moore's canonical study of fascist, socialist, and liberal-democratic pathways to modernity, which associated the emergence of liberal-democratic regimes with either the displacement of feudal landlords by an agricultural bourgeoisie, as in England, or their destruction by an alliance between bourgeois and popular classes, including peasants, as in France. Liberalism was in this view a bourgeois ideology, though one that occasionally found support in non-bourgeois social sectors. Moore, *Social Origins of Dictatorship and Democracy*, chapters 1, 2, and 7. The argument that liberalism had its origins in commercial and manufacturing sectors seeking to protect themselves against a predatory monarchy is also associated with the influential study of Douglass North and Barry Weingast, "Constitutions and Commitment: The Evolution of Institutions Governing Public Choice in Seventeenth-Century England," *Journal of Economic History* 49/4 (1989), which reaches this conclusion in part by using property rights as a proxy for personal rights per se.

22 This literature has become far too large to cite exhaustively. Examples not previously cited include Greg Grandin, *The Blood of Guatemala: A History of Race and Nation* (Durham, NC: Duke University Press, 2000); Ricardo Salvatore, *Wandering Paysanos: State Order and Subaltern Experience in Buenos Aires during the Rosas Era* (Durham, NC: Duke University Press, 2003); Marixa Lasso, *Myths of Harmony: Race and Republicanism during the Age of Revolution, Colombia, 1795–1831* (Pittsburgh: University of Pittsburgh Press, 2007); and Reuben Zahler, *Ambitious Rebels: Remaking Honor, Law, and Liberalism in Venezuela, 1780–1850* (Tucson: University of Arizona Press, 2013).

23 For different approaches to the question of whether and how modern Latin America was shaped by its colonial history, see Jeremy Adelman (eds.), *Colonial Legacies: The Problem of Persistence in Latin American History* (New York: Routledge, 1999).

understand a good deal less than we thought we did about the political history of Latin America in the nineteenth century.[24]

Theoretically, much of the work on popular politics in Latin America has drawn on conceptions of hegemony that emphasize the capacity of lower-class actors to engage with the political idioms imposed on them by elite oppressors. In a much-cited definition, William Roseberry proposes to use the term "hegemony" to designate "the ways in which the words, images, symbols, forms, organizations, institutions, and movements used by subordinate populations to talk about, understand, confront, accommodate themselves to, or resist their domination are shaped by the process of domination itself."[25] Because political concepts and practices exist in a field of contention, and cannot be entirely controlled by either dominant or subordinate groups, their meaning is always dynamic. It can only be grasped within the context of particular struggles and histories.

Let us explore the historical argument of perhaps the most influential work about the popular dimensions of Latin American politics in the nineteenth century. Florencia Mallon's *Peasant and Nation*, first published in 1995, uses a concept of hegemony much like Roseberry's to frame an investigation into popular participation in the civil and international warfare of the Reform War (1858–1861) and War of the French Intervention (1862–1867) in Mexico and the War of the Pacific (1879–1883) in Peru.[26] Mallon shows that indigenous peasants in parts of both countries were not mere spectators to conflicts in which they saw no stakes for themselves. On the contrary, taking hold of "the universal promise of a national-democratic project," and investing the discourse of liberal democracy with local meanings, indigenous peasants were willing to go to war and die for their concepts of the nation.[27]

Mallon thus dispels powerful stereotypes about the parochialism of peasants' political vision. Rather than rejecting liberalism and democracy as alien to their needs or culture, peasants in Peru and Mexico often welcomed their promise of equality. However, once the wars were over, their elite allies turned against them. In Mexico, victorious liberal elites took the side of estate owners in local land conflicts, attempted to disarm National Guard units they perceived as a threat to social peace, and in the state of Puebla, where popular participation in the war effort had been

24 A point recently made for the Peruvian case – but with a broader Latin American perspective also in mind – by Paul Gootenberg, "Fishing for Leviathans? Shifting Views on the Liberal State and Development in Peruvian History," *Journal of Latin American Studies* 45/1 (2013), 125–131.

25 William Roseberry, "Hegemony and the Language of Contention," in *Everyday Forms of State Formation*, eds. Gilbert Joseph and Daniel Nugent, 355–366.

26 Mallon, *Peasant and Nation*, especially 7–8 for Mallon's definition of "hegemony."

27 Mallon, *Peasant and Nation*, 17.

particularly critical, manipulated state elections against a popular candidate. Mallon fits these findings into a three-stage narrative scheme she borrows from Partha Chatterjee's analysis of colonial and post-colonial nationalism in India: in a "moment of departure" elite sectors of the colonized population become aware of the possibility of a "national-democratic project"; in a "moment of maneuver" they build a coalition with popular sectors against colonial or old-regime interests; and, having gained power, in a "moment of arrival" they forsake their lower-class allies and rewrite the history of their struggle to clear it of its contradictions.[28] In Mexico and Peru, the same liberal commanders who had first fought alongside popular forces were often later sent to repress them, and Mallon's dramatic unpacking of the stories of intimate betrayal buried under the victors' official discourse contributes some of the most haunting pages to scholarly attempts to come to grips with the nineteenth century's squandered promise of emancipation.

While Mallon proposes that the nineteenth century's liberal-democratic spirit foundered on the choices of a liberal elite that was too ill at ease with its social base to fulfill its promise of emancipation, there are elements even in her own study that strain against this interpretation. If peasants were drawn to the Enlightenment promise of equality, why did they adopt conservative as well as liberal positions? Mallon deals with instances of popular conservatism mostly in an ad hoc fashion. Apart from reiterating familiar arguments about the religiosity of peasants and indigenous villagers – which "[opened] potential spaces for Conservative populisms through the connection of religion to ritual" – she suggests that popular-conservative alignments in areas of Puebla represented tactical choices in local power struggles, and that those in areas of Morelos may have expressed the interests of higher strata within local society.[29] Most important, Mallon argues that peasants often joined conservative forces not for ideological reasons but in response to their disillusionment with the perceived betrayals of liberal elites.[30] This argument allows her to accommodate the fact of popular conservatism inside Chatterjee's historical stage model, though at the price of a loss in methodological consistency: her analysis of popular liberalism, based on close readings of peasant texts and actions, is fleshed out and empirical in a way that her analysis of popular conservatism is not. Moreover, one might find evidence of a conservative political practice even where peasants supported the liberal side in the war:

28   Mallon, *Peasant and Nation*, 13. Note that Chatterjee develops his analysis specifically to explain the trajectory of nationalist thought from native colonial to post-colonial elites, a trajectory missing in Mexico and Peru in the second half of the nineteenth century. Partha Chatterjee, *Nationalist Thought and the Colonial World: A Derivative Discourse* (London: Zed Books, 1993).
29   Mallon, *Peasant and Nation*, 29, 33, 92–96, 169, here 94.
30   Mallon, *Peasant and Nation*, 45–47, 139–141.

National Guard soldiers' expectation of rewards for themselves and punishment for their enemies at the end of the war, which Mallon reads as a sign of republican fervor, can also be seen as an appeal to an old-regime "economy of favor" according to which rulers were expected "to reward good subjects and punish the bad ones."[31]

Subsequent studies of nineteenth-century Latin America have found popular nationalist idioms in a variety of circumstances much wider than Mallon's story would allow for. In a departure from Mallon's chronological argument, investigations of popular politics in Mexico have shown that lower-class actors began appropriating liberal-democratic goals as early as the War of Independence, decades before the civil and international warfare of the 1850s and 1860s.[32] Mallon's association of native communities with popular forms of liberalism, and hacienda residents with a more conservative outlook, has also been challenged. For example, in Colombia's Cauca Valley, James Sanders has detected the greatest support for a liberal politics among Afro-Colombian hacienda workers while finding that indigenous towns were especially drawn to a conservative defense of corporate landholding regimes.[33] In Mexico, too, indigenous as well as mestizo (mixed-race) peasants were often attracted to conservative positions and at times gave whole regions a strongly anti-liberal stamp.[34]

While studies on popular political culture have vastly expanded our empirical knowledge, they have also tended to move away from broader questions about the process of post-colonial state formation. Much of the recent literature on nineteenth-century Latin America has been driven by a rescue ethos. Earlier scholarship, as Marcela Echeverri puts it in her examination of the Colombian independence war, "often assumed that

31 Alejandro Cañeque, *The King's Living Image: The Culture and Politics of Viceregal Power in Mexico* (New York: Routledge, 2004), 159, and more generally chapter 5.

32 Guardino, *Peasants* and *Time of Liberty*; Serrano Ortega, *Jerarquía territorial*; Claudia Guarisco, *Los indios del valle de México y la construcción de una nueva sociabilidad política, 1770–1835* (Zincantepec: El Colegio Mexiquense, 2003); Ducey, *Nation of Villages*.

33 Sanders, *Contentious Republicans*.

34 Benjamin Smith, *The Roots of Conservatism in Mexico: Catholicism, Society, and Politics in the Mixteca Baja, 1750–1962* (Albuquerque: University of New Mexico Press, 2012); Luis González y González, *Pueblo en vilo: Microhistoria de San José de Gracia* (Mexico City: El Colegio de México, 1968); Brian Hamnett, "Mexican Conservatives, Clericals, and Soldiers: The 'Traitor' Tomas Mejía through Reform and Empire, 1855–1867," *Bulletin of Latin American Research* 20/2 (2001); Will Fowler and Humberto Morales Moreno (eds.), *El conservadurismo mexicano en el siglo XIX* (Puebla: Benemérita Universidad Autónoma de Puebla, 1999); Jean Meyer, *Esperando a Lozada* (Mexico City: CONACYT, 1984); Zachary Brittsan, "In Faith or Fear: Fighting with Lozada," PhD dissertation, University of California San Diego (2010); K. Aaron Van Oosterhout, "Confraternities and Popular Conservatism on the Frontier: Mexico's Sierra del Nayarit in the Nineteenth Century," *The Americas* 71/1 (2014).

popular groups were not drawn to anticolonial politics, either because they had little awareness of the larger political context or because their interests were fundamentally different from the modernizing thrust of the elites."[35] New histories of popular politics, by contrast, explore lower-class actors' engagement with republican politics in situations that range from household quarrels and village politics to riots, rebellions, and, as in Mallon's work, full-blown civil and international warfare. Thematically, then, this approach is apt to stress all manifestations of political awareness in popular speech or action and tends toward what Eric Van Young has termed an "apotheosis of agency." It assumes a concept of personhood that takes little account of the habituated or non-creative side of human behavior.[36] And while it is probably true that all historical approaches contain an implicit epistemological bias in favor of the significance of their own subject-matter, the field of popular political history in Latin America has so far done little to differentiate, prioritize, or otherwise order the profusion of forgotten voices, projects, and mentalities that regional and judicial archives have now made available for historical scrutiny.

Existing scholarship also treats popular politics predominantly in a mode of conflict.[37] That is no less true of works dealing with the quotidian concerns of domestic or village life than of those that have party-politics or civil war as their central topic. Political identities appear defined by whom they confront and what they oppose; their more positive content, relating to the kind of world people try to project, is, at best, intimated through the prism of their antagonistic relationships. There are, of course, good reasons for this emphasis. Conflicts produce the documents on which historians rely. They possess an air of inherent significance and dramatize the tensions that give history much of its texture. At the same time, conflicts are often sui generis in a way that makes it hard to see around their edges: it is no accident that research on popular politics is seldom more than regional in scope. A focus on conflict is apt to obscure more positive themes and concerns that bound lower-class Latin Americans from different regions and settings into common political projects.

The approach that has shaped recent scholarship on nineteenth-century Latin America is at once too broad and too narrow. Too broad,

---

35   Marcela Echeverri, "Popular Royalists, Empire, and Politics in Southwestern New Granada, 1809–1819," *Hispanic American Historical Review* 91/2 (2011), 239.

36   Eric Van Young, "The New Cultural History Comes to Old Mexico," *Hispanic American Historical Review* 79/2 (1999), 243; and *The Other Rebellion: Popular Violence, Ideology, and the Mexican Struggle for Independence, 1810–1821* (Stanford: Stanford University Press, 2001), 14. See also Alan Knight, "Subalterns, Signifiers, and Statistics: Perspectives on Mexican Historiography," *Latin American Research Review* 37/2 (2002), 141–142.

37   Notable exceptions are Guardino, *Time of Liberty*, especially chapter 6; Guarisco, *Los indios*, chapter 7; and Caplan, *Indigenous Citizens*, especially chapters 3 and 5.

because it lacks criteria by which to order or prioritize the manifestations of political awareness found, if viewed from up close, in almost any popular speech or action. Too narrow, because it isolates evidence of open political behavior from the larger patterns of meaning suffusing people's lives and guiding their engagement with the post-colonial state. Historians have yet to find an interpretive framework capable of making sense of the complex and varied political cultures they have recently discovered.

III Law and Revolution

There is now a rich body of work exploring how and why citizens of Latin America's post-colonial republics participated in their nations' political lives. This book seeks to contribute to that scholarship – and, more tentatively, to move beyond some of its limitations – by exploring the legal framework that connected republican politics to the realms of speech, thought, and habit in which people in nineteenth-century Mexico conducted their everyday affairs. Aldo Schiavone has described law and politics as separate domains that lie together "in an unbroken contiguity bristling with complicity and tension."[38] The revolutions that at the beginning of the century toppled or undermined old-regime structures and gave Spain's colonies their independence were first of all legal revolutions; they replaced systems in which rights and prohibitions attached to peoples' membership in estates, ethnic groups, and corporations with systems in which rights and prohibitions were equally shared between adult male citizens.[39] Ordinary life tasks became imbued with political meaning as people's choices about which structures of rights to appeal to in pursuit of their goals could prop up old-regime structures or give life to new ones.

38 Aldo Schiavone, *The Invention of Law in the West*, trans. Jeremy Carden and Antony Shugaar (Cambridge: Harvard University Press, 2012), 13–14.

39 There are a number of important studies of popular legal behavior in Mexico for the colonial period, e.g. Woodrow Borah, *Justice by Insurance: The General Indian Court of Colonial Mexico and the Legal Aides of the Half-Real* (Berkeley: University of California Press, 1983); Susan Kellogg, *Law and the Transformation of Aztec Culture, 1500–1700* (Norman: University of Oklahoma Press, 1995); and Brian Owensby, *Empire of Law and Indian Justice in Colonial Mexico* (Stanford: Stanford University Press, 2008). The only comparable study on the nineteenth century that I am aware of is Laura Shelton, *For Tranquility and Order: Family and Community on Mexico's Northern Frontier, 1800–1850* (Tucson: University of Arizona Press, 2011). For an essay that emphasizes the subject-forming power of the early nineteenth-century legal revolutions in Latin America, including Mexico, see Victor M. Uribe-Uran, "The Great Transformation of Law and Legal Culture: 'The Public' and 'the Private' in the Transition from Empire to Nation in Mexico, Colombia, and Brazil, 1750–1850," in *Empire to Nation: Historical Perspectives on the Making of the Modern World*, eds. Joseph W. Esherick, Hasan Kayali, and Eric Van Young (Lanham, MD: Rowman & Littlefield Publishers, Inc., 2006).

The codes and institutions that restructured the private realm in terms of a new, egalitarian conception of justice did not abolish the distinction between private and public domains but rather produced the characteristically modern instability of the boundary between the two: they endowed the sphere of legalized social relations with a utopian orientation that might always erupt into politics.[40] This legal dimension of popular life experiences, I will argue throughout this book, formed a common ground for Mexicans' political behavior in the nineteenth century and can help us make sense of the thicket of projects and voices that studies on popular politics have recently brought to light.

The book proceeds by way of a comparative study of the legal cultures of three social settings that in the nineteenth century were home to a vast majority of Mexican citizens: mestizo towns, indigenous towns, and hacienda (agricultural estate) settlements. It argues that in each of those settings struggles over the shape of the new legal order, and over the institutions responsible for its preservation, turned on competing conceptions about the ethical foundations of law. Egalitarian institutions flourished to the extent that they were able to mobilize social values centered on the practice of labor and care for the family. Yet egalitarian institutions were everywhere challenged by the attraction of alternative systems of value: in hacienda settlements, systems of value based on the principle of private property; in indigenous towns, systems of value based on the principle of corporate identity; and in mestizo towns, systems of value based on the principles of wealth, education, and social prominence. In nineteenth-century Mexico, the success of liberal state formation thus depended on the primacy of values and interests associated with work – and more particularly work in the service of familial care and duty – over other values and interests.

My argument rests on the premise of the non-autonomy of Mexico's legal system. It assumes that legal institutions are always connected to, and draw some of their substance from, an extra-legal fabric of values and interests. Because no state has the capacity to monitor the behavior of most citizens at most times, a functioning legal system must be more than a collection of executive orders backed by the threat of sanctions – the minimalist definition of law advanced by legal positivists like John Austin.[41] The threat of sanctions is not by itself a sufficient condition for

40 See E. P. Thompson, *Whigs and Hunters: The Origin of the Black Act* (London: Allen Lane, 1975), for a canonical interrogation of the relationship between legal expectations and the micro-politics of local social relations.

41 John Austin, *The Province of Jurisprudence Determined* (New York: B. Franklin, 1970). For critical discussions of Austin, see H. L. A. Hart, *The Concept of Law* (London: Oxford University Press, 1961), 18–25; and Ronald Dworkin, *Law's Empire* (Cambridge: The Belknap Press of Harvard University Press, 1986), 33–34.

a rule to become socially immanent. A more plausible definition sees the law as a codified system of rules that most people, most of the time, follow as a matter of habit and that is backed by social norms as much as by state coercion.[42] A study of legal culture can therefore not avoid being also a study of habits and values.

Paying attention to habits and values is doubly important in studies of transitional legal orders that are still searching for consent and institutional stability. In nineteenth-century Mexico, the post-independence state depended heavily on popular goodwill. Ordinary Mexicans – peasants, day workers, artisans, local merchants – contributed to "the practical articulation of the law" not only as interlocutors of new public institutions but as direct participants in the town governments and civic militias that were the local faces of the state's legal and coercive authority.[43] Because Mexico's early republican state was fragile, and because it depended on the approval, and sometimes the active participation, of a wide array of social actors, it was peculiarly responsive to the values and interests espoused by its citizens. For the country's political classes, this dependence was a cause of anxiety and a motive for taking a keen interest in the lives of the poor. The enforcement of social morality – carried out by means of the military draft – in nineteenth-century Mexico became a key function of the state. The public recognition of the social value of labor thus had a robust disciplinary dimension. It allowed the poor to claim new rights and protections and the state to enforce a demanding normative code.

By tracing the origins of the liberal state to ethical imaginaries associated with labor, or industriousness, this book challenges a widespread perception of liberalism as, most fundamentally, a bourgeois ideology. Scholars have long shown – against both Marxist and liberal orthodoxies – that in nineteenth- and twentieth-century Europe and Latin America it was the working classes who were the most reliable supporters of democratization; the bourgeoisie, according to a classic comparative study, was a politically less predictable actor, appearing sometimes as an

---

42 The classic statement on the internalizing, subject-forming character of the law is Hart, *Concept of Law*, 40. The relationship between the law and normatively coded structures of habit is stressed in Northrop Frye, "Crime and Sin in the Bible," in *Northrop Frye on Religion: Excluding The Great Code and Words with Power*, ed. Northrop Frye (Toronto: University of Toronto Press, 1996); and Harold Berman, *Law and Revolution: The Formation of the Western Legal Tradition* (Cambridge: Harvard University Press, 1983). The importance of perceived legitimacy for achieving citizen compliance with the law is stressed in Tom Tyler, *Why People Obey the Law* (Princeton: Princeton University Press, 2006).

43 Mae Ngai, *Impossible Subjects: Illegal Aliens and the Making of Modern America* (Princeton: Princeton University Press, 2004), 12.

ally of democratic movements but often putting its weight behind authoritarian forces.[44] Yet the same study goes on to contrast the inclusive and
mobilizing tendencies of democracy with the mere "formalism of liberal
law" and, following traditional accounts, to associate the latter with only
bourgeois interests and aspirations.[45] Such a view may be intuitive because
it finds support in the self-understanding of influential nineteenth-century
liberal thinkers – men like François Guizot in France or José María Luis
Mora in Mexico.[46] But it hews closer to bourgeois mythology than to any
empirical evidence.

At the broadest level of argument, this book posits a causal relationship between the strength of a system of values and interests centered
around the practice of labor and the success of liberal institution
building. It does not link liberalism to structural indicators of class.
For in the revolutionary era, when even in advanced economies factory
work remained uncommon, labor and property had not yet been fixed on
opposite sides of a political antinomy. In post-colonial Mexico workers
and capitalists, farmers and agricultural laborers were equally capable of
espousing liberal principles. Only at the end of my period of study,
during the Porfirian dictatorship, did property owners as a class incline
toward a markedly illiberal position, repudiating the principle of legal
equality. Rather, the book links liberalism to radical cultural patterns
that valorized work and domestic rectitude and rejected idleness, rent-
seeking, and sexual misbehavior.[47] People who shared in such patterns
were welcoming to the accumulation of property by diligent workers
or skillful entrepreneurs. But they were wary of the anti-social uses

44   Dietrich Rueschemeyer, Evelyne Huber Stephens, and John Stephens, *Capitalist Development and
     Democracy* (Chicago: University of Chicago Press, 1992). See also Göran Therborn, "The Rule of
     Capital and the Rise of Democracy," *New Left Review* 103 (1977); and Geoff Eley, *Forging
     Democracy: The History of the Left in Europe, 1850–2000* (New York: Oxford University Press,
     2002). Studies stressing the anti-democratic politics of entrepreneurial property owners,
     whether in England, continental Europe, or the Americas, include Evelyne Huber,
     "Introduction," in *Agrarian Structure and Political Power: Landlord and Peasant in the Making of
     Latin America*, eds. Evelyne Huber and Frank Safford, 3–20 (Pittsburgh: University of
     Pittsburgh Press, 1995); Theda Skocpol, "A Critical Review of Barrington Moore's Social
     Origins of Dictatorship and Democracy," *Politics and Society* 4/1 (1973), 19–22; and
     Blackbourn and Eley, *Peculiarities of German History*.
45   Rueschemeyer, Huber Stephens, and Stephens, *Capitalist Development and Democracy*, 61.
46   On the thought of Guizot and other French doctrinaire liberals, see Aurelian Craiutu, *Liberalism
     under Siege: The Political Thought of the French Doctrinaires* (New York: Lexington Books, 2003).
     On the thought of Mora, see Charles Hale, *Mexican Liberalism in the Age of Mora, 1821–1853* (New
     Haven: Yale University Press, 1968).
47   See Stedman Jones, *Languages of Class*, 21–22, for a discussion of social interest as created through
     language.

to which wealth might be put and opposed to the idea, advanced by members of the propertied classes, that the laboring poor had no capacity for law-governed social life and no need for the rights protected by liberal institutions.

By advancing a thesis that is theoretically parsimonious and, perhaps, generalizable – but at least testable – beyond the Mexican case, I hope to establish conversations with scholars in non-historical disciplines and in different regional fields. However, the main concern of this book is to offer an original and detailed account of the legal cultures of mestizo towns, indigenous towns, and hacienda settlements in nineteenth-century Mexico. I use the term "legal culture" broadly, to designate the ways Mexicans practiced, talked about, and otherwise interacted with the law. The book pays particular attention to the work of local courts and police forces – the two institutions that most commonly brought ordinary Mexicans into contact with the law – and to the debates and controversies circling around those institutions. In the process, the book also brings new evidence to bear on a number of topics that have previously occupied historians of Mexico and Latin America: social conflict, military recruitment, property rights, land privatization, the role of the army in politics, the relationship between state and locality. About these matters I engage in the kinds of historiographical debates, and form the kinds of "lower-level hypotheses," that, according to Alan Knight, are the bread and butter of the historical profession.[48] It is thus my hope that in the pages that follow, scholars who are unconvinced by my comparative and theoretical concerns will still find something to reward their attention.

Most of the evidence for this book comes from Guanajuato and San Luis Potosí, two states with exceptional government archives lying largely north of the Mesoamerican cultural zone. Populated by Spanish and indigenous settlers as well as some African slaves, in colonial times both of these states had developed rich mining industries which, in turn, had powered agricultural sectors containing both smallholder and hacienda production. However, Guanajuato, which occupied a large part of the fertile Bajío plains, was more prosperous and economically diverse than its more arid neighbor and, by the beginning of the nineteenth century, contained an important textile industry as well as Mexico's densest network of medium-sized towns. In Chapter 4, I also make use of material from the southern state of Oaxaca, where indigenous Mexicans, rather than having to hold their own in a landscape dominated by mestizo towns and haciendas, were the demographic majority.

---

48 Knight, "Subalterns, Signifiers, and Statistics," 156.

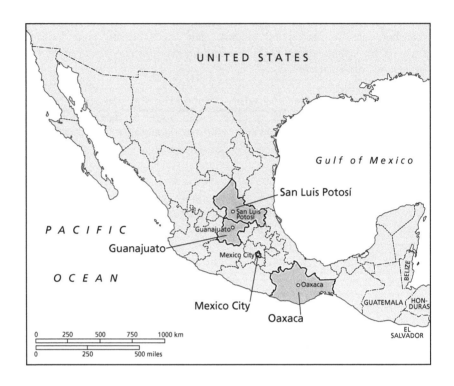

Although differences between the three regions were significant, I should warn readers that they will not receive a great deal of emphasis in this book. In moving beyond the single-region focus of most recent scholarship, my purpose has been not to emphasize Mexico's much-vaunted diversity but to uncover patterns of speech and action that were shared across the country's varied ethnic and social geography. The inevitable loss of nuance in my treatment of regional politics will, I hope, be outweighed by the benefits of a broader perspective and a surer sense of what was shared and typical in Mexicans' experiences of the post-colonial state.

The structure of this book is simple and may be quickly anticipated. Chapters 1 and 2 examine the legal culture of Mexican mestizo towns between the 1820s and 1850s; Chapters 3 and 4 do the same with hacienda settlements and indigenous towns. Chapter 5 picks up the story after the civil war period of the Reform era – which interrupted the workings of legal institutions, rendering their future uncertain – to look at the mixture of continuity and innovation that characterized the legal order of the illiberal

Díaz regime. Finally, the conclusion summarizes the findings and presents a theoretical account of the relationship between liberal institutions and cultural patterns established in Mexico's early republican decades and the regime of privilege through which elites reasserted their power in the final years of the century.

I

Mestizo Towns

I Politics

Mexico first experienced constitutional government under Spanish rule, though at a time when the War of Independence (1810–1821) was well underway. The 1812 Spanish Constitution, written in Cádiz by a liberal assembly that included delegates from the empire's overseas territories, stated in article 248: "In common, civil, and criminal affairs, there will be no more than one single jurisdiction for any class of persons."[1] At a stroke the legal distinctions that for centuries had defined imperial social relations were abolished; only members of the Church and the army would be able to hold on to their accustomed prerogatives. Concretely, the constitution located the operation of legal sovereignty in a hierarchy of judicial institutions that on the lowest level, where it would be encountered by the majority of citizens, was represented by the mayor (*alcalde*) and other members of the town council (*ayuntamiento*).[2] In charging municipal governments with the protection of a new civic equality, the Cádiz Constitution set a precedent that Latin America's post-independence republics would eagerly follow.[3]

---

1 "En los negocios comunes, civiles y criminales, no habrá más que un solo fuero para toda clase de personas." *Constitución política de la monarquía española: Promulgada en Cádiz a 19 de marzo de 1812* (Cádiz: Imprenta Real, 1812), articles 248–250. Quote from article 248.

2 *Constitución política de la monarquía española*, article 275.

3 The study of the institutional impact of the Cádiz Constitution on Mexican state formation goes back to Nettie Lee Benson, *The Provincial Deputation in Mexico: Harbinger of Provincial Autonomy, Independence, and Federalism* (Austin: University of Texas Press, 1992 [1955]). Important subsequent works include Virginia Guedea, "The Process of Mexican Independence," *American Historical Review* 105/1 (2000); Antonio Annino, "Soberanías en lucha" and "Pueblos, liberalismo, y nación en México," in *Inventando la nación: Iberoamérica. Siglo XIX*, eds. Antonio Annino and François-Xavier Guerra, 152–184 and 399–430 (Mexico City: Fondo de Cultura Económica, 2003); and "The Two-Faced Janus: The Pueblos and the Origins of Mexican Liberalism," in *Cycles of Conflict, Centuries of Change: Crisis, Reform, and Revolution in Mexico*, eds. Elisa Servín, Leticia Reina, and John Tutino, 60–90 (Durham, NC: Duke University Press, 2007); and the essays collected in Juan Ortiz Escamilla and José Antonio Serrano Ortega (eds.), *Ayuntamientos y liberalismo gaditano*

In colonial Latin America, town councils had been formed in urban centers with enough wealthy, creole (Spanish-descended) inhabitants to occupy all positions of government. The Cádiz Constitution, by contrast, demanded the installation of town councils in all towns with more than a thousand inhabitants as well as in smaller settlements "in which their existence is advisable."[4] In Mexico the consequences of this provision were profound. In regions with large indigenous majorities, like Oaxaca, it meant that constitutional municipalities were to take the place of indigenous *repúblicas* (corporate governments), creating a uniformity of local political institutions across the country's principal ethnic division. In ethnically mixed regions, like much of San Luis Potosí, it meant that populations who used to arrange their affairs through separate administrative channels would have to participate in a single legal and political framework.[5] And in regions with predominantly mestizo populations, it meant that local governments sprang up in places where none had existed before. In Guanajuato there were seven town governments in 1800, nine after 1804, and twenty-three by the early 1820s, when the Cádiz Constitution had begun to be followed.[6] Settlements that had previously been governed from afar, as dependencies of bigger, wealthier towns, for the first time became independent administrative seats.

The realization that a large share of responsibility for the construction of a post-colonial Mexican state rested with people whose main theater of action was the municipality has made the study of local political cultures a central task for historians of the period. How did small-town residents evaluate the nature of their bond to the polity at large? What implications did their ideas have for the construction of a liberal republic? One way in which historians have approached these questions has been to analyze the cultural and intellectual traditions by which local actors understood the

---

en México (Zamora and Xalapa: El Colegio de Michoacán and Universidad Veracruzana, 2007); and in *Cabildos, Repúblicas y Ayuntamientos Constitucionales en la Independencia de México*, eds. Moisés Guzmán Pérez (Morelia: Comisión institucional para la conmemoración del bicentenario de la independencia y el centenario de la revolución mexicana, 2009). For discussions of the importance of the Cádiz Constitution for the Spanish American independence process as a whole, see Jaime Rodríguez O., *The Independence of Spanish America* (Cambridge: Cambridge University Press, 1998); and Roberto Breña, *El primer liberalismo español y los procesos de emancipación de América, 1808–1824* (Mexico City: El Colegio de México, 2006).

4   "[E]n que convenga que haya." *Constitución política de la monarquía española*, article 310.

5   Juan Carlos Sánchez Montiel, "Nuevos ayuntamientos y reformulación de la representación política: San Luis Potosí, 1812–1835," PhD dissertation, Instituto de Investigaciones Doctor José María Luis Mora (2007), 124–130.

6   José Antonio Serrano Ortega, *Jerarquía territorial y transición política: Guanajuato, 1790–1836* (Zamora: El Colegio de Michoacán, Mexico City: Instituto Mora, 2001), 147.

changes they lived through. By way of carefully contextualized reconstruc-
tions of instances of anti-Spanish violence in the first years of Mexico's
independence war, Eric Van Young has shown that larger ideas associated
with the liberal Enlightenment and to some extent present in the programs
of insurgent leaders and Spanish liberals in Cádiz, like national sovereignty
or legal equality, were often far from the minds of the rural poor who killed
and rioted under their banners. For example, in November 1810 crowds
from the mestizo town of Atlacomulco and the nearby indigenous hamlet of
San Juan de los Jarros broke into the home of a Spanish-born merchant and
killed him together with his son, his son-in-law, and his estate administrator. This merchant had in previous decades accumulated land in the area,
making enemies of peasants on whose fields he was encroaching. According
to Van Young, in such an instance of popular violence the objective of
rebels or rioters was nothing as distant as national independence or the
establishment of a constitutional republic. Rather, peasants took advantage
of the chaos of war to attack those they considered their enemies: land-
usurping hacendados, abusive state officials, Spaniards, the local rich.[7]
What was ultimately at stake for them was "the continued political
viability of peasant communities and their existence as substantially autonomous producers of local ethnic culture."[8] Van Young suggests that much
of the participation of the rural poor in the War of Independence was
attributable to similar motives.

The idea that in Mexico most local interests were barely touched by
liberal and nationalist strands of thinking has also been influential in
scholarship on the post-colonial period. For example, Antonio Annino
has argued that after independence Mexicans' political loyalties continued
to belong to their municipalities before they belonged to the nation.
Political sovereignty, according to a common understanding going back
to the colonial period, resided not in an abstract nation but was territorially
anchored in the corporate bodies of the municipalities. Annino argues that
instability in nineteenth-century Mexico was largely a result of this early
modern understanding of politics. Small-town actors allied themselves
with military insurgents, and declared the national contract broken, whenever they thought that the central government was infringing on their
autonomy.[9]

Van Young and Annino emphasize the tensions between locally shaped
values and the demands of a liberal polity – between peasants for whom

7   Eric Van Young, *The Other Rebellion: Popular Violence, Ideology, and the Mexican Struggle for
    Independence, 1810–1821* (Stanford: Stanford University Press, 2001), chapters 15–17.
8   Eric Van Young, "Agrarian Rebellion and Defense of Community: Meaning and Collective
    Violence in Late-Colonial and Independence-Era Mexico," *Journal of Social History* 27/2 (1993), 249.
9   Annino, "Soberanías en lucha" and "Pueblos, liberalismo, y nación," esp. 168–177 and 410–414;
    and "The Two-Faced Janus."

politics was a field of established reciprocities and cosmopolitan lawmakers for whom it was a means for implementing exalted ideas. Other historians have developed a less skeptical view about peasants' interest in the political universe outside their towns or villages. In regional studies of the states of Guerrero and Veracruz, Peter Guardino and Michael Ducey examine political culture not as a reservoir of habits but as an evolving set of practices and expectations.[10] Guardino and Ducey highlight the dispersion of liberal ideas of citizenship and show that - whatever the resilience of the cultural and ideational systems described by Van Young and Annino - municipal politics underwent dramatic changes under the impact of national events like the War of Independence. Ordinary citizens not only adapted the categories of elite liberal discourse to their own interests but participated in cross-class and cross-regional coalitions that allowed them to project those interests into the arena of national politics. They took active and, sometimes, instrumental roles in the policy disputes occupying the country's political classes – disputes about land reform, trade policy, taxation, or the treatment of Spaniards still residing in Mexico. While peasant demands were typically mediated by regional strongmen like Juan Alvarez of Guerrero or Mariano Olarte of Veracruz, they were united both by a common set of grievances and by a common idiom through which to express them. If we treat "class" as a discursive construction rather than an ontological presence – as a result, in the phrase of Gareth Stedman Jones, of "the production of interest, identification, grievance and aspiration within political languages themselves" – then it is hard not to understand the politics of post-colonial Mexico as at least partly a class struggle.[11] And to the extent that people in different parts of the country understood their grievances and interests through a common language of class it becomes possible to describe not only the many local histories but the national history of nineteenth-century Mexico from their perspective.

There were, in particular, two moments when varieties of class-based struggles pushed clearly defined policy initiatives onto Mexico's national stage. The first of these came in 1829 and coincided with the populist presidency of Vicente Guerrero. Confronted with a Spanish invasion attempt, the Guerrero administration gave in to popular pressure and ordered the expulsion of all Spaniards from the country. Apart from its immediate context, the initiative, like a similar though weaker expulsion bill that had been passed two years earlier, was prompted by the widespread

---

10 Peter Guardino, *Peasants, Politics, and the Making of Mexico's National State: Guerrero, 1800–1857* (Stanford: Stanford University Press, 1996); Michael Ducey, *A Nation of Villages: Riot and Rebellion in the Mexican Huasteca, 1750–1850* (Tucson: University of Arizona Press, 2004).

11 Gareth Stedman Jones, *Languages of Class: Studies in English Working Class History 1832–1982* (Cambridge: Cambridge University Press, 1983), 8, 22.

perception that Spaniards, often the richest people in town, continued to dominate the economy through their control of the commercial sector.[12] In the first decade and a half after independence, perhaps three-quarters of Mexico's Spaniards were forced to leave the country due to various expulsion laws passed at the state and federal levels, of which the 1829 law was the most effective.[13]

A second broad, class-based movement began in the 1840s when peasants in various parts of the country – Guerrero, Morelos, the Sierra Gorda, the Huasteca region – started rebellions or became embroiled in rebellion-like skirmishes with haciendas they accused of usurping land or exploiting workers and tenants. Pacified by a mixture of force and concessions, many rebels once more took up arms in the Revolution of Ayutla, which in 1855 overthrew a short-lived conservative dictatorship. In the revolution's aftermath, peasant rebels found spokesmen in social liberals like Ponciano Arriaga, who presented a detailed program for agrarian reform to the 1856–1857 Constituent Congress.[14] In this case, too, popular demands with an important class dimension, though first articulated in dispersed mobilizations and rebellions, achieved enough collective force to attract a national audience and, through the use of political intermediaries, to influence national debates and policy schemes.

But the most vital issue around which local actors mobilized again and again in early republican Mexico was the defense of the municipality as an independent political space. Here, the findings of Guardino and Ducey converge with those of Van Young and Annino. Before the reform-era civil wars, Mexico's political culture organized loyalties around two basic constitutional options. A federalist constitution, in effect from 1824 to 1835 and again from 1846 to 1853, devolved a great deal of power to the states and, within the states, to the municipalities. This constitution relied on near-universal male suffrage in order to fill local, regional, and national

12   Silvia Arrom, "Popular Politics in Mexico City: The Parian Riot, 1828," *Hispanic American Historical Review* 68/2 (1988), 257–263; Guardino, *Peasants*, 115–119, 122–123, 127, and *The Time of Liberty: Popular Political Culture in Oaxaca, 1750–1850* (Durham, NC: Duke University Press, 2005), 183–86, 204–205; Ducey, *Nation of Villages*, 132–133; Rosalina Ríos Zúñiga, "Popular Uprising and Political Culture in Zacatecas: The Sombrerete Uprisings (1829)," *Hispanic American Historical Review* 87/3 (2007), 504–509, 518–519, 524, 529–530, 534; Margaret Chowning, *Wealth and Power in Provincial Mexico: Michoacán from the Late Colony to the Revolution* (Stanford: Stanford University Press, 1999), 131–133.

13   Harold Dana Sims, *The Expulsion of Mexico's Spaniards, 1821–1836* (Pittsburgh: University of Pittsburgh Press, 1990), 6.

14   John Tutino, *From Insurrection to Revolution in Mexico: Social Bases of Agrarian Violence, 1750–1940* (Princeton: Princeton University Press, 1986), 249–258; Leticia Reina, "The Sierra Gorda Peasant Rebellion, 1847–50," in *Riot, Rebellion, and Revolution: Rural Social Conflict in Mexico*, eds. Friedrich Katz, 269–294 (Princeton: Princeton University Press, 1988); Guardino, *Peasants*, 191–209. Ducey, *Nation of Villages*, 145–158, 165–167.

government posts. By contrast, two centralist constitutions, in effect from 1836 to 1846 and again from 1853 to 1855, concentrated power in Mexico City, arranged for regional and local government posts to be filled by appointment, and limited voting rights to people with property or significant incomes. Apart from elite groups based in Mexico City and a few large provincial towns, the military was the strongest supporter of centralism and provided the system with a country-wide institutional base. But the majority of Mexicans viewed centralism as an attack on municipal freedom – even, Ducey writes, "a neocolonial project" – and resisted it fiercely.[15] By confirming the local focus of ordinary Mexicans' political commitments, regional studies of popular political culture complicate the class-based assessment of Mexico's post-colonial state that they also invite.

Must we conclude that Mexican popular actors launched their most important interventions in national politics only to protect old, corporate solidarities, even if they used a liberal vocabulary to do so? In this book I would like to explore a different possibility. Rather than study the way in which towns were involved in national political struggles, I would like to explore how national ideologies found traction in municipal politics. To do this it is necessary to consider provincial towns not just as repositories of local interests and identities but as centers of social and political life in their own right. And it is necessary to do this not just in times of heightened tension, such as the Guerrero presidency or the peasant wars of the 1840s, but also in times of social and political tranquility. If most Mexicans supported the federalist form of government, what did federalism mean to them, not in their relationship to a distant center of power but in their relationship to their neighbors and fellow citizens, and not as a political slogan but as a day-to-day framework of life?

In this and the following chapter, I will ask this question of the inhabitants of mestizo towns in Guanajuato and San Luis Potosí. I am using the term "mestizo towns" as a shorthand for municipal townships that did not carry on indigenous corporate traditions, even where indigenous people made up a substantial part of their population, as was often the case in San Luis Potosí. Mestizo towns had often been founded to take advantage of ecological and geological niches: the mineral deposits of the Sierra de Guanajuato, Sierra de Catorce, and other mountain ranges, or the fertile agricultural land of the Bajío basin, which made Guanajuato into one of the colony's principal areas of wheat, corn, and livestock production and, over time, gave rise to subsidiary leather and textile industries. Mestizo towns tended to be ethnically diverse and, compared to other settlement types, socially fluid. They thus lacked the sharpness of definition by which both indigenous towns and haciendas had been fixed in place in the political and imaginative

---

15   Ducey, *Nation of Villages*, 172.

edifice of colonial rule: the first as wards of the Crown in need of guidance and protection, the second as symbols and, often enough, realizations of settler dominance, opulence, and independence. In mestizo towns, inequality and privilege had been less firmly rendered into the formal structure of life.

This does not mean that in these places the federalist system was universally accepted. Federalist ideals were challenged both by an old class of patrician elites, who had dominated town politics in the colonial period, and by a new class of soldiers and officers who continued to enjoy colonial-era immunities under the jurisdiction of the *fuero militar*. In the clashes local federalists fought with these adversaries, their ideas acquired sharpness and definition, allowing us to discern – as it were from the outside – some of the vital realities that, beyond the protection of local solidarities, were at stake in local mobilizations for a federalist constitutional project.

II Soldiers

The Mexican army was a formidable adversary of legal rule in nineteenth-century Mexico. Old-regime Spain, like other countries in early modern Europe, had been crisscrossed by an assortment of special legal statuses that limited the application of the ordinary royal jurisdiction, the *fuero real ordinario*. In the eighteenth century, at least thirty-four privileged jurisdictions had existed, including "those of the military, the clergy, the corporations of merchants, and the mining industry." These fueros or jurisdictions, Lyle McAlister writes, had been "the juridical expression of a society in which the state was regarded not as a community of citizens enjoying equal rights and responsibilities, but as a structure built of classes and corporations, each with a unique and peculiar function to perform."[16] In colonial Mexico, the formal division between conquerors and conquered had added a further dimension of jurisdictional complexity to this situation.[17]

In the course of the eighteenth century, New Spain's legal pluralism was increasingly called into question. Spain's so-called Bourbon reforms were, among other things, attempts to reduce the reach of special jurisdictions and streamline the Empire's judicial apparatus. Designed to enhance the power of the Crown against other, rival sources of authority,

---

16 Lyle McAlister, *The 'Fuero Militar' in New Spain 1764–1800* (Gainesville: University of Florida Press, 1957), 5–6. See pp. 5–12 for McAlister's full discussion of the various types of *fueros* in Spain and colonial Mexico. See also Lauren Benton, *Law and Colonial Cultures: Legal Regimes in World History, 1400–1900* (Cambridge: Cambridge University Press, 2002), 43–45.

17 The classic account of Spanish attempts to come to grips with the legal implications of its New World conquests is Silvio Zavala, *Las instituciones jurídicas en la conquista de América*, 3rd ed. (Mexico City: Editorial Porrua, 1988 [1935]).

they also addressed a need to simplify adjudication procedures in cases that crossed jurisdictional boundaries – a need becoming more urgent with the growing volume of interactions between different social and cultural groups.[18] But the Bourbon attempt to create a more unitary state existed alongside short-term policy objectives that muted much of its impact. Thus, the same geopolitical debility that partly motivated Spain's imperial reforms made it paramount for the Empire to raise a credible army in its overseas territories. At the end of the colonial period the army, strengthened in number and insisting on its legal prerogatives, clashed more and more often with civilian authorities.[19] And while the Bourbon project of concentrating legal sovereignty in a unitary state found its final fulfillment after Mexico's independence from Spain, the special jurisdiction of the army, together with that of the Church, survived the transition to republican rule.

Because the *fuero militar* removed soldiers from the claims of civilian justice, it threatened to undermine the rule of law wherever soldiers and civilians shared social space together. In the early republican period the abuses – sometimes the outright crimes – committed by soldiers were among town councils' most intractable problems. In Villa de la Soledad, two soldiers beat up a butcher on the grounds that he had refused to debone a piece of meat he was selling; the mayor of Villa de la Soledad managed to arrest one of the assailants but had to surrender his prisoner to a sergeant, who claimed him as one of his men, a few minutes later.[20] In Villa de Valle, a soldier injured a civilian; authorities were unable to arrest him as he had found protection in the house of an officer. "No delinquent in these towns," the mayor wrote to the governor of San Luis Potosí in 1825, "in order to exonerate himself from punishment for his offences needs to do anything but to be an *urbano* [soldier in the urban militia]."[21] Civilian authorities who refused to surrender offending soldiers to their officers might be made to do so by force: in 1825 the military commander José María Terán broke into Aquismón's town jail and liberated a soldier who had been imprisoned for committing unnamed "excesses."[22]

18 Benton, *Law and Colonial Cultures*.
19 A process described in detail in McAlister, *'Fuero Militar' in New Spain*. On civilian-military conflicts in late-colonial Mexico, see also Christon Archer, *The Army in Bourbon Mexico, 1760 – 1810* (Albuquerque: The University of New Mexico Press, 1977), 16, 125–128, 171–175, 181–185.
20 Letter from Pantaleón Trujillo, Villa de la Soledad, 30 May 1835, in AHESLP-SGG, Caja 530, Expediente without number.
21 "Ningún delincuente en estos pueblos . . . necesita de otra cosa para exonerarse de la pena de sus delitos, que de ser urbano." José María González to Gobernador, Villa de Valle, 6 June 1825, in AHESLP-SGG, Caja 17, Expediente 8, Folios 8–9. The urban militia in 1825 was probably a holdover from the War of Independence and had at any rate not yet been brought under civilian control as it would be a few years later.
22 Juan José Velarde to Gobernador, Tancanhuitz, 7 April 1825, in AHESLP-SGG, Caja 17, Expediente 10, Fojas 1–3.

Not only ordinary soldiers were guilty of abuses. Often enough men on the higher rungs of the military hierarchy themselves violated the rights of their fellow-citizens. Town authorities were then reduced to reporting the issue to the governor of their state and awaiting whatever remedial action he, in turn, might be able to secure from the commandant general of the army. Such reports describe a broad range of misbehaviors: an officer who nearly whipped to death a worker on his estate; another who, bypassing the channels of civil law, settled a land dispute through simple occupation; another who, upon learning that his brother had been jailed, in the dark of night appeared before the house of the responsible mayor, uttering threats and curses; another who sent his soldiers to break into and search the houses of citizens whom he suspected of having stolen corn from his field.[23] To those affected by this behavior, it was little consolation that military judges by and large decided cases professionally and without corporate bias. [24] Military courts existed only in the *comandancias generales*, or army headquarters, located in state capitals, and were no realistic means of redress for most people suffering the abusive behavior of officers and soldiers.

The misbehavior of soldiers remained manageable as long as it consisted of instances that could be addressed, coped with, or even grudgingly ignored on a case-by-case basis. From the point of view of municipal authorities, worse than the inability to punish specific offences was the general erosion of legal standards wherever soldiers appeared in public. "Equality before the law," wrote the mayor of Dolores Hidalgo, "cannot allow that in the society of a peaceful town there are privileged citizens dedicated to maintaining themselves, working, and living side by side with others who do not enjoy such favors, because [in such a case] there could never be peace, harmony, or happiness."[25] The mayor of Xilitla in 1825

---

23   José María de Ayala y Soto to Gobernador, Pénjamo, 4 July 1834, in AGEG-J, Caja 23, Expediente
     5; Mariano Rodríguez to Gobernador, Pénjamo, 9 October 1835, in AGEG-J Caja 25, Expediente
     7; Luis Ramirez to Gobernador and Comandante General, Romita, 16 September 1839, in AGEG-
     J Caja 35, Expediente 13; Manuel Juncal to Gobernador, Yuriria, 19 November 1826, in AGEG-
     M Caja 28, Expediente 2. For further examples of reported abuses by military officers, see Rafael
     García to Gobernador, Silao, 8 December 1830, in AGEG-J, Caja 14, Expediente 14. "Noticia de
     los puntos que há tratado el Ylustre Ayuntamiento de Xichú en sus acuerdos del presente més,"
     30 June 1827, in AGEG-M Caja 38, Expediente 16. José María Fernández to Gobernador, San
     Felipe, 23 July 1836, in AGEG-G Caja 66, Expediente 6.

24   Linda Arnold, "Privileged Justice? The *Fuero Militar* in Early National Mexico," in *Judicial
     Institutions in Nineteenth-Century Latin America*, ed. Eduardo Zimmermann, 49–4 (London:
     Institute of Latin American Studies, 1999).

25   "La igualdad ante la ley no puede permitir que en la sociedad de un pueblo pacífico haya
     ciudadanos privilegiados dedicados a mantenerse, a trabajar, y a vivir unidos a otros que no
     gozan tales gracias, porque nunca habría paz, harmonía, ni felicidad ... " José Agustín Villegas
     to Gobernador, Dolores Hidalgo, 27 August 1824, in AGEG-G, Caja 2, Expediente 3.

complained about four town residents who, after joining the company commanded by José María Terán, let it be known "that being soldiers of the said company they wouldn't have to respect anyone in the town; that the *ayuntamiento* to them would be nothing." Lately, one of the offenders had taken to running through the streets and challenging the authorities, saber in hand.[26] The mayor of Salamanca also reported that "[v]arious individuals," protected by the military fuero, "are guilty of misconduct, which although I notice I cannot correct since if I do so I expose my authority and compromise [public] tranquility; because the *aforados* [people covered by the military *fuero*] say that the mayors are not their judges."[27] The mayor of Bizcocho simply complained about "the repeated scandals that those in the military commit" under cover of their *fuero*.[28] Such complaints tell us a lot about the kind of legal order that town governments thought it was their task to protect. They insisted on equality as the fundamental principle of republican law. From their point of view, the *fuero militar* removed wrongdoers and criminals, if not from all accountability then from any legal process that through its neutrality might vindicate the rights of those who had suffered harm and the authority of the laws that had been violated.

Two instances of conflict shed special light on the structural tension between civilian authorities and members of the military in post-colonial Mexico. One Sunday night in August 1826, a municipal patrol in Villa de la Soledad, San Luis Potosí, came upon a dance [*fandango*] hosted by the soldier Lugardo Mesquitic.[29] As they walked past his house, members of the patrol saw that Mesquitic was attempting to force his sister-in-law to dance with him. When the woman resisted her kinsman became aggressive, demanding to know on whose orders she refused him a dance. The patrol intervened and a violent scuffle ensued in which Mesquitic injured two officers and a female bystander with a knife. Mesquitic's companions meanwhile fought with other members of the patrol. The story ends the way many such stories ended, with the offender arrested and jailed – it is not clear whether during the confrontation or at a later time – and his superiors demanding his surrender.

---

26 Tomás Chávez [to Gobernador], Xilitla, 20 April 1825, in AHESLP-SGG, Caja 15, Expediente 22, Foja 2.

27 "Varios individuos . . . cometen algunas faltas, que aunque yo las advierto, no puedo corregirlas, porque de hacerlo, tanto expongo mi autoridad, como comprometo la tranquilidad; pues dicen los aforados que no son sus jueces los alcaldes. . . ." Marcelo Estrada to Gobernador, Salamanca, 16 May 1827, in AGEG-G, Caja 14, Expediente 7.

28 "[L]os repetidos escándalos que cometen los militares." Manuel Ignacio de Caballero to Secretario del Gobierno, San Miguel de Allende, 10 October 1847, in AGEG-G, Caja 82, Expediente 1.

29 José María Santuján to Gobernador, Soledad, 23 August 1826, in AHESLP-SGG, Caja 56, Expediente 5, Fojas 4–5.

Protecting women from the aggression of drunkards, often their husbands or lovers, was a common enough task for town patrols to perform.[30]
Unless the victims pressed charges, men who were caught beating up
women could expect to spend a night or at most a few days in jail before
being sent home. But whereas Mesquitic's behavior was unexceptional as
far as it related to his sister-in-law, his and his companions' attack on town
officers was not: challenging, threatening, and in rare cases physically
assaulting civilian authorities belonged to a pattern of behavior that was
common only in members of the military classes. In the army, the kind of
anarchic aggression that in Mexico has long been associated with masculine
culture was directed not only at disobliging women or perceived male rivals
but was enclosed in a self-sufficient milieu whose members were insulated
from civilian demands for good conduct and were willing to attack the
forces of order.[31]

Aggression against civilian functionaries and, by extension, against the
normative sphere they represented was also a feature of a second case. In Ojo
Caliente, San Luis Potosí, a group of officers had "infinitely oppressed these
quiet inhabitants" by pressing military-age men into their army units.[32]
In 1827, at a time when the state's military structure was in the process of
being streamlined and armed groups from the independence era were being
disbanded, the town mayor thought that the units the officers claimed to
belong to might recently have been abolished. He wondered if the officers
were still covered by the military *fuero*: if not, he would be able to proceed
against them. Putting an end to the officers' behavior was urgent, not
least because they encouraged criminal behavior in their men. One of
the soldiers, the mayor reported, "having gravely injured ... a man and
a woman," had recently found shelter under their protection.[33] The officers,
in other words, not only forced men into their military units but also
turned them against the world of rules and civility from which they had
been taken.

Things came to a head when the mayor, José Eligio de Jauregui, went to
the house of one of the commanders and demanded to see his military
papers. As de Jauregui was making his demand, ten soldiers appeared from

---

30 *Ronda* report from January 1829, San Luis Potosí, in AHESLP-SGG, Caja 204, Expediente 2;
    Ronda report from 6 July 1829, AHESLP-SGG, Caja 240, Expediente 1; *Ronda* reports from 18,
    20, and 22 July 1829, AHESLP-SGG, Caja 240, Expediente 3.

31 On the opposition between military and civilian masculine codes of conduct in post-independence
    Mexico, see Peter Guardino, "Gender, Soldiering, and Citizenship in the Mexican-American War
    of 1846–1848," *American Historical Review* 119/1 (2014), esp. 30–35, 41–42.

32 "[T]iene ... oprimidos hasta lo infinito ... a estos quietos vecinos." José Eligio de Jauregui to
    Gobernador, Ojo Caliente, 8 February 1827, in AHESLP-SGG, Caja 79, Expediente 3, Folios
    8–10.

33 "[H]abiendo herido gravemente ... a un hombre y una mujer," and "burlándose de la justicia."

inside the house and menaced the mayor with their bayonets. De Jauregui claimed that it was only thanks to "the prudence with which I made them see the illegality with which they took arms against authority" that he managed to escape unharmed. The soldiers, he implied, were restrained by something like the memory of their former, civil selves.[34] In his communication with the governor, de Jauregui made it clear that he did not stand alone in this confrontation:

Today since six o'clock in the morning I have been receiving protestations from the town's citizenry to help me in case it were necessary, but I have told them that I will do nothing except denounce this outrage against justice, against the law, and against my person before the superior authorities.[35]

The governor responded by clarifying the status of the officers: although the provincial militia had indeed been disbanded, the officers had been transferred to the reserve army and hence continued in possession of the *fuero militar*; their legal immunity was a fact the mayor would have to find a way to cope with. The officers did not, however, retain the right to recruit soldiers. To the conflict at hand the governor offered at best half a solution: he forwarded the mayor's complaint to San Luis Potosí's commandant general, who promised to tell the officers in Ojo Caliente to refrain from committing "similar outrages" in the future. He also ordered them to hand over the offending soldier to the mayor, who, in turn, was instructed to remit the soldier to the commander-in-chief after forming a preliminary investigation. That meant that the prisoner would be given a military judgment even though, if the mayor's initial report was right, he had been enlisted by men with no authority to do so. It also meant that the intimidation that de Jauregui had suffered at the officer's house would go without retribution. "But neither my personal honor," the mayor protested, "nor the office I have been given by the people of the town allow me to stop insisting that the outrages must be adequately punished."[36] Emphasizing the public source of his authority, de Jauregui demanded a vindication not

34 "[L]a prudencia con que les manifesté la ilegalidad con que se armaban en contra de la autoridad." De Jauregui's version of the occurrences inside the officer's house was supported by his two companions in a separate report: Apolinar Mendoza and Tomás Villalpando, Ojo Caliente, 8 February 1827, in AHESLP-SGG, Caja 79, Expediente 3, Folio 11.

35 "Hoy mismo desde las seis de la mañana estoy recibiendo protestaciones del vecindario de ayudarme en caso necesario, pero les he dicho que no hago otra cosa que reclamar ante la superioridad este ultraje a la justicia, a la ley y a mi misma persona." José Eligio de Jauregui to Gobernador, Ojo Caliente, 8 February 1827, in AHESLP-SGG, Caja 79, Expediente 3, Folios 8–10).

36 "Pero ni mi honor particular ni la investidura que obtengo por el pueblo me permiten dejar de insistir en que los atentados sean corregidos como debe ser." José Eligio de Jauregui to Gobernador, Ojo Caliente, 15 February 1827, in AHESLP-SGG, Caja 79, Expediente 3, Folio 18.

only of his personal honor but also of the transparency of justice that had been put into question. There is no indication that he received either.

The incidents I have cited are culled from biased and hostile reports written in moments of crisis. Their version of events cannot be taken at face value. But the tension that propelled them was not only real, it also looked much the same from the opposite side of the civilian-military divide. Appealing to his superiors to save him from the clutches of civilian justice, a soldier in Villa de Valle asserted that "only my [military] chief has legal dominion over me according to ordinance."[37] Neither civilian nor military authorities ever doubted that their differences derived from struggles over jurisdictional boundaries. Officers regularly protested when civilian authorities interfered in army matters, which included the punishment of delinquent soldiers.[38] If descriptions of conflict penned by military men tended to be shorter than those of their civilian counterparts, that was because their task was simpler: for the most part they acted within the letter of the law, which really did afford them a wide range of legal prerogatives, including criminal jurisdiction over army personnel.[39] They had no need to invoke larger principles, or describe pernicious chains of cause and effect, in order to justify their demands. They were also the men with the guns. As long as they stood their ground, it was likely that they would come out on top in local jurisdictional wrangles. Thus, José Delgado, military commander of Ojo Caliente, in a letter to town authorities capped his insistence on taking charge of the punishment of a soldier, accused of gravely injuring two civilians, with a veiled threat: "for . . . I will sustain as far as is possible the duty to which I am called by a legitimate authority, and [if you don't hand over the soldier] in no way will I be responsible for the results that might occur."[40]

In the first decades following Mexican independence, the problems created by the existence of a privileged military jurisdiction were to an extent held in check by the rarity of sustained civilian-military contact. Once the irregular forces of the war era had been disbanded or incorporated

37   "[S]ólo mi jefe tiene dominio potestad sobre mi según ordenanza." Letter from Juan Esteban Cruz to Comandante General, [1826], in AHESLP-SGG, Caja 43, Expediente 11, Foja 11.

38   José María Terán to Juan Velarde, Huehuetlan, 3 April 1825, in AHESLP-SGG, Caja 17, Expediente 10, Foja 4; Manuel María Alcalde to Señor Alcalde 2.o Constitucional, San Felipe, 19 October 1834, in AGEG-G, Caja 62, Expediente 7.

39   Further examples are Esteban Moctezuma to Alcalde 1.o de la Villa de Alaquines, Rioverde, 7 February 1832, in AHESLP-SGG, Caja 369, Expediente 1; and Juan Nepomuceno Canalizo to Alcalde 1.o de Acámbaro, Comandancia Militar de Salvatierra, 24 February 1824, in AGEG-G, Caja 3, Expediente 15.

40   "[P]ues . . . sostendré hasta donde me sea posible el deber a que estoy constituido por una autoridad legítima, y de ninguna manera seré responsable a los resultados que haya." José Delgado to Señor Alcalde primero de esta Villa, Ojo Caliente, 7 February 1827, in AHESLP-SGG, Caja 79, Expediente 3, Fojas 1–2.

into formal military structures – a process that in Guanajuato and San Luis Potosí was completed by the late 1820s – army battalions were stationed in large urban centers and other places of strategic interest. Most Mexicans encountered soldiers only when they were on their way to being deployed. Before the intensification of domestic and foreign military strife in the late 1840s, the tensions between soldiers and civilians largely remained at the margins of local political life.

In Guanajuato this was less true than elsewhere. Here, a military organization that dated from the anti-insurgent mobilization of the independence war, the *milicia auxiliar*, continued to operate in the post-war decades and became an important power base for the state's established elites.[41] Most military abuses reported in the state were committed by *auxiliares*, who had a reputation for being a particularly violent and unruly bunch, given to extreme disturbance whenever they appeared in any numbers. For example, in December 1832 the mayor of Irapuato wrote that a troop of *auxiliares*, passing through on their way to Querétaro,

> have spread themselves through this territory, robbing and committing excesses that cannot be tolerated, with such shamelessness and audacity that in the outlying parts of this town, the night of the fourth of the present month, a number of twelve or fourteen gathered together, they insulted as many women as they encountered, and knocked down those unhappy people who had the misfortune to get in their way.

He added that the *auxiliares* had now been joined by other men "who, perhaps in their support, practice the same criminalities."[42]

---

41 On the origin and history of Guanajuato's milicia auxiliar, see "Memoria del Secretario de Estado y del despacho de la Guerra presentada a las Camaras en enero de 1825" (Mexico City: Imprenta del Supremo Gobierno de los Estados-unidos mexicanos, en Palacio, 1825), 17–18. A copy of this booklet can be found in AGN-Gobernación, Sin Sección, Caja 87, Expediente 14. "Esped.te promovido sobre si deben gozar fuero las mugeres de los ausiliares del Egercito," Council of State, session from 3 March 1825, in AGEG-G Caja 7, Expediente 15; Report from the town council of Pénjamo dated 27 April 1824, in AGEG-G, Caja 3, Expediente 11; and José Estanislao Gallardo to Gobernador, Pueblo Nuevo, 4 November 1826, in AGEG-G, Caja 9, Expediente 8. An indispensable work on the organization of local military companies during the independence war is Juan Ortiz Escamilla, *Guerra y gobierno: Los pueblos y la independencia de México* (Seville, Spain: Instituto Mora, El Colegio de México, Universidad Internacional de Andalucia, and Universidad de Sevilla, 1997). On the role of the *auxiliares* in Guanajuato's post-war politics, see José Antonio Serrano Ortega, "El ascenso de un caudillo en Guanajuato: Luis de Cortázar, 1827–1832," *Historia Mexicana* 43/1 (1992), and *Jerarquía territorial*, 257–263.

42 "[S]e han diseminado por este territorio, robando y haciendo excesos que no pueden tolerarse, con tal descaro y osadía, que en los suburbios de esta Villa; la noche del 4 del corriente, reunidos en número de doce o catorce, se burlaron de cuantas mujeres encontraron, y atropellaron a los infelices que tuvieron la desgracia de topar con ellos"; and, "que acaso en su apoyo, ejercitan las mismas criminalidades." Manuel Valenzuela to Gobernador, Irapuato, 6 December 1832, in AGEG-M, Caja 112, Expediente 6.

Auxiliary soldiers, who unlike regular soldiers lived among the civilian population rather than in special barracks, were a thorn in the side of local authorities even when not on campaign. In 1823, the government of San Felipe accused a resident auxiliary commander of collecting provisions for his private use – in effect, stealing – and of giving his soldiers license to do the same.[43] At the beginning of 1824, the mayor of Amoles reported that the commander of the local auxiliary company had, "by his own authority," confiscated three pieces of livestock from a resident who he claimed was owing him money. The mayor further wrote that men belonging to the auxiliary company refused to obey any authority other than that of their commander.[44] In 1827 the mayor of Uriangato wrote that the auxiliary militia in his town "is harmful because of its total indiscipline and the ineptitude of its officials," who "enlist delinquents persecuted by [the public authorities] into their companies," shielding them from punishment.[45] Drunkards, thieves, or adulterers, once they fell afoul of the civil authorities, could sign up with the *auxiliares* and continue their behavior with little fear of being sanctioned. The association of the auxiliary militia with depraved behavior was strong enough for some town governments to become concerned that so many bad and idle men had joined the militia that none were left to be pressed into the regular army.[46]

The political implications of the strain between *auxiliares* and local governments are most clearly revealed in two episodes in which soldiers belonging to auxiliary companies came to blows with members of the civic militia – the non-professional police corps that was the principal enforcer of law in mestizo towns. Documentation of the first of these cases comes from the auxiliary commander Tiburcio Balbueno. On the evening of March 13, 1825, Balbueno wrote, a member of the *cívicos* of Salamanca walked up to the auxiliaries' barracks and "insulted the troops with injurious words."[47] The following evening an unknown group of men, who Balbueno had no doubt belonged to the *cívicos*, knocked at the door of the barracks and, when

---

43   José Ignacio Espinosa to Jefe Superior Político, Villa de San Felipe, 25 August 1823, in AGEG-G, Caja 1, Expediente 23.

44   Antonio José Reyes to Jefe Político, Amoles, 17 January 1824, in AGEG-M, Caja 7, Expediente 1.

45   "[E]s nociva por su total indisciplina e ineptitud de sus oficiales"; and "alistan en sus compañías, delincuentes que aquellas [las autoridades públicas] persiguen .... " In "Espediente instruido á consecuencia de una esposicion hecha por el Alcalde Constitucional de Uriangato sobre los males que causa la falta de subordinacion y disciplina de la tropa auxiliar de aquel distrito," 1827, AGEG-G, Caja 15, Expediente 9.

46   Ayuntamiento Constitucional to Gobernador, Silao, 13 September 1840, in AGEG-G, Caja 72, Expediente 13; Francisco Abalo to Gobernador, San Luis de la Paz, 8 June 1845, in AGEG-G, Caja 78, Expediente 1; Gerónimo Calatanón to Gobernador, Celaya, 22 June 1854, in AGEG-G, Caja 119, Expediente 2.

47   "[C]on palabras injuriosas estuvo insultando la tropa." Letter from Tiburcio Balbuena, Salamanca, 15 March 1825, in AGEG-G, Caja 4, Expediente 11.

someone opened the window, fired a shot inside. Aside from the general hostility that Salamanca's *cívicos* were said to feel for the *auxiliares*, Balbuena provided no contextual information. The conflict, at any rate, does not appear to have escalated.

The second episode took place in 1827 and was reported by Ignacio Sierra, mayor of Irapuato. Sierra described how a group of auxiliary soldiers arrived at a dance apparently organized by the civic militia – the civic drummers provided the music for the entertainment – and started a fight that left seven people injured, three of them so gravely they were not expected to live. By the time Sierra had been informed of the fight, the civic militia had sounded the alarm; when he arrived at the militia barracks he found more than 200 *cívicos* already assembled, ready to move against the *auxiliares*. Yet in contrast to the *auxiliares*, the *cívicos* did not allow their passions to get the better of their discipline: "Thanks to the discipline that reigns among these worthy *cívicos*, their officers were able to contain the intense fury caused by a faction of villains."[48] As a result, Sierra wrote, he managed to take the offending *auxiliares* into custody while avoiding further bloodshed.

The military commander of Salamanca, Rafael Vélez, and the mayor of Irapuato stylized their accounts of the two clashes around competing assumptions about the sources of public order. Enclosing the report of auxiliary officer Balbuena with his own assessment of the situation, Vélez called Salamanca's civic militia "a body without order or discipline" and "a monster of society."[49] He went on, "in it you find assassins; thieves; bums without profession or known means of livelihood . . .: with the beautiful cloak of citizenship crimes are covered, and in conclusion there is neither order nor discipline."[50] It was no wonder that, since the time of the company's formation, public tranquility in Salamanca had been "exposed to a terrible and bloody disruption."[51] The problem was not simply that soldiers were drafted from the lower classes of the town – that was expected, and Vélez did not attempt to argue that the *auxiliares* were made from finer stuff. The problem was that men who entered the civic militia were driven by a desire "to get themselves exalted as chiefs." As a result, politics in

---

48 "A merced de la subordinación que reina en estos cívicos beneméritos, lograron sus oficiales contener el furor altamente irritado, por una facción de malvados." Ignacio Sierra to Gobernador, Irapuato, 5 June 1827, AGEG-G, Caja 20, Expediente 6.

49 "[U]n cuerpo sin orden ni disciplina'" "[U]n monstruo de la sociedad." Rafael Vélez to Gobernador, Salamanca, 19 March 1825, in AGEG-G Caja 4, Expediente 11.

50 "[E]n él se hallan asesinos; ladrones; holgazanes sin oficio ni modo de pasar conocido . . .: con la hermosa capa de la ciudadanía se cubren los crímenes." Rafael Vélez to Gobernador, Salamanca, 19 March 1825, in AGEG-G Caja 4, Expediente 11.

51 "[E]xpuesta a un trastorno horroroso, y sangriento." Rafael Vélez to Gobernador, Salamanca, 19 March 1825, in AGEG-G Caja 4, Expediente 11.

Salamanca had been taken over by a cabal of unscrupulous men who, combining administrative and military positions, used their power "to absolutely make themselves into monarchs, oppressing the peaceful citizens."[52] Vélez's problem, in other words, was democracy and its flip side, despotism. Composed of base people who were "in everything governed by private passions and interests," the civic militia was also a conduit through which the lowest behavior could flow into the public sphere.[53] Auxiliary soldiers, by contrast, had no say in the choice of their officers and were prevented from disturbing the social peace by the workings of the military hierarchy.

Now contrast Vélez's account with the second story, as told by the mayor of Irapuato. In the mayor's account, the anger of more than 200 *cívicos* who had convened in support of their comrades expressed not a mob mentality but the solidarity of a body of citizens who identified with their institutions and submitted without a murmur to the commands of their elected authorities. The action of the *auxiliares*, on the other hand, exposed the weakness of a system dependent on imposed discipline. Left unattended by their commanders, the soldiers wandered the town "like Moors without a master" and, the mayor implied, behaved as mercenaries with no commitment to the cause they were paid to protect. They "need to be taught a lesson," he demanded, "and with an exemplary punishment, so they will learn to respect the parts [*sic*] of National Sovereignty by whose expenses they subsist."[54] In an exact reversal of the military discourse, Irapuato's mayor associated national sovereignty with local civilian institutions and saw in the auxiliary forces a subsidiary instrument always in danger of spinning out of control.

These accounts suggest that the conflict between soldiers and civilian institutions, including the civic militia, drew meaning from the ideological matrix of national politics. In Guanajuato, the *auxiliares* were an important base of support for the rise of Luis de Cortázar, the landowner and military commander who in the 1830s dominated politics in the state. Belonging to a prominent landowning family, de Cortázar became a moderate federalist who kept the central government at arm's length from Guanajuato's internal affairs while suppressing popular revolts and intervening against

---

52 "[D]e hacerse exaltar como jefes"; and "[P]ara amonarcarse absolutamente oprimiendo a los ciudadanos pacíficos." Rafael Vélez to Gobernador, Salamanca, 19 March 1825, in AGEG-G Caja 4, Expediente 11.

53 "[D]irigido en todo por las pasiones e intereses particulares." Rafael Vélez to Gobernador, Salamanca, 19 March 1825, in AGEG-G Caja 4, Expediente 11.

54 "[C]omo moros sin señor"; and "[N]ecesitan ser escarmentados, y con un castigo ejemplar para que aprendan a respetar las secciones de la Soberanía Nacional a cuyas expensas subsisten." Ignacio Sierra to Gobernador, Irapuato, 5 June 1827, AGEG-G, Caja 20, Expediente 6.

more radical politicians in neighboring states.[55] This association between *auxiliares* and a particular political tendency, though uncommonly strong and straightforward, exemplified the role of the army in politics across the nation. There were features of army life – the military *fuero*, the rivalry with the civic militia, the strict attention to hierarchy – that inclined the military as an institution toward a distinct ideological position: one that exalted order, abhorred the conflicts caused by squabbling politicians, and celebrated the army's role in the foundation and defense of the nation.[56] And while some aspects of this ideology gave it a unique place within Mexico's post-colonial political spectrum, it clearly had more in common with moderate and conservative positions than with radical liberal ones.[57] In the small-town settings we have observed, soldiers and officers disdained the authority of elected functionaries and resented the civic militias. In sensibility, they were far closer to the patrician than to the democratic tendency in municipal politics.

III Patricians

José Antonio Serrano Ortega's study of the territorial hierarchy of post-independence Guanajuato describes a deep factional division in the municipal politics of the early republican period. On one side stood powerful families who continued to dominate the social life of colonial-era administrative centers, on the other side a rising class of shop owners, farmers, and craftsmen who often resided in smaller urban congregations and who under the Cádiz Constitution could for the first time aspire to positions in the

55 Serrano Ortega, "El ascenso de un caudillo."
56 Will Fowler, *Military Political Identity and Reformism in Independent Mexico: An Analysis of the Memorias de Guerra (1821–1855)*, Research Paper No. 47 (London: Institute for Latin American Studies, 1996), 11–21, 32–35, 40–54; Will Fowler, *Mexico in the Age of Proposals, 1821–1853* (London: Greenwood Press, 1998), chapter 6; and for a political biography of Mexico's leading general of the period, Will Fowler, *Santa Anna of Mexico* (Lincoln: University of Nebraska Press, 2007); Frank Samponaro, "The Political Role of the Army in Mexico," PhD Dissertation, State University of New York at Stony Brook (1974), 73–75, 79–80, 171–240; José Antonio Serrano Ortega, *El contingente de sangre: los gobiernos estatales y departamentales y los métodos de reclutamiento del ejército permanente mexicano, 1824–1844* (Mexico City: Instituto Nacional de Antropología e Historia, 1993), "El ascenso de un caudillo," 63–69; and, *Jerarquía territorial*, chapter 6.
57 This interpretation is borne out by Donald Stevens's analysis of 26 politicians who had come into politics after a military career. Of 11 politicians identified with a radical-liberal position, all had served in state or civic militias and none in the National Army; of 5 politicians identified with a moderate position, 2 had served in state or civic militias and 3 in the National Army; and of 10 politicians identified with a conservative position, only 1 had served in state or civic militias and 9 in the National Army. Donald Fithian Stevens, *Origins of Instability in Early Republican Mexico* (Durham, NC: Duke University Press, 1991), 53–54, table 4.4.

governments of their towns.[58] The opposition between established patricians and a rising bourgeoisie expressed itself in a number of conflicting positions on concrete policy issues: the patricians wished to abolish property taxes, the newcomers wished to retain them; the patricians wished to restrict the franchise, the newcomers wished to keep it open; the patricians wished to demobilize the civic militias, as far as was possible without compromising public safety, the newcomers wished to make them stronger. Most importantly, the patricians in the early 1830s began supporting a centralist constitutional project that would restore their own towns to primacy in Guanajuato's regional politics, whereas the newcomers defended the federalist model to which they owed their political relevance.[59]

What was the patricians' attitude toward the egalitarian orientation of Mexico's legal regime? Historians have recently emphasized the principled liberalism of the centralist constitutions and their intellectual backers. According to this interpretation, the anti-populism of the centralist project was driven by a concern for the same protection of rights and liberties that, a decade earlier, the country's first constitution-makers had tried to bring to life in a federalist system.[60] Confronted with the instability of post-colonial politics, intellectual and political leaders came to believe that

---

58 Serrano Ortega, *Jerarquía territorial*. Other scholars have shown that similar political struggles took place inside single mestizo towns in Oaxaca and Michoacán: Guardino, *Time of Liberty*, chapter 5; and Ramón Alonso Pérez Escutia, "Angangueo, Michoacán: Un ayuntamiento de mineros, 1820–1838," in *Cabildos, Repúblicas y Ayuntamientos Constitucionales* ed. Guzmán Pérez. Donald Stevens has shown that at the level of national politics, too, political convictions to an extent could be predicted by the wealth and social positions of their holders, with radicals occupying "the lower rungs of the social elite," conservatives holding "the uppermost social positions with the largest households and greatest profusion of household servants," and moderates fitting somewhere in the middle. Stevens, *Origins of Instability*, 105.

59 Serrano Ortega, *Jerarquía territorial*, chapters 4–6.

60 Reynaldo Sordo Cedeño, *El Congreso en la primera República Centralista* (Mexico City: El Colegio de México, Instituto Tecnológico Autónomo de México, 1993); Will Fowler, *Mexico in the Age of Proposals, 1821–1853* (London: Greenwood Press, 1998); Will Fowler, *Santa Anna of Mexico* (Lincoln: University of Nebraska Press, 2007); William Fowler and Humberto Morales Moreno, "Introducción: Una (Re)definición del conservadurismo Mexicano del siglo diecinueve," and Josefina Zoraida Vázquez, "Centralistas, conservadores y monarquistas 1830–1853," in *El Conservadurismo Mexicano en el Siglo XIX (1810–1910)*, eds. Humberto Morales and William Fowler, 115–133 (Puebla: Benemérita Universidad Autónoma de Puebla, Saint-Andrews University, and Gobierno del Estado de Puebla, 1999); Chowning, *Wealth and Power*, chapter 3; Erika Pani, "La 'innombrable': monarquismo y cultura política en el México decimonónico," in *Prácticas populares, cultural política y poder en México, siglo XIX*, ed. Brian F. Connaughton, 369–394 (Mexico City: Universidad Autónoma Metropolitana and Casa Juan Pablos, 2008); and Josefina Zoraida Vázquez, *Dos décadas de desilusiones: En busca de una fórmula adecuada de gobierno (1832–1854)* (Mexico City: El Colegio de México, 2009). For a similar argument about the ideological orientation of elites across Spanish America in this period, see Karen Racine, "'This England and This Now': British Cultural and Intellectual Influence in the Spanish American Independence Era," *Hispanic American Historical Review* 90/3 (2010), 423–454.

democratic "equality" was undermining "liberty" and that the appointment of judicial authorities by a central power would provide a more reliable framework for the protection of liberty than their election. Administrative rationality, rather than popular passion, was needed to make the law secure in the country. The switch to centralism, these historians argue, was a symptom of disenchantment – a reaction to the inability of the federalist system to bring peace and law to the nation. In this section, I would like to problematize this account. I want to show that the operative archives of municipal politics can give us a more immediate and, perhaps, a less mystifying view of the ideological concerns that animated elite reactions to the federalist experiment than statements and arguments made in public forums or aimed at a public audience.[61]

In 1824 the patrician town council of León, Guanajuato, reported to the state governor that

a misfortune [that is] the daughter of ignorance and lack of enlightenment has impressed on the majority of inhabitants [the belief] that liberty consists in acting according to their passions; as a result of this we have the multitude of thefts, murders, and other excesses, to the extreme of offending the authorities, who without support blushingly tolerate insults which, apart from offending their authority, are causes of bad examples for others.[62]

The town jail, wrote the patricians, was insufficiently large to hold all delinquents, so that authorities were obliged to free people arrested for minor offences. Local judges were overwhelmed with the number of cases to try. The concept of liberty, newly installed in the mind of every last ruffian, had become a public danger. In a post-war context in which public authority remained weak and social violence rampant, the liberal-egalitarian paradigm thus served as a ready-made explanation for what had gone wrong with the country. The writers pleaded with the governor "to pass measures capable of imposing on the people their subjection to the

61 Robert Buffington proposes that Mexican criminological discourse already showed a tendency to criminalize, and hence exclude from the benefits of citizenship, whole population groups in the late colonial and early republican periods. Before the second half of the nineteenth century, however, this tendency existed as "an unacknowledged subtext" and was most prominent in writings "not intended for a general literate audience." Internal administrative reports and queries are, of course, a prime example of such an elite transcript largely hidden from public view. Robert Buffington, *Criminal and Citizen in Modern Mexico* (Lincoln: University of Nebraska Press, 2000), 10, 15.

62 "[U]na desgracia hija de la ignorancia y falta de la ilustración ha impresionado a la mayoría de habitantes que la libertad es extensiva a obrar conforme a sus pasiones; de aquí resulta la multitud de robos, muertes, y otros excesos hasta el extremo de faltar a las autoridades que sin apoyo toleran ruborosamente, insultos que a más de ofender su autoridad, son causa del mal ejemplo de otros. " Alcaldes Constitucionales to Montes de Oca, León, 11 August 1824, in AGEG-M, Caja 8, Expediente 3, Foja 59.

authorities, and the means to make swift and effective the punishment of those who, [having strayed] off the course of the law ..., disturb the tranquility of the peaceful citizens and threaten their safety."[63] Their town, they implied, was about to succumb to mob rule.

The mayor of San Miguel de Allende, another of Guanajuato's old administrative centers, was equally anxious. The people of his town

> have badly understood the sacred rights that man enjoys in a free state, they have falsely persuaded themselves that liberty is the same as libertinage; that not to be held in despotism, is not to respect the authorities, nor obey the laws; and that subordination, the love of work, and the conservation of good order is typical of the *serviles* [Spanish loyalists].[64]

The mayor interpreted the high number of homicides in the countryside as a direct consequence of this mentality. The people, he wrote, had "abandoned themselves to the grossest and most antisocial vices, filling their fatherland with mourning and dishonoring liberty, which should impress on them the purest and most generous sentiments and the keenest and most efficient desire to conserve [public] order." For him, too, liberty was a concept too hard to handle to be made widely available. He went on to explain that San Miguel's civic militia was without weapons, and at any rate "experience has taught us that with it [the civic militia] one cannot conserve the public order."[65] And he asked for the mobilization of the auxiliary militia in order to establish law and order in his jurisdiction.

As descriptions of social violence the reports from León and San Miguel were hardly unusual. Everywhere in the country local governments faced the challenge of reestablishing order after the upheavals of the independence war.[66] Everywhere jails were overflowing. Prison conditions were

---

63   "[D]e dictar las providencias capaces a imponer al Pueblo en la sujeción a las autoridades, y el medio de hacer prontos, y efectivos los castigos de aquellos que desviados de la ley ... turban la tranquilidad de los ciudadanos pacíficos, y atentan contra su seguridad." Alcaldes Constitucionales to Montes de Oca, León, 11 August 1824, in AGEG-M, Caja 8, Expediente 3, Foja 59.

64   "[H]a entendido mal los sagrados derechos que el hombre goza en un estado libre, falsamente se ha persuadido que libertad es lo mismo que libertinaje: que no estar sujeto al despotismo, es no respetar las autoridades, ni obedecer a las leyes; y que es propio de los serviles la subordinación, el amor al trabajo, y la conservación del buen orden." Ignacio Cruces to Montes de Oca, San Miguel el Grande, 8 October 1824, in AGEG-M, Caja 5, Expediente 4, Foja 15.

65   "[S]e han abandonado a los vicios más groseros y antisociales, llenando de luto a su Patria y deshonrando a la Libertad que les debía imprimir los más puros y generosos sentimientos, y el más vivo y eficaz deseo de conservar el orden"; and "y la experiencia nos ha enseñado que con ella [la milicia cívica] no se puede conservar el orden público." Ignacio Cruces to Montes de Oca, San Miguel el Grande, 8 October 1824, in AGEG-M, Caja 5, Expediente 4, Foja 15.

66   For a discussion of rising crime rates as well as the manner in which they were interpreted in Mexico City in the post-independence period, see Michael Scardaville, "Los procesos judiciales y la autoridad del estado: Reflexiones en torno a la administración de la justicia criminal y la legitimidad en la ciudad de México, desde finales de la Colonia, hasta principios del México

such that suspected murderers often managed to escape or else, to avoid overcrowding, were released on bail until a time could be fixed for their trials.[67] Describing a situation in which "a thousand crimes are committed and these offences remain unpunished," the mayor of Silao asked permission to organize a bull run in order to raise funds for building an adequate jail.[68] He also reported that council members were barely able to cope with their tasks: "The load of criminal cases in this court and the scarcity of lettered advisors with whom to consult in order to proceed legally in [these cases] means that they proceed slowly, to the detriment of the unfortunate prisoners."[69] Following close on the heels of a civil war whose most unambiguous result – apart from the fact of independence – had been the dismantling of most judicial institutions, a different situation could probably not have been expected, least of all in towns that had not previously served as legal and administrative seats.

The reports from León and San Miguel were unusual not for their descriptive but for their ideological content. By denouncing the leveling impulse of the new system of government, they already expressed, in the first year of the federalist system, an affinity with the kinds of restriction that the 1836 centralist constitution would place on political participation. They also expressed a more diffuse disaffection. When patricians argued that an excess of liberty was at the root of the current crisis of authority, or that the instruments of law-enforcement envisioned by the new political system, of which the civic militia was the most important, were ineffective, they challenged the viability not only of particular laws or constitutional articles but also of the entire legal structure of what even under centralist constitutions would remain a liberal republic. The suggestion, made by mayor of San Miguel, that only the auxiliary militia could bring population to order is particularly revealing. We already saw that auxiliary militia had close ties to the state's patrician elites and were notorious for abusing their *fuero militar* and assaulting civilians. To almost anyone else in the state it would have been obvious that to deploy the

---

independiente," in *Poder y legitimidad en México en el siglo XIX: Instituciones y cultural política*, ed. Brian Connaughton, 405–422 (Mexico City: Biblioteca de Signos, 2003).

67 "Relacion de los presos pendientes." Jeréquaro [1824], in AGEG-M, Caja 7, Expediente 6, Foja 4. "Relacion de los procesos pendientes," Irapuato, 13 July 1824, in AGEG-M, Caja 7, Expediente 10, Foja 1; "Relacion de los reos," Salamanca, 23 July 1824, Caja 7, Expediente 13, Foja 5. "Noticia de los Reos q. hay en esta carcel," San Felipe, 14 July 1824, in AGEG-M, Caja 7, Expediente 15, Foja 8.

68 "[M]il crímenes lo verifican y quedan impunes sus delitos." José Mariano Reynoso to Gobernador, Silao, 9 October 1824, in AGEG-M, Caja 9, Expediente 10, Foja 20.

69 "El recargo de causas criminales que hay en este Jusgado y la escases de letrados con quien consultar para proceder en ellas legalmente hacen que estando atrasadas, sufran los infelices reos perjuicios." José María Reynoso to Gobernador, Silao, 10 June 1824, in AGEG-J, Caja 3, Expediente 25.

auxiliares was more likely to multiply instances of legal impunity than to
stop them.

In 1824 authorities in León and San Miguel understood social unrest not
as a contextual phenomenon, best battled by strengthening the new institutions, but as an intrinsic dimension of the egalitarian conception of
liberty. They assumed that plebeian Mexicans were too mean not only to
participate in the nation's political life but also to live by its laws.
Patricians continued to view the world through colonial assumptions:
before God all people may have been equal, but the law could ill afford to
treat weavers, miners, or sharecroppers – who would mistake liberty for
license and were ruled by passion rather than reason – with the same respect
it quite properly offered to merchants, notaries, or even master craftsmen.
The administrative discourse employed by Guanajuato's urban oligarchs
thus reveals a disaffection with the basic premises of Mexican constitutionalism. Politicians who wielded it were troubled not by the fragility of the
post-colonial legal system but by the principles on which, all around them,
they saw it being constructed.

At least until the 1840s, the patrician discourse was not a prominent
aspect of local politics. More common in Guanajuato than in San Luis
Potosí, even the archives of the former state yield only isolated examples.
Outside elite strongholds – León, Celaya, San Miguel de Allende, the state
capital, and perhaps Salvatierra – it appears to have existed not so much as
a discreet ideological program but as a submerged structure of attitude that
would rise to the surface at times of impasse or frustration.[70] For example,
in 1825 a certain Gil de Jesús Nolasco walked into the courtroom of Yuriria
with a glass of *aguardiente* (cane liquor), interrupting the mayor's attention
to a complaint made by a group of women. "[W]ith the greatest publicity
and shamelessness," reported the mayor, "and without showing me due
respect, [Nolasco and the women] took to drinking [the *aguardiente*] in the
same courtroom and in my presence." The mayor was moved to register
a larger complaint. He feared that the ideology of independence fostered
a culture of insolence: mocking the authorities, he wrote, had of late
become a habit in his town, whose residents defiantly declared "that we
are no longer in the time of the *gachupines* (Spaniards)."[71] Or consider the
opinion given by Mariano de Santiago, a member of the government of
Jerécuaro, when opposing a motion to "severely punish" inhabitants who

70 Buffington helpfully speaks of the "dispersed" and "disorderly" nature of certain criminological
    tropes in this period. He nevertheless suggests that these tropes amounted to an "intertextual
    discourse" that "was more convincing, more functional, and ultimately more influential than any
    of its individual components." Buffington, *Criminal and Citizen*, 11–12.

71 "[Y] con la mayor publicidad y descaro, sin atender a mi respeto se pusieron a tomarlo dentro del
    mismo juzgado y a mi presencia"; and "que ya no estamos en tiempo de los gachupines." Rafael
    Aranda to Gobernador, Yuriria, 8 March 1825, in AGEG-J, Caja 4, Expediente 21.

failed to follow a municipal bylaw. De Santiago argued that such people acted not from carelessness or malice but from "the supreme ignorance in which they are wrapped, it being evident that most citizens don't know what law is nor to what its fulfillment obliges them."[72] He concluded that it would be unfair to punish people for a fault that their lack of understanding gave them no possibility of remedying. While pleading for greater leniency, de Santiago shared the patrician assumption that lower-class Mexicans were not competent to fully assume their legal responsibilities under a republican system of government.

Defensive more than dynamic, and defining an attitude more than a project, in the daily workings of municipal politics the patrician discourse appears to have done little more than animate a few measures and proposals, largely ad hoc and not always consistent between themselves. The patrician discourse had its greatest impact not on the practice of local governance but on the higher-order question of which, and how many, settlements should be allowed to form local administrations in the first place. While the Cádiz Constitution had ordered the creation of town councils in all settlements of more than a thousand inhabitants, many Mexican states eventually removed municipal status from towns – often indigenous – whose populations they considered unsuitable for self-government.[73] In Guanajuato, where thirty towns formed local governments under the provisions of the Cádiz Constitution, eight of these had their municipal status revoked in 1826.[74] Reducing the number of local governments had the predictable consequence of stacking the legal system in favor of people with money and leisure: a hacienda owner could easily travel an extra eight or nine leagues to get to the nearest court of justice, whereas a day laborer might not be able to make the same trip without letting his children go hungry.

In debates over the municipal status of two particular towns, we can get a fuller view not only of the understanding of social power that motivated the patrician discourse but also of the republican challenge against which it reacted. Citizens of Cerritos, in San Luis Potosí, petitioned to have their town elevated to the status of a municipality in 1826. They began their request by citing the state constitution, which had adopted the Cádiz formula of demanding *ayuntamientos* in all towns of more than a thousand inhabitants. The petitioners wrote that Cerritos, together with surrounding hamlets or smaller settlements (*ranchos*), counted 2,341 current residents. "[D]esiring the splendor and progress of this state," they argued that

---

72 "[C]astigarlos severamente"; and "por la suma ignorancia en que se hallan envueltos, siendo evidente que los mas ciudadanos no saben qué cosa es ley ni a lo que los obliga su cumplimiento." Actas de Ayuntamiento, Jerécuaro, 7 October 1830, in AGEG-M, Caja 91, Expediente 1.

73 Guardino, *Peasants, Politics*, 86, 97; Claudia Guarisco, *Los indios del valle de México y la construcción de una nueva sociabilidad política, 1770–1835* (Zincantepec: El Colegio Mexiquense, 2003), 198–199.

74 Serrano Ortega, *Jerarquía territorial*, 158–159, 305.

the town was in need of a local government in order to realize the social project intended by the constitution.[75] Justice was central to that project. "Cases are very common in which a citizen needs to come before constitutional mayors in their respective courts, for the determination of their [the citizens'] affairs." Yet in order to reach the nearest court, in the municipal seat of Guadalcázar, "we have to walk the eight leagues that there are to the said Guadalcázar, of which the greatest part is impassable because it is rocky mountain land."[76] Under such conditions the rule of law could not be said to exist for inhabitants of Cerritos in the same way that it did for other Mexican citizens.

The town council of Guadalcázar responded by collecting statements from influential residents of nearby hamlets who expressed their desire to remain under Guadalcázar's jurisdiction. The council intimated a history of conflict between residents of Cerritos and those of the surrounding countryside, so that the attempt to form a government in Cerritos appeared merely as a strategy of conquest. But the writers devoted the largest part of their argument to a demonstration that the establishment of a court in Cerritos would be undesirable from the point of view of legal rule. If it were granted, citizens falling under Cerritos's new jurisdiction would be forced "to appear before and submit themselves to the judgment or decision of rustic and reckless mayors, compromising the outcome of their business." Law was a delicate science, difficult even for those trained in its technicalities. How, then, could one expect simple country folk – people "who have never even seen the alphabet, and suddenly find themselves [called?] to the difficult dignity of judges" – to understand it? Guadalcázar's authorities foresaw a disastrous result. "Miserable people," they exclaimed, "governed by people incapable of distinguishing the just from the iniquitous!"[77]

75 "[D]eseando el esplendor y progresos de este Estado." "Exped.te instruido por este Gobno. a solicitud de los vecinos del Puesto de los Serritos sobre creacion de Ayuntam.to en dho. punto, jurisdiccion de Guad.r," in AHESLP-SGG, Caja 44, Expediente 1.

76 "Son muy presentes los casos en que todo ciudadano necesita ocurrir a los alcaldes constitucionales en sus respectivos juzgados, para la decisión de sus asuntos"; and "tenemos que andar ocho leguas que hay para dicho Guadalcázar, de las que la mayor parte son intransitables por ser una fragosa sierra." "Exped.te instruido," in AHESLP-SGG, Caja 44, Expediente 1. Similar arguments about the difficulty of taking legal business to far-away municipal seats were made by the inhabitants of some settlements in federalist-era Yucatán. See Arturo Güémez Pineda, "El establecimiento de corporaciones municipales en Yucatán y los mayas: de la Constitución de Cádiz a la guerra de castas," in *Poder y gobierno local en México, 1808–1857*, eds. María del Carmen Salinas Sandoval, Diana Birrichaga Gardida, and Antonio Escobar Ohmstede, 274–275 (Mexico City: El Colegio Mexiquense, 2011).

77 "[D]e comparecer y someterse al juicio, o decisión de unos alcaldes rústicos, y temerarios, comprometiendo el éxito de sus negocios"; "que jamás han visto, siquiera el alfabeto, y repentinamente se hallan [llamados?] a la dificultosa dignidad de jueces"; "¡Miserables pueblos, gobernados por hombres incapaces de distinguir lo justo, de lo inicuo!" Luciano Posadas to Gobernador, Guadalcázar, 23 December 1826, in AHESLP-SGG, Caja 44, Expediente 1.

The authorities of Guadalcázar based their arguments on an uncompromising social vision. They thought that it was nonsensical to grant the request of Cerritos's citizens because, as a rural settlement, Cerritos belonged to a sphere of life far removed from conditions in which the law could be practiced. "Generally," they wrote, "rural people lack principles, and are absolutely ignorant of the first elements, or general notions, of law." The settlement even lacked the territorial requirements for proper participation in the constitutional legal order: because its inhabitants rented their house plots from a confraternity in Guadalcázar, they would be removed from the site if they ever failed to make their annual payments. Consequently, the projected *ayuntamiento* "would not have a fixed location, rather it would be an ambulant body." Instead of creating a new jurisdiction that would do damage to the very principles of justice, it was preferable "that the postulants come before the constitutional mayors of [Guadalcázar] to resolve their (by no means frequent) affairs."[78] The authorities of Guadalcázar thus did not see the people of Cerritos as full participants in the realm of social exchange enclosed and protected by the law. The town's population had no need for the presence of local judicial institutions; infrequent trips to Guadalcázar would suffice.

We find a sharper formulation of the patrician vision in the 1835 response from San Luis de la Paz to a request from citizens of San Pedro de los Pozos, a mining town of more than five thousand inhabitants, to be granted permission to elect a constitutional mayor and municipal solicitor (*alcalde constitucional* and *procurador síndico*) for their population. Guanajuato's state constitution had created the offices of the *alcalde constitucional* and *procurador síndico* for towns that lacked the number of literate inhabitants necessary to fill and annually replace a whole town council but were nevertheless too large to rely on auxiliary officials appointed by the nearest head town.[79] In the past, the inhabitants of San Pedro de los Pozos had been allowed to elect such officers. At that time, they wrote, the officeholders had "fulfilled their duties to the satisfaction of the respectable residents and of their superiors, who did not find faults of crass ignorance in them." Like the petitioners from Cerritos, those from San Pedro de los Pozos hoped that the presence of legal and political authorities would result in "the prompt administration of justice" for

---

78 "Por lo común las gentes rurales carecen de principios, e ignoran absolutamente los primeros elementos, o generales nociones, de Derecho "; "no tendría radicación fija, sino que sería un ente ambulante"; and "que los postulantes ocurran a los alcaldes constitucionales de la cabecera para resolver sus asuntos (nada frecuentes)." Luciano Posadas to Gobernador, Guadalcázar, 23 December 1826, in AHESLP-SGG, Caja 44, Expediente 1.

79 *Constitución política del Estado libre de Guanajuato*, article 147.

inhabitants of their town. They also hoped it would allow them to hold a Sunday market, as they had done under the colonial government, and to establish a primary school.[80]

The town council of San Luis de la Paz gave two arguments to oppose the idea of upgrading San Pedro's political status. First, none of the men who lived in the settlement were capable of holding the requested government posts. In San Pedro, wrote the aldermen, only a few individuals knew how to read and write, and those "are so miserable that it is to be feared that, on account of their lack of social standing, they would be exposed to derision and contempt, and that if they behave honestly [i.e., not accept bribes] they will perish of hunger."[81] Second, the council argued that the funds that local functionaries could hope to derive from renting out public land would be insufficient for the salary of a secretary and other administrative costs. The council also dismissed the desire of San Pedro's residents to reinstate the weekly market that had been held in the town before 1810. It was necessary to understand that

in that epoch there intervened circumstances that now are missing: that the business of the mines gave it momentum, and the lieutenant of justice with other respectable residents authorized it and prevented excesses, and [also took care that] the sales taxes were not being defrauded as must happen today.

In response to their petition, the citizens of San Pedro should be told that it was not to be expected that the establishment of a weekly market "would benefit the residents, but to the contrary it would harm them, because of the excesses that would be committed deriving from the drunkenness" that a market would attract.[82] The mayor of San Miguel de Allende, who forwarded the report to the governor in Guanajuato City, was particularly impressed with this last objection. In his own note, he repeated that, should a market be established in San Pedro, "we would be exposed to suffering disturbances to public quietude as a result of the drunkenness and other

80 "[H]an llenado la órbita de sus deberes, a satisfacción de los vecinos de propiedad y de los superiores quienes no han encontrado en aquellos faltas de crasa ignorancia"; and "la pronta administración de justicia." "Espediente instruido á consecuencia de la solicitud q. hacen varios vecinos del Mineral de S. Pedro de los Pozos . . .," [1835], in AGEG-M, Caja 132, Expediente 8.

81 "[S]on tan miserables que se teme que por la ninguna representación que tienen, exponerlos a la burla y al desprecio, y que si se portan con honradez perezcan de hambre." Joaquín Valdez, San Luis de la Paz, 9 May 1835, copied in San Miguel de Allende, in AGEG-M, Caja 132, Expediente 8.

82 "[Q]ue en aquella época mediaban circunstancias que ahora faltan: que el giro de las minas le daba impulso, y el teniente de justicia con otros vecinos de respeto lo autorizaban e impedían los excesos y no se defraudaban como ahora debe suceder los derechos de alcabalas"; and "no se considera que . . . resulten beneficiados sus vecinos, sino que por el contrario perjudicados, por los excesos que se deben cometer provenidos de la embriagues." Joaquín Valdez, San Luis de la Paz, 9 May 1835, copied in San Miguel de Allende, in AGEG-M, Caja 132, Expediente 8.

excesses that would be committed with impunity."[83] He also seconded the council's recommendation to allow, and even encourage, the establishment of a local primary school, whose oversight would rest with the authorities in San Luis de la Paz. As so often in nineteenth-century Mexico, vague encouragements about the provision of popular education served above all as justifications for denying the non-educated a voice in politics.

The arguments of the town council of San Luis de la Paz amounted to an anti-popular fantasy about the character of plebeian sociality. If the government of Guadalcázar believed that the people of Cerritos could do without a local court because of the infrequency of their legal business, that of San Luis believed that, absent the large-scale mining operations that before 1810 had boosted the town's commerce under the watchful eyes of colonial officers, allowing a market in San Pedro would create not a new ease of commerce but rather tax evasion and public scandal. People would see the market as an opportunity to drink and brawl, not exchange their corn for chilies or their wages for firewood. This allegation was particularly egregious because it was made in the same letter that denied San Pedro the presence of local legal officers who would be tasked with checking such excesses. The inhabitants of San Pedro, was the unstated assumption, needed no judicial presence because they had no capacity for the kind of social life that a judicial presence would regulate. For the authorities of San Luis de la Paz, the existence of a literate public sphere was a prerequisite not only for the responsible exercise of political rights but for the creation of republican legality as such. They frankly acknowledged the propertied, exclusive character of that public sphere by arguing that only men whose wealth put them apart from others would ever be able to demand the necessary respect to serve in positions of authority. Only where such men lived in any numbers could the rule of law be established.

It is this exclusiveness that justifies the use of the term "patrician" to describe an ideology that, while often originating in colonial-era family networks of local elites, no longer insisted on the God-given hierarchy of castes and estates to which those elites had first owed their rise to political and economic prominence. Creole elites who professed a belief in liberal principles were not therefore willing to accept lower-class pretensions to equal treatment before the law. From the very first years of Mexico's independence, they responded to the egalitarian tendencies of the country's new institutions by elaborating a social ontology that cast doubt on the capacity of Mexico's poor majorities to participate in the republican system of law-governed social relations. To cast their reaction as a defense of the

83   "[E]staríamos expuestos a sufrir las alteraciones de la quietud pública consiguientes a la embriagues y otros excesos que se cometerían impunemente." José María Terán to Gobernador, San Miguel de Allende, 15 May 1835, in AGEG-M, Caja 132, Expediente 8.

principle of "liberty" against that of "equality," as intellectual historians have sometimes done, is to misunderstand the nature of the disagreement between patrician and non-patrician sectors of mestizo society. The question was not whether the protection of "liberty" should or should not prevail over other political objectives. The question was whether liberty would be a right of citizenship or a privilege for the wealthy. In the end, the people of Cerritos were granted their request to become a municipal seat while those of San Pedro de los Pozos were denied theirs to elect an *alcalde constitucional* and *procurador síndico*. But in the petitions from both we get a first idea of the concrete meaning that federalism came to assume for many of its local supporters: it meant that the institutions charged with the protection of liberty must be open to all.

IV   Municipalities

Patricians and soldiers represented a danger to republican institutions of which other Mexicans were sure to be mindful. At a time when both colonial rule and the independence war were still within living memory, the heirs of colonial and independence-era power elites could expect to be taken seriously. Their actions and pronouncements forced adherents of liberal or federalist ideas to clarify their own commitments. When inhabitants of settlements like Cerritos or San Pedro de los Pozos explained their desire to be granted local governments in terms of residents' lack of access to the republican system of law, or when local officials attempted to defend their sphere of influence against military impunity, the need to respond to patrician or military adversaries drove them to articulate positions that went well beyond a desire to protect local interests or solidarities. Let us now look more closely at the municipal powers they defended or wished to establish.

Representing the state administratively, municipal governments carried out some of its most indispensable functions.[84] They were in charge of putting on annual independence-day celebrations, of organizing the election of local, regional, and national governments, and of collecting many of the state's taxes. They were responsible, too, for building and repairing public structures like roads, bridges, aqueducts, and fountains.[85] Some ran

---

84   See also Juan Ortiz Escamilla and José Antonio Serrano Ortega, "Introducción," in *Ayuntamientos y liberalismo gaditano*, eds. Ortiz Escamilla and Serrano Ortega, 9–18.

85   See, e.g., José Pablo Gómez to Gobernador, Apaseo, 19 August 1824, in AGEG-M, Caja 1, Expediente 1; Ignacio Romero to Gobernador, Silao, 23 December 1826, in AGEG-M, Caja 29, Expediente 18. Bartolomé Hernández to Gobernador, Dolores Hidalgo, 10 June 1826 and 12 June 1826, in AGEG-M, Caja 33, Expediente 1; Juan Méndez to Gobernador, Salvatierra, 24 January 1828, in AGEG-M, Caja 64, Expediente 9; Actas de Ayuntamiento, Acámbaro, 6 March 1829, in AGEG-M, Caja 77, Expediente 2; Manuel Vásquez to Jefe de Partido de

public granaries.[86] In Guanajuato, a few built public clocks.[87] Town governments also took charge of cleanliness and sanitation, passing edicts or bylaws (*bandos de policía*) that required residents to keep dogs and pigs off the streets, dispose of garbage in designated areas, and, on specified week days, sweep down and water the road in front of their houses.[88] They were partly addressing health-related concerns: in these years smallpox and cholera repeatedly swept the country, and – following the medical reasoning of the time – authorities attempted to free their towns of "mires from whose rotting arise corrupt miasmas that infect the atmosphere."[89] In Guanajuato and San Luis Potosí, these sanitation measures were paralleled by a smallpox vaccination campaign and probably contributed to a reduction in the incidence of epidemic disease in the nineteenth century.[90] But sanitation laws also had an aesthetic function. The authorities of Valle de San Francisco wrote that keeping pigs from roaming the

Celaya, Apaseo, 18 June 1838, in AGEG-M, Caja 144, Expediente 1; Manuel Vásquez to Gobernador, copying letter from the *ayuntamiento* of Yuriria, Celaya, 19 May 1838, in AGEG-M, Caja 144, Expediente 1; Ayuntamiento de Catorce to Gobernador, [1825], in AHESLP-SGG, Caja 24, Expediente 6; Report from Villa de Cerritos, enclosed with Anastasio Quiros to Gobernador, Guadalcazar, 13 January 1832, in AHESLP-SGG, Caja 369, Expediente 2. "Cuenta general de las cantidades imbertidas," Catorce, 19 December 1839, in AHESLP-SGG, Caja 732, unnumbered Expediente. Juan de Ugarte to Secretario del Superior Gobierno, Venado, 29 November 1841, in AHESLP-SGG, Caja 755, Expediente 3.

86   Citizens of Mineral del Pozo to Gobernador, [1826], in AHESLP-SGG, Caja 34, Expediente 7; Ramón Sáenz de Mendiola to Secretario del Superior Gobierno, copying from first and second judges of Cedral, Venado, 11 May 1841, in AHESLP-SGG, Caja 755, Expediente 4; Actas de Ayuntamiento, Villa de San Felipe, 28 March 1827, in AGEG-M, Caja 44, Expediente 5; "Diligencias practicadas p.ra conceder permiso del gasto de reparar las Casas Consistoriales y Alhondiga de S.n Mig.l el Grande á solicitud de su Ayuntamiento," [1825], in AGEG-M, Caja 12, Expediente 12; Actas de Ayuntamiento, Dolores Hidalgo, 17 May 1834, in AGEG-M, Caja 126, Expediente 6; José Martínez de Lejarra to Secretario del Superior Gobierno, San Luis de la Paz, 20 November 1851, in AGEG-M, Caja 179, Expediente 6.

87   Actas de Ayuntamiento, Dolores Hidalgo, 1 August 1828, in AGEG-M, Caja 64, Expediente 5; Actas de Ayuntamiento, Acámbaro, 12 January 1829, in AGEG-M, Caja 77, Expediente 2; Juan Pastor to Gobernador, copying from Jefe de Partido de San Felipe, San Miguel de Allende, 22 March 1841, in AGEG-M, Caja 152, Expediente 5.

88   For Guanajuato, see the following bandos de policía in AGEG-M: Silao, 1825, Caja 21, Expediente 8; Salvatierra, [1826], Caja 32, Expediente 9; Dolores Hidalgo, 20 October 1827, Caja 38, Expediente 3; Silao, 11 January 1833, Caja 112, Expediente 13; Acámbaro, 21 February 1833, Caja 120, Expediente 1; Salamanca, 1833, Caja 121, Expediente 5; Silao, 22 September 1842, Caja 154, Expediente 15; and Salvatierra, 1857, Caja 196, Expediente 4. For San Luis Potosí, see the following bandos in AHESLP-SGG: Coscatlan, 8 January 1826, and Tancanhuitz, 4 January 1826, Caja 33, Expediente 10; Valle de San Francisco, 10 February 1826, Caja 37, Expediente 5; Axtla, 6 March 1826, Caja 40, Expediente 1, Foja 3; Coscatlan, 19 January 1827, Caja 75, Expediente 19, Fojas 3–4; Charcas, 10 June 1841, Caja 755, Expediente 4.

89   "[L]os fangos de cuya pudrición dimanan miasmas corrompidas que inficionan la atmósfera." Bando de Policía, Salvatierra, [1826], in AGEG-M, Caja 32, Expediente 9.

90   Angela Tucker Thompson, *Las otras guerras de México* (Guanajuato City: Ediciones La Rana, 1998).

streets was a first step toward assuring "the cleanliness of a town that counts itself among those [towns] of some cultivation."[91] They regarded cleanliness as a public good requisite for upholding a collective moral pretension.

The most important function carried out by municipal governments, and the one that soldiers and patricians were most likely to obstruct, was the dispensation of justice. An 1812 law passed by the Cádiz parliament charged town mayors with correcting "insults and misdemeanors that deserve no other punishment than a reprimand or light correction" and with resolving civil disputes concerning values of less than fifty pesos.[92] While the law ordered graver matters to be tried by trained judges – one was supposed to be installed in any town of more than five thousand people – this provision was too impractical to be put into effect in wartime. In most places, municipal officers probably assumed the functions of first-instance judges in all civil and criminal matters that did not directly implicate public officeholders. After 1824, under the federalist system, the state constitutions of both Guanajuato and San Luis Potosí confirmed the role of mayors as first-instance judges but ordered state governments to hire a small number of judicial experts to advise, oversee, and, if necessary, correct their legal activities.[93]

The centralist constitutions of 1836 and 1843 curtailed the powers of local judges and altered the manner of their selection. In inland towns of more than eight thousand or port towns of more than four thousand inhabitants, mayors would now be elected under a limited franchise. In smaller towns, judicial functions were vested in unelected justices of the peace, to be appointed, from among local residents, by the state governments.[94] Mayors and justices of the peace were made responsible for facilitating the conciliation of feuding parties and, if unsuccessful, of verbally trying disputes about goods or services that did not exceed one hundred pesos in value.[95] In criminal matters, they would deal with all

---

91   "[L]a limpieza de un pueblo que se numera entre los de algún cultivo." Bando de Policía, Valle de
     San Francisco, 10 February 1826, in AHESLP-SGG, Caja 37, Expediente 5.
92   "[S]obre injurias y faltas livianas que no merezcan otra pena que alguna represión o corrección
     ligera." "Reglamento de las audiencias y juzgados de primera instancia," 9 October 1812, chapter
     3, article 5, in Manuel Dublán and José María Lozano (eds.), *Legislación Mexicana, ó, Colección
     completa de las disposiciones legislativas expedidas desde la independencia de la República*, vol. 1 (Mexico
     City: Imprenta del Comercio, 1876), 394.
93   *Constitución política del Estado libre de Guanajuato*, section 4, articles 193, 197. *Constitución política del
     Estado libre de S. Luis Potosí* (Mexico City: Imprenta del águila, 1826), articles 212, 215.
94   *Leyes Constitucionales*, 1836, part 6, articles 22, 23, 24, 28.
95   *Leyes Constitucionales*, part 6, articles 26, 29. The maximum amount of 100 pesos was fixed in an
     1837 law, "Arreglo provisional de la administracion de justicia en los juzgados y tribunales de
     fuero comun," 23 May 1837, article 113, in Dublán and Lozano (eds.), *Legislación Mexicana*,
     vol. 3, 403. The 1843 Constitution contained no provisions to replace the earlier arrangement of
     local judicial administration.

cases the district judges decided to leave in their care – in most cases probably the same "insults and misdemeanors" already invoked by the Cádiz law. They would also be responsible for intervening against disturbances of the public order and for carrying out initial inquiries in criminal cases.[96] Though their powers were diminished, local justices remained indispensable for the working of the republican legal system, and town halls with their respective courts of justice continued to be built, repaired, and renovated in the centralist era – even in small towns like Cedral, San Luis Potosí, where justices of the peace were the only local functionaries.[97]

The proliferation of legal functionaries in Mexican mestizo towns was part of a transformation in Latin America's legal culture that historians have only recently begun to investigate. In his study of nineteenth-century Venezuela, Reuben Zahler has identified three major legal innovations during the transition from the colonial to the republican era: because jurisdictional boundaries were for the first time clearly demarcated, legal processes became more efficient; because procedural rights were beginning to be codified, and judges lost their discretionary power, legal processes became more transparent, and judges more vulnerable to challenge on the ground of due-process violations; finally, because evidentiary standards became focused more tightly on the cases in question, rather than on the rank or reputation of the interested parties, legal processes became more empirical and unbiased.[98]

In Mexico, too, early republican judges were guided by shared standards of efficiency, due process, and empiricism. Consider a typical homicide case. Most often dealing with the outcome of a drunken brawl, such a case would begin with a written disposition, sometimes composed by auxiliary officers stationed in outlying ranchos or haciendas, that summarized the incident as

---

96 *Leyes Constitucionales*, part 6, article 26. "Arreglo provisional de la administracion de justicia en los juzgados y tribunales de fuero comun," 23 May 1837, article 102, in Dublán and Lozano (eds.), *Legislación Mexicana*, vol. 3, 402.

97 Oficio from first alcalde of Santa Cruz copied by Manuel Vásquez, Celaya, 26 July 1838, in AGEG-M, Caja 144, Expediente 1. "Presupuesto del costo que deben tener los útiles p.a la oficina del Juzgado de letras de este Partido," San José de Iturbide, 1 December 1851, in AGEG-M, Caja 179, Expediente 5; Ramón Reynoso to Gobernador, Celaya, 25 June 1845, copying from alcalde of Santa Cruz, in AGEG-M, Caja 166, Expediente 5; Crescencio Escobar to Prefecto del Distrito de Rioverde, Lagunillas, 6 May 1840, in AHESLP-SGG, Caja 740, Expediente "Las autoridades de Lagunillas, solicitan la licencia respectiva para el cambio de un terreno que pretende hacer D. José M. Olvera con los fondos de propios de dha. villa"; and, for the case of Cedral, Ramón Saenz de Mendiola to Secretaría del Superior Gobierno, Venado, 16 April 1841, copying from sub-prefecto of Catorce, copying from first and second justices of the peace of Cedral, in AHESLP-SGG, Caja 755, Expediente 8.

98 Reuben Zahler, *Ambitious Rebels: Remaking Honor, Law, and Liberalism in Venezuela, 1780–1850* (Tucson: University of Arizona Press, 2013), 107–119. Note that Zahler treats the issues of "transparency" and "due process" under different headings; to me they appear to belong together.

it had first been reported. Based on this document, the acting judge would order the arrest of the reputed perpetrator and the interrogation of witnesses. He would also commission a local surgeon to provide an expert opinion on the cause of death and the type and gravity of the victim's wounds. If the guilt of the accused could be established, the judge would then decide on a sentence – usually between two and twelve years of imprisonment with forced labor – based on considerations about intent, premeditation, and, if the murder was inflicted in the course of a fight, level of responsibility for the dispute and its escalation.[99] Practiced with a high degree of procedural routine, such processes met all three of the criteria that Zahler describes as marking the transition from a colonial to a republican culture of justice.

Whether in Mexico, as in Venezuela, such procedural uniformity was largely an innovation of the post-colonial period is a more difficult question. The most abrupt change from an old-regime to a post-revolutionary legal culture in Mexico was brought about by the abolition of corporate privileges. A standardized and routinely efficient legal procedure was, by contrast, already being followed in some criminal courts at the end of the eighteenth century: concerned with lower-class criminality in Mexico City, Viceroys Martin de Mayorga and Count Revillagigedo had created a well-staffed system of municipal tribunals, which came to handle the vast majority of the city's criminal cases. According to Michael Scardaville, the tribunals employed "court procedures [that] were generally impartial and predictable" and "sentenced 90 percent of all offenders within three days of their arrest, with at least one-half receiving punishment on the day following apprehension."[100] The trial procedures of the *acordada*, a police force tasked not just with catching but also with judging bandits in all parts of the colony, had remained less regular than those of the Mexico City tribunals, but after 1790 for the first time were subjected to routine judicial review in capital cases.[101]

---

99 Selections of injury and homicide cases from the early republican period can be found in AHESLP-STJ and AHML-Justicia-Causas Criminales. For a discussion of the varied sources of law and jurisprudence Mexican criminal judges drew on in the immediate post-independence period, see Elisa Speckman Guerra, *Crimen y castigo: Legislación penal, interpretaciones de la criminalidad y administración de justicia* (Mexico City: El Colegio de México, 2002), 23–30.

100 Michael Scardaville, "(Hapsburg) Law and (Bourbon) Order: State Authority, Popular Unrest, and the Criminal Justice System in Bourbon Mexico City," in *Reconstructing Criminality in Latin America*, eds. Carlos Aguirre and Robert Buffington, 1–18 (Wilmington: Scholarly Resources Inc., 2000), 8; and "Los procesos judiciales y la autoridad del estado: Reflexiones en torno a la administración de la justicia criminal y la legitimidad en la ciudad de México, desde finales de la Colonia, hasta principios del México independiente," in *Poder y legitimidad en México en el siglo XIX: Instituciones y cultural política*, ed. Brian Connaughton, 379–428 (Mexico City: Biblioteca de Signos, 2003).

101 Colin MacLachlan, *Criminal Justice in Eighteenth-Century Mexico: A Study of the Tribunal of the Acordada* (Berkeley: University of California Press, 1974), 84–87.

Reforming the old-regime justice system had thus been a concern, and sometimes an active project, of late-colonial bureaucrats decades before it became a task for republican politicians. However, reformist bureaucrats had been influential in few places outside of Mexico City. In most of the country, justice in the late-colonial period had been dispensed in the first instance either by town-council officers or by the viceregal administrators known as *corregidores* and *alcaldes mayores* and, after 1786, *intendentes* and *subdelegados*.[102] About the actual workings of this system we still know little. Even if we assume that these magistrates, too, had been influenced by novel ideas about procedural justice – at best a doubtful assumption – their presence had, at any rate, been confined to urban centers. The lieutenants they had appointed in some smaller towns had been without salaries, staff, and, apart from their private residences, buildings in which to hold court; it is hard to imagine that they had contributed much to the dispensation of justice, much less to the implementation of any kind of legal reform.[103]

A post-independence surge in the construction of jails and town halls, which also functioned as courts of justice, is perhaps the most tangible sign of a substantial shift in Mexican legal culture during the country's transition from a colonial to a republican regime. Together with the schoolhouse, jails and town halls were the only buildings owned – or, rarely, rented – by almost all local governments at almost all times in Mexico's post-independence nineteenth century. They were also the workplaces of municipalities' only permanent employees: the secretary, the jailer, and the teacher. But schools, while dependent on town councils and, in the minds of many, indispensable to the civic enterprise they embodied, in their daily operation were semi-separate organisms with no bearing on the business of government. Town halls and jails served the immediate needs of local administrations.

In the mestizo towns of Guanajuato and San Luis Potosí town councils took great care to acquire solid and attractive buildings, suited to the dignity of their purpose. In 1824, on the occasion of "the grandiose act of the swearing-in of our constitution," the government of León argued for the need to construct a new meeting room [*sala capitular*] because the old one, on account of "its smallness and shabbiness," was incompatible with "the decorum of a body that represents this great population."[104] In 1828, the

---

102 Horst Pietschmann, *Las reformas borbónicas y el sistema de intendencias en Nueva España: Un estudio político administrativo*, trans. Rolf Roland Meyer Misteli (Mexico City: Fondo de Cultura Económica, 1996), 118–125. Serrano Ortega, *Jerarquía territorial*, 42–45.

103 On the tenientes in smaller settlements, see the few remarks in Serrano Ortega, *Jerarquía territorial*, 43; and Pietschmann, *Las reformas borbónicas*, 180–181.

104 " [El] grandioso acto del juramento de nuestra constitución "; "su poca extensión y desaliño"; and "el decoro de un cuerpo que hace la representación de esta gran población." Manuel Antonio de Lizardi to Gobernador, León, 27 November 1824, in AGEG-M, Caja 8, Expediente 8.

government of Purísima del Rincón, about to move from rented rooms into a town hall then under construction – in a phrase hinting at the aesthetic weight placed on the appearance of municipal buildings – wrote that the finished work would give "presence and beauty" to the town square.[105] The casual visitor, the artisan's wife selling *atole* in the town square, the farmer seeking out a functionary to attend to legal business, all would, it was hoped, be impressed and perhaps humbled by the respectability of the edifice. The size and lay-out of town halls varied considerably and depended on a town's financial capacity. The mayor of Casas Viejas in 1846 presented Guanajuato's governor with a drawing of a new town hall his government had built, in part by employing the voluntary labor of some of the town's artisans. The structure included an entryway, guards' room, meeting hall, archive, court room, secretariat, and courtyard.[106] But the majority of *ayuntamientos* could not afford such spacious lodgings, and some, especially in the post-war years, had trouble finding any suitable location. In the poorer state of San Luis Potosí, the authorities of Lagunillas in 1840 were still trying to replace a building they described as in an advanced state of decay.[107] But that also was rare. Typical town halls probably resembled the one for whose construction the government of San Francisco del Rincón proposed a budget in 1826, and which would contain a big room or hall and an adjacent office: the first no doubt for weekly council meetings and public business, including civil and criminal proceedings, and the second for administrative work and correspondence.[108] Town-hall furniture consisted of desks, shelves, and chairs, and sometimes included carpets and other "decorations."[109] Town halls, then, were functional buildings that lent the municipality, and through it the national polity to which it belonged, a worldly and symbolic permanence transcending the brief terms of office of

---

105　"[S]er y hermosura." [Facundo?] Aguirre to Jefe Político del Departamento, Purísima del Rincón, 13 January 1828, in AGEG-M, Caja 64, Expediente 7.

106　"Ynforme relativo á la Casa Consistorial de San José Casas Viejas. Año de 1846," in AGEG-M, Caja 168, Expediente 1.

107　Ángel Torrín to Jefe Superior Político, Irapuato, 5 July 1823, in AGEG-M, Caja 2, Expediente 3, Foja 14; Juan Nepomuceno Barragán to Gobernador, Valle del Maíz, 10 January 1826, in AHESLP-SGG, Caja 35, Expediente 12; Crescencio Escobar to Prefecto del Distrito de Rioverde, Lagunillas, 6 May 1840, in AHESLP-SGG, Caja 740, Expediente "Las autoridades de Lagunillas, solicitan la licencia respectiva para el cambio de un terreno que pretende hacer D. José M. Olvera con los fondos de propios de dha. villa."

108　Domingo Hernández to Gobernador, San Francisco del Rincón, 14 December 1826, in AGEG-M, Caja 21, Expediente 4.

109　Actas de Ayuntamiento, Chamacuero, 26 January 1829, in AGEG-M, Caja 78, Expediente 4. Oficio from first alcalde of Santa Cruz copied by Manuel Vásquez, Celaya, 26 July 1838, in AGEG-M, Caja 144, Expediente 1; "Presupuesto del costo que deben tener los útiles p.a la oficina del Jusgado de letras de este Partido," San José de Iturbide, 1 December 1851, in AGEG-M, Caja 179, Expediente 5.

particular local or national administrations, or even of particular constitutional regimes. In the same way that parish churches represented the spiritual body of the universal Church, town halls represented the secular body of the republic.

Jails, too, reflected the values of Mexico's post-colonial political order. According to the Cádiz Constitution, jails should be constructed "to secure and not molest the prisoners," who in particular must not be held in "subterranean or unhealthy dungeons."[110] In Guanajuato and San Luis Potosí, there remained some jails that were cramped and dark, and others that lacked security, throughout the period under study.[111] But town governments made persistent efforts to build new ones or improve the ones that existed.[112] New jails were typically built with an entrance room, a chamber for the warden, two or three cells, and an enclosed patio in which the prisoners could take air.[113] Women's jails (*recojidas*), while a lower priority, were also built or expanded in most towns and looked essentially the same as the men's jails. The existence of an outside space for the use of the inmates was considered indispensable. When the justice of peace of

---

110 "[P]ara asegurar, y no molestar a los presos" and "calabozos subterráneos ni malsanos." *Constitución política de la monarquía española*, article 297.

111 On dark or cramped jails, see, e.g., Ramón García to Jefe Político Superior, San Pedro Piedra Gorda, 27 March 1824, in AGEG-M, Caja 4, Expediente 7, Foja 1; Crescencio Escobar to Prefecto del Distrito de Rioverde, Lagunillas, 6 May 1840, in AHESLP-SGG, Caja 740, Expediente "Las autoridades de Lagunillas, solicitan la licencia respectiva para el cambio de un terreno que pretende hacer D. José M. Olvera con los fondos de propios de dha. villa"; Juan del Ugarte to Secretario del Superior Gobierno, Venado, 29 November 1841, in AHESLP-SGG, Caja 755, Expediente 3. On jails that lacked security, see, e.g., José Vicente Gayaga to Jefe Político, Pénjamo, 29 February 1824, in AGEG-M, Caja 5, Expediente 5, Foja 5; José Apolonio Alonso to Jefe Superior Político, Casas Viejas, 18 October 1824, in AGEG-M, Caja 6, Expediente 3, Foja 3; José María García to Gobernador, Tancanhuitz, 5 March 1830, in AHESLP-SGG, Caja 272, Expediente 28.

112 See, e.g., Felipe Neri Guillén to Gobernador, Rioverde, 12 July 1826, in AHESLP-SGG, Caja 52, Expediente 10; José María Nuñez to Gobernador, Cedral, 9 January 1832, in AHESLP-SGG, Caja 369, Expediente 4; Mariano de Pano to Secretario del Gobierno Superior, Rioverde, 4 February 1841, in AHESLP-SGG, Caja 755, Expediente 1; Juan del Ugarte to Secretario del Superior Gobierno, Venado, 29 November 1841, in AHESLP-SGG, Caja 755, Expediente 3; R.L. Medellín to Secretario del Gobierno, Tancanhuitz, 29 January 1845, in AHESLP-SGG, Caja 1845.2, unnumbered Expediente; Josef Francisco Gómez to Jefe Superior Político, Yuriria, 12 March 1824, in AGEG-M, Caja 5, Expediente 7, Foja 2. Pedro Sánchez to Jefe Superior Político, Chamacuero, 2 May 1824, in AGEG-M, Caja 6, Expediente 7, Foja 1; José Calisto Gutiérrez to Gobernador, San Francisco del Coecillo, 21 May 1826, in AGEG-M, Caja 24, Expediente 1; "Lista de lo contribuido, p.r los individuos que en ella se acientan, p.a la costrucion de un cuarto p.a carcel de Pueblo Nuebo," in AGEG-M, Caja 43, Expediente 2; Actas de Ayuntamiento, Ciudad Fernández, 8 April and 15 April 1839, in AMCF, Caja 34, Expediente CDF 90.

113 For descriptions and drawings, see Domingo Hernández to Gobernador, San Francisco del Rincón, 14 December 1826, in AGEG-M, Caja 21, Expediente 4; "Ynforme relativo á la Casa Consistorial de San José Casas Viejas. Año de 1846," in AGEG-M, Caja 168, Expediente 1; José Miguel de Avila to Secretario del Gobierno, Catorce, 4 November 1841, in AHESLP-SGG, Caja 755, Expediente 6.

Cedral reported in 1841 that the town's one-cell jail was getting little traffic and remained sufficient for the needs of the population, he took care to assure his superiors that the jail included a yard [*corral*] "so that the prisoners may be out in the sun."[114] The creation of decent jail conditions, apart from serving a general humanitarian function, may also have been intended to diminish the social stigma associated with temporary imprisonment. Whereas convicted thieves and murderers were sent to federal prisons or labor camps, persons convicted of offences considered minor, like gambling, domestic violence, or public inebriation, usually served short sentences in local jails before returning to their roles as parents, neighbors, and citizens.

The presence, even in small towns, of a permanent penal and judicial apparatus, located in the jail and town hall, made republican legal institutions far more accessible than – outside of Mexico City and at best a few other large towns – they had been in the colonial period. Let us look at two situations in which inhabitants of mestizo towns routinely sought the support of local judges. First, judicial backing was often necessary to enforce the terms of minor financial and commercial transactions. Some of the values concerned in such suits were very small and appear to have belonged to the sphere of the household economy: a debt of twenty reales (two and a half pesos); an even smaller one of eighteen reales, to be paid over the course of the following month; a debt of four and a half pesos to be paid over four months or, failing that, the mortgaging to the creditor of "a black pig of [the debtor's] property."[115] Records from San Luis Potosí and the neighboring state of Querétaro show that larger values were contested in business relationships in which labor or goods had been advanced by one of the contracting parties: fourteen pesos for a fence, thirty pesos for the sale of four fattened pigs, thirty pesos for taking a team of mules on a commercial journey.[116] Laura Shelton's summary of a few hundred verbal judgments in the frontier state of Sonora suggests the centrality of petty credit-relationships to the working and artisan classes of early republican Mexico.[117] These were cases in which "a few pesos, some bushels of grain,

114   "[P]ara que se asoleen los presos." Ramon Sáenz de Mendiola, copying from first and second judges of Cedral, Venado, 11 May 1841, in AHESLP-SGG, Caja 755, Expediente 4.

115   "[U]n marrano prieto de su propiedad." "Conocimientos del Juzgado que es a mi cargo," entries of 12 April, 14 July, and 18 November 1842, in AMRV, Caja 1842, Expediente R3.

116   "Libro de Juicios civiles vervales que se selebran por el Ciudadano J. Nepomuceno Guzmán Alcalde 1.o Constitucional de la Villa del Armadillo en el año de 1836 y 1837," entry from 20 April 1836, in AHESLP-STJ, Civil, Enero 1836 (1); "Libro de juicios verbales," Jalpan, entries from 28 June 1838 and 19 March 1840, in AHPJEQ-DJ, Criminal, 9–265.

117   Laura Shelton, *For Tranquility and Order: Family and Community on Mexico's Northern Frontier, 1800–1850* (Tucson: University of Arizona Press, 2011), 105.

or a couple head of livestock were usually at stake."[118] While the details of the debt relationships tend to remain murky, they highlight the function of local courts as guarantors of contractual obligations that served to enlarge the range of subsistence strategies and entrepreneurial possibilities available to non-elite Mexicans.

Mexicans also frequently sought court intervention in the domestic sphere. Here, it was primarily women who came before municipal judges in order to seek support against violent or negligent husbands.[119] When María Candelaria Izaguirre's husband beat her during a domestic quarrel, "with this she came immediately to present herself in this court so that it may proceed in the manner it finds best-suited to remedy the many ills that afflict her with her said husband, for various times he has beaten her like a beast."[120] The court responded by condemning the husband to six months of public works. María Dominga Torres proceeded against her husband for having beat her – cruelly enough to leave her injured – and spending his time in the home of his mistress. Her husband was lucky that she pleaded with the judge to sentence him to no more than four months of public work: his treatment of Torres, opined the court assessor, "both because she is his wife and because of the weakness of her sex, shows a graver misconduct that is worthy of greater punishment."[121]

Women often went to court not to have their husbands punished but to deliver a warning against further abuses. The wife of Domingo Turiñan noted her husband's formal behavior toward her on the day after a quarrel, "and fearing some bad treatment she wanted to assure herself of him, and only for the sake of the peace between the two spouses did she go to the present señor judge."[122] She specifically denied that she desired a prison term for her husband, and the judge complied by letting him off with a warning. In another case, María Antonia Hernández retracted a lawsuit for domestic abuse on the grounds that "[a]ny punishment ... must surely also result in detriment to [María Antonia] for lacking the support of her husband." She hoped "that this kindness will be recognized by her husband

118 Shelton, *For Tranquility and Order*, 104.

119 For important studies of Latin American women's use of the new, republican court systems established after the region's independence in order to liberalize domestic gender relations, see Christine Hunefeldt, *Liberalism in the Bedroom: Quarreling Spouses in Nineteenth-Century Lima* (University Park: Pennsylvania State University Press, 2000); and Arlene Díaz, *Female Citizens, Patriarchs, and the Law in Venezuela, 1786–1904* (Lincoln: University of Nebraska Press, 2004).

120 "[C]on esto se vino inmediatamente a presentarse a este Juzgado para que proceda como mejor convenga en remedio de tantos males que le afligen con dicho su marido pues que varias veces la ha golpeado como a una bestia." AHESLP-STJ, Caja 120, Expediente 9, Fojas 2–3.

121 "[A]sí por ser su esposa, como por la debilidad de su sexo manifiestan una falta más notable y digna de mayor castigo." AHESLP-STJ, Caja 117, Expediente 5.

122 "[Y] recelando algún mal trato quiso asegurarse de él, y por solo medio de paz entre ambos consortes se dirijo al presente Sr. Juez." AHESLP-STJ, Caja 5, Expediente 22, Foja 8.

and he will leave off the custom of hitting her in the future, which if it doesn't happen and she is again attacked she declares that she will formally sue him so that he will suffer the punishment," even though, she added, in that event she would have "to go begging."[123] María Josefa Padierna similarly sued her husband only to retract the suit – "anxious for the peace and quiet of her house" – with the warning that she would proceed in all seriousness should he mistreat her again.[124]

Shelton's examination of a larger set of court records from Sonora makes it clear that vindications of the rights of battered women were by no means the only norm in Mexico's early republican judicial system. Mexico in the nineteenth century remained an openly patriarchal society. According to the dominant gender culture, men, as the rulers of households, were allowed and even expected to "correct" wives who were disobedient or lacking in wifely diligence. Moderate corporal punishment was considered an ordinary aspect of the domestic union, and husbands, writes Shelton, had "tremendous latitude" for interpreting when a woman was "disobedient" or what kinds of beatings were "moderate" and hence permitted.[125] Men who wounded their wives with knives might still walk free if the victims' wounds were quick to heal.[126] Judges were particularly sympathetic to husbands who suspected their wives of infidelity – even if the suspicion was found to be baseless. While it is likely that judges were more willing to excuse male violence in the frontier state of Sonora than in other parts of the country, forms of domestic abuse were everywhere part of the fate that married women were expected to bear. In return, husbands were expected to fulfill the roles of protectors and breadwinners, and Shelton shows that judges tended to take the woman's side in a lawsuit if a husband's violence had been accompanied by economic neglect. Josefa Donijan, for instance, in

123   "Cualquiera pena . . . debe refluir también en perjuicio de la exponente por carecer del auxilio de su marido"; "[Q]ue de esta bondad sea reconocido por su esposo y se enmienda de la costumbre de golpearla en lo sucesivo lo que si no sucediere y fuere de nuevo ofendida protesta demandarlo formalmente entonces para que sufra el castigo"; and "[A] pedir limosna." "Conocimientos del Juzgado que es a mi cargo," entry of 15 May 1842, in AMRV, Caja 1842, Expediente R3.

124   "[D]eseosa de la paz y tranquilidad de su casa." "Conocimientos del Juzgado que es a mi cargo," entry of 18 June 1842, in AMRV, Caja 1842, Expediente R3.

125   Shelton, *For Tranquility and Order*, 63. On domestic violence and its ideological underpinnings in colonial Mexico and Latin America, see Richard Boyer, "Women, *La Mala Vida*, and the Politics of Marriage," in *Sexuality and Marriage in Colonial Latin America*. Edited by Asunción Lavrin, 252–286 (Lincoln: University of Nebraska Press, 1989); Steve Stern, *The Secret History of Gender: Women, Men, and Power in Late Colonial Mexico* (Chapel Hill: University of North Carolina Press, 1995), chapter 4; and Susan Migden Socolow, *The Women of Colonial Latin America* (New York: Cambridge University Press, 2000), 67. The best discussion of the laws governing domestic violence in nineteenth-century Mexico is Ana Lidia García Peña, *El fracaso del amor: Género e individualismo en el siglo XIX mexicano* (Mexico City: El Colegio de México: 2006), 66–70.

126   Shelton, *For Tranquility and Order*, 64.

1835 left her husband because "everyone in Arizpe knew that [he] was a notorious drunk who could not support his family," and the judge supported her wish for a separation.[127] The importance of the judicial option was therefore not that it protected women from violence per se but that it opened what Steve Stern has called the "contested patriarchal pacts" of domestic gender relations to the possibilities of public scrutiny and intervention.[128] Men could continue to beat their wives as long as they also put food on the table and refrained from causing serious injuries. From the perspective of Mexican women, this was, at least, preferable to a situation in which no courts existed to limit the mistreatment they received from their spouses.

Lower-class Mexicans who asked municipal courts to enforce credit agreements they could not themselves enforce, or to correct abuses of power in the domestic sphere, were among those who benefited most from the transformation of Mexico's legal culture in the post-colonial period. The absence of documentation of colonial cases in the archives I have consulted makes it impossible to confirm whether the nature of the judicial process changed to the same extent in provincial Mexico as it did in the Venezuelan case examined by Zahler. But the codification of citizen rights in successive constitutions, the vesting of judicial powers in elected magistrates under the federalist system, and, above all, the proliferation of local courts testify to a new concern with the regularity and accessibility of the judicial process at all levels of the country's political and administrative apparatus.

In the early republican period, flaws in the administration of justice became the most common reason for citizens to launch complaints against local officials. For example, in 1826 residents of Rincón de Tamayo, Guanajuato, reported that their town council, having come to power in a flawed election, was making a mockery of the impartial application of the law: "we have not seen justice administered with energy and disinterestedness; prestige, repute, influence, and forcefulness always occupying the first place in the court."[129] In the same year, the aldermen of Axtla, San Luis Potosí, accused the presiding mayor of a dereliction of duty. On the one hand, "without first presenting a summary notification of the charge, driven only by the most refined pride, he imprisons whomever he likes without having legitimate cause," yet on the other "he leaves those whom because of their misdeeds he would properly need to castigate

---

127 Shelton, *For Tranquility and Order*, 67.   128 Stern, *Secret History of Gender*, 85, 110.

129 "[N]o hemos visto administrar la justicia con desinterés y energía; ocupando siempre el primer lugar en el juzgado, la consideración, el respeto, el influjo y la preponderancia." "Expediente promovido p.r el ciud.o Lazaro Martinez y otros vecins del Rincon de Tamayo," in AGEG-M, Caja 13, Expediente 12.

unpunished."[130] In 1836, now under a centralist constitution, a group of citizens from Villa de la Palma rejected what they alleged had been a fraudulent election because they believed, on the basis of the mayor-elect's previous behavior, "that he will not be a judge of order nor of peace, nor will he hold justice in one hand and charity in the other, that he will make this town not happy but unhappy."[131] Whether made by adversaries or by disgruntled citizens, virtually all attacks on municipal office holders extolled a similar ideal of justice: expectations about the fairness of the legal system had become central to Mexicans' relationship with the institutions of their home towns, or *patria chica*.

The egalitarian tendencies embodied in the municipal legal system found their fullest expression in the federalism of the immediate post-independence years; under centralism they faced special challenges. In Salvatierra, Guanajuato, the centralist coup consolidated the power of a political clique who harassed their opponents and soon became the target of a flurry of anonymous complaints accusing them of tyranny, nepotism, and grave irregularities in the application of the law.[132] I have found no similar accusations from other towns in the two states. However, some smaller towns reported that the drastic reduction in the number of government officials meant that crimes could no longer be adequately prosecuted.[133] These assertions are intuitively plausible and accord with the perceptions of residents of Cerritos and San Pedro de los Pozos who, as we saw, considered the presence of elected authorities indispensable for the prompt administration of justice.

Even if we assume that the effects of the centralist reorganization of Mexico's legal system were minimal, that reorganization, and the

---

130   "[P]ues sin preceder notificación sumaria del hecho, valido solamente del más refinado orgullo, aprisiona al que le parece sin que haya causa legítima para ello"; and "deja impunes a los que debidamente por sus delitos debía de castigar"; Regidores to Gobernador, Axtla, 5 April 1826, in AHESLP-SGG, Caja 44, Expediente 10, Fojas 1–2.

131   "[Q]ue no será juez del orden ni de la paz, ni que tendrá la justicia en una mano y la caridad en otra, que no hará feliz este pueblo sino infeliz." To subprefecto of Ciudad del Maíz, Villa de la Palma, in AHESLP-SGG, Caja 591, Expediente 1.

132   Los quejosos de siempre to Gobernador, Salvatierra, 25 June 1835; Los de siempre to Gobernador, Salvatierra, 16 October 1835; and Los de siempre to Gobernador, 6 March 1839, all in AGEG-M, Caja 130, Expediente 9; Anonymous letters from Salvatierra, 15 March and 1 August 1838, in AGEG-J, Caja 33, Expediente 10; Varios perseguidos to Gobernador, Salvatierra, 12 April 1840, in AGEG-J, Caja 36, Expediente 9; Los que claman por justicia to Gobernador, Salvatierra, 18 December 1841, in AGEG-M, Caja 153, Expediente 13. For some background on the conflict, see also the various documents from Salvatierra in AGEG-M, Caja 126, Expediente 10.

133   Juan Pastor to Gobernador, San Miguel de Allende, 6 November 1840, copying from Jefe de Partido of San Luis de la Paz, in AGEG-J, Caja 36, Expediente 3; Juan Pastor to Secretaria de Gobierno, San Miguel de Allende, 20 July 1853, copying from Juez de Paz of San Felipe, in AGEG-M, Caja 185, Expediente 2; and José Linares to Gobernador, Celaya, 11 September 1855, copying from Subprefecto of Yuriria, in AGEG-M, Caja 190, Expediente 1.

anti-popular rhetoric by which it was accompanied, would still have laid bare the vulnerability of local legal institutions to political interference. To a new group of politicians drawn from a small-town middle class, it showed that the liberal institutions in which they were invested existed only on sufferance. We can now see why the issue of local democracy loomed so large in non-elite Mexicans' political programs. In mestizo towns, the protection of municipal rights was indistinguishable from a meaningful preference to place one's life under the rule of law. Citizens who fought for a federalist system of government did so not because they were parochial or hostile to a liberal political culture but because in post-colonial Mexico only local, popular governments were able to guarantee the rights and freedoms that independence had promised.

In an age famed for its volatility, town governments developed administrative routines that provided residents with a steady horizon of expectations about social rules and their enforcement. These findings shift the burden of historical explanation to questions that have not often been addressed by scholars of Mexican history. Historians writing about the first half of the nineteenth century have most often looked for ways to explain the instability of national politics, yet when we look at Mexico's post-colonial trajectory from the vantage point of town politics, it is not the instances of conflict but the long stretches of tranquility that confront us with a puzzle and require a special effort of understanding.[134]

---

134 Will Fowler has shown that Mexican rebellions and *pronunciamientos* before the 1850s, with the exception of the 1832 federalist revolt, affected the lives of only small minorities of Mexicans. See Will Fowler, "Civil Conflict in Independent Mexico, 1821–1857: An Overview," in *Rumours of Wars: Civil Conflict in Nineteenth-Century Latin America*, ed. Rebecca Earle, 49–86 (London: Institute of Latin American Studies, 2000).

2

Family and Legal Order

I Families

Little is known about the provision of public security in nineteenth-century Mexico. The most detailed study about the subject, Paul Vanderwood's *Disorder and Progress*, investigates the famous rural police force, the *rurales*, of the late-century Díaz dictatorship. Vanderwood argues that the *rurales* were in method and character hardly to be distinguished from the bandits they chased. Formed by the government of Benito Juárez in 1861, many of the first generation of *rurales* were, in fact, former brigands who switched sides.[1] While later recruits came from the peasant and artisan sectors, the *rurales* remained notorious for their lax morals, abuse of power, illegal use of force – especially the extrajudicial execution of criminals under pretext of preventing their escape –, and loyalty to the dictator rather than the constitution or the rule of law.[2] Vanderwood describes this situation as the logical culmination of Mexico's post-independence political trajectory. The colonial state gone, Mexicans had taken advantage of the "unprecedented opportunities for self-advancement" offered by independence and sought only their personal, local, or sectoral advantages. Many drifted into crime.[3] The country's early republican decades, Vanderwood surmises, were characterized by "an epidemic of banditry" hardly held in check by local policing bodies more adept at serving special interests than at "disciplined law enforcement."[4]

If Vanderwood's interpretation were true, the transformation of the legal culture of mestizo towns described in the previous chapter might not have been very meaningful: the creation of a widely accessible network of municipal courts could bind citizens into a new legal system only as long as those courts had the means to enforce their jurisdictional claims. However, we have reason to be skeptical of Vanderwood's account, which

---

1 Paul Vanderwood, *Disorder and Progress: Bandits, Police, and Mexican Development* (Lincoln: University of Nebraska Press, 1981), chapter 5.
2 Vanderwood, *Disorder and Progress*, chapters 9–10.   3 Vanderwood, *Disorder and Progress*, 25.
4 Vanderwood, *Disorder and Progress*, 6, 34.

draws sweeping conclusions about the nature of law enforcement while summarily dismissing the importance of local police operations. Yet it was in Mexico's municipalities that, as we saw, the post-colonial state had its most vital institutional presence. In this chapter, we will examine the contribution of local police forces, or civic militias, to the provision of public order in early republican Mexico. We will also discuss the replacement of those militias with other types of armed forces during the civil wars of the 1850s and 1860s. But looking at social discipline only from the perspective of law enforcement affords too narrow an understanding of the sources of order in post-colonial Mexico. We will therefore begin by considering the ordering impulses contained in nineteenth-century social life as such, and in particular in the institution of the family.

Families, with their clannish loyalties, unaccountable leaders, and private codes of deference, have sometimes been cast as special adversaries of the rule of law in nineteenth-century Mexico.[5] However, in recent decades scholars have shown that families often played a disciplinarian, rather than anarchic, role in Mexican public life. According to this scholarship, the patriarchal family acted both as a principle and an instrument of order. It acted as a principle of order because it contained hierarchies and reciprocities that mirrored those at work in society at large. Steve Stern has called attention to the "processes of echo, resonance, and temporary fusion" between domestic and political cultures in late-colonial Mexico: as the family father demanded obedience from his wife and children yet was the object of reciprocal expectations of benevolence, sustenance, and shelter, so colonial officials demanded obedience from their subjects yet were the objects of expectations of fairness, magnanimity, and protection.[6] Familial and political structures of meaning continued to reflect each other in the republican period, perhaps most emphatically in frontier states like Sonora and Chihuahua. There, republican officials equated the orderly hierarchy of domestic life with civilization while associating promiscuity and an absence of a gendered division of labor with the "savage" indigenous populations who defied state control during much of the century.[7]

---

5 François-Xavier Guerra, *México: Del Antiguo Régimen a la Revolución*, vol. 1, trans. Sergio Fernández Bravo (Mexico City: Fondo de Cultura Económica, 1988); Fernando Escalante Gonzalbo, *Ciudadanos imaginarios: memorial de los afanes y desventuras de la virtud y apología del vicio triunfante en la República Mexicana: tratado de moral pública* (Mexico City: Centro de Estudios Sociológicos and Colegio de México, 1992). For a review of the abundant literature on family networks in the colonial period, see Pilar Gonzalbo Aizpuro, "La familia en México colonial: Una historia de conflictos cotidianos," *Mexican Studies/Estudios Mexicanos* 14/2 (1998), 397–400.

6 Steve Stern, *The Secret History of Gender: Women, Men, and Power in Late Colonial Mexico* (Chapel Hill: University of North Carolina Press, 1995), 211.

7 Laura Shelton, *For Tranquility and Order: Family and Community on Mexico's Northern Frontier, 1800–1850* (Tucson: University of Arizona Press, 2011), 39–48; Ana María Alonso, *Thread of Blood: Colonialism, Revolution, and Gender on Mexico's Northern Frontier* (Tucson: University of Arizona

The family was also an instrument of order. By directing the activities of its members, punishing their bad behavior, and satisfying their material needs, it converted the bare productivity of labor into a rule-governed social world.[8] According to Sonya Lipsett-Rivera, Mexicans in the eighteenth and nineteenth centuries thought of their homes as "oases of morality and order."[9] This ordering impulse made the family a crucial ally of the state. A world in which patriarchs disciplined women and children, distributed labor and resources, and adjudicated domestic conflicts was one in which the work of public institutions was manageable rather than overwhelming.[10] It is no wonder that judges employed harsh sanctions against people who broke the rules of family life: wives who resisted their husbands, children who struck their parents, husbands who not only beat but failed to provide for their wives and children.[11] Such behaviors were perceived not as breaches of this or that moral precept but as attacks on the moral foundation of society. Mexicans' attitude toward the domestic sphere shows that Partha Chatterjee's argument about the role of the family in modern liberal thought – as a natural unit whose existence allowed thinkers to ground anemic accounts of contractual rights in an ethics of affective and immediate belonging – applies as much to the sphere of practical reason as to that of high philosophy.[12]

The reliance of the Mexican state on the family as an instrument of social control raises an important question. The rules and routines of domestic life did not much change between the late colonial and early republican periods.[13] How, then, could the patriarchal family contribute to the specifically republican legal regime we encountered in the previous chapter? In the following section, we will address this question by examining the relationship between domestic life and the emerging practices of a disciplinary state. In the European context, the influential work of Michel

Press, 1995), chapter 3; Sarah Chambers has also called attention to the prevalence of familial metaphors in Chile's post-independence state-building project in *Families in War and Peace: Chile from Colony to Nation* (Durham, NC: Duke University Press, 2015).

8 Alonso, *Thread of Blood*, 87. William French, *The Heart in the Glass Jar: Love Letters, Bodies, and the Law in Mexico* (Lincoln: University of Nebraska Press, 2015), 30–32.

9 Sonya Lipsett-Rivera, *Gender and the Negotiation of Daily Life in Mexico, 1750–1856* (Lincoln: University of Nebraska Press, 2010), 35.

10 Thus, early republican intellectuals and statesmen often imagined familial neglect as a prime cause in the formation of criminal elements. See Robert Buffington, *Criminal and Citizen in Modern Mexico* (Lincoln: University of Nebraska Press, 2000), 20–21.

11 Shelton, *For Tranquility and Order*, 116–118; Deborah Kanter, *Hijos del Pueblo: Gender, Family, and Community in Rural Mexico, 1730–1850* (Austin: University of Texas Press, 2008), chapter 5; French, *Heart in the Glass Jar*, section 1.

12 Partha Chatterjee, *The Nation and Its Fragments: Colonial and Postcolonial Histories* (Princeton: Princeton University Press, 1993), 230–234.

13 Lipsett-Rivera, *Gender and the Negotiation of Daily Life*, 20; Kanter, *Hijos del Pueblo*, chapter 7; Peter Guardino, *The Time of Liberty: Popular Political Culture in Oaxaca, 1750–1850*, (Durham, NC: Duke University Press, 2005), 246–249.

Foucault has drawn attention to just such a relationship. Foucault argued that in the course of the eighteenth and nineteenth centuries, establishments like schools and hospitals extended their "disciplinary mechanisms" into the home and the family through the diffusion of powerful norms of behavior.[14] According to Foucault, the modern state was ultimately the "general design or institutional crystallization" of such diffused disciplinary procedures.[15]

In the Mexican and, more broadly, the Latin American context, evidence for the emergence of a muscular and state-backed disciplinary apparatus begins to appear only late in the nineteenth century.[16] But while Latin America's early republics lacked the capacity to regulate their citizens' behavior at the level of most of their European counterparts, they did wield a crude but powerful instrument of social control in the military draft. Peter Beattie and Ricardo Salvatore have shown that military recruitment in nineteenth-century Brazil and Argentina was about more than staffing the army. Targeting men who did not meet norms of a settled life, hard work, and familial responsibility, recruitment also served as a method of punishment that allowed authorities to eliminate undesirable masculine behavior without worrying about legal niceties.[17] In Mexico, too, the draft allowed republican institutions to put forward an ideal of citizenship that served the needs of social discipline.

II Recruitment

The task of army recruitment in early republican Mexico rested in the hands of town governments. Of all the instruments of discipline at their

---

14 Michel Foucault, *Discipline and Punish: The Birth of the Prison*, trans. Alan Sheridan (New York: Vintage Books, 1995), 211–212, and *The History of Sexuality*, vol. 1, trans. Robert Hurley (New York: Vintage Books, 1990), 106–113.

15 Foucault, *History of Sexuality*, 93.

16 On efforts by state-supported mining companies to shape the domestic life of their workers through the provision of schools and hospitals during the Porfirian dictatorship, see William French, *A Peaceful and Working People: Manners, Morals, and Class Formation in Northern Mexico* (Albuquerque: University of New Mexico Press, 1996), chapter 2. On the emergence of a late nineteenth-century disciplinary state in urban Mexico, see Pablo Piccato, *City of Suspects: Crime in Mexico City, 1900–1931* (Durham, NC: Duke University Press, 2001); and Mark Overmyer-Velazquez, *Visions of the Emerald City: Modernity, Tradition, and the Formation of Porfirian Oaxaca, Mexico* (Durham, NC: Duke University Press, 2006).

17 Peter Beattie, *The Tribute of Blood: Army, Honor, Race, and Nation in Brazil, 1864–1945* (Durham, NC: Duke University Press, 2001), 28–29; Ricardo Salvatore, *Wandering Paysanos: State Order and Subaltern Experience in Buenos Aires during the Rosas Era* (Durham, NC: Duke University Press, 2003), 264–267. For an overview of recruitment in Latin America – albeit one that privileges the Colombian perspective, see Malcolm Deas, "The Man on Foot: Conscription and the Nation-State in Nineteenth-Century Latin America," in *Studies in the Formation of the Nation-State in Latin America*, ed. James Dunkerley, 77–93 (London: Institute of Latin American Studies, 2002).

disposal, it was without doubt the harshest. Apart from any punishments the law might prescribe for particular crimes or misdemeanors, the practice of military recruitment opened the possibility of expelling offenders from the civic community altogether. From the perspective of town politicians, the draft doubled as a measure of social engineering. It allowed them to rid society of idlers and troublemakers – men who produced no wealth and supported no families – and thus to externalize their social ills.[18] In this way, the army became instrumental in defining the negative boundaries of Mexican citizenship.

During the first decades of Mexico's republican experiment, captive recruits marched along the country's highways in constant trickles. Apart from volunteers and deserters, the 1824 law that regulated recruitment in Guanajuato listed four categories of people from which town authorities were to draft soldiers: those without professions or jobs [*oficios*]; those with professions or jobs who didn't exercise them; those who, though working, were "habitually immoral"; and those who were married or widowed but lived "apart from their families, without maintaining them nor looking after the education of their children."[19] Other men could be drafted if those categories did not yield the requisite numbers.

The law gave town authorities a language with which to describe their recruitment choices. In a group of six recruits conducted from Casas Viejas to the state capital of Guanajuato in 1829, authorities described the first as "a professional gambler [who] doesn't support his mother"; the second as "a professional gambler"; the next as "an idler with no profession"; the next as "an idler [who] has a profession [but] doesn't exercise it"; the fifth as "an idler [who] lives with a woman out of wedlock"; and the last as "a professional gambler [who] continuously lives with a woman out of wedlock."[20] Some authorities gave more detailed explanations for why they had picked up particular men. Antonio García of Dolores Hidalgo was sent to the army for being "immoral, drunk, and a gambler, and he doesn't sustain his family"; Juan Martín Urbano of Yuriria for "consum[ing] everything he earns in his habitual gambling, [and he is] scandalous, provocative, boastful, he opposes the patrols and the authorities and finally [he is] incorrigible in all his vices"; and Vicente Montes of Casas Viejas not only "for [being]

---

18 See Peter Guardino, "Gender, Soldiering, and Citizenship in the Mexican-American War, 1846–1848," *American Historical Review* 119/1 (2014).

19 "[H]abitualmente viciosos "; and "viviendo separados de sus familias sin mantenerlas, ni cuidar de la educación de sus hijos. "Law from 17 September 1824, articles 6 and 7, in AGEG-Leyes y Decretos. For the extension of the provisions of that law to recruitment for the reserve army, see the law from 26 January 1828, in AGEG-Leyes y Decretos.

20 "[T]ahúr de profesión no asiste a la madre"; "tahúr de profesión"; "vago sin oficio"; "vago tiene oficio no lo ejerce"; "vago y amancebado"; "tahúr de profesión y amancebado." Recruitment list from Casas Viejas, 10 September 1829, in AGEG-G, Caja 33, Expediente 3.

disobedient and not supporting his father," but also "for an injury that he inflicted with a large knife, being furthermore a drunkard and gambler."[21] In these reports the legal categories of the recruitment law served as a loose conceptual framework for the description of all kinds of anti-social behavior.

Broadly speaking, the most important distinction in the motives that local authorities gave for sending men to army was between idleness and immorality, the latter understood as neglect of the family. People sent to the army for the first reason were called *vagos*: idlers or vagrants. Of 619 men described in 83 recruitment lists from Guanajuato, 378, or 61.1 percent, were described by the use of this word or, in a few cases, an equivalent description.[22] In a group of recruits from Dolores Hidalgo, four men had

21   "[V]icioso, ebrio y jugador y no mantiene a su familia"; "consume todo cuanto adquiere en el juego es consuetudinario tahúr de profesión, escandaloso, provocativo, baladrón, contra las rondas se opone, y a las autoridades y finalmente incorregible en todos sus vicios"; "por desobediente y que no asiste a su padre ...; y herida que infirió con belduque, yendo además ebrio y jugador." Recruitment lists from Dolores Hidalgo, 10 September 1830, in AGEG-G, Caja 41, Expediente 2; Yuriria, 4 August 1830, in AGEG-G, Caja 42, Expediente 7; and Casas Viejas, 9 July 1827, in AGEG-G, Caja 19, Expediente 3.

22   The numbers in this and the following paragraphs are based on information from these eighty-three recruitment lists:

In AGEG-J: Dolores Hidalgo, 1 October 1826, Caja 6, Expediente 6.

In AGEG-M: Pénjamo, 25 April 1825, Caja 18, Expediente 2, Foja 26; Acámbaro, [1826], Caja 25, Expediente 1; Acámbaro, [1828], Caja 65, Expediente 1; Acámbaro, [1829], Caja 77, Expediente 2.

In AGEG-G: Acámbaro, 14 October 1824, Caja 2, Expediente 2; Casas Viejas, 7 December 1824, Caja 3, Expediente 3; Pénjamo, 15 January 1824, Caja 3, Expediente 11; Pénjamo, 17 September 1826, Caja 8, Expediente 10; Piedragorda, 8 November 1826, Caja 8, Expediente 10; San Luis de la Paz, 2 October 1826, Caja 8, Expediente 17; Dolores Hidalgo, 1 October 1826, Caja 10, Expediente 6; Casas Viejas, 21 November 1826, Caja 12, Expediente 4; Casas Viejas, 9 September 1826, Caja 12, Expediente 4; Jerécuaro, 22 October 1827, Caja 14, Expediente 3; Santa Cruz, 3 October 1827, Caja 14, Expediente 11; Casas Viejas, 4 October 1827, Caja 15, Expediente 1; Xichú, 9 October 1827, Caja 15, Expediente 10; Pénjamo, 3 December 1827, Caja 16, Expediente 9; San Luis de la Paz, 16 October 1827, Caja 16, Expediente 17; Acámbaro, 28 April 1827, Caja 19, Expediente 2; Casas Viejas, 9 July 1827, Caja 19, Expediente 3; Apaseo, 27 April 1827, Caja 20, Expediente 2; Dolores Hidalgo, 5 February 1827, Caja 20, Expediente 5; Apaseo, 13 June 1828, Caja 27, Expediente 2; Dolores Hidalgo, 28 November 1828, Caja 27, Expediente 6; Dolores Hidalgo, 10 September 1828, Caja 27, Expediente 6; Irapuato, 30 April 1828, Caja 27, Expediente 7; Silao, 22 May 1828, Caja 27, Expediente 19; San Luis de la Paz, 2 December 1828, Caja 27, Expediente 23; Casas Viejas, 10 September 1829, Caja 33, Expediente 3; Dolores Hidalgo, 8 October 1829, Caja 34, Expediente 2; Irapuato, 14 June 1829, Caja 34, Expediente 3; Apaseo, 4 September 1829, Caja 34, Expediente 4; San Luis de la Paz, 9 December 1829, Caja 34, Expediente 4; Valle de Santiago, 3 September 1829, Caja 34, Expediente 8; Valle de Santiago, 18 December 1829, Caja 34, Expediente 8; Apaseo, 22 August 1829, Caja 35, Expediente 1; Apaseo, 16 September 1829, Caja 35, Expediente 1; Apaseo, 22 September 1829, Caja 35, Expediente 1; Apaseo, 13 July 1829, Caja 35, Expediente 1; Chamacuero, 4 June 1829, Caja 35, Expediente 2; Pénjamo, 4 July 1829, Caja 35, Expediente 4; Silao, 16 July 1829, Caja 35, Expediente 11; Pénjamo, 17 February 1830,

been convicted as *vagos*: one who, although having a profession, "does not exercise it," and three who claimed to be farmers [*labradores*] but were unable to prove that they were cultivating their lands.[23] The descriptions show the concept's malleability. To have a job and not exercise it, or to own land and not work it, could not, in practice, mean anything but a relative lack of gainful application; everyone needed to eat, and the word was not intended for the well-off sitting on idle money. Even men described as lacking a profession would still have been doing work of some sort, either hopping from job to job or helping out in the family business. Thirty-two men (5.2 percent) on the lists were described as thieves and thirty-five (5.7 percent) as gamblers, including some "professional gamblers," but it is unlikely that anybody with a fixed residence, known to authorities and neighbors, was able to make a full living from such activities. Only among the thirty-four men (5.5 percent) described as foreigners or as having no homes might there have been a few who kept themselves afloat entirely by preying on others. Most commonly the term *vago* referred to someone who worked irregularly, or only for his dissipation, rather than for domestic prosperity.

A related but distinct category of vice referred to neglect of the family. The word typically employed to designate this failing in a general sense, *vicioso* (immoral), appeared in 16 percent of the description of recruits in my sample, and roughly equivalent terms such as *malo, de malas costumbres,* or *mal entretenido* in another 2.9 percent. Such terms were especially likely to

Caja 39, Expediente 1; Pénjamo, 13 July 1830, Caja 39, Expediente 1; Pénjamo, 19 June 1830, Caja 39, Expediente 1; Salvatierra, 5 June 1830, Caja 39, Expediente 3; Salvatierra, 24 February 1830, Caja 39, Expediente 3; Salvatierra, 19 August 1830, Caja 39, Expediente 3; Silao, 28 July 1830, Caja 39, Expediente 6; Silao, 14 August 1830, Caja 39, Expediente 6; Chamacuero, 14 July 1830, Caja 41, Expediente 1; Dolores Hidalgo, 17 November 1830, Caja 41, Expediente 2; Dolores Hidalgo, 10 September 1830, Caja 41, Expediente 2; Dolores Hidalgo, 28 April 1830, Caja 41, Expediente 2; Irapuato, 31 May 1830, Caja 41, Expediente 3; Irapuato, 10 July 1830, Caja 41, Expediente 3; Irapuato, 10 July 1830, Caja 41, Expediente 3; Salamanca, 7 June 1830, Caja 41, Expediente 3; Irapuato, 20 February Caja 41, Expediente 3; Apaseo, 5 March 1830, Caja 42, Expediente 1; Apaseo, 2 June 1830, Caja 42, Expediente 1; Casas Viejas, 18 June 1830, Caja 42, Expediente 1; Casas Viejas, 18 June 1830, Caja 42, Expediente 1; Salamanca, 10 March 1830, Caja 42, Expediente 6; Salamanca, 25 July 1830, Caja 42, Expediente 6; Salamanca, 21 April 1830, Caja 42, Expediente 6; Yuriria, 4 August 1830, Caja 42, Expediente 7; Yuriria, 6 March 1830, Caja 42, Expediente 6; Yuriria, 3 August 1831, Caja 45, Expediente 3; Salamanca, 26 August 1833, Caja 56, Expediente 8; San Luis de la Paz, 3 July 1833, Caja 60, Expediente 5; Yuriria, 26 September 1840, Caja 73, Expediente 19; Pénjamo, 16 January 1841, Caja 74, Expediente 9; Santa Cruz, 30 December 1841, Caja 74, Expediente 15; Apaseo, 4 January 1842, Caja 75, Expediente 3; Dolores Hidalgo, 24 February 1842, Caja 75, Expediente 6; Salamanca, 24 February 1843, Caja 75, Expediente 15; Silao, 27 March 1842, Caja 75, Expediente 17; Silao, 22 February 1843, Caja 75, Expediente 17; Valle de Santiago, 14 February 1843, Caja 75, Expediente 19.

23 "[N]o lo ejerce." List from Dolores Hidalgo, 1 October 1826, in AGEG-J, Caja 6, Expediente 6.

be supplemented with more specific descriptions of wrongdoing. In the group of recruits from Dolores Hidalgo already mentioned, a fifth recruit had been picked "for being *vicioso*, having abandoned his wife without providing for her."[24] A recruit from Casas Viejas had earned his place in the army as somebody "married who does not support his family because [he is] *vicioso*."[25] Not taking proper care of one's wife, children, or aged parents was specifically given as a reason for recruitment in 10.3 percent of all cases in the sample, sometimes with situational variations: Anselmo Romero was "a *vago* and *mal entretenido* who, although he has a profession, does not exercise it, having a mother he doesn't support her and [instead supports] his mistress"; José María Ramírez "abuses his wife, continually beating her"; Rafael Hernández "does not support his wife, nor does he educate his children"; and Vicente Naranjo, "his father and mother being sick and already old, doesn't support them nor provide them relief."[26] A further 4.8 percent of recruits were charged with making trouble for other families, or even the abstract idea of the family, by having sex outside of wedlock.

Concerns about men's work ethic and familial conduct were mutually sustaining. Masculine labor supported the care for home and family. The family home and its attendant responsibilities in turn assured that work had a moral content, that the interests it satisfied were beneficial rather than harmful to society.[27] At the height of the old regime, and well into the eighteenth century, labor in Mexico had been viewed as a dishonorable activity. Not only had it signified low social status – the paradigm of the laboring man had been the slave – but it had been associated with a rude, self-aggrandizing, and antisocial form of masculinity. In his study of devil worship in New Spain, Fernando Cervantes found that laboring men invoked the help of the devil for the attainment of

---

24   "[P]or ser vicioso, teniendo a su esposa abandonada sin socorrerla." List from Dolores Hidalgo, 1 October 1826, in AGEG-J, Caja 6, Expediente 6.

25   "[C]asado que no asiste a su familia por vicioso." List from Casas Viejas, 21 November 1826, in AGEG-G, Caja 12, Expediente 4.

26   "[P]or vago y mal entretenido que aunque tiene oficio i no lo ejerce teniendo madre no le asiste y si a la amasia"; "da mala vida a su mujer golpeándola de continuo"; "no asiste a su mujer, ni les da educación a sus hijos"; "teniendo a su padre y madre con enfermedades y ya ancianos, no los socorre ni les facilita alivio." Lists from Casas Viejas, 4 October 1827, in AGEG-G, Caja 15, Expediente 1; Casas Viejas, 10 September 1829, in AGEG-G, Caja 33, Expediente 3; San Luis de la Paz, 2 October 1826, in AGEG-G, Caja 8, Expediente 17; and Santa Cruz, 3 October 1827, in AGEG-G, Caja 14, Expediente 11.

27   Such associations of virtue and domesticity suggest parallels not only with other Latin American countries but also with the European novelistic imagination of the period. See Sandra Lauderdale Graham, *House and Street: The Domestic World of Servants and Masters in Nineteenth-Century Rio de Janeiro* (Austin: University of Texas Press, 1992); and Nancy Armstrong, *Desire and Domestic Fiction: A Political History of the Novel* (New York: Oxford University Press, 1987).

masculine skills including the seduction of women, the winning of knife fights, and superiority at work tasks such as carding wool, herding cattle, and carrying loads.[28] Thus, the normative reversal by which labor became elevated from a mean and degrading to an honorable activity in the public estimation, still fragile in Mexico's post-independence decades, was only possible as long as labor had the family as its object. Where it did not, men of the laboring classes were described as "scandalous" or "boastful," disobeying their parents, mocking authorities, and engaging in anti-social activities that ranged from gambling and heavy drinking to carrying weapons and hurting others – in short, as behaving with the kind of egotistical savagery that during much of the colonial era had been considered their natural state of being.

The law governing recruitment in San Luis Potosí was less detailed than its Guanajuatan counterpart, calling only for the recruitment of those "without a known way of living."[29] The lists that town authorities sent along with their recruits were similarly inexpressive. They gave recruits' names and sometimes their provenance, but not the reasons for their apprehension. However, town authorities challenged about their decisions by recruits or recruits' families named motives similar to those found in recruitment lists from Guanajuato. Rafael Rocha, apart from not providing for his mother, was described as "scandalous, drunk, provocative, a constant litigator, insubordinate, he doesn't want to apply himself to working."[30] Anselmo Obispo was "an idler and good-for-nothing, with no more occupation than to walk from billiard hall to billiard hall, and from game to game, fighting with any unfortunates he encounters, and furthermore also stealing."[31] In descriptions of twenty-four recruits, all submitted by recruitment juntas in response to petitions for the men's freedom, the concept of the *vago* is invoked eight times and that of immorality seven times. Five men were accused of having sex outside of wedlock, four of

28 Fernando Cervantes, *The Devil in the New World: The Impact of Diabolism in New Spain* (New Haven: Yale University Press, 1994), 87–91.

29 "[L]a gente que no tenga modo de vivir conocido." Law from 7 November 1824, article 4, in AHESLP-SGG-Leyes y Decretos. For a discussion of recruitment laws from a larger variety of states – all of them similar to the ones discussed here – see José Antonio Serrano Ortega, *El contingente de sangre: los gobiernos estatales y departamentales y los métodos de reclutamiento del ejército permanente mexicano, 1824–1844* (Mexico City: Instituto Nacional de Antropología e Historia, 1993), 44–47.

30 "[E]scandaloso, borracho, provocativo, pleitista, insubordinado, no quiere aplicarse a trabajar." Response to a petition from María de Jesús Galicia, in AHESLP-SGG, Caja 29, Expediente 3, Fojas 45–46.

31 "[U]n hombre vago y mal entretenido, sin más oficio que andar de billar en billar, y de juego en juego, peleando a cuantos pobres encuentra, y además robando también." Response to a petition from Juana Santa María, San Luis Potosí, 1 December 1825, in AHESLP-SGG, Caja 29, Expediente 3, Fojas 17–19.

being "scandalous," three of not obeying their parents, and three more of having participated in popular riots. Two men each were described as thieving, disrespecting authority, and not providing for their families, and one man each of gambling, drinking, and having caused injuries. Lastly, one man had been committed simply because he was single and had no parents to support, and another, in spite of the objection of his family, was said to be a volunteer.[32]

Military recruitment in nineteenth-century Mexico was a tool in an ambitious project of aligning the disciplinary function of family life with the legal objectives of the post-colonial state. In the details of its operation it is not difficult to discern the "spectral mixture" between law-preserving and lawmaking violence that Walter Benjamin has associated with the modern police. According to Benjamin, a mythical, lawmaking power is inherent in any exercise of violence and shows itself clearly in the phenomena of the general strike and international warfare – deployments of violence that aim to create new legal orders rather than serve existing ones. While in established states the lawmaking power of violence is to an extent superseded by its law-preserving function, Benjamin argued that the performative, foundational dimension of violence nevertheless lives on in the state's prerogative to take life through the institution of capital punishment and, especially, in the power of the police to pass decrees without legislative oversight. In their use of law-preserving violence, the police are granted a level of discretion that allows them to partially act outside of legal strictures and repeat, in ghostly form, the original violent act that posited the validity of one particular legal order against all possible others.[33]

32 Based on responses by recruitment juntas to letters from the following petitioners, all in AHESLP-SGG: María Antonia Morales, Caja 17, Expediente 1, Fojas 8–9; María de la Luz, Caja 28, Expediente 11, Foja 15; Marcelino Castro, Caja 29, Expediente 3, Fojas 1–2; María Dionisia Reyna, Caja 29, Expediente 3, Fojas 3–6; María Perfecta Guevara, Caja 29, Expediente 3, Fojas 8–10; Lorenza de Jesús Portana, Caja 29, Expediente 3, Fojas 13–15; María Valentina Chávez, Caja 29, Expediente 3, Fojas 13–15; Juana Santa María, Caja 29, Expediente 3, Fojas 17–19; Eugenia and Dionicia Tamayo, Caja 29, Expediente 3, Fojas 20–23; Juana Francisca Rivera, Caja 29, Expediente 3, Fojas 24–27; Juan Pablo Caperillo, Caja 29, Expediente 3, Fojas 28–29; Mariana de la Luz Dimas, Caja 29, Expediente 3, Fojas 38–41; Maria de Jesús Galicia, Caja 29, Expediente 3, Fojas 45–46; María Rojas, Caja 29, Expediente 3, Fojas 49–54; María Diega Galván, 1 December 1825, Caja 35, Expediente 1; José Nicolás Paulín, Caja 51, Expediente 2, Fojas 1–2; Isabel Álvarez, 23 April 1836, Caja 591, Expediente 3; Miquelia de Torres, 29 June 1836, Caja 618, Expediente 3; Lorenza Campillo, 28 June 1836, Caja 618, Expediente 3; María Eleuteria Camacho, 17 October 1836, Caja 620, Expediente 3; the letters from José María Terán to Gobernador, Huehuetlán, 19 January 1837, Caja 645, Expediente 4; José Ignacio Rivera to Gobernador, Huehuetlán, Caja 722, Expediente 10; and José María Fas y Cardona to Secretario del Superior Gobierno, San Luis Potosí, 17 January 1845, Caja 1845.4, Expediente 1.

33 Walter Benjamin, "Critique of Violence," trans. Edmund Jephcott, in Walter Benjamin, *Reflections: Essays, Aphorisms, Autobiographical Writings*, ed. Peter Demetz, 277–300 (New York: Harcourt Brace Jovanovich, 1978). My reading of Benjamin owes something to that by

While recruitment procedures in nineteenth-century Mexico were legal in the sense that they rested on laws passed by elected legislatures, they nevertheless retained what, following Benjamin, we can recognize as a foundational or performative relationship to the law by virtue of two systematic deviations from standards of due process, scrupulously adhered to in all other judicial routines. First, recruitment juntas proceeded from an initial assumption not of innocence but guilt.[34] Town authorities who sat on the juntas, and their officers in outlying barrios and adjunct hamlets and haciendas, persecuted men based on hearsay and reputation. For example, Felipe Santiago, Jacinto Sanchez, and José María Peña of Casas Viejas were sent to the army because they were "reputed as *vago*," and Pedro Arias of Pénjamo because, among other things, he was "accused as a thief."[35] José María Trejo was committed to the military for attempted rape. In an ordinary criminal investigation, only a scrupulous taking and weighing of evidence could have upheld so serious an allegation, yet in the recruitment process it was sufficient that Trejo, "although he presented witnesses," was unable to prove that he had not committed the crime.[36]

Once someone was chosen for examination, the law – which authorities did not always follow – gave him three days to find witnesses to clear his character; if he was unsuccessful, or his witnesses unpersuasive, his guilt was assumed.[37] Thus, in 1827 the junta of Jerécuaro summarized the result of its examination of four recruits:

Carlos Martínez ... for [being] a *vago* who, although he has a profession, doesn't exercise it, and [for being a] habitual drunk. To which he responded, that although

Jacques Derrida in, "Force of Law: The 'Mystical Foundation of Authority,'" trans. Mary Quaintance and Gil Andijar, in Derrida, *Acts of Religion*, 228–298 (New York: Routledge, 2002).

34   Michael Scardaville argues that the burden of proof had been squarely put on the prosecution in the late colonial period by a 1796 decree of Charles IV aimed at curbing "the danger of oppressing innocence [el peligro de oprimir la inocencia]," and he shows that processual standards aimed at protecting the innocent were scrupulously followed in thousands of criminal cases in Mexico City during the late-colonial and independence period. Michael Scardaville, "Los procesos judiciales y la autoridad del estado: Reflexiones en torno a la administración de la justicia criminal y la legitimidad en la ciudad de México, desde finales de la Colonia, hasta principios del México independiente," in *Poder y legitimidad en México en el siglo XIX: Instituciones y cultural política*, ed. Brian Connaughton, 379–428 (Mexico City: Biblioteca de Signos, 2003), here 397.

35   Lists from Casas Viejas, 21 November 1826, in AGEG-G, Caja 12, Expediente 4; and Pénjamo, Penjamo, 25 April 1825, AGEG-M, Caja 18, Expediente 2, Folio 26.

36   List from Casas Viejas, 25 October 1829, in AGEG-G, Caja 33, Expediente 3.

37   It is not clear that all recruits were actually given the three days to clear their names. The practice is mentioned in a number of Guanajuato's recruitment lists, for example, Dolores Hidalgo, 10 September 1828, in AGEG-G, Caja 27, Expediente 6; San Luis de la Paz, 2 December 1828, in AGEG-G, Caja 27, Expediente 23; and San Luis de la Paz, 9 December 1829, in AGEG-G, Caja 34, Expediente 4.

he is a drunk he exercised his profession of blanket maker, which he didn't prove and he was graded as a *vago*.

José María Bellojín ... for [being] a *vago* without profession. He responded that although he doesn't have a profession he worked as a laborer on the Hacienda de [Zatemalle?], which he didn't prove and he was graded as a *vago*.

Ignacio Rosales ... for [being] a *vago* who, though he is a farmer, doesn't exercise [that profession]: to which he responded that he had a piece of land that he worked on, which he didn't demonstrate, and he was graded as a *vago*.

José Rafael Fuentes ... Fuentes [is a] *vago* and although he has the profession of blanket maker he doesn't exercise it and [he is] a habitual drunk, he responded that he had a profession and exercised it and finally didn't show it, he was graded as such [a *vago*].[38]

While we cannot know what kind of opportunity for proving their good character these recruits were given, nor what kind of contrary evidence would have satisfied the members of the junta, it is clear that the burden of evidence rested entirely on the shoulders of the accused.

The second irregularity in the recruitment operation shows just how little recruitment served as a calibrated response to specific legal infractions. Recruitment juntas judged not deeds but character: not thieves but idlers, not fornicators but men who were immoral were sent to the army. Specific acts, like thieving or fornication, most often appear in recruitment documents to establish general, adjectival failings, denoted by words – including the central *vago* and *vicioso* – that were ill-defined and elastic. Under such circumstances, innocence and guilt could only be relative notions. For example, men were sent to the army for the vices of drunkenness or gambling in a culture where everybody sometimes drank and a large number of perfectly respectable family men sometimes gambled.

More than the procedural irregularities of the recruitment process, it was this indeterminacy of the categories employed to measure guilt that prompted a steady number of recruits and their families to dispute the juntas' decisions. In Guanajuato and San Luis Potosí, effectively written petitions, accompanied by sworn statements testifying to the good character of a recruit and directed to the governor, could lead to the freedom of the recruit – not often, but often enough for people to keep trying – if the

---

38 "Carlos Martínez .... por vago que aunque tiene oficio no lo ejerce y briago consuetudinario. A lo que respondió, que aunque es briago ejercía su oficio de mantero, lo que no probó y fue calificado por vago./ José María Bellojín .... por vago sin oficio. Respondió que aunque no tiene oficio trabajaba de peón en la Hacienda de [Zatemalle?], lo que no probó y fue calificado por vago./ Ignacio Rosales ... por vago que aunque es labrador no lo ejerce: a lo que respondió que tenía labor que trabajaba en ella, lo que no hizo ver, y fue calificado por vago./ José Rafael Fuentes ... Fuentes vago y aunque tiene oficio de mantero no lo ejerce y briago de costumbre, respondió que tenía oficio que lo ejercía y al fin no hizo constar, fue calificado por tal." List from Jerécuaro, 22 October 1827, in AGEG-G, Caja 14, Expediente 3.

recruitment juntas were unable to justify their decisions by presenting contrary evidence.[39] Naturally, juntas and recruits had different ideas about what qualified as evidence for good character. When María Felipa Tapia attempted to vindicate the conduct of her brother, she presented witnesses who all agreed that the recruit worked in a shoemaking workshop and took care of a sister as well as, in one account, a niece. But three out of four witnesses also said that they had seen Tapia drinking. One of them went as far as to say that Tapia "was prone to drinking liquor every week," although, the witness added, he did not know that Tapia "became provocative when drinking."[40] In another case a witness acknowledged that the recruitment junta had been correct to say that Gerónimo Granada lived apart from his wife. Granada, however, was blameless, for it was the perverse character of his wife that had caused their separation.[41] It was not enough: Tapia and Granada both had to remain in the army. But on other occasions men who submitted positive character dispositions won back their liberty in spite of the faults for which they had at first been committed.[42] The recruitment junta of Acámbaro sent José María Oliveros to the army for entertaining illicit relations with a woman. In response, Oliveros's mother presented an array of witnesses who, while sometimes admitting the occasion of sexual misconduct, attested to the general excellence of Oliveros's life. Oliveros "is a farmer by profession, and with this occupation he provides for his mother and brothers," the recruitment junta heard from one of his neighbors, and "he [the speaker] does not know of any vice [in Oliveros]."[43] In this case, Guanajuato's governor overturned the junta's decision, and Oliveros walked free.

Notwithstanding these irregularities, the *leva* – the forced recruitment of the idle and depraved – aroused little active opposition in post-colonial Mexico. At best, and very rarely, a municipal government

---

39 For cases where recruitment juntas successfully presented additional evidence after their initial recruitment decision had been contested, see, for example, the cases concerning José Ignacio Rosales in AGEG-M, Caja 65, Expediente 2; and José Mariano Vasquez in AGEG-G, Caja 8, Expediente 13.

40 Petition from María Felipa Tapia, [1827], in AGEG-J, Caja 9, Expediente 15.

41 Statement of Mariano López, San Agustin, 8 August 1830, in AGEG-G, Caja 35, Expediente 6.

42 For a few examples of petitions that were successful in gaining recruits back their freedom, see those from María Guevara, in AHESLP-SGG, Caja 29, Expediente 3, Folios 8–10; María Valentina Chávez, in AHESLP-SGG, Caja 29, Expediente 3, Folios 13–15; María Francisca Espejo and María Juliana Espejo, San Luis Potosí, 15 April 1826, in AHESLP-SGG, Caja 46, Expediente 1; Juan Higinio Ortiz, Ramos, 7 October 1836, in AHESLP-SGG, Caja 620, Expediente 3; and José María Salazar in AGEG-G, Caja 27, Expediente 6.

43 "[Q]ue es de profesión labrador, y que con este ejercicio mantiene a la madre y hermanos, que no sabe [el declarante] que [Oliveros] tenga vicio alguno." Statement of Francisco Delgado, Acámbaro, 9 October 1826, in AGEG-J, Caja 6, Expediente 2.

might allege an absence of suitable men in its jurisdiction.[44] It was the periodic attempts to forego moral distinctions and base army recruitment on a lottery system (*sorteo*) that emptied the countryside of able-bodied men and called forth protest and foot-dragging on the part of local officials.[45] The lottery system of recruitment – modeled on a Spanish decree from 1767 and favored by officers and politicians who were concerned about the quality of an army composed of vagrants and idlers – was used for the reserve army (*milicia activa*) in the 1820s and for all parts of the military under the centralist administrations in power between 1835 and 1846.[46] According to a law from 1837, *vagos* were now to be sent to special prison camps or forced to work for industries willing to take them on.[47] For the most part, these directives do not appear to have been followed. The states of Puebla and Michoacán simply refused to adopt the centralist recruitment laws and continued to draft soldiers by means of the *leva*.[48] In centralist-era Guanajuato and San Luis Potosí, town governments sometimes, and possibly routinely, continued to recruit soldiers by means of the *leva*, whereas documentation of routine applications of the *sorteo* is non-existent in both state archives; politicians wrote

---

44 Even this was extremely rare. The three instances I have found in Guanajuato and San Luis Potosí are Policarpo Ruiz to Gobernador, Salvatierra, 26 February 1830, in AGEG-G, Caja 39, Expediente 3; Ignacio Lortada to Gobernador, 22 November 1825, in AHESLP-SGG, Caja 27, Expediente 1, Folio 19; and Pedro Bocanegra to Gobernador, Coscatlan, 28 February 1825, in AHESLP-SGG, Caja 38, Expediente 33.

45 Ignacio Cruces to Gobernador, San Miguel de Allende, 11 March 1825, in AGEG-M, Caja 15, Expediente 9, Folios 3–4; Baltasar de Pesquera et.al. to Gobernador, Silao, 9 May 1825, in AGEG-M, Caja 15, Expediente 12, Folios 1–3; Baltasar de Pesquera to Gobernador, Silao, 14 February 1826, in AGEG-M, Caja 28, Expediente 2; report from José Pedro de Arios, Rioverde, 3 September 1835, in AHESLP-SGG, Caja 530, unnumbered expediente. On the same point, see also Manuel Muro, *Historia de San Luis Potosí*, vol. 2 (San Luis Potosí: Sociedad Potosina de Estudios Históricos, 1973), 201–202.

46 *Real Declaración sobre puntos esenciales de la ordenanza de Milicias Provinciales de España, que interin se regla la formal, que corresponde á estos Cuerpos, se debe observar como tal en todas sus partes* (Mexico City: D. Felipe de Zúñiga y Ontiveros, calle de la Palma, 1781 [1767]). On recruitment for the active militia based on this law, see "Plan bajo el que deben formarse los cuerpos provinciales de infantería" [16 Septiembre 1823], Artículo 28, in Joaquín Ramírez y Sesma (ed.), *Colección de decretos, ordenes y circulares: espedidas por los gobiernos nacionales de la Federación Mexicana desde el año de 1821 hasta el de 1826 para el arreglo del ejército de los Estados-Unidos Mexicanos* (Mexico City, Imprenta a cargo de Martin Rivera, 1827), 234; and "Ordenanza de la milicia activa" [5 Mayo 1824], in *Colección de las leyes y decretos expedidos por el Congreso General de los Estados-Unidos Mejicanos, Tomo III, que comprende los del Segundo Constituyente*, Segunda Edición (Mexico City: Imprenta de Galvan á cargo de Mariano Arévalo, 1829). On the switch to a lottery system of recruitment for the regular army in the 1830s and 1840s, see Serrano Ortega, *Contingente de sangre*, 72–73.

47 "Reglamento provisional para el gobierno interior de los departamentos," 20 March 1837, articles 6 and 69, in Dublán and Lozano (eds.), *Legislación Mexicana*, vol. 3, 325, 330.

48 Serrano Ortega, *Contingente de sangre*, 79–80.

about the *sorteo* only to say that they needed more time, or even the presence of government soldiers, in order to be able to carry it out.[49]

Recruitment by the *leva* caused no such collective rejection. Instead, it gave rise to disputes about particular decisions that served to reinforce the criteria on which the recruitment process rested. Throughout the country, men or the families of men who were drafted into the army authored petitions and collected testimonial evidence attesting to their *hombría de bien*, or good character. For example, in 1845 María de San Juan Ferrer, from the municipality of San Nicolás Tolentino, San Luis Potosí, wrote that her son José María had

worked as a day laborer near Rioverde, by our [his parents'] will, and on his way back from that point to his legitimate residence ... he was [arrested and] handed over to the Señor Judge of Catarina, who judged him as an idler, but, Señor Prefect, my son does not behave like that ... I respectfully beg you to consider the indigence in which I could be left with my family in the absence of a son who will certainly be the comfort of our old age.[50]

In 1825 María Antonia Morales, resident of a small hamlet in the municipality of Guadalcázar, San Luis Potosí, pleaded for the liberty of her son,

who is the only one who maintains me with his modest labor since I remain a widow and with such a large family as [mine] is and furthermore of maiden girls

49　For the continuation of the *leva* under centralism, see Juan de Obregón to Gobernador, León, 19 May 1838, in AGEG-M, Caja 142, Expediente 5; Tomás Yllanes to Gobernador, León, 14 July 1842, in AGEG-M, Caja 156, Expediente 3; Juan Pastor to Gobernador, San Miguel de Allende, 30 June 1840, in AGEG-J, Caja 36, Expediente 3; Mariano de Mena to Gobernador, Irapuato, 10 December 1836, in AGEG-G, Caja 66, Expediente 4; the recruitment lists from the years 1840–1843 in AGEG-G, Caja 73, Expediente 19; Caja 74, Expedientes 9 and 15, and Caja 75, Expedientes 3, 6, 15, 17, and 19; Vicente Valenzuela to Pedro Cortázar, Irapuato, 15 August 1844, in AGEG-M, Caja 162, Expediente 3; and a great number of petitions from 1845 in AHESLP-SGG, Caja 1845.4, Expediente 1. For apologetic mentions about the difficulties of implementing the *sorteo*, see José María Alcocer to Secretario del Gobierno, León, 18 August 1853, in AGEG-M, Caja 186, Expediente 8; [Illegible name] to Juez de Paz of Romita, San José, 7 July 1854, and Ignacio Soto Maldonado to Gobernador, Romita, 8 July 1854, in AGEG-M, Caja 186, Expediente 9. The *ayuntamiento* of Mexico City was similarly reluctant to carry out the *sorteo*. See Sonia Pérez Toledo, *Trabajadores, espacio urbano y sociabilidad en la Ciudad de México, 1790–1867* (Mexico City: Universidad Autónoma Metropolitana – Unidad Iztapalapa, 2011), 178–179.

50　"[E]staba en albercas de Rioverde trabajando de jornalero, por voluntad nuestra, y al regresarse de aquel punto para su legítima residencia ... lo pusieron a disposición del Señor Juez de Catarina, el que juzgándolo, por un hombre vago, lo cual Señor Prefecto, no tiene mi hijo esa conducta ... A V.S. rendidamente suplico se digne a atender a la indigencia, en que puedo quedar con mi familia, en la falta que me hará un hijo que ciertamente será el báculo de nuestra vejes." Petition from María de San Juan Ferrer, 16 January 1845, in AHESLP-SGG, Caja 1845.4, Expediente 1.

exposed to infinite dangers . . . no no Señor he is not an immoral man nor a drunk nor a gambler nor is he a slacker. [He is] only immersed in his work.[51]

And in 1825 María Antonia Ramírez from Salamanca, Guanajuato, attempted to win back the freedom of her husband:

I can affirm, first of all that [my husband] is married to me; that he has the profession of weaver . . . and that is the second thing; third, that he has a family which he has the obligation to assist with what he earns by his work, consisting of me, and two small children which we have had from our union.

"And how is it," she went on, "that he should be torn from the bosom of his family, and from his profession, so that he may serve as a soldier?"[52] Hundreds of similar documents could be cited: authored with the help of professional or semiprofessional scribes, these petitions constituted perhaps the principal genre of lower-class writing in early republican Mexico.

By describing men as hardworking rather than idle, sober rather than drunk, and altruistic rather than selfish, petitioners deplored not just the loss of freedom but also the moral injury effected by recruitment. Some evoked the absurdity of being arrested for idleness at moments when they were, in fact, hard at work. Manuel Alonzo of Cerro de San Pedro, San Luis Potosí, wrote that he was "surprised" and arrested by his *alcalde* "as I was with the plough in my hand working for the subsistence of my family."[53] The wife of a sharecropper on the Hacienda de Talpa, in Guanajuato, reported at length how her husband, busily plowing his land, was asked to help out with the hacienda's wheat harvest, "where having gone for the accustomed Sunday pay they caught him" to send to the army.[54] Reyes Pérez of San Luis de la Paz, Guanajuato, similarly reported being arrested at

---

51   "[E]l cual es el único que me mantiene con su corto trabajo desde que quedo viuda y con la familia tan crecida como es y más de niñas doncellas expuestas a infinitos peligros . . . no no Señor no es ningún hombre vicioso ni es borracho ni es jugador ni él anda de flojo. Solo metido en su trabajo." Petition from María Antonia Morales, San Luis Potosí, 11 April 1825, in AHESLP-SGG, Caja 17, Expediente 1, Fojas 8–9.

52   "Y sí puedo afirmar, que es lo primero casado conmigo; que tiene el oficio de obrajero . . ., y es lo segundo; lo tercero, que tiene familia forzosa a que asistir, con lo que gana con su trabajo, como soy yo, y dos tiernos hijos, que hemos tenido de nuestro matrimonio. ¿Y como así se le ha de arrancar del seno de su familia, y de su oficio para que vaya a servir plaza de soldado?" Petition from María Antonia Ramírez in AGEG-G, Caja 8, Expediente 13.

53   "[F]ui sorprendido por el alcalde auxiliar de aquella fracción al tiempo mismo que me hallaba con el arado en la mano trabajando en busca de la subsistencia de mi familia." Petition from Manuel Alonzo, 4 June 1836, in AHESLP-SGG, Caja 620, Expediente 5.

54   "[E]n donde habiendo concurrido a la acostumbrada paga del domingo lo aprehendieron." Petition from María Atanasia Galván, in AGEG-J, Caja 14, Expediente 11.

a time when he was working and when, he added, "I was neither involved in any scandal nor offending anybody."[55]

Women pleading on behalf of their sons or husbands might also stress their apprehension in domestic settings: the *alcalde* and his officer arrested her husband "surprising my house," wrote one woman; they "snatched [my son] from his house, they did not take him on the street," wrote another; and another, "they snatched [my son] from his workshop, and his house, where a man should always be respected."[56] If military recruitment carried a kind of patriotic stigma – recruits were deemed guilty of failing not just their families but the nation at large – then petitioners turned this accusation on its head: by tearing men from their productive or familial settings, they argued, it was the recruitment juntas, and not the recruits, who did damage to the moral fabric of the nation. While such petitions did much to encumber the work of recruitment, they also gave dramatic depth to the idea that society was constituted through the practice of masculine labor. As a scripting of the normative foundations of Mexico's post-colonial legal order, military recruitment was effective precisely because it involved popular groups in a ceaseless moral performance.

Military recruitment was an area in which civilian and military authorities, rather than clashing over jurisdictional boundaries, worked together and even depended on one another. The army counted on local governments to provide it with recruits. Local governments counted on the army to rid their towns of undesirable elements, so much so that at times when recruitment was temporarily halted, or replaced with a lottery system, some professed themselves helpless to cope with the results. For example, at a time when Guanajuato's yearly recruitment quota had been filled, the mayor of Tarandacuao begged the governor to allow him to draft at least a few more men "who don't respect any authority and are enemies of public tranquility."[57] Our examination of military recruitment thus compels us to look at military-civilian tensions from a different, and broader, perspective than that of wounded civil society. The military's standing outside the realm of lawfulness flowed in part from decisions made by the same municipal governments that throughout the nation were the principal

---

55   "[N]i yo andaba escandalizando, ni ofendiendo a ninguna persona." Petition in AGEG-G, Caja 12, Expediente 17.

56   "[S]orprendiendo mi casa." "Lo sacaron de su casa, no lo cogieron en la calle .... " And "... lo sacaron de su taller, y de su casa, donde el hombre siempre debe ser respetado"; Petition from María Perfecta Guevara, in AHESLP-SGG, Caja 29, Expediente 3, Folios 8–10; Petition from María Valentina Chávez, in AHESLP-SGG, Caja 29, Expediente 3, Folios 13–15; and Petition from María Luisa Domínguez, Villa de San Francisco, 4 July 1836, in AHESLP-SGG, Caja 620, Expediente 3.

57   "[L]os cuales no respectan autoridad ninguna, y son unos enemigos de la tranquilidad pública"; José María Perea to Gobernador, Tarandacuao, 19 May 1827, in AGEG-G, Caja 14, Expediente 16.

purveyors of law and justice. By impressing citizens into the army, municipal governments displaced major instances of what they considered rowdy, immoral, or anti-social behavior from the contexts in which they arose and concentrated them in an institution that became, as it were, compositionally defined by its members' banishment from the ordinary legal order. Soldiers who cloaked themselves in the military *fuero* and caused trouble for civilian authorities had first been expelled from the community of law that now they menaced.

III   The Civic Militia

A brutal and constitutionally dubious measure, army recruitment fostered a culture of work and domesticity and allowed local authorities to expel perpetrators of socially undesirable behaviors from the community of citizens. But it did not release them from the necessity of developing an effective law-enforcement routine. In Mexico's immediate post-independence years, the force tasked with establishing such a routine was the civic militia: a non-professional citizen police organized by municipal governments on the basis of an 1822 national law and further regulations passed by the various states.[58] In an age of chronic fiscal insolvency, vesting the defense of the law in a civic militia was above all a pragmatic choice; only in a few urban centers did town councils have enough money to hire professional policemen.[59] It was nevertheless a choice that put the republican notion of popular sovereignty directly to the test. Whether it would work depended on the answers to two questions that for local politicians became a source of considerable worry: would enough men enlist in the militias to make them viable? And, if they did, would the bodies of armed plebeians sustain the rule of law rather than damage it further?

A number of government reports from the 1820s, listing the strength of all municipal militias, allows us to address the first question in some

58   "Reglamento de la milicia cívica," 3 August 1822, article 1, in Manuel Dublán and José María Lozano (eds.), *Legislación Mexicana, ó, Colección completa de las disposiciones legislativas expedidas desde la independencia de la República*, vol. 1 (Mexico City: Imprenta del Comercio, 1876), 619; José Antonio Serrano Ortega, *Jerarquía territorial y transición política: Guanajuato, 1790–1836* (Mexico City: El Colegio de Michoacán, Instituto Mora, 2001), 86–96, 250, 254–55; Juan Ortiz Escamilla, "Las fuerzas militares y el proyecto de estado en México, 1767–1835," in *Cincuenta años de historia en México*, eds. Alicia Hernández Chavez and Manuel Miño Grijalva, 261–282 (Mexico City, 1991), vol. 2, 272–275. On the organization of local militias during the independence war, see also Juan Ortiz Escamilla, *Guerra y Gobierno: Los pueblos y la independencia de México* (Seville, Spain: Instituto Mora, El Colegio de México, Universidad Internacional de Andalucia, and Universidad de Sevilla, 1997).

59   The classic work on fiscal instability in post-independence Mexico is Barbara Tenenbaum, *The Politics of Penury: Debts and Taxes in Mexico, 1821–1855* (Albuquerque: University of New Mexico Press, 1986).

detail for the state of Guanajuato. The same reports contain municipal population counts, making it possible to calculate the percentage of residents who participated in their towns' militia duties. Unfortunately I have found no good ways to arrive at a precise estimate of the proportion of people who fell into the 16–50 years age group or who lived in the urban parts of their municipalities and were thus expected to serve in the infantry-companies rather than in the cavalry, responsible for policing in the countryside. Even the proportion of males in the population may, in the aftermath of the independence war, have been smaller than the expected 50 percent. However, we may not be too far off the mark if we take 50 percent as the ratio of people who were male, 45 percent as the ratio of people who were between 16 and 50 years old, and 40 percent as the ratio of men who lived in municipal seats.[60] We can then take 9 percent as a rough estimate of the proportion of Guanajuato's total population that was eligible to serve in the infantry companies of local militias.

Table 1 shows that the percentage of estimated eligible men who did militia service in the urban areas of Guanajuato ranged widely at the edges, between 2.5 percent in León in 1826 and 83.1 percent in Acámbaro and Celaya in 1824–1825. These variations can be explained by a number of factors: local politics, unreliable information-gathering, differences in the proportion between urban and rural residents in different municipalities. A relatively low proportion of urban to rural residents is almost certainly responsible for the nonsensical percentage result for Jerécuaro in the years 1824–1825. Most of the numbers, however, fall between 10 and 35 percent, and the average of eligible men in the entire state of Guanajuato who served in their towns' civic militias is estimated as 24.4 percent in 1824–1825, 22.3 percent in 1826, and 24.9 percent in 1829.

If a little less than a quarter of all eligible men in fact served in the civic militia, it is clear that whether to serve or not involved a large element of choice. Those who wanted to shirk militia duties had two options.[61] First,

60 David Brading, *Miners and Merchants in Bourbon Mexico, 1763–1810* (New York: Cambridge University Press, 1971), 227, has estimated that in 1793 a third of Guanajuato's population lived in towns with more than 5,000 inhabitants. I have adjusted this number upwards because towns with fewer than 5,000 inhabitants nevertheless featured among municipal capitals in the late 1820s. The estimate of a 40 percent urban population for the state as a whole, however, is not only highly uncertain, it also masks large differences between regions and individual municipalities. For my estimate of the percentage of the male population between 16 and 50 years of age, I have slightly adjusted the number of 46.5 percent of men who fell within the age span of 15 to 49 years in the only recorded census by age group, taken in Oaxaca in 1777, of the colonial and early republican periods, reproduced in Sherburne F. Cook and Woodrow Borah, *Essays in Population History: Mexico and the Caribbean*, vol. 1 (Berkeley: University of California Press, 1971), 207, Table 16b.

61 Law nr. 95, 2 April 1828, article 2, in AHESLP-Leyes y Decretos.

Table 1: *Milicia cívica infantry in Guanajuato, 1824–1829*[62]

	Number of milicianos 1824–1825	Total population/ Percentage of estimated eligible population	Number of milicianos 1826	Total population/ Percentage of estimated eligible population	Number of milicianos 1829	Total population/ Percentage of estimated eligible population
Guanajuato	1,455	33,488/48.3	1,631	34,611/52.4	2,166	37,265/64.6
Salamanca	646	15,053/47.7	481	15,838/33.7	538	18,335/32.6
Irapuato	381	16,054/26.4	256	17,111/16.6	564	19,503/32.1
Silao	450	16,694/29.9	545	17,832/34.0	471	21,221/24.7
Valle de Santiago	214	14,677/16.2	180	15,226/13.1	282	17,834/17.6
Celaya	716	9,571/83.1	708	16,453/47.8	779	25,021/34.6
Salvatierra	102	16,284/7.0	192	16,620/12.8	296	18,501/17.8
Acámbaro	620	8,292/83.1	245	8,288/32.8	266	8,923/33.1
Yuriria and Uriangato			631	28,834/24.3	542	30,582/19.7
Chamacuero	80	4,482/19.8	119	5,200/25.4	124	6,156/22.4
Casas Viejas			111	9,571/12.9	50	11,373/4.9
Jerécuaro	1,080	10,252/117.0	557	10,252/60.4	607	11,478/58.8
Apaseo			166	10,108/18.2	83	17,470/5.3
Santa Cruz	500	9,007/61.7	340	9,418/40.1	109	10,698/11.3
San Miguel de Allende	1,168	39,092/33.2	839	30,321/30.7	633	33,556/21.0
Dolores Hidalgo	300	31,710/10.5	231	22,500/11.4	142	24,841/6.4
San Felipe and Bizcocho			400	20,583/21.6	340	22,571/16.7
San Luis de la Paz					156	14,254/12.2

(Continued)

62 Based on *Memoria que presenta el Gobernador de Guanajuato al Congreso Constituyente del estado de los negocios públicos que han estado á su cuidado, desde 10 de Mayo de 1824 hasta 31 de Diciembre de 1825* (Guanajuato: Imprenta del supremo Gobierno en Palacio, 1826); *Memoria que el Gobernador del Estado de Guanajuato formo para dar cumplimiento a la parte 8.a del articulo 161 de la Constitucion Federal, ampliandola en otros ramos para conocimiento del Congreso del mismo Estado, todo por lo respectivo al año de 1826* (Mexico City: Imprenta y librería a cargo de Martin Rivera, 1827); and *Memoria que presenta el Gobernador del estado de Guanajuato, de su administracion publica correspondiente al año de 1829, para cumplir con lo dispuesto en el artículo 161 fraccion 8.a de la constitucion federal, y en el 82 de la particular del mismo Estado* (Guanajuato: Imprenta del Supremo Gobierno a cargo del C. Jose Maria Carranco, 1830).

Table 1: *(Continued)*

	Number of *milicianos* 1824–1825	Total population/ Percentage of estimated eligible population	Number of *milicianos* 1826	Total population/ Percentage of estimated eligible population	Number of *milicianos* 1829	Total population/ Percentage of estimated eligible population
Xichú	102	7,469/15.2	94	7,469/14.0		
León	100	39,468/2.8	99	43,485/2.5	1,031	48,270/23.7
Pénjamo	240	20,941/12.7	73	21,839/3.7	146	23,689/6.8
Piedragorda	240	12,485/21.4	88	12,686/7.7	335	14,594/25.5
San Francisco del Rincón					147	
Purísima del Rincón					175	
Total	8,394	382.829/24.4	7,991	397,635/22.3	9,977	444,441/24.9

if they were public employees, ecclesiastics, day workers, low-income salaried workers, or students, they could apply for an exemption.[63] It was the categories of day work and low-income salaried work that left poor and middling Mexicans with a good deal of room for maneuver. These categories were not flexible enough to capture the realities of people who sometimes worked for a salary while also owning or renting land, or keeping shop, or working a trade, or engaging in any other form of private enterprise. Because town authorities lacked the resources to inquire into the exact circumstances of everybody claiming an exemption, people were relatively free to describe their work as best fitted their purpose.[64]

63 "Reglamento de la milicia cívica," 3 August 1822, article 1, in Dublán and Lozano (eds.), *Legislación Mexicana*, vol. 1, 619; Law nr. 48, 28 May 1828, part 1, article 2, in AGEG-Leyes y Decretos. Law nr. 95, 2 April 1828, article 2, in AHESLP-Leyes y Decretos.

64 For examples of town governments trying to cope with the complexities of the laws' application to peoples' real-life situations, see José Antonio Robles to Gobernador, Bizcocho, 24 August 1824, in AGEG-M, Caja 2, Expediente 16, Foja 18; Actas de Ayuntamiento, Irapuato, 19 January 1828, in AGEG-M, Caja 63, Expediente 3; Actas de Ayuntamiento, Salamanca, 28 April, 2 June 1829, in AGEG-M, Caja 77, Expediente 8; Actas de Ayuntamiento, Piedragorda, 14 January 1830, in AGEG-M, Caja 84, Expediente 3; Juan de la Vega to Gobernador, Pénjamo, 26 June 1849, in AGEG-M, Caja 175, Expediente 5; Rafael Arambures to Gobernador, Irapuato, 28 August 1827, in AGEG-M, Caja 16, Expediente 5; Ayuntamiento to Gobernador, Acámbaro, 27 June 1827, in AGEG-G, Caja 19, Expediente 1; Luis Villalpando to Gobernador, Acámbaro, 8 August 1827, in AGEG-G, Caja 19, Expediente 2; Eduardo Mendosa to Gobernador, Celaya, 15 October 1828, in AGEG-G, Caja 25, Expediente 1; "Espediente promovido por el Ciudadano Lucas Estrello vecino del Pueb.o de Acambaro," 1828, in AGEG-G, Caja 27, Expediente 1. For a case in which

The second way to avoid service in the civic militia was simple evasion. Like applying for exemptions, evasion depended on the limited capacity of town authorities to engage in surveillance and persecute contraveners.[65] Also like applying for exemptions, it was an option that was most realistic for the poor and unsettled, who could elude official notice by moving between jobs, dwellings, and municipalities. We may assume that the rich had their own means to avoid militia service, and that therefore the civic militia was most properly the preserve of the middle sectors of provincial society. This, however, was only a tendency: there are records of day workers who served in the militias for years before attempting to get out, and of others who kept on serving in spite of the possibility of gaining legal exemptions.[66]

Low recruitment numbers meant that towns sometimes struggled to keep enough men under arms. In the early 1820s the militia of Valle de Santiago was so small that individual soldiers had to stand guard and go on patrol on four days each month, even though, the mayor wrote, they were "unfortunate people who depend on their physical labor to support their families."[67] In Casas Viejas the high number of citizens claiming exemption from militia service made it necessary to temporarily suspend the preventive guard and the Sunday patrol in 1829 and, once again, in 1830.[68] The militia of Jerécuaro in 1833 was able to provide a permanent guard only at the jail. Public safety, the mayor reported, suffered from the absence

poor farmers were granted a seasonal reprieve from militia service while they were sowing their fields, see Actas de Ayuntamiento, Acámbaro, 15 June 1829, in AGEG-M, Caja 77, Expediente 2.

65   On citizens attempting to avoid militia service, see Actas de Ayuntamiento, Casas Viejas, 9 April 1829, in AGEG-M, Caja 77, Expediente 5; José Francisco Gamiño to Gobernador, Irapuato, 8 July 1826, in AGEG-G, Caja 8, Expediente 7; Miguel de la Peña to Jefe Político, Celaya, 11 September 1823, in AGEG-M, Caja 2, Expediente 13, Foja 16; José Estanislao Gallardo to Gobernador, Pueblo Nuevo, 9 May 1826, in AGEG-G, Caja 9, Expediente 8; Joaquín Galván to Gobernador, Celaya, 21 February 1837, in AGEG-M, Caja 139, Expediente 2; Lorenzo Bravo to Presidente del Ayuntamiento de este Pueblo Juan María Rodríguez, Pénjamo, 27 June 1838, in AGEG-G, Caja 69, Expediente 4.

66   For day workers or salaried workers receiving exemptions from militia service after they had already served, see Faustino Hernández to Gobernador, Venado, 2 March 1826, in AHESLP-SGG, Caja 41, Expediente 1; Actas de Ayuntamiento, Casas Viejas, 4 December, 22 December, and 29 December 1828, in AGEG-M, Caja 63, Expediente 1; Actas de Ayuntamiento, Casas Viejas, 24 August 1829, in AGEG-M, Caja 77, Expediente 5; Luis Rangel et al. to Gobernador, Acámbaro, 21 May 1827; and Ayuntamiento to Gobernador, Acámbaro, 28 May 1827, in AGEG-G, Caja 19, Expediente 1. For day workers who served in the civic militia in spite of their occupational status, see letter to Gobernador, Pénjamo, 16 February 1830, in AGEG-M, Caja 81, Expediente 2.

67   "[U]nos infelices, que solo están atendidos a su corporal trabajo para el sostén de sus familias"; Miguel González y Núñez to Intendente, Valle de Santiago, 10 December 1823, in AGEG-G, Caja 1, Expediente 27.

68   Actas de Ayuntamiento, Casas Viejas, 9 April and 11 June 1829, in AGEG-M, Caja 77, Expediente 5; and Actas de Ayuntamiento, Casas Viejas, 19 April and 26 August 1830, in AGEG-M, Caja 83, Expediente 1.

of a larger police presence.[69] And in 1838 an officer from Pénjamo reported that it was becoming difficult to motivate enlisted *cívicos* to take up their guard duties, since they were few and the duties they had to perform excessive. In this case the governor responded by suggesting the recruitment of more citizens into the militia, adding that "he who refuses to provide a service so little troublesome as that rendered [by the militias] inside the settlements, [the mayor] may send him to this government in order to put him into the permanent army."[70]

If it is clear that in Guanajuato a large number of eligible citizens were able to avoid militia service, most of the time enough people joined the civic militias to give them a preponderance of force that no criminal group was likely to match. However, whether the existence of this force would strengthen or undermine a liberal culture of law was by no means certain. For some town authorities, members of the civic militias raised the same concerns as regular soldiers. In 1840 Silao's town council reacted with alarm when the local militia asked to be reconstituted as an auxiliary force: the presence of auxiliary soldiers covered by the military *fuero*, wrote the council, "would be a seedbed of demoralization, of insubordination, and of disorder for the common class of citizens, the truth of which is sadly demonstrated by experience."[71] In 1842 Irapuato's militia commander informed the state governor of the shameless behavior of one of his sublieutenants, who – together with others – had been seen throwing stones at a tavern that had refused them service at two in the morning. The commander considered it necessary to demote the sub-lieutenant from the officer class "so that his misconduct will be punished and be a lesson to others."[72]

Complaints such as these were not politically innocent: in part they were driven by misgivings that the civic militias allowed men of poor or disreputable backgrounds to ascend to positions of power. Their social

---

69 A. Llaca Romero to Jefe Político of Celaya, Jerécuaro, 2 June 1833, in AGEG-G, Caja 56, Expediente 5.

70 "[A]quel que se niegue a dar un servicio tan poco molesto como el que se presta dentro de las poblaciones, puede mandarlo a este Gobierno para destinarlo al ejército permanente"; Lorenzo Bravo to Presidente del Ayuntamiento, Pénjamo, 27 June 1838, and undated response to that letter, in AGEG-G, Caja 69, Expediente 4.

71 "[P]ara la clase común de ciudadanos sería un semillero infinito de desmoralización, de insubordinación y de desorden cuyas verdades tiene tristemente demostradas la experiencia"; Ayuntamiento of Silao to Gobernador, 13 September 1840, in AGEG-G, Caja 72, Expediente 13.

72 "[Q]ue la insubordinación y prostitución de este individuo, todos los días se aumenta, y por lo mismo, no puede merecer mi confianza; a más de esto, que prevalido del empleo que tiene, como dejo a V.E. dicho se pasea de noche, hasta la hora que le da la gana en compañía de otros, y a los encargados de la policía les ha dicho, que ni alcaldes, ni nadie tienen que meterse con él"; and "para que queden castigadas sus faltas, y sirva de escarmiento a los demás." Nicolás Tejeda to Gobernador, Irapuato, 1 October 1842, in AGEG-G, Legajo 75, Expediente 7.

composition made the militias into natural exponents of class-based policy proposals. José Antonio Serrano Ortega has shown that between 1828 and 1834 Guanajuatan civic militias successfully pressured state governments to expel resident Spaniards, back the national presidency of Vicente Guerrero, and, in 1832, support the overthrow of the conservative Bustamante administration. Though originally supported by regional elites, by the early 1830s many militias had slipped from elite control and become centers of populist agitation.[73] At the level of town politics, militias' political sympathies might trump their subordination to municipal authorities. In 1833, in the heat of an argument over administrative competencies in Silao, a militia commander told the mayor "that [the commander's] troops belonged to the federation and that he did not have to lend me [the mayor] any help."[74] At the level of national politics, anxiety over the militias' capacity to channel and project lower-class sentiment was part of what drove the patrician coalition that in 1834 overthrew the radical Gómez Farías regime and turned the country toward centralism; putting a strict limit on the size of state militias was among the first actions of the coalition once it had taken power.[75]

Although militia companies sometimes promoted nonconformist political projects, we should not exaggerate the extent to which they did so. Fascination with the political implications of a citizen militia has often led historians to disregard the civic militia's actual functions and operational routines. But the main purpose of the militia was neither political – to defend state prerogatives or project lower-class voices – nor military – to put down rebellions or defend national sovereignty. In the civic-militia regulation of 1822, these objectives did not figure at all. Rather, the militias' tasks were to stand guard at municipal buildings; to patrol public spaces, especially during festivities that would draw large numbers of people; to catch and transport "deserters and wrongdoers"; to escort prisoners and public funds between towns; and to defend their towns against military attacks.[76] The state regulations of Guanajuato and San Luis Potosí

---

73 Serrano Ortega, *Jerarquía territorial*, 272–289. For examples of militia pronouncements, see Juan Méndez to Jefe de Policía de Celaya, Salvatierra, 14 December 1828, in AGEG-G, Caja 27, Expediente 15; Mariano Domenzain to Gobernador, Dolores Hidalgo, 11 January 1829, in AGEG-G, Caja 34, Expediente 2; Francisco Duque to Ayuntamiento de esta Villa, San Felipe, 3 September 1832, in AGEG-M, Caja 112, Expediente 9; Mariano Ramírez de Prado to Gobernador, San Felipe, 11 September 1832, in AGEG-G, Caja 49, Expediente 7; and Pronouncement of civic militia, San Felipe, 3 September 1832, in AGEG-G, Caja 53, Expediente 3.

74 "[Q]ue aquella tropa pertenecía a la federación y que no me había de dar auxilio alguno." Luis Gasca to Gobernador, Silao, 29 August 1833, in AGEG-G, Caja 56, Expediente 11.

75 Serrano Ortega, *Jerarquía territorial*, 272–293. Sordo Cedeño, *El Congreso*, 154–161.

76 "[D]esertores y malhechores." "Reglamento de la milicia cívica," 3 August 1822, articles 12–18, in Dublán and Lozano (eds.), *Legislación Mexicana*, vol. 1, 620.

repeated this list with slight variations: the militias in Guanajuato were not asked to provide guards for public buildings except in the state capital (though in practice they often did), and those of San Luis Potosí were specially enjoined to lend any service asked of them by their town governments or other public authorities.[77] The state regulations also foresaw the possibility that the militias would have to serve in a military role: it belonged to their functions, stated the law from Guanajuato, "to sustain national independence, the constitution of the republic, and the particular one of the state," and the law from San Luis Potosí contained a similar provision.[78] But the militia's principal task was that of policing.

In Guanajuato, where the work of the militias is well documented, militia detachments typically mounted guard at public buildings and, in many towns, routinely patrolled the streets. On their patrols *milicianos* sometimes worked under their own officers and sometimes went accompanied by civil authorities.[79] By rotating guard and patrol duties between soldiers, the *cívicos* were able to perform a vital public service without neglecting their private affairs. For example, in Chamacuero the number of *milicianos* who accompanied authorities on their nightly patrols in 1828 was given as five.[80] If there was a total of 124 *milicianos* – the number listed for the following year – each *miliciano* would have to serve one day out of twenty five.

In spite of occasional apprehensions about its trustworthiness, in most towns and at most times the Guanajuatan civic militia was recognized as a vital source of support for public authority. To have a militia guard at the ready meant, according to a politician from Chamacuero, that "the civil authorities have a place where they can find assistance when it is necessary."[81] The town council of Purísima del Rincón wrote that it was

---

77 Law nr. 95, 2 April 1828, article 52, in AHESLP-Leyes y Decretos. Law nr. 48, 28 May 1828, part 1, articles 48–50, 53, in AGEG-Leyes y Decretos.

78 "[S]ostener la independencia nacional, la Constitución de la República, y la particular del Estado." Law nr. 48, 28 May 1828, part 1, article 47, in AGEG-Leyes y Decretos. The same function is listed in Law nr. 95, 2 April 1828, article 58, in AHESLP-Leyes y Decretos.

79 Rafael de Herrera to Gobernador, Salvatierra, 22 September 1824, in AGEG-M, Caja 3, Expediente 7, Foja 116; Guadalupe Delgado to Gobernador, Salamanca, 27 May 1839, in AGEG-G, Caja 71, Expediente 11. Actas de Ayuntamiento, Casas Viejas, 16 August 1827, in AGEG-M, Caja 42, Expediente 3; Juan de Ontón to Gobernador, Dolores Hidalgo, 2 August 1826, in AGEG-G, Caja 10, Expediente 6; Isidro Chávez to Gobernador, Silao, 10 April 1846, in AGEG-M, Caja 168, Expediente 13; Letter from José Gerónimo de Salar, San Felipe, 10 March 1824, in AGEG-M, Caja 2, Expediente 18, Foja 4; and Letter from Ayuntamiento of Valle de Santiago, 1846, in AGEG-M, Caja 168, Expediente 16.

80 Actas de Ayuntamiento, Chamacuero, 7 January, 20 October and 23 October 1828, in AGEG-M, Caja 64, Expediente 3.

81 "[T]engan las autoridades civiles donde impetrar auxilio en caso necesario." Actas de Ayuntamiento, Chamacuero, 19 April 1827, in AGEG-M, Caja 39, Expediente 1.

on the promise of such assistance that its ability "to prevent calamities" depended.[82] The government of Apaseo, after praising the work of the local militia in "conserving the interior order [of the town]," described its function as "the support of the public authorities, helping them on the occasions in which it has been called, be it to conduct convict gangs from Querétaro to Celaya, be it with the apprehension of thieves."[83] Periodical recruitment failures stood out precisely because the militia had almost everywhere become an indispensable institution. In 1832, when militia troops were withdrawn from Purísima del Rincón, a town that had recently lost its status as an independent municipality, a local functionary warned that "the interests of the public treasury are exposed, as are those of the residents"; if a militia guard was not reinstated, it was to be feared that bandit gangs would emerge from among the town's population.[84] The town council of Silao, ordered in 1846 to send thirty armed soldiers to Querétaro as the country prepared for war, protested in the strongest terms. Two years earlier, General Santa Anna had passed through Silao and robbed its militia of most of its weapons. Town residents had nonetheless managed, with the greatest difficulty and by means of a private collection, to keep a patrol of *milicianos* under arms. If those weapons were also lost, the militia contingent left in town

would remain without being able to provide the accustomed police patrols and temerity will lose its inhibition; without being able to go on nocturnal rounds, and vice and insecurity will make disastrous forays unpunished; without being able to guard the jail and the prisoners therefore will make natural attempts to gain their liberty, since the building in which they are contained is flimsy and situated outside of town.[85]

That the civic militias were effective providers of public security is also attested by reports from the state government. In 1831, Guanajuato's governor wrote that the presence of civic militias, together with the work of civil authorities, "have been enough to keep the towns in quietude and to

82   "[E]vitar las desgracias." Felipe Espinosa to Jefe Político of León, Purísima del Rincón, 30 November 1827, in AGEG-G, Caja 16, Expediente 11.

83   "[C]onservar el orden interior"; "es el sostén de las autoridades, auxiliándolas las ocasiones que han sido llamados, ya para conducir cuerdas de Querétaro a Celaya, ya para la aprensión de ladrones." "Ynforme que el Ayuntamiento del Pueblo de S. Juan Bautista de Apaseo, dio al Señor Vice Gobernador," 11 May 1830, in AGEG-M, Caja 101, Expediente 1.

84   "[E]stán expuesto los intereses de la hacienda pública, así como los de los vecinos." Ignacio García to Gobernador, Purísima del Rincón, 4 December 1832, in AGEG-G, Caja 49, Expediente 6.

85   "[Q]ueda ... sin poder dar las patrullas de policía acostumbradas y la osadía usará de sus desenfrenos; sin poder dar las rondas nocturnas y el vicio e inseguridad harán funestos ensayos impunemente; sin poder dar la guardia de la cárcel y la prisión en el acto hará los esfuerzos naturales por su libertad, cuando el edificio que la contiene es débil y situado en extramuros"; Isidro Chávez to Gobernador, Silao, 10 April 1846, in AGEG-M, Caja 168, Expediente 13.

persecute the thieves that, under cover of night, committed their petty robberies."[86] A year later, the governor opined that the militias "may today be truly esteemed as the bulwark of the institutions and the liberties of the state."[87]

When looked at from the perspective of Guanajuato's provincial towns, the common perception of early republican Mexico as a place lacking in law and order is largely unfounded. While we lack evidence to reconstruct actual crime figures, it is hard to doubt that Guanajuato saw a strong trend toward the consolidation of law and the containment of crime and violence in the first republican decade. At a time when the optics of state formation added visibility to violence and delinquency, municipal and state politicians were unanimous in their depiction of a situation of lawfulness inside urban settlements, and in the attribution of that state of affairs to the work of the civic militias. Whether this situation was typical for mestizo towns everywhere in post-independence Mexico is not a question that can be answered at present. In San Luis Potosí, where civic militia companies owned or rented barracks in a number of towns – including Real de Catorce, Ciudad del Valle, Valle del Maíz, and Ramos – I have not found sufficient information to reconstruct the companies' operational routines. It is nevertheless worth noting that in the 1830s municipal reports from all regions of that state, with very minor exceptions, depicted situations of public peace and security.[88]

In Guanajuato, the gamble of vesting law-enforcement in a body of armed plebeians clearly paid off. While local magistrates at times expressed concern about the political militancy of the *cívicos*, far more commonly they praised them as men who exemplified the most desirable traits of citizenship and masculinity. According to town leaders from Pénjamo, the *cívicos* were "honorable" and "decent" folk.[89] The commander of the companies of

---

86   "[H]an sido bastantes para mantener a los lugares en quietud, y perseguir a los rateros que al abrigo de la noche, ejecutaban sus pequeños robos." *Memoria instructiva, que en cumplimiento de la parte 4.a del articulo 109 de la Constitucion del estado de Guanajuato, presenta al Superior Gobierno del mismo su primer Vice-Gobernador Constitucional, Año de 1830* (Guanajuato: Imprenta del Supremo Gobierno administrada por el C. Ruperto Rocha, 1831), 17.

87   "[P]uede hoy día estimarse verdaderamente como el baluarte de las instituciones y de las libertades del Estado." *Memoria de la administracion publica del Estado de Guanajuato, correspondiente al año de 1831, que el Vice-Gobernador Constitucional, en ejercicio del poder ejecutivo, presenta en cumplimiento del articulo 82 de la Constitucion del mismo Estado* (Mexico City: Imprenta del Aguila, 1832), 12.

88   See the documents collected in "Partes mensales remitidos á este Gobierno por los Prefectos y Sub-Prefectos de los cuatro Departamentos del Estado en cumplimiento de las dispuesto en la Circular de 2 de Mayo de 831 recordada posteriormente con fha. 8 de Setiembre de 834," in AHESLP-SGG, Caja 530, unnumbered Expediente.

89   Rafael de Chávez to Jefe Político interino, Pénjamo, 7 October 1823, in AGEG-G, Caja 1, Expediente 18. José Francisco Rodríguez to Gobernador, Pénjamo, 16 November 1824, in AGEG-G, Caja 3, Expediente 11.

Casas Viejas described his men as "hardworking individuals, burdened with large families," who "when the law calls them they lend themselves, they lend themselves with enthusiasm, full of joy, animated by their interest for our mother *patria*."[90] The mayor of San Luis de la Paz wrote of the local militia that it was composed of men "in whom can be detected a general enthusiasm for the military service which, when it is added to their honesty, makes them worthy of the regard of their leaders."[91] Decency, honesty, patriotism, hard work: these were the attributes of a masculine type that, point by point, was the opposite of that represented by the army recruit. Militia soldiers embodied the republican values that army recruits threatened and, through their service, gave them a permanent institutional expression.

IV Civil War

Mexico's civic militias were the protective arm of a society whose chief values were labor and domesticity and whose chief foil was an aggressive, egotistical model of masculinity. We saw, however, that the militias, too, could be a source of political anxiety. Like the regular army, they contained, at one end of the spectrum of their potential, the capacity to suspend the authority of elected officials and project alternative principles of power. If the militias ultimately came to embody the protection of the law and not its subversion that was because of the operation of at least three institutional safeguards: the civic militias (1) were under the command of civilian authorities; (2) fulfilled functions that were of immediate public benefit, including that of their members; and (3) relied on a model of citizen participation that was temporary, close to home, and largely voluntary. We can contrast these points, one by one, with the modus operandi of the regular army, which was largely – at the local level, completely – removed from civilian oversight, fulfilled a function that except during times of war was highly abstract, and, most important, forced its soldiers into multiple-year terms of service away from home and family.

The civic militias and regular army could exist as opposed institutional and even cultural worlds as long as the need for cooperation between them was rare. By the end of the 1840s, this condition no longer held.

---

90 "[U]nos individuos laboriosos, cargados de familia numerosa."; "cuando la ley los llama se prestan, se prestan con entusiasmo llenos de júbilo animados del interés de nuestra Madre Patria."; "Sobre quejas del Comandante de Cívicos de Casas Viejas, contra el Alc.e 1.o de aquel lugar, p.r ecsigirles éste á aquellos, servicios q. no están designados en el reglamento," Guanajuato, 1827, in AGEG-G, Caja 15, Expediente 2.

91 "[S]e les advierte un general entusiasmo al servicio militar que reunido éste a su honradez, los hace acreedores al aprecio de sus jefes." Leandro Cardenas to Comandante General and Gobernador, San Luis de la Paz, 17 June 1838, in AGEG-G, Caja 69, Expediente 3.

The Mexican-American War (1846–1848), together with a number of internal uprisings that prompted military responses, made the army increasingly reliant on the support of locally raised forces. Sometimes companies of *cívicos* tried to take advantage of the wartime situation to mimic the behavior of the regular army. In February 1847, the mayor of Jerécuaro complained about the "great disorder" caused by local militias who, claiming the military *fuero* – which technically they did not at the time possess – "many times upset public tranquility and impede the administration of justice."[92] In 1849 the mayor of Silao reported that militia officers regularly excused themselves from accepting public duties to which they were called by the town government, such as that of defenders in criminal trials, "by saying that they have the *fuero*, and that they cannot fulfill nor admit any commission that the *ayuntamiento* might give them, nor any authority other than the military commander."[93] But these were exceptions, and most militia soldiers experienced the approximation of militias and regular army as a frightening development. Many refused to go on campaign. They were reluctant not so much to join the national war effort against the American invaders, for which many expressed great enthusiasm, as to be forced into a military formation in which they would be treated as regular soldiers.[94]

To this situation, Mexico's government responded by forming the National Guard as a permanent alternative to the civic militias. Two ordinances, from 11 September 1846 and 15 July 1848, governed the formation of the National Guard during and after the Mexican-American War. The difference between the National Guard and the civic militias has not received much attention from historians, who have been satisfied to treat both as similar examples of popular participation in the project of Mexican nation building. But while the new ordinances mandated the internal election of National Guard officers, they departed from the regulations that had governed the civic militias in two fundamental ways.[95] First, they ordered harsh penalties – confinement of up to thirty days in prison or fines of up to 15 pesos in 1846 and 100 pesos in 1848, in addition to the loss

---

92 "[U]n gran desorden"; and "perturban muchas veces la tranquilidad pública y entorpecen la administración de justicia"; José Martínez de Lejarza to Secretario del Supremo Gobierno, Celaya, 21 February 1847, copying from Jefatura of Jerécuaro, in AGEG-G, Caja 82, Expediente 2.

93 "[C]on decir que son aforados, y que no pueden hacer ni admitir ningún encargo que les nombre el ayuntamiento, ni ninguna otra autoridad, que no sea el Comandante militar." Isidoro Chávez to Gobernador, Silao, 11 July 1849, in AGEG-M, Caja 174, Expediente 8.

94 On the importance of this boundary for Mexican civic-militia soldiers, which had its counterpart among forces on the American side of the war, see Guardino, "Gender, Soldiering, and Citizenship."

95 "Reglamento para organizar la guardia nacional," 11 September 1846, articles 37, 38; and "Ley orgánica de la guardia nacional," 15 July 1848, article 32, both in Dublán and Lozano (eds.), *Legislación Mexicana*, vol. 5, 165, 417.

of active political rights – for non-exempt citizens who attempted to avoid enrollment.[96] Although serving in the civic militias had in principle also been mandatory, these rules attempted to close the space for negotiation and evasion that, as we saw, had characterized militia recruitment. They therefore brought National Guard recruitment closer to the coercive practices associated with the regular army. Second, depending on circumstances, the National Guard was placed under the command of either the state governors or the president of the republic, but never under that of local civilian authorities. The 1846 law ordered National Guard commanders only to notify town governments before assembling local troops, and the 1848 law made no mention of municipal politicians at all.[97] The formation of the National Guard was thus driven by a centralizing imperative even as it attempted to harness popular energies to the national war effort.[98] The implications of the new regulations bear emphasis. Removing Guard soldiers from local command structures, local purposes, and local domestic contexts, they did away with all three institutional safeguards that had ensured that the civic militias would enforce republican laws rather than subvert them.

To what extent these regulations were actually followed is a more complicated question. We know most about the workings of the National Guard in indigenous towns of the Puebla Sierra and the Oaxacan Sierra Norte. In these areas, where no civic militia companies had been formed in the early republican years, joining the National Guard pulled peasants into the great mid-century conflicts – the Revolution of Ayutla (1854–1855), the Three Years War (1858–1861), and the War of the French Intervention (1862–1867) – about the future of the nation. As Guy Thomson, Florencia Mallon, and Patrick McNamara have shown, indigenous National Guard companies remained close to local value systems and, politically speaking,

---

96 "Reglamento para organizar la guardia nacional," 11 September 1846, articles 3, 14; and "Ley orgánica de la guardia nacional," 15 July 1848, articles 7, 65, both in Dublán and Lozano (eds.), *Legislación Mexicana*, vol. 5, 162–63, 414, 420.

97 "Reglamento para organizar la guardia nacional," 11 September 1846, articles 4, 77; and "Ley orgánica de la guardia nacional," 15 July 1848, articles 43, 46, both in Dublán and Lozano (eds.), *Legislación Mexicana*, volume 5, 161, 168, 418. Separate laws passed in 1847 went even further, endowing National Guard soldiers with the military fuero when under arms and, against widespread public protest, subordinating the Guard to state-level military command posts (*comandancias*) of the regular army. These laws were abrogated in 1848. "Sobre que toca á los consejos de guerra de cuerpo ó de plaza, imponer las penas de Ordenanza á la guardia nacional," 17 June 1847; and "Ley orgánica de la guardia nacional," 15 July 1848, articles 45, 74, in Dublán and Lozano (eds.), *Legislación Mexicana*, volume 5, 286, 418, 421; Pedro Santoni, "The Failure of Mobilization: The Civic Militia of Mexico in 1846," *Mexican Studies/Estudios Mexicanos* 12/2 (1996), 184–185.

98 The anti-popular, anti-local character of the National Guard regulations has been noted by Alicia Hernández Chávez, *Las fuerzas armadas mexicanas: Su función en el montaje de la República* (Mexico City: El Colegio de México, 2012), 38.

gave the ideology of liberalism a rooted, popular dimension. The logic of civil war infused the relationship between liberal commanders and locally raised forces with high levels of tension and, ultimately, put important restraints on the level of control that the former could exercise over the latter. Army commanders were aware that guardsmen who felt imposed upon could, and did, withdraw from the struggle, or even offer their support to the conservative side.[99] In Puebla the result was that guardsmen mostly operated in their home region, where they could count on the logistical support of wives and families. The differentiation of the National Guard from the regular army – which the 1846 and 1848 regulations had threatened to abolish – in Puebla became a centerpiece of local military practice: peasants joined the National Guard with the understanding that they would fight under their own commanders and be shielded from impressment into other military forces.[100] National Guard regiments from Oaxaca were more likely to participate in joint operations with regular-army units and at times served away from their homes, including in Puebla.[101] In their internal organization, however, these battalions mirrored the political hierarchies of their home towns, so that Oaxacan National Guard soldiers were commanded by the same men who governed their lives as civilians.[102]

In practice, then, the deployment of the National Guard was often characterized by the kind of local embeddedness against which the 1846 and 1848 regulations had been directed. We must nevertheless be careful not to lose sight of the substantial differences that existed between the National Guards of the civil-war era and the earlier civic militias. The easiest way to mark that difference is to distinguish between the kinds of public good served by each institution.[103] In their daily task of enforcing the law – of combating and preventing its violation – the civic militias realized a good that flowed directly from their actions. This was true of the militias' response to particular crimes: arresting thieves, murderers, or brawlers created a world in which legal consequences predictably

---

99   Florencia Mallon, *Peasant and Nation: The Making of Postcolonial Mexico and Peru* (Berkeley: University of California Press, 1995), chapter 2; Guy Thomson with David LaFrance, *Patriotism, Politics, and Popular Liberalism in Nineteenth-Century Mexico: Juan Francisco Lucas and the Puebla Sierra* (Wilmington: Scholarly Resources Inc., 1999), 75–82.

100 Guy Thomson, "Bulwarks of Patriotic Liberalism: The National Guard, Philharmonic Corps, and Patriotic Juntas in Mexico, 1847–1888," *Journal of Latin American Studies* 22/1 (1990), 36–40; Mallon, *Peasant and Nation*, 76–77.

101 Patrick McNamara, *Sons of the Sierra: Juárez, Díaz, and the People of Ixtlán, Oaxaca, 1855–1920* (Chapel Hill: University of North Carolina Press, 2007), 40–42, 47–48, 51–55, 59–63.

102 McNamara, *Sons of the Sierra*, 35.

103 In this and the next paragraph, I draw on the contrast between internal and external goods described in Alasdair MacIntyre, *After Virtue* (Notre Dame: University of Notre Dame Press, 1981), 175–176.

followed from proscribed forms of behavior. But it was the militias' daily routines that had the greatest impact on the texture of life. Standing guard, patrolling the streets at night, telling those they encountered that it was time to go home: it was in part through these activities that republican law was converted from words on paper into a system of norms, and perhaps of habits, of how to behave in public.

The goods fought for by the National Guard stood in a different relationship to the guardsmen's immediate actions. Created in a context of military crisis, National Guard companies – in spite of the lawmakers' intentions – never replaced the civic militias as regular enforcers of the law. Rather, the indigenous companies studied by Thomson, Mallon, and McNamara were mobilized specifically to fight on the liberal side in the Reform-era civil wars and help it to victory. But military victory, as Mallon has shown, had no fixed and agreed-upon political meaning.[104] To liberal elites it meant property and free trade, to indigenous guardsmen local democracy and the recognition of land rights. The goods fought for by the National Guard were therefore external to their practice. They would have to be made concrete, through negotiations with the government, once the fighting was done – once the political process could resume and the spoils of victory be fought over. Thus, although the National Guard introduced local voices into debates about the meaning of liberal politics, these voices had no necessary stake in the kind of revolutionary liberalism – concerned with legal equality and the rule of law – that the civic militias had represented. To the contrary, after the civil wars National Guard companies in Puebla and Oaxaca became embroiled in a politics of trade-offs, shows of force, and negotiations that were partly concerned with creating new privileges for those who had contributed to the liberal victory.

The mobilization of National Guard companies appears to have been most successful in areas, often indigenous, with no previous history of militia organization. In Guanajuato, the National Guard, though clearly envisioned as a replacement for the civic militias – in times of peace as well as war, and for the purpose of police work as well as military operations – never achieved remotely similar levels of support. In the first half of the 1850s, under both conservative and liberal administrations, various towns reported on the impossibility of establishing National Guard companies when pushed to do so. In 1853, the town authorities of Celaya even caused a riot after sending out patrols to recruit men from their houses.[105]

---

104 Mallon, *Peasant and Nation.*
105 Genaro Ferrer de Herrera to Secretario del Gobierno, Celaya, 31 March and 10 April 1853, in AGEG-G, Caja 115, Expediente 2. For reports from 1855, see letter from Eusebio de la [Herran?], Salamanca, 10 December 1855, in AGEG-G, Caja 120, Expediente 13; Tomás Hernández to Gobernador, San Francisco del Rincón, 28 November 1855, in AGEG-G, Caja 120, Expediente 16; Antonio Ramírez to Gobernador, San Francisco del Rincón,

The National Guard, it appears, was permanently associated with a model of military service most citizens found repugnant. The civic militias, however, though not formally abolished, did not revive either, and law enforcement quickly slipped out of local control. Town governments faced with threats to their authority were now reduced to requesting support from the regular army – something they had never done before the 1850s.[106]

During the civil wars of the 1850s and 1860s some town governments in Guanajuato nevertheless attempted to reestablish their public-security forces. In June 1855, during Santa Anna's brief dictatorship, a "committee of neighbors" of Chamacuero came together "to agree on the measures for the defense of the town in the present circumstances." While a garrison of fifteen army soldiers was stationed in the town, that number was too small to resist "a gang of considerable size like the one that invaded us on the 31st of last March." The committee decided to collect contributions from all residents in order to buy one hundred guns, which would then be distributed among the population.[107] In San Miguel de Allende, "some residents with their own weapons" in 1857 formed a small force to protect the town from a "gang" that had already once entered the population and, it was feared, would return "with the aim of carrying out a general plunder, assisted by the rabble of this city."[108] In April 1858, the mayor of Moroleón reported about a meeting to which he had called "the principal residents and [public] employees of this place, with the exclusive aim to propose means of defense, to save the lives and interests of the residents, which find themselves threatened by the gangs of evil-doers." His letter received

    19 December 1855, in AGEG-M, Caja 190, Expediente 13. See also the 1855 episode from Irapuato described in Daniel Haworth, "The Mobile National Guard of Guanajuato, 1855–1858: Military Hybridization and Statecraft in *Reforma* Mexico," in *Forced Marches: Soldiers and Military Caciques in Modern Mexico*, eds. Ben Fallaw and Terry Rugeley, 49–80 (Tucson: University of Arizona Press, 2012), 63–64.

106 Guadalupe Maciel to Gobernador, Piedragorda, 5 May 1853, in AGEG-G, Caja 115, Expediente 6; José María Bribierra to Gobernador, Pénjamo, 28 December 1854, in AGEG-M, Caja 186, Expediente 6; Ignacio Soto Maldonado to Gobernador, Romita de Liceaga, 7 October 1855, in AGEG-M, Caja 190, Expediente 9; José María Rodríguez to Gobernador, Pénjamo, 13 December 1855, in AGEG-M, Caja 192, Expediente 4; Fernando Santana to Gobernador, Irapuato, [1856], in AGEG-M, Caja 195, Expediente 7; Nicolas Negreti to Gobernador, Cuitzeo de Abasolo, 24 February 1857, in AGEG-G, Caja 131, Expediente 1; Gregorio Hernández to Inspector, Romita, 5 December 1857, in AGEG-G, Caja 131, Expediente 6.

107 "[P]ara acordar los medios de defensa de aquella población en las presentes circunstancias"; and "una gavilla de consideración, tal como la que nos invadió el día 31 de Mayo último." "Acta de junta de vecinos," enclosed with Gerónimo Calatayno to Gobernador, Celaya, 21 June 1855, in AGEG-M, Caja 192, Expediente 2.

108 "[A]lgunos vecinos con sus propios armas"; and "con el fin de hacer un saqueo general, ayudado de la plebe de esta Ciudad." Manuel González Torres to Secretario de Gobierno, San Miguel de Allende, 8 November 1857, in AGEG-G, Caja 131, Expediente 8.

a favorable response from the conservative governor, who promised to send fifty guns to the town.[109] In May of the same year, the sub-prefect of San Felipe requested funds to pay a security force he had raised "with the object of resisting the bandits who threatened [this town]."[110]

Unlike the National Guard battalions of other parts of the country, the forces raised in this manner appear to have lacked an openly military purpose. In important respects, they resembled the pre-1846 civic militias. They met two of the three criteria that, I argued, had made the civic militias into law-sustaining rather than law-subverting organizations: they were active in public-security functions that were of broad local benefit, and they consisted of citizens-in-arms who continued in their domestic lives while serving in the militias. But in crucial areas the new militias differed from the old ones. The role of "distinguished" or "principal" residents in their foundation suggests an affinity with the patrician principles of property and distinction rather than the civic virtues of labor and domesticity. And while town residents' fear of banditry was no doubt genuine, the notion of what constituted banditry was itself dependent on the fortunes of war. The militias' function as local police forces was not so much replaced by military partisanship as it became indistinguishable from it: the militias would fight liberal "bandits" when the conservatives were in power and conservative "bandits" when the liberals were.[111] The distinction between law and politics had all but disappeared.

The civil wars of the 1850s and 1860s were a watershed in the social history of nineteenth-century Mexico. When the conservatives had been defeated, and the French driven out of the country, perhaps the greater part of a generation of men had known little of life but violence and plunder. Demobilizing a citizen army, hunting down bandits, and pacifying a countryside still riven by social conflict have often been described as the defining tasks for the governments of the 1870s. But the extent to which the experience of civil war also created a rupture in Mexicans' experience of the *legal* framework in which their lives were embedded has not yet been fully appreciated. In the pre-war decades the provision of order had

---

109 "[L]os vecinos principales y empleados de este lugar, con el exclusivo fin de proponer medios de defensa, para salvar las vidas e intereses de los vecinos, que se halla amagada de las gavillas de mal hechores"; Ignacio Silva to Gobernador, Moroleón, 5 April 1858, in AGEG-M, Caja 201, Expediente 5.

110 "[C]on objeto de resistir á los bandidos que la [esta villa] amagaban"; Juan Pastor to Secretario de Gobierno, San Miguel de Allende, 10 May 1858, copying from subprefecto of San Felipe, in AGEG-G, Caja 136, Expediente 2.

111 On this point, see also Raymond Buve, "Pueblos indígenas de Tlaxcala, las leyes liberales juaristas y la guerra de Reforma: una perspectiva desde abajo, 1855–1861," in *Los pueblos indios en los tiempos de Benito Juárez (1847–1872)*, ed. Antonio Escobar Ohmstede, 91–121 (Mexico City: Universidad Autónoma Metropolitana, 2007), 115–116.

depended both on the operations of local militias and on the promotion of a social practice centered on the values of labor and domesticity. Yet as early as the Mexican-American War, the institution that had most directly placed those values at the service of the state's disciplinary function, the civic militia, had been replaced by a different organization, the National Guard, whose responsiveness to civil authorities had been deliberately weakened and whose war-time practice had had little to do with the protection of shared legal rules. After 1867, Mexico's new political classes were themselves a product of the civil-war era. They did not remember the legal culture of the earlier era, and if they did they had little interest in its revival.

3

Haciendas

I Land and Revolution

Although historians of nineteenth-century Mexico have recently focused their attention on local manifestations of republican politics, the settlements situated on haciendas, or large agricultural estates, have largely remained outside their purview. The omission is not accidental. In colonial times, larger Mexican towns had already governed their internal affairs through patrician town councils, and indigenous villages theirs through communally constituted authorities. The radical innovations that independence brought to these settings can be considered in the context of a political tradition. Colonial haciendas, by contrast, had lacked the formal institutions of other social formations. To analyze them as political spaces makes little intuitive sense.[1]

The Mexican hacienda emerged in the late sixteenth and the seventeenth centuries when the Spanish Crown abolished forced indigenous labor (the *encomienda* and *repartimiento*) but recognized Spanish settlers' rights to territory over which they had established control by illegitimate and often violent means.[2] This meant, according to François Chevalier's classic study, that settlers were able to "withdraw, with their slaves, servants, and retainers, behind their own boundaries, where the sole authority was that

---

[1] The absence of political studies of hacienda life was noted more than twenty-five years ago by Bernardo García Martínez, "Los poblados de hacienda: Personajes olvidados en la historia del México rural," in *Cincuenta años de historia en México: En el Cincuentenario del Centro de Estudios Históricos*, eds. Alicia Hernández Chávez and Manuel Miño Grijalva, 331–370 (Mexico City: El Colegio de México, 1991), 332, and has recently been reiterated by Juan Carlos Sánchez Montiel, "De poblados de hacienda a municipios en el altiplano de San Luis Potosí," *Estudios de Historia Moderna y Contemporánea de México*, no. 31 (2006), 59. The lack of formal governing institutions in estate settlements has also been stressed by Eric Van Young, "Mexican Rural History since Chevalier: The Historiography of the Colonial Hacienda," *Latin American Research Review* 18/3 (1988), 19–20.

[2] François Chevalier, *Land and Society in Colonial Mexico: The Great Hacienda*, trans. Alvin Eustis (Berkeley: University of California Press, 1963); Herbert Nickel, *Morfología social de la hacienda mexicana*, trans. Angélica Scherp and Alberto Luis Gómez, 2nd ed. (Mexico City: Fondo de Cultura Económica, 1996), 42–47, 59–63, and 67–69; Charles Gibson, *The Aztecs under Spanish Rule: A History of the Indians of the Valley of Mexico 1519–1810* (Stanford: Stanford University Press, 1964), 58–81, 272–299.

exercised by the owner, the chaplain, and the handful of Spaniards and mestizos who controlled operations."[3] Later scholarship has shown that the actual power of hacendados, or hacienda owners, vis-à-vis their resident workforce fluctuated with changing market conditions.[4] It also depended on location, being strongest in areas of pre-Hispanic settlement like the Huasteca region in San Luis Potosí, where the relationship between Hispanic landlords and native workers was also that between conquerors and conquered, and much weaker on the remote cattle estates in the north of that state, which was worked and settled by mestizo cowboys who put a high premium on mobility and independence. In Guanajuato's rich Bajío basin, workers and tenants lost much of their negotiating power during the economic boom of the eighteenth century – when land became scarce and labor abundant – only to regain it after the country's independence.

Whatever their location, agricultural estates presented powerful obstacles to the spread of a republican political culture. Haciendas were privately owned. They owed their existence to economic considerations. They lacked a self-conscious political tradition. François-Xavier Guerra, whose speculations about the incompatibility of republican politics with popular culture in post-independence Mexico have largely been disproven by empirical research, is still worth our attention when he describes estate communities' social organization. Guerra argues that landownership in the nineteenth century was a social and political as well as an economic fact. By anchoring family clans to an ultimate source of patronage and authority, it made hacienda settlements into tightly-

3   Chevalier, *Land and Society in Colonial Mexico*, 81. Gibson, *Aztecs under Spanish Rule*, 59, makes a similar point. The relation between the earlier *encomienda* system, in which Spaniards were given control over indigenous labor but not over their land, at least juridically, and the later system of land grants under a condition of labor-freedom, was for a time a burning question in the historiography. For succinct statements of the conflicting positions, see James Lockhart, "Encomienda and Hacienda: The Evolution of the Great Estate in the Spanish Indies," *Hispanic American Historical Review* 49/3 (1969); and Robert Keith, "Encomienda, Hacienda and Corregimiento in Spanish America: A Structural Analysis," *Hispanic American Historical Review* 51/3 (1971). For a summary of the literature, see Magnus Mörner, "The Spanish American Hacienda: A Review of Recent Research and Debate," *Hispanic American Historical Review* 53/2 (1973), 186–188.

4   On social relations on colonial agrarian estates, see John Tutino, *From Insurrection to Revolution in Mexico: Social Bases of Agrarian Violence, 1750–1940* (Princeton: Princeton University Press, 1986), 55–90; D. A. Brading, *Haciendas and Ranchos in the Mexican Bajío: León 1700–1860* (New York: Cambridge University Press, 1978), 8–12, 21, 24–27, 34–38, 73–77, 197–199; Eric Van Young, *Hacienda and Market in Eighteenth-Century Mexico: The Rural Economy of the Guadalajara Region, 1675–1820* (Berkeley: University of California Press, 1982), chapter 11; Marta Eugenia García Ugarte, *Hacendados y rancheros queretanos (1780–1920)* (Mexico City: Consejo Nacional para la Cultura y las Artes, 1992), 64–65; Jan Bazant, *Cinco haciendas Mexicanas: Tres siglos de vida rural en San Luis Potosí (1600–1910)*, 3rd eds. (Mexico City: El Colegio de México, 1995), 29, 41; Nickel, *Morfología social*, 73–89; Gibson, *Aztecs under Spanish Rule*, 246–256. For the more coercive labor conditions on estates in southern and northern New Spain, see William Taylor, *Landlord and Peasant in Colonial Oaxaca* (Stanford: Stanford University Press, 1972), 144–152; and Charles Harris III, *A Mexican Family Empire: The Latifundio of the Sánchez Navarros, 1765–1867* (Austin: University of Texas Press, 1975), chapter 3.

knit and semi-autonomous centers of sociability – "the equivalent of what the *pueblo* [incorporated town] was to the other inhabitants of the countryside."[5] John Tutino's work on the colonial period, which has given us perhaps the first sustained description of the political structures that organized life and labor on Mexican estates, draws a strikingly similar picture.[6] Tutino shows that hacendados appointed estate administrators from among prosperous residents who stood at the head of large family clans. Through them, the owners "extended their power deep into estate communities."[7] The result was a system of rule organized around kinship, wealth, prestige, and charisma. That such a system could have migrated, undisturbed by intervening political changes, from the illiberal society of the colonial era to the illiberal society of the Porfirian dictatorship remains a credible proposition.

Against this static picture of the social relations in estate settlements stands our knowledge about the inversion of Mexico's agrarian structure in the early decades of the republic. Largely linked to the collapse of mining, Mexico's post-war economic depression left little room for the kind of estate-controlled production that, at least in the country's core regions, had predominated in the late eighteenth century. After independence, estate owners scaled down their role as agricultural producers, and the majority of hacienda residents, instead of working for their landlords, rented land to grow subsistence and market crops. As smallholding peasants came to dominate the rural economy, hacendados were demoted to a rentier class.[8]

Tutino has argued that these changes in agrarian social relations were partly brought about by peasants' political activism.[9] In Guanajuato,

5   François-Xavier Guerra, *México: Del Antiguo Régimen a la Revolución*, vol. 1, trans. Sergio Fernández Bravo (Mexico City: Fondo de Cultura Económica, 1988), 134.

6   John Tutino, *Making a New World: Founding Capitalism in the Bajío and Spanish North America* (Durham, NC: Duke University Press, 2011), 142–144, 352–402.

7   Tutino, *Making a New World*, 367.

8   This picture of the post-independence hacienda economy is now widely accepted. See John Tutino, *From Insurrection to Revolution*, 222–241; and "The Revolution in Mexican Independence: Insurgency and the Renegotiation of Property, Production, and Patriarchy in the Bajío, 1800–1855," *Hispanic American Historical Review* 78/3 (1998); François Chevalier, "Acerca de los orígenes de la pequeña propiedad en el occidente de México. Historia comparada," in *Despues de los latifundios: La desintegración de la gran propiedad agraria en México*, ed. Heriberto Moreno García, 3–12 (El Colegio de Michoacán, Fondo para Actividades Sociales y Culturales de Michoacán, 1981); García Ugarte, *Hacendados y rancheros*, 90–152, and especially 133–148 on the rise of a new smallholder class; Michael Ducey, *A Nation of Villages*, 102–103; Margaret Chowning, *Wealth and Power in Provincial Mexico: Michoacán from the Late Colony to the Revolution* (Stanford: Stanford University Press, 1999), 97, 119, 162–163; and Simon Miller, *Landlords and Haciendas in Modernizing Mexico: Essays in Radical Reappraisal* (Amsterdam: CEDLA, 1995), 29–32. In the terms of Eric Wolf's influential typology, land-renting tenants behaved as if they were peasants, and in control over their "processes of production." Eric Wolf, "Types of Latin American Peasantry: A Preliminary Discussion," *American Ethnologist* 57/3 (1955), 453–454.

9   Tutino, "Revolution in Mexican Independence."

hacienda peasants swelled the forces that in 1810 initiated Mexico's long War of Independence, turning an elite-led conflict over political power into a social revolution. During the war, they proceeded to drive landowners and administrators off their estates and divide the land between themselves. Landlords were able to charge rent from the peasants once the war was over but not to regain productive control over their properties. Tutino suggests that the new, tenant-dominated rural economy was more productive, dynamic, and entrepreneurial than is acknowledged in standard treatments by economic historians, who have often stressed the country's economic decline in the early republican period. Because assessments of the sluggishness of the post-war economy rely on official sources that did not capture subsistence production or trading in local and regional markets, the revolution in Mexico's agrarian relations may well have driven an expanding economy that existed beneath the radar of the state's rudimentary taxing procedures.[10] Hacienda tenants, Tutino concludes, entered Mexico's republican era as self-assertive farmers who "joined in the political and cultural construction of the nation."[11] The Mexican republic was, in part, their creation.

Tutino's evidence is stronger for the war years than for the period of national consolidation. Much of the force of his argument depends on a detailed reconstruction of production and tenancy arrangements on one particular hacienda in Guanajuato, the Puerto de Nieto estate.[12] But his data for this estate comes to an end only a few years into the republican era. It comes to an end, moreover, at a time when the owner was making a comeback: by 1825, he and his administrator had managed to reassert control not over production but over rental arrangements and payments, which tenants had unilaterally suspended during the war. If Mexico's agriculture remained dominated by smallholder production until the second half of the century, it may well be that the structure of the post-war economy, and not peasants' combativeness, was responsible for this result.[13]

---

10   Tutino, "Revolution in Mexican Independence," 409–414. For similar estimates of Mexican economic performance in these years, see Margaret Chowning, "The Contours of the Post-1810 Depression in Mexico: A Reappraisal from a Regional Perspective," *Latin American Research Review* 27/2 (1992); and Sergio Cañedo Gamboa, "Merchants and Family Business in San Luis Potosí, Mexico: The Signs of an Economic Upsurge, 1820–1846," PhD dissertation, University of California San Diego (2011). For more skeptical estimates, see John Coatsworth, "Obstacles to Economic Development in Nineteenth Century Mexico," *American Historical Review* 83/1 (1978); and Richard Salvucci, "Mexican National Income in the Era of Independence, 1800–40," in *How Latin America Fell Behind: Essays on the Economic Histories of Brazil and Mexico, 1800–1914*, ed. Stephen Haber, 216–242 (Stanford: Stanford University Press, 1997).

11   Tutino, "Revolution in Mexican Independence," 414.

12   Tutino, "Revolution in Mexican Independence," 375–397.

13   In an earlier work, Tutino himself attributed the change to economic depression. Tutino, *From Insurrection to Revolution*, 223–228; see also Chevalier, "Acerca de los orígenes," and García Ugarte, *Hacendados y rancheros.*

In order to evaluate the relationship between hacienda settlements and Mexico's revolution in law and government, we will need more information than given by either Guerra or Tutino. Where Guerra speaks of estate communities as lost to republican politics, Tutino depicts them as important participants in the nineteenth-century state. Yet neither Guerra nor Tutino pays much attention to the ways hacienda communities were, in fact, integrated into an emerging state apparatus, nor to the conflicts surrounding the manner of that integration. How did the republican system propose to deal with substantial human settlements that were entirely located on private land? What place in that system did hacienda owners imagine for themselves? And what place their tenants?

II Disorder

In early republican Mexico, haciendas were only loosely incorporated into the administrative structure of the state. While municipal governments appointed auxiliary officers, called *alcaldes auxiliares*, to guard the peace in the countryside, these officers were thinly spread. Single men often kept watch over various estate and smallholder (*ranchero*) settlements.[14] Yet unlike other rural settlements lacking in self-government, haciendas could be home to large populations. As spaces of sociability, they often had more in common with towns than with the dispersed agricultural settlements, or *rancherías*, to which they acted as social and economic centers.[15] Though privately owned, haciendas nevertheless were public spaces. They hosted large gatherings like cockfights, bullfights, dances, and weekly markets, sometimes with government license but often without.[16] In this

14 "Actas del Ayuntamiento de Dolores Hidalgo," 22 August 1828, in AGEG-M, Caja 64, Expediente 5; and Ignacio Romero to Gobernador, Silao, 30 May 1826, in AGEG-M, Caja 28, Expediente 2.

15 Guerra, *México*, vol. 1, 134. Zachary A. Brittsan, "In Faith or Fear: Fighting with Lozada," PhD dissertation, University of California San Diego (2011), 150–151.

16 For cockfights and bullfights, see "Actas de Ayuntamiento de Silao," March 1827, in AGEG-M, Caja 44, Expediente 8; and José Manuel Ortiz de Zarate to Gobernador, Valle de Maíz, 3 June 1826, in AHESLP-SGG, Caja 49, Expediente 4. For dances, see "Actas del Ayuntamiento de Casas Viejas," 4 December 1828, in AGEG-M, Caja 63, Expediente 1; "Actas del Ayuntamiento de Casas Viejas," 10 December 1839, in AGEG-M, Caja 77, Expediente 5; "Actas del Ayuntamiento de Casas Viejas," 27 May 1830, in AGEG-M, Caja 83, Expediente 1; and "Espediente formado para la aprobación de los reglamentos ...," in AGEG-M, Caja 170, Expediente 2. Dances on estates also turn up in criminal proceedings, since they could be the settings of brawls that led to homicides: see the cases in AHML, Justicia, Causas Criminales, Caja 3, Expediente 8, and Caja 4, Expediente 12. For markets, which were much harder to conceal, see letters from Piedragorda dated 14 June and 16 August 1824, in AGEG-M, Caja 4, Expediente 6, Fojas 6, 13; José Vicente Gayaga to Jefe Político, Pénjamo, 29 February 1824, in AGEG-M, Caja 5, Expediente 5, Foja 5; "Presupuesto," Salvatierra, 6 October 1824, in AGEG-M, Caja 7, Expediente 14, Fojas 32–33; "Espediente instruido á solicitud de los vecinos de Yrapuato, p.a

context an auxiliary officer, with no armed force or other institutional support, would be able to exert little real control.

Local politicians were well aware of estate settlements' institutional neglect. In 1822 the town council of Rioverde complained that haciendas, on account of their great dispersion, were without religious care and education. Hacienda youth, "because no curb holds them back, commit vices easily, giving themselves over to all kinds of disorder." The councilmen suggested that the whole country was harmed: because of the reigning anarchy on haciendas, the Mexican state "will never have any men that might be useful to it."[17] In 1825, an officer from San Felipe reported that on another hacienda, home to a community of 10,000 people, members of feuding social factions were able to commit crimes against each other in plain sight of the helpless *alcaldes auxiliares*.[18] In 1827, the town government of Alaquines, feeling that strong measures were required to combat disorder in the countryside, vainly petitioned San Luis Potosí's governor to reintroduce the use of stocks on a nearby hacienda in order to contain its inhabitants' "drunkenness and other excesses."[19]

The suppression of rural markets was a particular concern for local authorities, who feared a loss of commerce in their own towns and worried that outlying markets would attract immorality and crime.[20] When, in 1825, wealthy residents of Irapuato addressed Guanajuato's state congress with a complaint about the illegal markets formed on various haciendas, they named a whole host of ills that flowed from the lack of proper government on estate settlements: the state was defrauded of its fiscal rights, deserters walked free, religious duties were not regarded, prostitutes set up their trade, robbery flourished, stolen goods were openly sold. Wrongdoers knew that on haciendas "there are no judges they need to

estinguir los mercados q. se forman en las Haciendas y Rancherias," 1825, in AGEG-M, Caja 15, Expediente 6, Fojas 1–15; "Actas de Ayuntamiento de Casas Viejas," 5 April 1824, in AGEG-M, Caja 42, Expediente 3; "Actas de Ayuntamiento de Casas Viejas," 3 December 1829 and 10 December 1829, in AGEG-M, Caja 77, Expediente 5; "Espediente instruido . . . para suspender los mercados que se hacían en varios puntos de la municipalidad," in AGEG-M, Caja 159, Expediente 2; Bando published in Casas Viejas on 2 May 1836, in AGEG-M, Caja 134, Expediente 4; Juan Pastor to Gobernador, San Miguel de Allende, 26 June 1840, in AGEG-M, Caja 149, Expediente 6; and Juan Nepomuceno Guzmán to Gobernador, Armadillo, 8 August 1826, in AHESLP-SGG, Caja 55, Expediente 9.

17 "[C]omo no tienen freno que los contenga, se vician con facilidad dándose a toda clase de desórdenes"; and "Viven en la más crasa ignorancia y nunca el estado puede contar con unos hombres que le sean útiles." Report from Rioverde, 14 February 1822, photocopy in possession of the author.

18 AGEG-M, Caja 13, Expediente 14, letter from San Felipe dated 8 January 1825.

19 Juan Ignacio Azua to Gobernador, Alaquines, 13 March 1827, in AHESLP-SGG, Caja 74, Expediente 23.

20 "Espediente instruido a consecuencia de la aprobación que el Gefe de Partido de Jerécuaro pidió," Guanajuato, 1843, in AGEG-M, Caja 159, Expediente 2.

respect; there are no troops to intimidate them; there is nobody to watch over their conduct; nor are there jails in which they can be punished." The commission charged by congress with considering these allegations did not hesitate to accept them as well founded and true.[21] Authorities nevertheless found it hard to abolish outlying markets. The government of Casas Viejas reported longstanding but unsuccessful efforts to dissolve an illegal market on the Hacienda de Charcas:

[The market] becomes extinguished and little by little it reestablishes itself, beginning with a few indigenous people of both sexes who come with fruit and wild roots and foodstuff of little value . . ., which they carry under their arms so they can flee with them easily when they are pursued . . .; but in this way the market becomes formalized, until it contains bigger stands, something that it is impossible to prevent at a distance of five leagues.[22]

Only a permanent armed force would be able to suppress the market indefinitely, yet if such a force existed it would in fact be possible to regulate the market rather than suppress it.

The prejudice of provincial town dwellers against imagined peasant rustics, perhaps sharpened by the precariousness of their own claims to urban sophistication, may have accounted for the stridency of these denunciations. But complaints about the disorderliness of life on haciendas were more than ideological projections. Town governments were hard-pressed to keep haciendas within the orbit of republican law. They often relied on hacienda owners or administrators for carrying out such basic tasks as the convocation of estate residents to municipal elections; the publication of laws and decrees issued by Congress; the collection of population statistics; the collection of taxes; military recruitment; the overnight custody of recruits on their way to state capitals; the regulation of weights and measures on local markets; the repair of public roads running through estate properties; and – an issue to which we will return – the policing of estate communities and the surrounding countryside.[23] This practice was

21   "[N]o hay jueces a quien respetar: no hay tropas que los intimide: no hay quien cele sobre su conducta: ni tampoco cárceles en que se castiguen." "Espediente," in AGEG-M, Caja 15, Expediente 6, Fojas 1–15. For a similar list of complaints from San Luis Potosí, see Juan Nepomuceno Guzmán to Gobernador, Armadillo, 8 August 1826, in AHESLP-SGG, Caja 55, Expediente 9.

22   "Se llega a extinguir aquel [mercado] y poco a poco se restablece de nuevo, comenzando por unos cuantos indígenas de ambos sexos, que vienen con frutas y raíces silvestres, y víveres de poco valor . . ., que traen bajo del brazo, para poder huir con ello fácilmente cuando se les persigue . . .; pero así se va formalizando el mercado, hasta contener puestos de más importancia, cosa que es imposible evitar en una distancia de más de cinco leguas"; Juan Pastor to Gobernador, San Miguel de Allende, 26 June 1840, in AGEG-M, Caja 149, Expediente 6.

23   On the convocation for elections, see letter from Ignacio Vasquez Tejeda, Neutla, in AGEG-M, Caja 27, Expediente 4. On the publication of laws and decrees, see Santiago Quintanilla to

pragmatic and did not necessarily reflect a political alignment between landowners and municipal politicians. Rather, town governments wanted to maximize the chances that the tasks they set would be accomplished. Often they issued administrative orders to *alcaldes auxiliares* and estate owners at the same time, apparently reasoning that if one type of authority was not up to handling a particular issue, the other still might be.

Haciendas thus possessed a number of characteristics that marked them as unique territories in the spatial operationalization of legal sovereignty, as different from small villages and other agricultural settlements as they were from constitutional townships. Deprived of the conditions necessary to make republican law operative, they were left in what Miranda Spieler, writing about the French Caribbean during the second half of the 1790s, has called "a state of spatio-

Gobernador, Celaya, 4 November 1824, in AGEG-M, Caja 1, Expediente 2, Foja 28; circular letter dated 1 February 1822, in AHESLP-PSLP, Caja 2, Expediente 5. On the formation of statistics, see Actas de Ayuntamiento, Apaseo, 23 October 1829, in AGEG-M, Caja 78, Expediente 2, and Actas de Ayuntamiento, Acámbaro, 29 November 1830, in AGEG-M, Caja 99, Expediente 1; and the documents in AHML, JP-EST-COM Caja 1, Expediente 22, 1826, and JP-EST-CEN Caja 1, Expedientes 1–18, 1822–1828. On the collection of taxes, see Actas de Ayuntamiento, Chamacuero, 12 March 1827, in AGEG-M, Caja 39, Expediente 1; and Actas de Ayuntamiento, Casas Viejas, 3 December 1829 and 10 December 1829, in AGEG-M, Caja 77, Expediente 5. On weights and measures, see Actas de Ayuntamiento, August 1827, in AGEG-M, Caja 40, Expediente 3. On military recruitment, see Actas de Ayuntamiento, Casas Viejas, 6 August 1829, in AGEG-M, Caja 77, Expediente 5; José Francisco Gamiño to Gobernador, Irapuato, 12 October 1824, in AGEG-G, Caja 2, Expediente 11; list of recruits from Pénjamo dated 15 January 1824, in AGEG-G, Caja 3, Expediente 11; Isidro Andres to Gobernador, [1827], in AGEG-G, Caja 16, Expediente 2; and letter from Charcas, 9 December 1825, in AHESLP-SGG, Caja 29, Expediente 3. On the guarding of recruitment processions stopping for the night, see Juan Castro to Gobernador, Hacienda de Sauceda, 7 September 1825, in AHESLP-SGG, Caja 25, Expediente 12, Foja 19; letter from Charcas, 24 November 1825, in AHESLP-SGG, Caja 27, Expediente 1, Fojas 47–48; letter from Ojocaliente, 13 December 1825, in AHESLP-SGG, Caja 29, Expediente 7, Foja 11; and José Dionisio Mendoza to Gobernador, Hacienda de Bocas, 29 December 1825, in AHESLP-SGG, Caja 31, Expediente 10. On roads, see Actas de Ayuntamiento, Apaseo, 26 June 1829, in AGEG-M, Caja 4, Expediente 1, Fojas 13–14, Caja 8, Expediente 5, Foja 1, Caja78, Expediente 2; "Actas de Ayuntamiento de Apaseo," 26 June 1829; José Ignacio de Lara to Gobernador, Valle de San Francisco, 27 May 1826, in AHESLP-SGG, Caja 45, Expediente 15; Pedro Legorreta to Gobernador, San Luis Potosí, 20 September 1837, in AHESLP-SGG, Caja 103, Expediente 19; and García Martínez, "Los poblados de haciendas," 363–364. On policing, see Actas de Ayuntamiento, Casas Viejas, 22 April 1830, in AGEG-M, Caja 83, Expediente 1; Ignacio Rocha to Gobernador, 4 August 1841, AGEG-G, Caja 74, Expediente 1; and the documents in AMG-AG-M, Caja 11, Documento 978, and Caja 13, Documento 1135, Fojas 1–15. Something similar happened in the frontier state of Sonora. See José Marcos Medina Bustos, "El gobierno indígena en una zona de frontera durante la transición del Antiguo Régimen al liberalismo. El caso de la provincia de Sonora (1763–1831)," in *Poder y gobierno local en México, 1808–1857*, eds. María del Carmen Salinas Sandoval, Diana Birrichaga Gardida, and Antonio Escobar Ohmstede, 225–260 (Mexico City: El Colegio Mexiquense, 2011), 245.

legal indeterminacy."[24] Hacienda residents who wished to enjoy the rights and protections to which they were constitutionally entitled would first need to confront the absence of credible state institutions in the countryside. The solution to their problem was both obvious and difficult: they would have to convert their settlements into constitutional towns with their attendant courts of law and civic militias.

III Metamorphosis

In the decades following Mexican independence, tenants from a number of haciendas demanded to have their settlements turned into municipal seats.[25] These tenants faced an ambivalent legal situation, for they lived on territory that, while formally covered by the state's constitutional order, did not therefore cease to be private property. When claiming their rights as Mexican citizens, estate tenants therefore confronted a right no less positive

---

24 Miranda Spieler, "The Legal Structure of Colonial Rule during the French Revolution," *William and Mary Quarterly* 66/2 (2009), 401.

25 A no doubt partial list of haciendas or settlements involved in such attempts includes, in Oaxaca, the Hacienda Valdeflores in 1822; in Guanajuato, the Haciendas de la Laja and Bizcocho in the early 1820s, the Hacienda San Nicolás in 1857, and the Hacienda de la Quemada in 1866; in Veracruz, the settlements El Chico, Corral de Piedras, and La Estanzuela, belonging to haciendas owned by local strongman and, on various occasions, President of Mexico, Antonio López de Santa Anna, in the 1840s; in Querétaro, the estate settlements of Boyé and San José Bizarrón in 1847; in San Luis Potosí, the Haciendas Albercas, Concordia, Bocas, and Santo Domingo between the 1840s and 1860s; in Puebla, the Haciendas La Manzanilla and Xochiapulco during the Reform-era civil wars; and in Coahuila, the settlements of Lerdo, Matamoros, and San Pedro in the same period. For the case from Oaxaca, see "Sobre ereccion en pueblo el barrio de S.ta Getrudis de Oaxaca," in Archivo General de la Nación (AGN)-Gobernación, Sección Fomento, Caja 18, Expediente 1, Fojas 1–25; for Veracruz and Querétaro, see Sánchez Montiel, "De poblados de hacienda," 61–62; for Veracruz, see also Francisco Zarco, *Historia del Congreso Extraordinario Constituyente {1856–1857}* (Mexico City: El Colegio de México, 1956), session from 23 May 1856, 201–202; for Querétaro, see also García Ugarte, *Hacendados y rancheros*, 318. For Guanajuato, see "Expediente formado á consecuencia de la solicitud hecha ante S.M. el Sr. D.n Agustín 1.o Emperador de Mexico . . .," Guanajuato, 1822, in AGEG-M, Caja 1, Expediente 3; "Cuaderno 2.o del Expediente que siguen los vecinos de San Diego del Biscocho con Don Narciso Alday . . .," Guanajuato, 1825, in AGEG-M, Caja 15, Expedientes 7, and "Cuaderno Num. 3.o del Esped.te q. e siguen los vecinos del Viscocho con D. Narciso Alday, sobre erigirse en Pueblo," in AGEG-M, Caja 15, Expediente 8; "Espediente provoido por los vecinos de la Hacienda de San Nicolas de Agustinos, en jurisdiccion de Salvatierra, para que se erija en Pueblo dicha Hacienda," Guanajuato, 1857, in AGEG-M, Caja 196, Expediente 11. For Puebla, see Florencia Mallon, *Peasant and Nation: The Making of Postcolonial Mexico and Peru* (Berkeley: University of California Press, 1995), 30, 61–62. For Coahuila, see María Vargas-Lobsinger, *La hacienda de "La Concha": Una empresa algodonera de La Laguna 1883–1917* (Mexico City: Universidad Nacional Autónoma de México, 1984), 18–20. Only the cases in San Luis Potosí have been the subject of detailed historical scholarship: see Sánchez Montiel, "De poblados de hacienda," and *De poblados de hacienda a municipios en San Luis Potosí* (San Luis Potosí: Comisión del Bicentenario de la Independencia Nacional y Centenario de la Revolución Mexicana, 2011).

than their own. How to adjudicate between these conflicting rights was far
from clear. The Cádiz Constitution, while endowing towns (*pueblos*) of more
than one thousand inhabitants with the right to form municipal governments, had nowhere specified what constituted a *pueblo*. Subsequent Mexican
Constitutions offered no more detailed definition. Did a *pueblo* require
a certain density of population? A compactness of settlement? Colonial law
at least suggested that urban status required a terrain for house plots and
a commons (*ejido*) as a territorial foundation – a requirement that landlords,
tenants, and political authorities involved in disputes over the erection of
new townships appear to have taken as axiomatic. Although in Guanajuato
and San Luis Potosí there existed at least a couple of municipal seats that were
situated entirely on hacienda lands, they were perhaps too vulnerable to the
whims of their landlords and, lacking rental income from town lands, too
fiscally weak to serve as models for the creation of new ones.[26] To establish
new municipal governments on rural estates would thus require the expropriation of private property, allowed by the Cádiz and subsequent
Mexican Constitutions, with prior indemnification of the owners, "for
reasons of known utility."[27] What constituted public utility was a matter
of interpretation for which the law offered no guidance.

   Behind such legal conundrums lurked larger questions about the social
depth of liberal politics. Across Europe and Latin America, wherever old
regimes had relied on the mediation of landed magnates to extend state
power, landlords' political power did not get abolished at the same time as
their feudal rights or their posts in colonial governing structures. As long as
whole settlements continued to exist on private domains, the fact of landownership was a source of social control with which estate tenants – if they
wished to exercise their rights as citizens – inevitably came into conflict.
For example, between 1848 and 1851 French peasants joined a radical
national movement among other reasons to fight for the right to sit on
municipal councils still dominated by landed magnates.[28] In Colombia's
Cauca Valley Afro-Colombian estate laborers participated in liberal
clubs that challenged the stranglehold landlords continued to exercise
over the lives of tenants and workers after the abolition of slavery.[29]

26 *Recopilación de leyes de los Reynos de las Indias*, book 4, title 7, laws 7 and 13. The town in Guanajuato
    located on estate land was Casas Viejas, today San José Iturbide; the town in San Luis Potosí was
    Cedral. See "Ynforme relativa a la Casa Consistorial de Casas Viejas," in AGEG-M Caja 168,
    Expediente 1. Letter from Cedral dated 7 June 1832, in AHESLP-SGG, Caja 380, Expediente 9.
27 *Constitución ... promulgada en Cádiz*, article 172, paragraph 10.
28 Peter McPhee, *The Politics of Rural Life: Political Mobilization in the French Countryside, 1846–1852*
    (New York: Oxford University Press, 1992); and Ted Margadant, *French Peasants in Revolt:
    The Insurrection of 1851* (Princeton: Princeton University Press, 1979).
29 James Sanders, *Contentious Republicans: Popular Politics, Race, and Class in Nineteenth-Century
    Colombia* (Durham, NC: Duke University Press, 2004), 43.

In both countries the repression of these peasant movements would mark a rightward shift in national politics and the deterioration of institutional safeguards for the impartial administration of law.

Mexican peasants who wished to form townships on private land thus contributed to controversies about the foundations of the legal state that spanned the Atlantic World. To explore the form these controversies took in the Mexican case, let us look at the conflicts provoked by the attempts of tenants of two Guanajuatan haciendas to convert their settlements into municipalities. The first of these attempts, made in 1822 by José Encarnación Rodríguez on behalf of the more than two thousand inhabitants of the de la Laja hacienda and its immediate surroundings, was unsuccessful, in part because of Rodríguez's inefficiency as a legal operator.[30] The second attempt, expertly conducted by a lawyer on behalf of residents of the Bizcocho hacienda, had the advantage of a stronger initial position. At the end of Mexico's War of Independence, these residents had already been congregated and formed into a township, under the auspices of the Cádiz Constitution and with the backing of a royalist military commander.[31] When the landowner challenged the new status quo, they fought back and, in 1826, gained a significant legal victory: they would be allowed to purchase the territory on which their settlement stood at a fair price – though not the other lands they were renting – and they were confirmed in the possession of their municipal government.

In order to explore what was at stake in these cases, we can begin by attending to the arguments made by the tenants' adversaries. The hacendados at once repeated and amplified the reasoning employed by urban patricians who combated the establishment of *ayuntamientos* in dependent towns like Cerritos in San Luis Potosí and San Pedro de los Pozos in Guanajuato. Like the patricians, hacendados alleged a lack of education, civility, and financial resources in the settlements built on their properties. "They are very ignorant, they lack morals, they are mired in the greatest poverty," the de la Laja owners wrote about their tenants. The Bizcocho owner's lawyer asserted that there were not enough literate men on the estate to renew an *ayuntamiento* each year, as required by law.[32]

But for the hacendados these were rhetorical routines meant to bolster a more important line of argument. The lawyer of the Bizcocho estate

30 The case can be found in "Expediente formado á consecuencia ...," in AGEG-M Caja 1, Expediente 3.

31 For more details on these cases, see Timo Schaefer, "Law of the Land? Hacienda Power and the Challenge of Republicanism in Postindependence Mexico," *Hispanic American Historical Review* 94/2 (2014), 207–212.

32 "Son muy ignorantes, les faltan costumbres, se hallan sumidos en la más grande pobreza." "Expediente formado á consecuencia ...," in AGEG-M, Caja 1, Expediente 3, Foja 31r; "Cuaderno Num. 3.0," in AGEG-M, Caja 15, Expediente 8, Foja 9v.

argued that his client's tenants had given up all links to political society, to which each one of them had been vertically attached by virtue of the landlord's benevolent care, when they had left their dispersed rental sites and formed themselves into a settlement. "These inhabitants, for the reason that they are for the main part farm hands [*gañanes*], are more in need of the quiet of the countryside for their daily work than of the bustle that warps and distracts them."[33] The landlord's argument gained support from the tenants' actions during the legal proceedings. In order to raise their legal fees, the case's main promoters engaged in what the hacendado's lawyer claimed was an act of extortion, threatening that tenants unwilling to pay up would not be able to keep living on town land once the case had been won. The tenants' lawyer did not deny the accusation but argued that the method was inevitable in legal cases involving multiple beneficiaries.[34] The Bizcocho lawyer took it as evidence for a despotism by which a handful of well-off peasants imposed their will on an ignorant multitude, a taste of the reign of injustice awaiting Bizcocho should the tenants' solicitude be granted.[35]

If the Bizcocho lawyer's argument was circumstantial rather than principled, the owners of the de la Laja estate defended their rights with a mix of exposition, argument, and rhetoric that moved seamlessly from the personal shortcomings of Encarnación Rodríguez to the legal and intellectual shortcomings of his project, and from there to a terse discussion of the propertied bases of political liberty. Rodríguez was "an idle person, from an outside jurisdiction, ambitious to boss people around." Without authority from any of the more substantial neighbors of the estate, he "carried the voice of a few day workers designated by him," yet was unable to produce his credentials even as these people's representative.[36] Rodríguez's complaint that the landlords had begun evicting his supporters proved the baselessness of his demands. For the owners, forcing non-paying tenants off the land was a matter of principle:

We believe that they [Rodríguez and one of his allies] and those who direct them are ignorant of [the new republican laws], because only that way is it possible to explain the complaint they have and express, that we charge [our tenants] the rents

---

33 "Aquellos habitantes por lo mismo que en su mayor parte son gañanes, necesitan más de la quietud del campo para sus diarios ejercicios, que del concurso que los vicia, y los distrae." "Cuaderno 2.o," in AGEG-M, Caja 15, Expediente 7, Foja 16r.

34 "Cuaderno 2.o," in AGEG-M, Caja 15, Expediente 7, Foja 82v-82r.

35 "Cuaderno Num. 3.o," in AGEG-M, Caja 15, Expediente 8, Fojas 5r-6v, 8r-9r.

36 "[U]n hombre vago, vecino de extraña jurisdicción, ambicioso de ser mandón ... llevando la voz por unos cuantos jornaleros que el designa." "Expediente formado á consecuencia," in AGEG-M, Caja 1, Expediente 3, Foja 29r.

that they justly have to pay us, and of which they judge that their disordered attempt to form a township has already freed them.[37]

Conflating the tenants' request to be granted a municipal government and their complaint about politically motivated evictions, the hacendados claimed that the petitioners wanted to turn the world upside down – "to bring about . . . an astonishing metamorphosis by which we are left despoiled of our worthy rights, and our renters or tenants are converted into the owners of houses, lands, etc."[38] The landlords contrasted the illegitimacy of such a project with the immutability of individual rights, which were "independent of any political authority." Even tyrants protected property.[39] The owners were confident enough to acknowledge that it was in principle possible for a liberal government to expropriate property, given evidence of an urgent public need and proper indemnification of the owners. But for the time being the irregularity of Rodríguez's proceedings made any discussion about the public utility of granting their tenants' request irrelevant. The idler Rodríguez and his day workers had failed to establish their right to appear before the state politically, while property's right to state protection was "one of the bases of the liberal system."[40]

In making these arguments, the landowners moved the debate from the level of constitutional legality to that of its operation in particular settings. The de la Laja day workers had proven themselves incapable of legally challenging property's *a priori* right to state protection; the Bizcocho tenants would lose any political attributes once they cut their links to the institution of landownership, represented by the hacendado. Heirs to Edmund Burke's pragmatic conservatism, the landlords opposed the utopianism of the constitutions' social premises with the evidence of the world as it existed: a world held together by their propertied power.

If the landlords argued that their tenants were incapable of self-rule, the tenants countered that the principle of private property, far from being a solution to the problem of lawlessness on haciendas, was in fact its root cause. Irreconcilable conceptions about property's role in the social order

---

37 "Creemos que ellos y quien los dirige todo lo ignoran por qué solo así puede cohonestarse la queja que tienen y expresan de que les cobremos las rentas que justamente nos deben pagar, y de que ellos se juzgan ya libres con solo el conato desordenado que han hecho para la formación de Pueblo." "Expediente formado á consecuencia," in AGEG-M, Caja 1, Expediente 3, Foja 30r.

38 "[D]e que . . . se hace . . . una metamorfosis admirable por la que nosotros quedamos despojados de nuestros respetables derechos, y nuestros inquilinos o arrendatarios convertidos en dueños de casas tierras etc." "Expediente formado á consecuencia," in AGEG-M, Caja 1, Expediente 3, Foja 29r.

39 "[I]ndependientes de toda autoridad política." "Expediente," in AGEG-M, Caja 1, Expediente 3, Foja 30v.

40 "[U]na de las bases del sistema liberal," "Expediente formado á consecuencia . . .," in AGEG-M, Caja 1, Expediente 3, Foja 30r.

emerge from the way that the question of rental eviction inserted itself into the struggle over the erection of a municipal seat on the Hacienda de la Laja. According to Encarnación Rodríguez, the eviction of estate residents was part of the landowners' strategy in opposing their tenants' demand to be granted a municipal government. A number of tenants – "on account of their misery and the calamities of the weather" – had fallen into arrears with rental payments, giving the landowners a pretext for "the expulsion of the old tenant, and settlement of the new one, who has offered to oppose himself to the project of creating a township on the hacienda."[41] But the issue of tenant eviction had come up even before the landlords could have started taking reprisals: in a document that Rodríguez inserted into his original request for the creation of a local government, the estate resident Hilario López had argued that the hacienda owners, clinging to powers they had enjoyed under colonial laws, now "want to take away the farms, of their sweat and blood, of all the poor laborers and field hands."[42] López's phrase contrasted the idleness of mere ownership with the ethical value of labor, here rendered in an image of painful bodily toil.

The ability to buy house plots at non-arbitrary prices, won by the residents of the Bizcocho hacienda, represented a significant victory because it broke the landlords' control over the conditions of the private lives of their tenants; residents unable to rent agricultural land might now work for their neighbors, or exercise other trades, without losing their place in the world. In the de la Laja case, Rodríguez never clarified how he imagined the transition from settlement to township would work out with respect to ownership rights. Would hacienda land be expropriated and made public? Would house plots be distributed to residents? Beyond such practical details, Rodríguez was concerned to show that the greatest source of social precariousness on the estate was the power wielded by the landlords. As long as the owners could banish residents from their homes at a whim, the idea of a lawful social existence would be no more than wishful thinking.

The Bizcocho tenants more explicitly framed their dispute with the landlord as a struggle for freedom from tyranny. These tenants had congregated in a settlement and formed a town government already at the end of the independence war. Now they argued that dismantling their township would return them to a life under despotism. About the landlord's assertion that only he was able to impose order on his estate, the tenants' lawyer commented:

41   "[P]or su miseria, y calamidades de los tiempos" and "la expulsión del arrendatario antiguo, y colocación del nuevo, que ha ofrecido oponerse a la pretensión, de que la Hacienda se erija en pueblo." "Expediente formado á consecuencia . . .," in AGEG-M, Caja 1, Expediente 3, Foja 26r.

42   "[Q]uieren levantar sus fincas, de su sudor y sangre, de todos los pobres operarios y gañanes," "Expediente formado á consecuencia . . .," in AGEG-M, Caja 1, Expediente 3, Foja 5v.

But with what power will he be invested? Not the power of the judge, for our system knows of no class [of judge] except the one whose authority comes from the election of the people . . . Will he be granted an oppressive omnipotence, and given a position like a sultan, so that he may order and judge with absolute power? We thank señor Alday [the landowner] for such heroic aims . . . His very language is no other than that of a tyrant.[43]

The lawyer's allusion to "our system," or form of government, picked up on the mixture of liberal and democratic elements that, in the context of early nineteenth-century political thought, was among the most radical features of Mexico's federalist constitution. It was a common idea of the period – in Europe as well as in Mexico – that democracy, since it was based on the will of an ignorant multitude, was inimical to lawful government. But according to the lawyer of the Bizcocho tenants, to have public officials elected by the people, far from creating a state of anarchy, was indispensable for defeating rural lawlessness. Only government by the people could establish true legal rule.

The lawyer proposed a thought experiment designed to show that, on the Bizcocho estate, forming a municipality would have a dynamic effect on a reality stunted by centuries of landlord oppression. Suppose for a moment that the Bizcocho settlement really did consist only of idle troublemakers, as the landowner had suggested. The question the government then needed to ask was "whether it is useful to the state that Bizcocho be properly organized as a township, so that those inhabitants can achieve the benefits of society and be brought under obedience of the law."[44] To answer his question, he drew a bold sketch of the benefits to be gained from confirming the population's municipal status:

the presence of just and severe judges destroys offences; order and vigilance bring an end to insubordination; society fosters education, as isolation destroys it, and fortunes grow with calmness, order, and prosperity. All these are goods that any government must seek for the citizens who trust in its rectitude, and they cannot be achieved without forming a township that will work for their attainment.[45]

43 "¿Pero con que investidura se le ha de poner? No con la de juez por que nuestro sistema desconoce toda clase que no sea la que tiene autoridad provenida por eleccion del pueblo. . . . ¿Se le dará una omnipotencia opresora, y se le colocará como a un vizir, para que mande y juzgue con poder absoluto? Se agradecen al Señor Alday tan heroicos fines. . . . Su lenguaje mismo no es otro que el de los tiranos." "Cuaderno 2.o," in AGEG-M, Caja 15, Expediente 7, Foja 85v-85r.

44 "[S]i es útil al Estado, que el Bizcocho sea Pueblo organizado rectamente, para que aquellos habitantes logren de los beneficios de la sociedad, y sean contenidos en la obediencia de la ley," "Cuaderno 2.o," in AGEG-M, Caja 15, Expediente 7, Foja 82v; see Foja 86r for a different formulation of the same point.

45 "[L]os delitos se destruyen por la presencia de jueces rectos y severos, la insubordinación se acaba con el orden y la vigilancia: la educación se fomenta con la sociedad, como se destruye en el aislamiento, y las fortunas crecen con la quietud, el orden, y la prosperidad. Todos estos son bienes

The lawyer went on to suggest that hacienda residents who had testified on behalf of the landowner were in fact troublemakers moved by hatred against local authorities, who in the last few years had finally begun to check their misconduct.[46]

Ultimately, the lawyer of the Bizcocho tenants argued that the private ownership of large tracts of land, on which the livelihood of many people depended, was at odds with the principle of liberty. He described the estate owner as a tyrant and colonial relic but his clients as "the useful, productive classes of citizens, those [classes of citizens] which should be seen with the just consideration deserved by [people] who profess honorable professions that promote production, supplying the well being of all."[47] According to the lawyer, the creation of social wealth, and not the ownership of property, was the true basis of republican legality. Like the Abbé Sieyes on the eve of the French Revolution, or English working-class leaders in the first half of the nineteenth century, the lawyer evoked the value of labor to oppose the hereditary power of the idle and privileged.[48]

IV Despots

The radical position articulated by the Bizcocho lawyer was not that of a minority. We saw in previous chapters that politicians in mestizo towns tended to identify with a liberalism that celebrated labor and thought of idleness as the capital vice. If this identification was in part a rebuke of the rowdy lifestyle of plebeians, it was equally directed against the unearned power of hacienda owners. In their comments on rural social relations, local politicians praised the work ethic of the peasantry and lambasted the stranglehold that idle ownership exerted over the agricultural economy. Examples are legion. The mayor of Pénjamo, Guanajuato, charged that landlords discouraged peasant investment by raising rents whenever their tenants made improvements to the land. Although the more than 400 farms comprising the two biggest local haciendas were "susceptible to all kinds of produce," he argued that

> que todo gobierno debe procurar a los ciudadanos que confían en su rectitud, y ellos no se pueden lograr sin que allí se forme un Pueblo que proporcione su consecución." "Cuaderno 2.o," in AGEG-M, Caja 15, Expediente 7, Foja 87v-87r.

46 "Cuaderno 2.o," in AGEG-M, Caja 15, Expediente 7, Fojas 80v-81v, 88r.

47 "[S]on de las clases útiles y productoras, de aquellas que deben verse con la consideración justa que merecen los que profesan ejercicios honrosos que fomentando la producción, proporcionan el bien estar de todos." "Cuaderno 2.o," in AGEG-M, Caja 15, Expediente 7, Foja 86v-86r.

48 See William Sewell, Jr., *A Rhetoric of Bourgeois Revolution: The Abbé Sieyes and "What Is the Third Estate?"* (Durham, NC: Duke University Press, 1994); Gareth Stedman Jones, *Languages of Class: Studies in English Working Class History, 1832–1982* (Cambridge: Cambridge University Press, 1983).

the people who possess [i.e., rent] them don't risk spending any money on them . . ., for even the smallest improvement that a tenant makes on his farm . . . already serves as a powerful motive for increasing his rent or taking the farm away from him.[49]

According to a report from San Luis de la Paz, the threat of eviction could be effective even absent a strong market for land rentals because hacendados had the option of converting fields into cattle pastures; tenants went along with increased payments in order "not to lose homesteads which for so many years they have watered with their sweat."[50] Local magistrates across Guanajuato cited exorbitant rents as powerful depressants of the economy and exalted the labor of the peasantry – "a class of people," in the words of the mayor of Silao, "deserving of every privilege and attention."[51]

In San Luis Potosí, urban politicians responding to a 1822 request to describe local social conditions made similar arguments about the distorting effects of estate ownership on rural social relations.[52] Without agricultural work, wrote the government of San Francisco del Valle, "the principal means for the conservation of life would be missing," and yet hacienda laborers were paid so little that they "do not have . . . enough to feed themselves, nor for covering their nudity, and thus it is that they are always hungry, and their flesh always uncovered."[53] Private wretchedness begot public decadence. The governments of Valle de Matehuala, Minas de

---

49 Although the farms "son susceptibles de toda clase de producciones los sujetos que los poseen no se arriesgan a hacer gastos en ellos . . ., pues con la más pequeña mejora que haga un arrendatario en su rancho . . . ya es un motivo poderoso para subirle la renta o quitarle el rancho." "Estado que manifiesta los ramos en que consiste la Agricultura," Pénjamo, 1826, in AGEG-M, Caja 29, Expediente 11.

50 "[P]or no desamparar unos hogares, que han regado tantos años con el sudor de su rostro," "Observaciones q.e el Ayuntamiento de San Luis de la Paz, tiene hechas sobre los hacendados, y arrendatarios de esta demarcasion," 7 December 1824, in AGEG-M, Caja 6, Expediente 11, Fojas 52–53.

51 "[C]lase de gentes que se merecen todo privilegio y atención." José Agustín Villegas to Gobernador, Dolores Hidalgo, 27 March 1827, in AGEG-M, Caja 46, Expediente 4; Fermín Sosa et al. to Gobernador, Silao, 7 December 1829, in AGEG-M, Caja 77, Expediente 14; Municipal report, Acámbaro, 28 May 1830, in AGEG-M, Caja 99, Expediente 1; Ignacio Romero to Gobernador, Silao, 21 November 1826, in AGEG-M, Caja 29, Expediente 17.

52 These reports are discussed in José Alfredo Rangel Silva, "Las voces del pueblo. La cultura política desde los ayuntamientos: San Luis Potosí (1820–1823)," in *Poder y gobierno local*, eds. Salinas Sandoval, Birrichaga Gardida, and Escobar Ohmstede, 123–149. I am grateful to Professor Rangel Silva for allowing me the use of his photocopies of the town council reports. The present location of most of the original documents in the AHESLP-SGG is unknown due to a recent reorganization of the archive.

53 "[S]in ellos faltaría lo principal para la conservación de la vida," and "no tienen . . . para alimentarse suficientemente, ni para cubrir su desnudez, y de ahí proviene el que siempre estén con hambre y siempre descubiertas sus carnes." Report from Valle de San Francisco, 9 February 1822, photocopy in possession of the author.

Santa María, Tlaxcalilla, Alaquines, Cedral, and Rioverde all argued that the ability of landlords to evict tenants and manipulate rents acted as a disincentive to agricultural entrepreneurship. It caused peasants to be miserable and local economies to be depressed:

[on those occasions] when [the landlords] . . . rent out a farm, when least expected they throw out [the old] tenant in order to give [the farm] to another, with the result that each year new pleas are necessary; and in this way no peasant makes an effort to come up with ideas for advancing his husbandry because he fears to lose [the results of] his work.[54]

Exorbitant land rents, coupled with the fear of sudden eviction, had the result that "the tenant never cultivates or looks after the land with interest, and from that comes the decadence of the important branch of agriculture, and as a result also that of crafts, industry, commerce, etc."[55] Thus was peasant industry squandered on a class of parasites. According to the *ayuntamiento* of Rioverde, landowners in the region were renting out uncleared mountain land only to evict the tenants once the land had been put under cultivation.[56] The *ayuntamiento* of Cedral allowed itself to imagine the boost that would be given to the local economy if estate lands were distributed among town residents: "everybody dedicating himself to work, with love and care, on that [land] that would be really his, without the haste [resulting from the fear that] the landlord might take it away tomorrow and give it to someone else."[57]

Some governments made suggestions of how to remedy the situation. The town council of San Luis de la Paz recommended a legal ceiling on land rents so as "to contain the arbitrariness of the hacendados," while that of Pénjamo proposed a forced sale of hacienda lands to tenants; should that be impracticable, enforcing a nine-year minimum term for land rentals would at least curb the worst of landlord abuses.[58] The government of Valle de San

54   "Otras ocasiones como . . . arriendan un rancho, y al menos pensar despojan a aquel arrendatario para dárselo a otro, de suerte que cada año es necesario nuevas súplicas; y de este modo ningún labrador se empeña en proyectar ideas para adelantar sus labranzas por que teme perder su trabajo." Report from Alaquines, 10 April 1822, photocopy in possession of the author.
55   "[A]sí jamás el arrendatario cultiva, ni cuida el terreno con interés, y de allí resulta la decadencia del importante ramo de la agricultura, y por consiguiente la de las artes, industria, comercio etc." Report from Tlaxcalilla, 25 February 1822, photocopy in possession of the author.
56   Report from Rioverde, 14 February 1822, photocopy in possession of the author.
57   "[D]edicándose entonces a labrar con amor, y empeño cada uno lo que será propiamente suyo, sin el afán de que se lo quitará mañana el dueño para darselo a otro. . . ." Report from Cedral, 26 February 1826, photocopy in possession of the author. See also the reports from Valle de Matehuala, 13 February 1822, and Minas de Santa María, 14 February 1822, photocopies in possession of the author.
58   "Observaciones," 7 December 1824, in AGEG-M, Caja 6, Expediente 11, Fojas 52–53. "Estado que manifiesta los ramos en que consiste la Agricultura," Pénjamo, 1826, in AGEG-M, Caja 29, Expediente 11.

Francisco demanded a government-mandated wage increase for hacienda workers (*gañanes*) and a law that would require landowners to rent out uncultivated lands. It also proposed to legislate against "the iniquitous and usurious quotas that have become too common [i.e., in sharecropping arrangements]."[59] The town councils of Rioverde and Minas de Santa María suggested using the legal instrument of the *censo enfiteusis* to restrict the power of landlords, giving them the right to receive an annual payment whose amount would be fixed by the government but not to increase rents or arbitrarily evict tenants.[60] Many *ayuntamientos* argued that hacienda lands close to town boundaries should be designated as *ejidos* and either used in common – as pasture or woodland – or rented out by the municipality.[61]

In the eyes of small-town politicians, landlords were despots as well as exploiters. Hacendados "oppress" their renters "with servitude" according to the town government of San Luis de la Paz, they "imagine that all others were born to be their slaves, and perpetually at their service" according to a group of citizens claiming to speak on behalf of the peasants [*labradores*] of Silao. The government of Rioverde wrote that peasants were "tyrannized" by local landlords and that of Dolores Hidalgo that estate owners "convert their [economic] rights into a power that they do not and cannot have over the persons and interests of their miserable [tenants]."[62] A sense of anger and outrage is palpable in such formulations: people were miserable, it was averred, because landlords were behaving badly. The government of Rioverde talked of landowners' "usurious abuses," that of Tlaxcalilla of their "avarice" and "covetousness." The town government of Palma, surrounded by indigenous villages whose land during the independence war had been invaded by hacendados, in a more measured tone accused the landlords of lacking "charity and justice."[63]

59 "[E]xterminándose con severas penas los inicuos y usurarios partidos que demasiado se han generalizado." Report from Valle de San Francisco, 9 February 1822, photocopy in possession of the author.

60 Reports from Rioverde, 14 February 1822, and Minas de Santa María, 14 February 1822, photocopies in possession of the author. On the censo enfiteusis and its place in the hispanic legal tradition, see Margarita Menegus Bornemann, *La Mixteca Baja entre la Revolución y la Reforma: Cacicazgo, territorialidad y gobierno siglos XVIII–XIX* (Oaxaca City: Universidad Autónoma "Benito Juárez" de Oaxaca, 2009), 114.

61 Reports from Salinas del Peñon Blanco, 8 February 1822; Real de San Francisco, 3 February 1822; Cedral, 26 February 1822; Alaquines, 10 April 1822; and Matehuala, 13 February 1822; photocopies in possession of the author.

62 The landowners imagined "que nacieron los demás para su esclavos y perpetuos a su servidumbre"; and "convirtiendo sus derechos en un poder que no tienen ni pueden tener sobre las personas e intereses de los infelices." "Observaciones," 7 December 1824, in AGEG-M, Caja 6, Expediente 11, Fojas 52–53; Fermin Sosa et al. to Gobernador, Silao, 7 December 1829, in AGEG-M, Caja 77, Expediente 14; Report from Dolores Hidalgo, 1830, in AGEG-M, Caja 100, Expediente 1; Report from Rioverde, 14 February 1822, photocopy in possession of the author.

63 Reports from Rioverde, 14 February 1822, and Tlaxcalilla, 25 February 1822, photocopies in possession of the author. Report from Palma in AHESLP-PSLP, Caja 3, Expediente 14.

Compared to these adversaries of the hacienda economy, the number of municipal officeholders who defended estate owners was minute. Nostalgia for the coercive possibilities of the colonial period is implied in a suggestion by the town council of Tancanhuitz that indigenous families living dispersed in the surrounding mountains should be forced to resettle and grow specified amounts of corn, black beans, and sugarcane so as to leave behind "the dark state in which they live." Those failing to meet their quotas would have to hire themselves out "at the going rate" – in other words, would form a pool of forced labor for surrounding haciendas.[64] José Antonio Rangel notes that this opinion expressed the political dominance of landowners in the Huasteca region, where Tancanhuitz was located.[65] The situation had few parallels elsewhere in the state but may have been common in parts of southern Mexico, where social relations were more strongly marked by a history of racial violence.[66] In Puebla, for example, the authorities of the town of Atlixco in the 1820s and 1830s supported the right of nearby haciendas to lock up indigenous workers so as to prevent their escape before their labor contract had been fulfilled.[67] In most areas of Guanajuato and San Luis Potosí, such a practice would have been unthinkable.

The overwhelming identification of what we might now call the middle-class interests of small-town politicians with the plights of the rural poor, and against the dominance of the hacendado class, is a striking feature of the political landscape in large parts of early republican Mexico. To explain it, we can point to certain structural features. Estate agriculture was detrimental to a wide variety of people: merchants were harmed by a lack of competition in the provision of foodstuffs, medium-sized farmers by the lack of a dynamic land market, and politicians by a scarcity of town lands whose rent would help cover the costs of municipal government.[68] The business of medium-sized farmers, moreover, was perfectly compatible with a labor force of small-holding peasants periodically hiring themselves out in order to supplement their family harvests. It also appears that the provincial middle classes, and especially middling farmers, remained close to the production process. Local politicians often took leaves of absence during harvest time in order to attend to their agricultural operations.

---

64 Report from Tancanhuitz, 28 February 1822, photocopy in possession of author.

65 Rangel Silva, "Las voces del pueblo."

66 On the difference between social relations in the southern and northern parts of Mexico, see Tutino, *Making a New World*, 32–33.

67 Elizabeth Terese Newman, "From Prison to Home: Labor Relations and Social Control in Nineteenth-Century Mexico," *Ethnohistory* 60/4 (2013), 663–664, 667–668.

68 Alan Knight has noted the tension between hacienda owners and provincial middle-class interests – particularly those of shopkeepers – during the Porfiriato. Alan Knight, *The Mexican Revolution:* vol. 1, *Porfirians, Liberals, and Peasants* (Cambridge: Cambridge University Press, 1986), 98.

In this context, labor and industry became closely associated in local class imaginaries. As monopolists of land, seekers of rent, and, like the army, perpetuators of a culture of privilege, hacendados were the enemies of both.

If there was a strong consensus about the deleterious effects of landed estates on local legal and political cultures, why were so few measures taken to curb the power of hacienda owners? Municipal governments were legal and administrative bodies with no legislative powers. But anti-hacienda positions, though hegemonic on the level of municipal politics, became increasingly scarce as one moved up the scale from local to regional and national politics, where wealthy landowners were more likely to have influence. Estate owners' power did not go completely unchallenged. At the level of state politics, the government of Zacatecas took measures to break up hacienda lands under the liberal government of Francisco García (1829–1835), while in San Luis Potosí a struggle between liberal and conservative factions in the late 1820s and early 1830s revolved at least partly around the liberal attempt to pass laws that would protect small-holding tenants from arbitrary land evictions.[69] At the level of national debate, proposals aiming at the redistribution of large landholdings were made during the War of Independence and in the immediate post-independence period, including at the 1823 Constituent Congress, and again during the radical liberal administration of Valentín Gómez Farías from 1833 to 1834.[70] They all came to nothing. For the most part, conflicts between hacienda owners and their tenants took place at the margins of national politics.

This changed in the late 1840s, when a string of popular revolts for the first time brought questions about the country's agrarian structure to

---

69 On Zacatecas, see Brading, *Haciendas and Ranchos*, 202–203; Chevalier, "Acerca de los orígenes de la pequeña propiedad," 6–7; and Mercedes de Vega, "La opción federalista en Zacatecas, 1820–1835," in *Cincuenta Años*, vol. 2, eds. Hernández Chávez and Miño Grijalva, 254–255; and Jesús Reyes Heroles, *El liberalism mexicano*, 2nd ed.: vol. 3, *La integración de las ideas* (Mexico City: Fondo de Cultura Económica, 1974), 563–566. In San Luis Potosí, a number of ambitious legal attempts to regulate estate tenancies between 1827 and 1829 were canceled by a new administration in 1831. See AHESLP-Leyes y Decretos, circular núm. 22 from 27 February 1827, circular número 103 from 5 May 1828, circular from 20 May 1829, circular núm. 50 from 30 September 1829, and circular núm. 10 from 28 February 1831.

70 The most extensive discussion of agrarian ideas in Mexico's independence and post-independence period is, to my knowledge, Reyes Heroles, *El liberalismo mexicano: vol. 1, Los orígenes*, 127–132 and 138–146, and vol. 3, *La integración de las ideas*, 542–568. See also Costeloe, *Central Republic*, 33, and Charles C. Griffin, *Los temas sociales y económicos en la época de la Independencia* (Caracas: Fundación John Boulton, 1962), 47–48. On agrarian radicalism during the Gómez Farías presidency, see Michael Costeloe, *The Central Republic in Mexico, 1835–1846*: Hombres de Bien *in the Age of Santa Anna* (Cambridge: Cambridge University Press, 1993), 33. On the origins of such ideas in eighteenth-century Spain, see Fernando Perez Montesinos, "Poised to Break: Liberalism, Land Reform, and Communities in the Purépecha Highlands of Michoacán, Mexico, 1800–1915," PhD Dissertation, Georgetown University (2014), 55–61.

sustained national attention. The most famous is the Maya rebellion in Yucatán, which after 1847 established an autonomous indigenous polity that would last until the end of the century. Closer to the centers of power, a decades-long fight for municipal rights in Guerrero acquired an agrarian dimension when local elites pressed their claims to the ownership of territory they had long contested with indigenous towns.[71] In nearby Morelos longstanding conflicts between peasants and landlords in the 1850s escalated into a low-level class war claiming various deaths on both sides.[72] In Veracruz, a dispute between a hacienda and nearby indigenous towns in 1848 prompted the outbreak of a large-scale rebellion that elites classified as a caste war and were only able to pacify in the following year, by a mixture of repression and concessions.[73] And in the Sierra Gorda, a mountain area occupying parts of Querétaro, Guanajuato, and San Luis Potosí, a shifting coalition of rebels fought the state from 1847 to 1850 and in 1849, with the Plan of Rioverde, composed one of the most radical agrarian programs written in nineteenth-century Mexico: any estates with populations of more than 1,500 would be converted into self-governed townships; the owners of other estates could charge only "moderate" rents for the use of agricultural land and had no right to their tenants' labor or shares of their tenants' harvests; and landowners would not be allowed to charge rent for tenants' usage of common wood and pasture land, nor for the space merely occupied by house plots.[74]

The rebellions of the 1840s and 1850s were precipitated by a renewed resource competition between hacendados and peasants, perhaps as a result of an economic "mini-boom" such as Margaret Chowning has diagnosed for the regional economy of Michoacán in this period.[75] The same years saw a resurgence of tenant attempts to transform their settlements into municipal

---

71 On the role played by local land conflicts in the development of Guerrero's "popular federalism", see Guardino, *Peasants*, 150–151.

72 Guardino, *Peasants*, 201–209. Florencia Mallon, "Peasants and State Formation in Nineteenth Century Mexico: Morelos, 1848–1858," *Political Power and Social Theory* 7 (1988); and *Peasant and Nation*, chapter 5; Jesús Sotelo Inclán, *Raíz y razón de Zapata*, 2nd ed. (Mexico City: Fondo de Cultura Económica, 1970), 253–269.

73 Ducey, *Nation of Villages*, chapter 6.

74 "Plan político y eminentemente social: proclamado en Rio Verde por el Ejército Regenerador de Sierra Gorda," Rioverde, 14 March 1849, in *Planes en la nación Mexicana* (Mexico City: Cámara de senadores de la República Mexicana, 1987), vol. 4, articles 11–14. For an account of the rebellion, see Leticia Reina, "The Sierra Gorda Peasant Rebellion, 1847–50," in *Riot, Rebellion, and Revolution: Rural Social Conflict in Mexico*, ed. Friedrich Katz, 269–294 (Princeton: Princeton University Press, 1988).

75 Margaret Chowning, "The Contours of the Post-1810 Depression in Mexico: A Reappraisal from a Regional Perspective," *Latin American Research Review* 27/2 (1992), 121. On the relationship between economic recovery and peasant rebellion, see also Tutino, *From Insurrection to Revolution*, chapters 6 and 7; and Perez Montesinos, "Poised to Break," 117–118.

seats. Let us once more consider a particular example. In 1857, tenants of the Bocas hacienda in San Luis Potosí petitioned the state's Constituent Congress for municipal status. Their petition described a situation of rapidly deteriorating tenancy conditions on the hacienda: rent used to be moderate, now it was excessive; plots used to be decent, now they were marginal; foraging in wastelands used to be tolerated, now it was persecuted.[76] Worst of all, the landowner forced residents to work on his land in the harvest months, causing their own crops to go to waste. The petition lingered on the abusiveness of this situation:

the Señor Hacendado, since he sows so much, obliges us by force to help him bring in his harvest, which he does in the months of January and February, and all this time our own harvest is exposed in the fields, and the punishment for whoever dares to bring it in without the permission of the hacendado is to be robbed of his plot: he is seen with such contempt that even his dwelling is taken away from him.[77]

The tenants reported that in 1854 and 1855 people had died of hunger as a result of the loss of their harvest. Should their wish for the creation of a township not be granted, they demanded at least that the government put a ceiling on land rents and protect them from the landlords' illegal labor demands.

In political terms, the tenants framed their plight as a struggle not for social justice but for freedom or liberty. Like the Bizcocho tenants before them, they stressed the despotism governing life on a hacienda. "Neither for having invested our bodily labor," they wrote, "nor for paying our rent, are we free to enjoy the fruits or products that [our fields] give us."[78] The Bocas tenants thus gave the idea of personal freedom a radical social inflection. They adapted it to the concrete conditions of hacienda life, where in order to protect tenants' freedom to work it would be necessary to put restrictions on the tenancy conditions imposed by their landlords.

Taking advantage of a favorable political context – the recent overthrow of Santa Anna's dictatorship in the Revolution of Ayutla – the tenants also

76 José María Aguilar et al. to Gobernador, 6 October 1857, in AHESLP-SGG, Caja 1857.21, unnumbered Expediente. The Bocas tenants achieved the hacienda's conversion to an incorporated township in 1857. However, the new municipality was unable to meet its fiscal obligations and was abolished in 1871. See Sánchez Montiel, *De poblados de Hacienda*, 169–184.

77 "[E]l Señor Hacendado como siembra tanto, nos obliga esforzadamente a que le ayudemos a levantar su cosecha que viene hacer por los meses de enero y febrero, y todo este tiempo está tirada la nuestra en el campo, con pena de que el que se atreviere a levantarla sin voluntad del hacendado, éste se le despoja de su labor: sele ve con desprecio hasta el grado de despojarle de su habitación." José María Aguilar et al. to Gobernador, 6 October 1857, in AHESLP-SGG, Caja 1857.21, unnumbered Expediente.

78 "No por habernos costado nuestro corporal trabajo, ni por pagar nuestra renta, somos libres para gozar ampliamente los frutos o productos que ellas dan." José María Aguilar et al. to Gobernador, 6 October 1857, in AHESLP-SGG, Caja 1857.21, unnumbered Expediente.

established a direct relationship between their struggle and that of the victorious liberals. They suggested that the hacendados were making a mockery of the republican justice system: past attempts to bring the tenants' plight to the attention of public officials had failed "because these *señores* with their threats have won over the people ..., and before the authorities their reliable witnesses are all their dependents." Furthermore, the rental contracts between landlord and tenant were a travesty, drawn up "without legal authorization of any kind except by him [the hacendado]."[79] This complaint went beyond the position, familiar from the de la Laja and Bizcocho cases, that haciendas were semi-stateless territories in which the legal sovereignty of the republic was not truly established. The Bocas tenants alleged that hacendados had been able to extend their abuses into courts of law and legal instruments like the rental contract. Only now, under a new government committed to "the happiness of man, the glorious triumph of his rights, and the severe punishment against those who break his sacred laws," could the tenants finally hope to find justice.[80]

A concern with legal abuses, such as those expressed by the inhabitants of the Bocas estate, also informed the programs of the agrarian insurgencies of the 1840s and 1850s. Agrarian rebels in Guerrero, Morelos, and Veracruz fought for a federalist constitution in part because they thought that centralist politicians were stacking the legal system against them.[81] In the Plan of Rioverde, those of the Sierra Gorda made legal reform one of their core demands: the privileges of the Church were to be abolished, the army disbanded and replaced by a National Guard, and, in an article directly aimed at the ability of the powerful to influence the courts in their favor, all trials were henceforth to be by jury.[82] The demand for legal reform was an aspect of "popular liberalism" in nineteenth-century Mexico whose importance historians have yet to fully acknowledge.

The agrarian rebellions of the 1840s and 1850s finally brought the contradiction between estate ownership and legal rule to sustained national attention, where it entered a broader polemic about the future of the country. In the aftermath of the disastrous defeat in the Mexican-American War (1846–1848), conservatives, rather than attempt to accommodate their illiberal convictions within a republican framework of law, for

79   "[P]orque estos señores con sus amenazas han ganado el Pueblo ...., y ante las autoridades sus fidedignos testigos son todos los dependientes"; and "sin más habilitación de ninguna clase, que por solo él." José María Aguilar et al. to Gobernador, 6 October 1857, in AHESLP-SGG, Caja 1857.21, unnumbered Expediente.

80   "[L]a felicidad del hombre, el glorioso triunfo de sus derechos: y el severo castigo contra los infrasitores de sus sagradas leyes." José María Aguilar et al. to Gobernador, 6 October 1857, in AHESLP-SGG, Caja 1857.21, unnumbered Expediente.

81   Guardino, *Peasants*, 150–151; Ducey, *Nation of Villages*, chapter 6.

82   "Plan político y eminentemente social," articles 4, 6, 8.

the first time formulated an explicitly anti-republican position. Some proposed a return to the corporate hierarchy of the colonial era, which they thought had guided the nation's ascent to a now-lost splendor. They argued that hacienda owners should be allowed to govern their tenants as they saw fit and interpreted the uprisings of the 1840s as expressions of debilitating social divisions, animated by the false ideal of equality.[83] During his dictatorship from 1853 to 1855, Santa Anna, who as a landlord in Veracruz had first-hand experience with the audacity of tenants attempting to form municipal governments, promulgated a decree that outlawed the transformation of settlements into townships without estate owners' explicit consent.[84]

In contrast to the conservative position, a group of radical liberals amplified the voices of agrarian rebels for a national audience. These politicians denounced not only the abuses of individual landlords but the structural injustices of rural life and the distortions they caused in the national polity.[85] In 1847, José María Lafragua, on behalf of the Ministry of the Interior, wrote:

The most decisive cause of our ills has been the extraordinary disproportion with which territorial property has been distributed, which, making fortunes unequal, makes the poor class victim of the opulent, not only in financial matters, because it subjects the political conduct of a multitude of citizens to the caprices of a landowner.[86]

After the defeat of Santa Anna's dictatorship, and coinciding with the demand for a township by the tenants of the Bocas hacienda, a group of liberals proposed a radical land-reform program during the 1856–1857 Constituent Congress. Ponciano Arriaga, the *potosino* lawyer who was their most eloquent spokesman, argued that as long as Mexico suffered from an extreme disparity in the distribution of land, its people "can be neither free nor republican." He proposed that the state take ownership of all landed properties larger than 15 square leagues that, within two years of the law's passing, had not been brought under cultivation. Where towns or settlements lacked proper lands, surrounding landholdings should be redistributed, and their owners indemnified for their losses, irrespective of whether

---

83 The classic discussion of the rise of Conservatism in late 1840s Mexico is Charles Hale, *Mexican Liberalism in the Age of Mora, 1821–1853* (New Haven: Yale University Press, 1968), 241–244. See also Guardino, *Peasants*, 190–194, and Will Fowler, *Mexico in the Age of Proposals, 1821–1853* (Westport, CT: Greenwood Press, 1998), 80–81.

84 Francisco Zarco, *Historia del Congreso Extraordinario Constituyente {1856–1857}* (Mexico City: El Colegio de México, 1956), sessions from 5 April and 19 May 1856, 181–182. Sotelo Inclán, *Raíz y razón*, 273–274.

85 Guardino, *Peasants*, 193–199; Sotelo Inclán, *Raíz y razón*, 258–261.

86 Quoted in Guardino, *Peasants*, 193.

the land was being cultivated. Arriaga argued that legislators unwilling to reign in hacienda power were blind to the material foundation of the social order. "How can one rationally imagine or expect that these unhappy people [hacienda tenants] will one day leave the sphere of abject tenants by legal means and, by the magical words of a written law, convert themselves into free citizens, who know and defend the dignity and importance of their rights?"[87] Agrarian reform was a question of legal as well as economic justice; under an unreformed system of land tenure, the universality of republican law would remain a chimera.

The failure of the social liberals' reform proposals has often been attributed to their intellectual isolation. The social liberals are then hailed as precocious precursors to the radical agrarianism of the early twentieth century rather than serious contenders for the attention of their contemporaries. That explanation is not convincing. By the time the Constituent Congress met in 1856, agrarian reform had been an important topic of liberal debate for at least a decade; we have seen that among estate residents and local politicians it had been a topic of debate since the very beginning of Mexico's life as a republic.[88] These residents, and the agrarian rebels who were their descendants, played the vital role in the construction of Mexican republicanism posited by John Tutino, and disprove François-Xavier Guerra's assumption that Mexico's rural masses were governed by old-regime cultural standards that cut them off from the liberal bent of elite politics. The social liberals of the Constituent Congress were not isolated precursors of a revolutionary future but rather custodians of a critique that had been voiced in provincial towns and villages for decades and that they put before the country's political elite in the form of explicit legislative proposals. They did not fail for lack of a social constituency.

V Regions of Refuge

If hacienda residents were as well equipped to participate in a liberal political culture as any other group in post-colonial Mexico, we need to ask why they did not do so more often. Initiatives to convert estate settlements into municipal seats, such as those undertaken by the de la Laja, Bizcocho, and

---

87 "¿Cómo se puede racionalmente concebir ni esperar que tales infelices salgan alguna vez por las vías legales de la esfera de colonos abyectos y se conviertan por las mágicas palabras de una ley escrita en ciudadanos libres, que conozcan y defiendan la dignidad e importancia de sus derechos?" Zarco, *Historia del Congreso*, session from 23 June 1856, 387–404, here 388–389. On Arriaga's political formation in early republican San Luis Potosí, see Sergio A. Cañedo Gamboa and María Isabel Monroy Castillo, *Ponciano Arriaga: La formación de un liberal 1811–1847* (San Luis Potosí: Gobierno del Estado de San Luis Potosí and Archivo Histórico del Estado, 2008).

88 Guardino, *Peasants*, 191–209; Reyes Heroles, *El liberalismo mexicano*, vol. 3, "La integración de las ideas," 576–585.

Bocas tenants, were scarce in relation to the total number of haciendas – even in states like Guanajuato and San Luis Potosí, where hacienda residents would have found sympathetic allies in most local politicians. It is easy to find reasons for this scarcity. At a minimum, challenging hacienda power required financial resources, a culture of solidarity, and enough determination to risk landlord reprisals such as the evictions complained of by de la Laja tenants. In the absence of a formal political tradition, these were not easy goods to muster. The difficulties of overcoming initial collective-action problems are suggested by the different trajectories of two of the cases examined in this chapter. If the de la Laja tenants were represented by a man with no legal expertise who may not have received any pay for his efforts, it was because they lacked a sustaining organizational culture. If the Bizcocho tenants were able to see their case to a moderately successful conclusion, it was because they had in fact been constituted as a township during the final years of the Spanish government; it was the established town authorities who initiated the tenants' defense, hired a lawyer, and collected the money to keep him paid.

These reasons seem weighty but not sufficient to explain why more estate populations did not push for the creation of constitutional townships. The threat of rental eviction, though certainly alarming for most tenants, did not pose an existential danger at a time of relative land abundance; evicted from one hacienda, peasants could find land on another. Moreover, evictions were a double-edged sword: rent had become the principal source of income for most hacendados, and only a few tenants could be replaced at a time.[89] Nor could acting in common to transform settlements into townships have presented an insuperable hurdle. Hacienda tenants did, after all, belong to large kinship networks and share religious and other cultural practices. And the inhabitants of a great number of other settlements – settlements not located on private land – did take advantage of Mexico's liberal revolution to demand the creation of local governments, sometimes against the opposition of bigger and more powerful towns.

The foundation of formal townships was in fact not the only area in which hacienda tenants displayed a relative absence of civic engagement. When state governments created the civic militias, they asked authorities to form rural cavalry as well as urban infantry companies. Yet local authorities, who did not always find it easy to organize militias inside their towns, found it much harder to do so outside, where they had little influence and no personal presence. They reported that people who lived in the countryside often took to their heels rather than sign up for militia service.[90] In Guanajuato, the number of men who served in the rural

89 Tutino, *From Insurrection to Revolution*, 233–234.
90 "Expediente instruido sobre si debe o no existir una compañía de milicia cívica formada en el pueblo del Huage," in AGEG-G, Caja 7, Expediente 12. Actas de Ayuntamiento, Casas Viejas, 22

cavalries – 1,078 in 1826 and 1,956 in 1829 – was more than five times smaller than that of men who served in urban militias, even though more people almost certainly lived in the countryside. While authorities sometimes managed to mobilize estate residents in response to specific banditry threats, their attempts to establish the kind of permanent guards who in the 1820s were becoming routine institutional fixtures in urban settings met with little success.[91] The tyranny of hacendados or the injustice of rural property relations were thus not the only factors that could be blamed for the debility of the rule of law on haciendas. There was also the unwillingness of rural residents to participate in republican civic institutions to anywhere near the extent as their urban counterparts.

Conservative politicians – those who mistrusted the egalitarian foundation of the post-colonial legal system – took advantage of the low recruitment numbers to put rural policing on a different social basis. In the 1830s, state governments in both Guanajuato and San Luis Potosí charged landowners with the organization of rural militia companies. On one level, they were trying to link the power of government to traditional forms of social control. But there was a pragmatic core to their efforts: as holders of large and immobile assets, landowners, unlike peasants, could not easily hide, nor ignore the call of authority. In Guanajuato, a policy of involving landowners in the formation of cavalry units, going back at least to 1830, was legally formalized in 1834. Owners of haciendas and ranchos were now responsible for outfitting – depending on their wealth – one, two, or three men for the rural militias, and for providing substitutes for any deserters.[92] In San Luis Potosí, an 1832 law even more completely collapsed the distinction between public and private authority: under its provisions, hacendados and their administrators were made responsible not only for finding recruits but for commanding rural militia units. An 1837 law set up small detachments of hacendado-led rural watchmen (*celadores rurales*) in all of the state's haciendas and ranchos.[93] A formal boundary between the power of the state and that of estate owners no longer existed.

and 29 April and 6 and 27 May 1829, in AGEG-M, Caja 83, Expediente 1; A. Llaca Romero to Jefe Poítico of Celaya, Jerécuaro, 2 June 1833, in AGEG-G, Caja 56, Expediente 5; "Nota de caballería rural de Casas Viejas," 25 May 1840, in AGEG-G, Caja 73, Expediente 3; F. García Valle to Gobernador, Salamanca, 16 April 1834, in AGEG-G, Caja 60, Expediente 1; and José María Durán to Jefe Político, Acámbaro, 17 June 1848, in AGEG-G, Caja 84, Expediente 1.

91 For examples, see Actas de Ayuntamiento, Silao, 26 May 1829, in AGEG-M, Caja 77, Expediente 14; and José Guerrera to Juan Castillo, Villela, 2 January 1829, in AHESLP-SGG, Caja 201, Expediente 2.

92 For the 1834 law, see AMG-AG-M, Caja 13, Documento 1135, Fojas 5–8, articles 1, 8, 11, 18, and 19. Mention of earlier policies is made in AMG-AG-M, Caja 11, Documento 978; and Antonio Ocampo to Gobernador, Salamanca, 18 January 1831, in AGEG-M, Caja 107, Expediente 8.

93 I have found no record of the law itself; it is mentioned in Vicente Hernández to Secretario de Gobierno, Rioverde, 8 January 1845, in AHESLP-SGG, Caja 1845.5, Expediente 1.

To what extent these laws were being followed is hard to determine. Many hacendados were no more willing than their tenants to comply with their new obligations. Francisco Guerrero, a landowner from Celaya, called the Guanajuatan law despotic and added that only by an act of force would he be able to impress a man into the cavalry.[94] The administrator of the Hacienda de Burras wrote that he could provide a recruit only if he were given military support. Pressed by the government, the hacienda's owner finally yielded and impressed two men into the militia. He nevertheless declared his concern that he had laid hands on the men

without any authority, and in fear that I will be reproached and incriminated for my conduct, and with the likely consequence of their early desertion for which, if it should happen, I must not be held responsible, and about [all of this] I declare to you my most formal and legal protest.[95]

In this particular case, the state government coerced landowners to coerce their tenants to serve on the forces charged with bringing order to the countryside.

Whatever their misgivings, many, and perhaps most, hacendados at least sometimes provided the state with men, horses, and money for the establishment of rural militias.[96] A few even took the initiative and approached the government with requests for permission to form rural guards on the civic-militia model.[97] The archival record allows only an impressionistic account of the workings of the forces put together in this

94 Antonio Ocampo to Gobernador, Salamanca, 18 January 1831, in AGEG-M, Caja 107, Expediente 8.

95 "[Q]ue sin tener autoridad, les he hecho, con el temor de que se me reclame y acrimine esta conducta, y con el correlativo de su pronta deserción, que si se verifica, no debo quedar responsable a ella, y sobre lo cual hago a V.S. la más formal y legal protesta." Letter from José Mariano Sardaneta, 8 January 1831, in AMG-AG-M, Caja 11, Documento 978.

96 See Francisco Rocha to Gobernador, Irapuato, 8 February 1858, in AGEG-M, Caja 201, Expediente 3; Letter from José María García del Valle, Guanajuato, 19 September 1831, in AGEG-G, Caja 45, Expediente 19; "Lista de los dueños, arrendatarios o administradores de las haciendas y ranchos," Salvatierra, 5 March 1836, in AGEG-G, Caja 66, Expediente 2; Letter from Jesus Aguilera, Irapuato, 25 February 1847, in AGEG-G, Caja 83, Expediente 7; Remigio Plancarte to Gobernador, Apaseo, 7 August 1853, in AGEG-G, Caja 115, Expediente 1; Antonio Roxas [Tabón?] to Secretario de Gobierno, Chamacuero, 3 October 1853, in AGEG-G, Caja 115, Expediente 3; Ramón Hernández to Secretario de Gobierno, Villa de Iturbide, 1 August and 13 August 1853, in AGEG-G, Caja 115, Expediente 4; Letters from 4 January, 13 January, 16 January, 17 January, 19 January, and 20 January 1845, in AHESLP-SGG, Caja 1845.4, Expediente 1; Manuel Montufar to Administrador de Rentas, Hacienda del Pozo, 15 January 1834, in AHESLP-SGG, Caja 468, Expediente 2.

97 Actas de Ayuntamiento, Acámbaro, 3 May 1830, in AGEG-M, Caja 99, Expediente 1; Letter from Lorenzo de Larrauri, Hacienda de Zesano, 14 October 1838, in AGEG-G, Caja 69, Expediente 11; Miguel de Obregón to Gobernador, León, 26 January 1845, in AGEG-G, Caja 78, Expediente 10.

manner. In February 1839, a militia commander from León assembled 100 rural guards to give chase to a reported band of 25 armed marauders. In November of that year, the same guards were patrolling highways that were unusually busy on account of an annual fair.[98] In 1840, cavalry units from Casas Viejas went on nightly patrols and regularly rode out to the Hacienda de Charcas in order to break up an illegal market.[99] And during the late 1830s and early 1840s, detachments of rural watchmen, numbering from four to eleven, each month reported for duty on most haciendas and large ranchos in San Luis Potosí, though it is unclear what actual tasks they performed.[100]

Nothing definitive can be concluded from so patchy a record. It seems at least clear that rural police forces, unlike their urban counterparts, did not establish themselves as a familiar public presence, capable of checking the behavior of drunkards, brawlers, wife-beaters, or petty thieves. They may, however, have been successful at limiting the spread of banditry and popular unrest. The strongest conclusion we can draw concerns the merging of public and private power in this crucial area of state formation: though the extent to which militia forces came to operate in the countryside is questionable, it is certain that when and where they did they largely relied on landowners for their organization. In rural parts of early republican Mexico, the provision of public security was thus built on a foundation of landed property. It is perhaps no wonder that, at the 1856–1857 Constituent Congress, landlords were such a formidable counterforce to the mobilized peasants who had brought down Santa Anna's dictatorship in the Ayutla Revolution. However reluctantly, they, too, had come to embody the legal state in a way that their tenants had not.

In order to explain the reluctance of hacienda residents to take part in civic tasks like community policing, let alone to challenge landowners' authority by attempting to form new municipalities, we may consider the options they had at their disposal. Estate tenants wishing to establish republican institutions first needed to challenge the control that landowners exercised over their property – a feat the de la Laja, Bizcocho, and Bocas tenants undertook by casting labor, and not property, in the leading role of the social founding narrative. But to argue for the social primacy of labor meant to encumber the notion of citizenship with a heavy burden.

98 Letter from Julian de Obregón, León, 13 February 1839, in AGEG-G, Caja 71, Expediente 8; Julian de Obregón to Gobernador, León, 11 November 1839, in AGEG-M, Caja 147, Expediente 5.

99 "Nota en estado de caballería rural de Casas Viejas," 25 May 1840, in AGEG-G, Caja 73, Expediente 3.

100 "Noticia de las listas de revista de Celadores rurales," San Luis Potosí, 14 September 1839, in AHESLP-SGG, Caja 721, Expediente 4. Watchmen lists from 1841 in AHESLP-SGG, Caja 756, Expedientes 3, 4, and 5; and C. Carrera to Secretario de Gobierno, Venado, 14 January 1845, in AHESLP-SGG, Caja 1845.5, Expediente 1.

Inhabitants of *ayuntamiento*-ruled towns lived in a setting of demanding civic duties and heightened social surveillance. Implied in the notion of the laboring citizen was the notion of the taxpaying citizen, who contributed to the costs of government; the breadwinning citizen, who raised and maintained a family while keeping his distance from the temptations of gambling, drinking, and other forms of all-male sociability; and the arms-bearing citizen, who ensured the observance of such strictures among his fellows by taking part in the duties of community-policing. Implied in it also was its antithesis: the idler, drunkard, or troublemaker whose forced service in the army would defend a national sovereignty from whose benefits he himself was excluded.

Haciendas, seen as zones of lawlessness by most contemporary observers, from the point of view of many of their tenants can be redescribed as "regions of refuge."[101] If haciendas were holdouts of colonial tyranny, they were also hiding places for popular actors unwilling to live up to the citizen-ideal of a liberal republic. Hacienda residents were not beyond the reach of the state, but they had heightened opportunities for evading its demands. They kept their distance from the republic's exigent civic culture and were able to engage in personal behavior – gambling, brawling, unrestrained marital violence – they would find it hard to get away with in municipal centers. They paid less taxes and probably sent fewer men to the army.[102] The visionary concept of labor summoned by some hacienda tenants thus also helps us understand why more tenants did not demand the creation of municipal governments on their estates. For most, it was a summons to be avoided.[103]

Let us now return to Guerra and Tutino's accounts of the relationship between hacienda settlements and republican political culture. Guerra's description of a self-enclosed peasant culture dominated by landlords

---

101 I am borrowing the concept from Gonzalo Aguirre Beltrán, *Regiones de Refugio: El desarrollo de la comunidad y el proceso dominical en Mestizo América* (Mexico City: Instituto Indigenista Interamericano, 1967). For a recent appropriation of the concept, see James Scott, *The Art of Not Being Governed: An Anarchist History of Upland Southeast Asia* (New Haven: Yale University Press, 2009).

102 On this point, see Raymond Buve, "Un paisaje lunar habitado por bribones y sus víctimas. Mirada retrospectiva al debate sobre las haciendas y los pueblos durante el Porfiriato (1876–1911)," in *Don Porfirio presidente ..., nunca omnipotente: Hallazgos, reflexiones y debates. 1876–1911*, eds. Romana Falcón and Raymond Buve, 121–152 (Mexico City: Universidad Iberoamericana, 1998), 140–141.

103 There is a parallel here to Juan Martínez Alier's discovery that Peruvian hacienda workers in the 1940s and 1950s were often unwilling to switch from what he calls "pre-modern" to "modern" labor relations, even if doing so offered tangible material benefits. Juan Martínez Alier, "Relations of Production in Andean Haciendas: Peru," in *Land and Labour in Latin America: Essays on the Development of Agrarian Capitalism in the Nineteenth and Twentieth Centuries*, eds. Kenneth Duncan and Ian Rutledge, 141–164 (New York: Cambridge University Press, 1977).

ignores the active principle at work in peasants' strategies of state evasion:
it was not the remoteness of the state but its closeness, its solicitude and
imposition, that formed the context for hacienda residents' political behavior through most of the nineteenth century.[104] By contrast, Tutino's
description of a peasantry contributing to the construction of a more
equitable state can help us make sense of the actions of the inhabitants of
the de la Laja, Bizcocho, and Bocas haciendas but ignores the failure of
residents on most other estates to lay claim to republican institutions.
Participation in a social revolution did not turn easily into participation
in the politics of nation building, and the allegiance of most tenants,
whether by default or volition, belonged to a propertied domain in which
republican law remained at least partly suspended. In the larger panorama
of Mexican history, this attitude makes them more at home under the Díaz
dictatorship at the end of the century than in their own present. In the
politics of liberal state formation, they were a corrosive anomaly.

---

104 James Scott has argued that we should see the social structures in what Aguirre Beltrán called
     "regions of refuge" not as holdovers of pre-colonial cultures but as adaptive responses to the
     threats emanating from state power. Scott, *Art of Not Being Governed.*

4

Indigenous Towns

I A Separate People

While no haciendas and only a few mestizo towns entered Mexico's constitutional era with a tradition of formal political organization, most indigenous towns did. In the colonial period, the Spanish Crown had isolated Latin America's indigenous peoples in their own "republic of Indians," separate from the "republic of Spaniards" and administratively divided into hundreds of self-governed towns. This spatial arrangement had satisfied both the secular and the spiritual, the material and the ethical pretensions of the Spanish Empire. Territorial separation had made it possible to subject the empire's native subjects to extractive measures like the tribute and, especially in the first century of colonial rule, the labor draft. It had also made it easier to regulate their participation in the imperial economy through the credit monopolies of the *reparto de mercancías* and to shield them from the abuses of individual settlers.

Endowing indigenous subjects with rights and protections, rather than merely incidental or ameliorative, had been fundamental to Spain's imperial project. In his study of post-conquest society in the Peruvian Andes, Steve Stern identifies three factors that explain the emergence of a "colonial hegemony" based on a partial "willingness," on the part of Peruvian Indians, "to accommodate to the 'reality' of colonial dominance."[1] First, the availability of judicial options to mitigate settler abuses gave Indians a stake in the institutions of the colonial state. Second, the progressive erosion of native self-sufficiency in the economic sphere – linked partly to the tribute demands of the colonists, partly to the costs of litigation, and partly to a desire for Spanish-made articles of consumption – made indigenous people increasingly dependent on the Spanish-controlled labor market and system of mercantile exchange. And third, the opportunities for advancement offered to a minority of indigenous people created or exacerbated divisions within Andean society and made it unlikely that

[1] Steve Stern, *Peru's Indian Peoples and the Challenge of Spanish Conquest: Huamanga to 1640* (Madison: University of Wisconsin Press, 1982), chapters 5–8, here p. 187.

native Andeans would oppose their exploitation as a group. Historians of colonial Mexico have documented a similar relationship between indigenous people and the Spanish imperial state.[2]

In the decades following Mexican independence, native citizens provided support for both the liberal and the conservative sides of the national political divide. Which side they chose depended in part on how they assessed the colonial past. For example, popular liberalism thrived among indigenous people in present-day Guerrero, who associated independence with the end of monopolistic credit relationships, racially specific taxes, and abuses committed by royal officials.[3] During the 1830–1831 War of the South, in which Guerrero's peasantry rose in arms against the anti-liberal Bustamante administration, rebel leaders like Juan Alvarez established direct links between that conflict and the earlier Independence struggle: the rebels' objective, in Alvarez's words, was "to sustain the sovereignty of the States, force the reinstatement of the deputies and prevent the federal system from being changed for the central [system], which is how the agents of the European tyrant desire to subjugate us."[4] For Alvarez and his followers, conservative or centralist positions thus remained associated with the tyranny of Spanish rule. Scholars have documented similar political perceptions in other parts of the country with large indigenous populations, including areas of Veracruz, Puebla, Morelos, San Luis Potosí, and the Yucatán.[5]

In Oaxaca's Mixteca Baja, however, a region directly adjacent to Guerrero, indigenous people remained attached to colonial-era social and religious institutions long into the republican period. Here, as Benjamin

2   The first of these mechanisms receives particular emphasis in Woodrow Borah, *Justice by Insurance: The General Indian Court of Colonial Mexico and the Legal Aides of the Half-Real* (Berkeley: University of California Press, 1983); Susan Kellogg, *Law and the Transformation of Aztec Culture, 1500–1700* (Norman and London: University of Oklahoma Press, 1995); and Brian Owensby, *Empire of Law and Indian Justice in Colonial Mexico* (Stanford: Stanford University Press, 2008); the second mechanism is emphasized in Jeremy Baskes, *Indians, Merchants, and Markets: A Reinterpretation of the Repartimiento and Spanish Indian Economic Relations in Late Colonial Oaxaca, Mexico, 1750–1821* (Stanford: Stanford University Press, 2000); and John Chance, *Conquest of the Sierra: Spaniards and Indians in Colonial Oaxaca* (Norman: University of Oklahoma Press, 1989), 103–121, 146–148; and the third mechanism is discussed in Yanna Yannakakis, *The Art of Being In-Between: Native Intermediaries, Indian Identity, and Local Rule in Colonial Oaxaca* (Durham, NC: Duke University Press, 2008); and Kevin Terraciano, *The Mixtecs of Colonial Oaxaca: Ñudzahui History, Sixteenth through Eighteenth Centuries* (Stanford: Stanford University Press, 2001).

3   Peter Guardino, *Peasants, Politics, and the Formation of Mexico's National State: Guerrero, 1800–1857* (Stanford: Stanford University Press, 1996).

4   Quoted in Guardino, *Peasants, Politics,* 134.

5   Florencia Mallon, *Peasant and Nation: The Making of Postcolonial Mexico and Peru* (Berkeley: University of California Press, 1996); Michael Ducey, *A Nation of Villages: Riot and Rebellion in the Mexican Huasteca, 1750–1850* (Tucson: University of Arizona Press, 2004); Mark Saad Saka, *For God and Revolution: Priest, Peasant, and Agrarian Socialism in the Mexican Huasteca* (Albuquerque: University of New Mexico Press, 2013); Terry Rugeley, *Yucatán's Maya Peasantry and the Origins of the Caste War* (Tucson: University of Texas Press, 1996).

Smith has shown in compelling detail, religious brotherhoods, or *cofradías*, blended Catholic dogma with local forms of devotion and were crucial providers of credit and mutual insurance.[6] As a result, indigenous peasants in the Mixteca Baja frequently supported centralist or conservative administrations and resisted liberal curtailments of their religious life. In 1859, after Mexico's liberal government had mandated the break-up of cofradía properties, the town council of Tequixtepec asserted that the expropriation law was "a sacrilege against the Mexican church, an attack on the Catholic cult, and an atrocious blow to Mexican society." The objective of its promoters was nothing less than to "deprive us of all morality, the only bond of fraternity and the base of all society."[7]

These examples might suggest a rather simple polarity: indigenous liberalism was defined by a rejection of the colonial heritage, indigenous conservatism by its acceptance. While not incorrect, such a reading neglects the substantive similarities in native appropriations of liberal and conservative politics. The discovery of such similarities is among the most significant results of the emergent scholarship on popular conservatism in nineteenth-century Mexico. The inhabitants of indigenous towns such as Tequixtepec at first welcomed the federalist system and its promise of protection for local institutions of governance.[8] They switched allegiance to what Smith calls a "selective centralism," and ultimately to the conservative side in the mid-century civil wars, partly to preserve their religious practices and partly to defend themselves against attacks from insurgent federalists who rose in arms in the valleys of Putla and Copala or entered the territory from neighboring Guerrero.[9] But the substance of their concerns was not too different from that of peasants in liberal-dominated areas. They sought control over municipal politics, freedom from interference in religious rituals, and protection of town lands, including those held by religious brotherhoods.

Historians have documented similar manifestations of popular conservatism in at least two other Mexican regions. Between 1856 and 1873, led by the erstwhile bandit Manuel Lozada, indigenous inhabitants of the Sierra del Nayarit,- in what was at the time the northernmost part of the state of Jalisco - fought successive liberal governments. Their support for Lozada ensued in part from the depredations committed by intruding liberal troops, in part from Lozada's interventions in land disputes with mestizos, and in part from the protection he offered, against both the church hierarchy and liberal politicians, to local brotherhoods and religious

---

6   Benjamin Smith, *The Roots of Conservatism in Mexico: Catholicism, Society, and Politics in the Mixteca Baja, 1750–1962* (Albuquerque: University of New Mexico Press, 2012), 36–46, 67–69, 99–103.
7   Quoted in Smith, *Roots of Conservatism*, 120, 149.   8   Smith, *Roots of Conservatism*, 124–131.
9   Smith, *Roots of Conservatism*, 108–116, 131–135.

cults.[10] In the 1847–1849 insurrection in the Sierra Gorda, a mountain region spanning parts of Guanajuato, San Luis Potosí, and Querétaro, the closeness of liberal and conservative positions was even more evident. The same rebellion that, as we saw in the Chapter 3, produced one of the most radical agrarian programs of the nineteenth century was partly led by Tomás Mejía, an indigenous leader who after 1848 moved toward a conservative politics centered on the defense of religion. In the 1850s and 1860s Mejía would become one of the country's most powerful conservative generals, and in 1867 he would die before a firing squad, side by side with the would-be Habsburg emperor Maximilian.[11] But Mejía's conservatism was highly attuned to the grievances of his rural constituency. During the 1847–1849 rebellion, he suspended the payment of taxes and repeatedly overruled government officials in areas under his control, even after he had gone over to the government side, and when, in 1856, Mejía led an uprising against the liberal Ayutla regime, his enemies feared the expropriation of hacienda lands and the beginning of a local caste war.[12] In national political terms, the Sierra Gorda may have become a conservative stronghold, but programmatically speaking, writes James Cypher, "Binary divisions between liberals and conservatives held little lasting significance in the Sierra."[13]

Recent research suggests that whether native Mexicans chose to align themselves with liberal or conservative positions most critically depended on whether local elites represented the protective or the exploitative face of state power. There were regions where, in the late colonial and early republican periods, predatory elites and Church officials put increased pressure on local resources and customs; here, indigenous citizens articulated their politics in a republican idiom that linked authority to the will of the people. And there were regions – typically poorer in resources and less

---

10 Zachary Brittsan, "In Faith or Fear: Fighting with Lozada," PhD dissertation, University of California San Diego (2010), 100–101, 106–108, 120–126 (on depredations committed by liberal troops), 129–133, 148–181 (on Lozada's intervention in land conflicts), and 115–116 and 130 (on his protection of religion). On Lozada's championing of local brotherhoods and cults, see K. Aaron Van Oosterhout, "Confraternities and Popular Conservatism on the Frontier: Mexico's Sierra del Nayarit in the Nineteenth Century," *The Americas* 71/1 (2014).

11 On Tomas Mejía, see Brian Hamnett, "Mexican Conservatives, Clericals, and Soldiers: The 'Traitor' Tomas Mejía through Reform and Empire, 1855–1867," *Bulletin of Latin American Research* 20/2 (2001). On the Sierra Gorda rebellion, see also Leticia Reina, "The Sierra Gorda Peasant Rebellion, 1847–50," in *Riot, Rebellion, and Revolution: Rural Social Conflict in Mexico*, eds. Friedrich Katz, 269–294 (Princeton: Princeton University Press, 1988); and James Cypher, "Reconstituting Community: Local Religion, Political Culture, and Rebellion in Mexico's Sierra Gorda, 1846–1880," PhD Dissertation, Indiana University Bloomington (2007).

12 Cypher, "Reconstituting Community," 44; Hamnett, "Mexican Conservatives," 191–192.

13 Cypher, "Reconstituting Community," 9–10. On the compatibility of liberal and conservative positions in local indigenous politics, see also Matthew O'Hara, *A Flock Divided: Race, Religion, and Politics in Mexico, 1749–1857* (Durham, NC: Duke University Press, 2010), 187–188.

integrated into nationwide commercial networks – where elites and Church officials remained closely involved in economic and cultural life and acted as protectors rather than predators; here, indigenous citizens articulated their politics in a quasi-colonial idiom that linked authority to social prestige and religious piety. In either case, native people struggled to improve their access to rights and protections, and decrease their vulnerability to assaults by powerful outsiders.[14]

If studies of indigenous support for liberal and conservative projects have often reached similar conclusions, that may be in part because they have tended to share a critical conceptual premise: they have treated indigenous towns, or "communities," as their central political actors while relegating the clash between individual interests within such towns to the margins of their analyses.[15] Challenging this premise requires acknowledging the reality it seeks to capture: because native-born residents of indigenous towns were usually given free access to land and other resources, and because they participated, much more than the residents of mestizo towns, in religious and administrative activities, indigenous towns really did have unusually strong collective identities. The first part of this chapter therefore explores the conflicts between indigenous collective identities and a new legal order premised on the primacy of individual rights. Yet it is a mistake to imagine that indigenous Mexicans had no individual interests of their own, or that those interests did not lead them into conflicts with relatives, neighbors, and other fellow residents of their towns; the chapter therefore moves on to examine how indigenous Mexicans received and used liberal property law, not as members of collectives or corporate groups but as individual citizens.

II Colonial Legacies

The legacies of a system of rule that had divided people by race, and assigned the "races" separate rights and even territories, were most strongly felt where natives and mestizos lived closely together, mingling as they went about their daily business. Such was the case in the north-central part of the country. In Guanajuato and San Luis Potosí, indigenous cultures had survived the period of conquest and colonial settlement only in isolated, and generally inaccessible, pockets of terrain like the Sierra Gorda and the tropical Huasteca region. But in most regions of those states, Spanish

---

14 The argument about the defensive nature of indigenous political concerns is perhaps most richly developed in Romana Falcón, *México descalzo: Estrategias de sobrevivencia frente a la modernidad liberal* (Mexico City: Plaza Janés, 2002).

15 Peter Guardino has begun to buck this trend in *The Time of Liberty: Popular Political Culture in Oaxaca, 1750–1850* (Durham, NC: Duke University Press, 2005).

settlers, together with their native allies from Central Mexico, had thoroughly disrupted the polities and societies they had encountered. These settlers had built their towns amidst the sedentary peoples of the northern frontier of the Mesoamerican cultural zone. And they had either displaced or exterminated the nomadic groups who had been living beyond it. Consequently, in the new colonial society, indigenous towns – most of them formed by the Spaniards' Otomí, Tarascan, and Tlaxcalan allies – were kept apart from the Hispanic world only by the institutions of the *república de indios* and not by any great physical distance.[16] Inhabitants of native and mestizo towns jostled each other on the streets, attended the same festivals, exchanged goods, and sued each other in court. Ethnic division was less an expression of distance than a means of managing proximity.

After independence, this proximity made ethnic identities more, not less, relevant than they were elsewhere. In a legal context that had abolished any formal differences between citizens, urgent questions – such as whether mestizo politicians could make indigenous people serve in their civic militias, or indigenous people keep mestizos off of pastures or out of woodlands that had belonged to now-defunct corporate groups – arose in regions where native and non-native geographies had long begun to blend together. In Guanajuato and San Luis Potosí, the legal erasure of ethnic difference ran up against at least three customary social practices: native towns continued (1) to hold land in common and (2) to govern themselves according to colonial-era corporate traditions; and mestizo politicians (3) continued to discriminate against indigenous people on the basis of their alleged racial inferiority. Between these practices and the republican ideal of equality, there developed a constant friction.

(1) **Collective landholding.** Indigenous and mestizo landholding practices in nineteenth-century Mexico shared important features: in both mestizo and indigenous towns, families or individuals owned and worked most available agricultural land; in both mestizo and indigenous towns, municipal governments owned – and regulated residents' use of – surrounding grazing, wood, and shrub lands (*ejidos*); finally, in both mestizo and indigenous towns, municipal governments often owned tracts of agricultural land that was either rented out or – in indigenous towns – worked collectively in order to defray civil and religious expenses.

But there were also substantial differences between mestizo and indigenous landholding practices. Indigenous towns, unlike mestizo ones, possessed distinct territorial identities, expressed in collective founding

16 David Frye, *Indians into Mexicans: History and Identity in a Mexican Town* (Austin: University of Texas Press, 1996), 43–50, 72–77; John Tutino, *Making a New World: Founding Capitalism in the Bajío and Spanish North America* (Durham, NC: Duke University Press, 2011), 77–90.

narratives and the possession of (usually forged) primordial titles; where such titles were absent, indigenous people often believed in their existence, claiming they had been lost in government archives.[17] Furthermore, in indigenous towns secular and religious administrations were closely intertwined. The landholdings of lay religious organizations, while not formally town property, were often regarded as an integral part of a town's patrimony.[18] Collective identities were the foundation of individual claims to landownership: residents of a town that lost land in litigation would lose whatever private claims to the land they had previously possessed. By the same token, residents' private claims to parts of a disputed territory, if based on a history of active usufruct, would strengthen the case for jurisdiction over the land by the town in which they resided. Private and collective forms of landownership were entangled in a way that they were not in mestizo towns.

Because of this entanglement, the abolition of the indigenous *república* after Mexican independence, and its replacement by the inclusive municipality, inevitably raised questions about the status of even privately owned indigenous land.[19] Consider the following conflict. In 1839 an *apoderado* (or attorney invested with formal powers of representation) of an indigenous quarter, known alternatively as Xihue or Pueblo de la Purísima Concepción, addressed the governor of San Luis Potosí with a number of complaints about the government of Ciudad del Maíz – the town in which the quarter was located. While the original representation has been lost, the source of friction appears clearly from the town council's response. The natives of Xihue lived in what the council described as a central section of Ciudad del Maíz: "the inhabitants of that quarter belong to the core of the town and many of them live in the same street that points South from the town square."[20] Others were separated from the central

---

17 Terraciano, *Mixtecs of Colonial Oaxaca*, 58–63; Guardino, *Time of Liberty*, 57–59; Paul Gillingham, *Cuauhtémoc's Bones: Forging National Identity in Modern Mexico* (Albuquerque: University of New Mexico Press, 2011), 162–163.

18 Claudia Guarisco, *Los indios del valle de México y la construcción de una nueva sociabilidad política, 1770–1835* (Zincantepec: El Colegio Mexiquense, 2003), 63–72, 259–262; Guardino, *Time of Liberty*, 51, 233, 243–244; Van Oosterhout, "Confraternities and Popular Conservatism"; Smith, *Roots of Conservatism*, 100–103.

19 A detailed discussion of the problem of dealing with communally owned goods under the republican regime takes up a large part of Andrés Lira's classic study, *Comunidades indígenas frente a la ciudad de México: Tenochtitlan y Tlatelolco, sus pueblos y barrios, 1812–1919* (Zamora: El Colegio de Michoacán, 1983). See also Guardino, *Peasants, Politics*, 103–107; and Norma Angélica Castillo, "Cambios y continuidades entre las repúblicas indias y los ayuntamientos constitucionales de Cholula, 1768–1865," in *Poder y legitimidad en México en el siglo XIX: Instituciones y cultura política*, eds. Brian Connaughton, 137–179 (Mexico City: Universidad Autónoma Metropolitana, 2003).

20 "[L]os vivientes en aquel barrio son del casco de esta Ciudad y muchos de ellos viven en la misma calle que sale de la plaza al rumbo del sur." Vicente Lozano to Sub-Prefecto, Ciudad del Maíz, 10 December 1839, in AHESLP-SGG, Caja 722, Expediente 9.

area only by a gully. Nevertheless, Xihue's inhabitants, as successors of a native *república*, continued to claim control over territory that now fell under the municipality's administrative purview. At stake was the use of uncultivated town lands, some of which the residents of Xihue used as an *ejido* for grazing animals and collecting firewood and building materials. While the town council had begun selling access to the land to non-indigenous residents, the natives regarded the *ejido* as their own and defended it against outsiders. A prospective renter found by the town council eventually cancelled the deal, being "afraid to be harmed by those [native] residents."[21] Through means the report didn't specify, the natives themselves derived an income from the *ejido*, investing the money in public infrastructure – badly, according to the town council. "[W]hat they attempt with their continuous representations," a council member wrote, "is to return to the bad management of the said lands and to avoid having to settle accounts, for if they did it would no doubt turn out that nothing has been done well, and that they have used up everything badly and without the assent of the others."[22] Better, the council argued, to assign the land to the municipal treasury, which would ensure "that its revenues will be exclusively invested for the benefit of the same quarter [of Xihue]."[23]

The fact that the municipal government, though claiming control over the *ejido*, nevertheless promised to use any money derived from it for the exclusive good of the indigenous quarter shows that it was aware of the legal ambiguity of its claim. The government further explained that its officials had "in no way prohibited [the people of Xihue from exercising] the free use of both the land that they have divided [for individual use] and of firewood, maguey, and pasture."[24] It even conceded that the inhabitants of Xihue "have a pre-eminent right to [the lands] by virtue of the donation [by the Spanish Crown] that was made to the first people who formed a congregation," from whom the natives were descended.[25] Thus, the

---

21 "[T]emeroso de recibir perjuicios de aquellos vecinos." Vicente Lozano to Sub-Prefecto, Ciudad del Maíz, 10 December 1839, in AHESLP-SGG, Caja 722, Expediente 9.

22 "[Y] lo que intentan con sus continuas representaciones es volver al mal manejo de dichas tierras y eximirse de rendir cuentas, como que por este medio resultaría sin duda alguna que nadie ha obrado bien, y que todo lo han consumido en sí muy mal y sin conocimiento de los demás." José Reyes Lara to Sub-Prefecto, Ciudad del Maíz, 5 December 1839, in AHESLP-SGG, Caja 722, Expediente 9.

23 "[Q]ue sus productos se invirtiesen exclusivamente en beneficio del mismo barrio." José Reyes Lara to Sub-Prefecto, Ciudad del Maíz, 5 December 1839, in AHESLP-SGG, Caja 722, Expediente 9.

24 "En nada se les ha prohibido el libre uso así de las tierras que tienen repartidas, como dela leña, maguey, y pastos." José Reyes Lara to Sub-Prefecto, Ciudad del Maíz, 5 December 1839, in AHESLP-SGG, Caja 722, Expediente 9.

25 "[T]ienen un derecho trascendental a ellas por la donación que se los hizo a los primeros que formaron congregación." José Reyes Lara to Sub-Prefecto, Ciudad del Maíz, 5 December 1839, in AHESLP-SGG, Caja 722, Expediente 9.

council acknowledged the existence of a strong legal bond between the native quarter and the *ejido* lands in question.

The conflict between the town council of Ciudad del Maíz and the indigenous quarter of Xihue illustrates the difficulties that were involved in attempts to reconcile indigenous land claims with a liberal property regime. Xihue's property rights were historically incontestable, yet they belonged to a collectivity with no remaining legal status. Should these rights be transferred to the ethnically mixed – but mestizo-controlled – municipality as the successor organization of the indigenous *república*? Or did they reside, not in a political body, but in the individuals who had composed the collectivity, so that the descendants of Xihue's indigenous founders retained exclusive ownership rights to the *ejido*? The town council of Ciudad del Maíz was torn between these approaches: it acknowledged the force of the latter insofar as it allowed indigenous residents to use *ejido* lands without payment, but acted according to the dictates of the former in as far as it attempted to make the same lands accessible to non-indigenous users. Other town councils were more uncompromising. For example, the government of Xilitla in 1827 decided to introduce a rental fee, to be paid in kind at harvest time, for the cultivation of mountain lands that native residents considered to be theirs and had previously been able to work without charge.[26]

Most indigenous people, when confronted with claims on their lands by the mestizo governments of ethnically mixed municipalities, refused to relinquish their own. The native villagers of San Nicolás de los Montes in 1841 continued to insist on their sovereign right to charge outsiders rent for the use of their lands, even though they were now a dependency of Ciudad del Maíz with no legal or administrative competency.[27] In other cases indigenous people began to articulate their rights in ways appropriate to the biases of the new era. In 1827, the authors of a letter bearing five signatures, but claiming to speak on behalf of all native residents of Santa María del Río, protested against the attempt of Santa María's town council to charge them rent for the use of lands "for the defense of whose boundaries [in the past] we have borne great expenses."[28] To this land the town's native inhabitants had a right on account of the original donation to their fore-fathers and "the services that all our *república* has rendered not only under the old [colonial] government but also under the present [post-colonial] one." They had always fulfilled their fiscal obligations and, two of the

---

26 Plan de Arbitrios, San Agustín de Xilitla, 16 March 1827, in AHESLP-SGG, Caja 81, Expediente 3, Fojas 22–24.

27 Letter from San Nicolás de los Montes, 25 September 1841, and Vicente Lozano to Secretario del Superior Gobierno, Ciudad del Maíz, 3 August 1841, in AHESLP-SGG, Caja 773, Expediente 7.

28 "[P]or cuya defensa de sus linderos hemos sufrido crecidos gastos." Undated letter in AHESLP-SGG, Caja 102, Expediente 8, Fojas 22–24.

authors wrote in a second letter, would continue to pay their municipal taxes "as long as they are in the right proportion and according to the law."[29] The petitioners thus named at least three reasons for considering the lands to be native property: the native community had been given legal title to the land; it had always defended it against encroachments; and it had fulfilled its obligations to the rights-granting institutions of first the colonial and then the republican state. "[I]t pains us," the authors wrote, "to be made into renters of our properties ... and it disturbs us even more that [these properties] are rented out to strangers."[30]

The complainants were not content with defending their claims on historical grounds. In a second letter, two of the indigenous leaders, José Dionicio Cadena and Juan Bautista Hernández, mobilized explicitly liberal principles in defense of their rights. They referred to the post-independence era as

the beautiful days of prosperity and glory that have succeeded the terrible [error?] of despotism, when a new and grand order of events prepared by the centuries has changed and ennobled the political stage of our peoples, when the wisest and most philanthropic laws restored to the indigenous people the precious rights owed to the dignity of man, removing them from the most shameful abjection and pupilage to which they had been reduced by the barbarous legislation of the former and ferocious conquerors.[31]

By refusing to recognize native property rights, the town council was continuing the work of the Spanish oppressors. Without embracing liberalism, Cadena and Hernández further argued, Santa María del Río would not be able to advance in civilization. In order to achieve the "enlargement and progress of this worthy state," it was necessary "to promote and cultivate the population, one of the principal means [for this objective] being the

29 "[L]os servicios que toda nuestra república tiene hechos no solo en el gobierno antiguo mas también en el actual." And "[C]on tal que sea con la debida proporción y con arreglo a las leyes." Undated letter and José Dionicio Cadena and Juan Bautista Hernández to Gobernador, San Luis Potosí, 27 August 1827, both in AHESLP-SGG, Caja 102, Expediente 8, Fojas 22–24, 26–28.

30 "[N]os es muy sensible constituirnos arrendatarios de nuestras propiedades ... y mucho más gravoso es para nosotros que se les arrienden a otros extraños." Undated letter in AHESLP-SGG, Caja 102, Expediente 8, Fojas 22–24.

31 "[L]os bellos días de prosperidad y de gloria que sucedieron al horroroso [error?] del despotismo: cuando un nuevo y grande orden de acontecimientos que habían preparado los siglos cambiaron y ennoblecieron la escena política de nuestros Pueblos: cuando los más sabias y filantrópicas leyes restituyeron a los indígenas, los preciosos derechos debidos a la dignidad del hombre, sacándolos de la más vergonzosa abyección y pupilaje a que los había reducido la bárbara legislación de sus antiguos y feroces conquistadores." José Dionicio Cadena and Juan Bautista Hernández to Gobernador, San Luis Potosí, 27 August 1827, in AHESLP-SGG, Caja 102, Expediente 8, Fojas 26–28.

enfranchisement and protection of property owners."[32] They described the municipality's decision to charge rent for indigenous land use as an attack on the town's native inhabitants, considered not as a corporate collective but as individual landholders. And they based their defense of these rights on a specifically republican law, passed earlier in the year by San Luis Potosí's state congress, according to which "the lands belonging to the communities of indigenous towns will remain the property of their current possessors, whatever their mode of acquisition."[33]

Cadena and Hernández's request failed to sway the state governor, who sided with the town council's alternative account of the situation. The council denied that it was charging Santa María's indigenous residents a fee for the use of their agricultural land, arguing instead that the lands at stake in the conflict were not individually owned parcels but the former *ejido*s of the native community. As wealthy descendants of a line of *caciques*, Cadena and Hernández had long monopolized these *ejido*s for their large herds of cattle, "with harm to the mass of *hijos del pueblo* [native inhabitants of the town] who dare not take a single *tuna* [cactus fruit] from the land."[34] In claiming the lands for the municipality, the town's concern was not to lay hands on indigenous property but, on the contrary, to break up a monopoly of which the town's native majority had been the principal victim. Although it is hard to assess the balance of truth between these accounts, the version of the town council seems the more credible: the vast majority of Santa María del Río's population was indeed indigenous and, under the democratic franchise of the 1820s, would hardly have elected a town council hostile to their interests, especially if they had found an alternative in politically savvy native leaders like Cadena and Hernández.[35]

Beyond the glimpse it offers into the ambiguities of indigenous politics, the disagreement between town council and indigenous leaders is notable

32 "[L]a experiencia de todos los Pueblos", "el engrandecimiento y progreso de este recomendable Estado"; and "promover y fomentar la población, siendo uno de los principales medios las franquicias y protección de los propietarios." José Dionicio Cadena and Juan Bautista Hernández to Gobernador, San Luis Potosí, 27 August 1827, in AHESLP-SGG, Caja 102, Expediente 8, Fojas 26–28.

33 "Que las tierras pertenecientes a las comunidades de los pueblos indígenas, permanecerán en propiedad de sus actuales poseedores sea cual fuere el modo de su adquisición." Quoted in undated letter in AHESLP-SGG, Caja 102, Expediente 8, Fojas 22–24. For a copy of the earlier law, see "Plan de fondos Municipales para los Pueblos," 17 January 1823, in AHESLP-SGG, Caja 102, Expediente 8, Fojas 35–36.

34 "[C]on perjuicio de la muchedumbre de hijos del pueblo que no osan tomar una tuna en las tierras." Rafael [Hernon?] to Gobernador, Santa María del Río, 9 October 1827, in AHESLP-SGG, Caja 102, Expediente 8, Fojas 39–45.

35 Cadena and Hernández give the number of indigenous inhabitants of Santa María del Río as more than 8,100, and we know that around 1820 the town had a total population of 8,815 people. Juan Carlos Sánchez Montiel, "Nuevos ayuntamientos y reformulación de la representación política: San Luis Potosí, 1812–1835," PhD dissertation, Instituto de Investigaciones Doctor José María Luis Mora (2007), 242.

for occurring on a factual rather than an ideological level. The town council did not challenge the idea that individual owners should be confirmed in their titles to communal indigenous lands, and the complainants accepted that the status of such lands had to be reconceived under a liberal property paradigm. In this instance, liberalism had become, in William Roseberry's sense, a "language of contention" – a shared idiom in which to debate the shape and quality of Santa María's transition from a corporate to a republican property regime.[36] In post-colonial Mexico, the territoriality of indigenous politics was a large but not, after all, an insuperable obstacle to the ascendancy of a culture of legal equality.

(2) **Corporate traditions.** One of the reasons the mestizo town council and native complainants of Santa María del Río could agree at least on the legal principles by which their conflict should be assessed was that the complainants, though speaking in the name of the town's indigenous population, made no attempt to represent that population as a collective legal or political actor. They did not presume to belong to a corporate body with special jurisdictional claims. But in many indigenous towns the protective structures of corporate governance remained in force long into the national period. Most commonly, indigenous towns paid lip service to the formal requirements of constitutional government while carrying on at least some of the political routines of a previous era. In mestizo-dominated areas like Guanajuato and San Luis Potosí, this usually meant that these towns acknowledged their formal dependence on non-indigenous municipal seats while jealously guarding their right to appoint local authorities: *alcaldes auxiliares* under the federal, *jueces de paz* under the centralist constitutions.[37] At the very least, they demanded to be given authorities who belonged "to their own class," that is, who were

---

36 William Roseberry, "Hegemony and the Language of Contention," in *Everyday Forms of State Formation: Revolution and the Negotiation of Rule in Modern Mexico*, eds. Gilbert Joseph and Daniel Nugent, 355–366 (Durham, NC: Duke University Press, 1994).

37 This phenomenon has been well studied in other parts of the country. See Guardino, *Peasants, Politics,* 91–92; Ducey, *Nation of Villages,* 97–102; Guarisco, *Los indios,* 222–232; Antonio Escobar Ohmstede, "Los ayuntamientos y los pueblos indios en la Sierra Huasteca: Conflictos entre nuevos y viejos actores, 1812–1840," in *La Reindianización de América, siglo XIX*, ed. Leticia Reina, 294–316 (Mexico City: Siglo Veintiuno, 1997); Antonio Escobar Ohmstede, "'Ha variado el sistema gubernativo de los pueblos'. La ciudadanía gaditana y republicana fue ¿imaginaria? para los indígenas. Una visión desde las Huastecas"; José Marcos Medina Bustos, "El gobierno indígena en una zona de frontera durante la transición del Antiguo Régimen al liberalismo. El caso de la provincia de Sonora (1763–1831)"; and Arturo Güémez Pineda, "El establecimiento de corporaciones municipales en Yucatán y los mayas: de la Constitución de Cádiz a la guerra de castas," in *Poder y gobierno local en México, 1808–1857*, eds. María del Carmen Salinas Sandoval, Diana Birrichaga Gardida, and Antonio Escobar Ohmstede, 261–301 (Mexico City: El Colegio Mexiquense, 2011).

indigenous.[38] Even in places where indigenous quarters were contiguous with larger mestizo towns, they often held on to separate administrative structures. For example, indigenous residents of Acámbaro in 1824 were persuaded – or perhaps coerced – to cede half of their fiscal income to the mestizo government of the municipality, by implication remaining in control of the other half.[39] The municipality of San Martín, San Luis Potosí, in 1837 possessed two public buildings: "one that serves as a municipal hall, school, and jail, and one that is a community building of the indigenous people."[40] Indigenous towns and congregations after the end of the colonial period did not lose a sense of the relevance of their ethnic particularity.

Mestizo politicians often alleged that the enduring power of colonial governing structures was a means for indigenous elites to impose themselves on helpless and unwilling commoners.[41] While such allegations were no doubt sometimes true, they overlooked the formative role that colonial traditions played in the lives of indigenous citizens. In the religious sphere, the conservation of festive and spiritual practices, which reform-minded outsiders described as forms of excess, left participants in control over an important site of cultural production.[42] In the political sphere, corporate institutions offered highly evolved mechanisms for allocating power, settling disputes, and coordinating collective action. These two spheres – the religious and the political – were united in the so-called *cargo* system or civil-religious hierarchy: a ladder of service positions, ascending from menial posts like message boy or church keeper to prestigious ones like

38 The indigenous residents of Neutla, belonging to the municipality of Chamacuero, refused to accept an appointed *alcalde auxiliar* "en virtud de que este nombramiento no recayó en sujeto que fuera de su clase" in 1828. Acuerdos de Ayuntamiento, Chamacuero, 21 January 1828, in AGEG-M, Caja 64, Expediente 3. For similar complaints, see "[Expediente] promovido por los naturales del Pueblo de Jarimoro, en pretencion de q. el Ylte. Ayuntamiento de Salvatierra nombre de entre ellos al alcalde aucsiliar, y no á los arrendatarios del mismo Pueblo," 1829, in AGEG-M, Caja 78, Expediente 7. "[Expediente] promovido por los CC. Antonio Soriano y Manuel Chavez vecinos del Barrio de S.n Juan Bautsita de Salvatierra, contra el C. Antonio Aldazava Alcalde ausiliar del mismo Bárrio," 1830, in AGEG-M, Caja 82, Expediente 1; and José María [Otahegui?] to Gobernador, San Luis Potosí, 13 October 1840, in AHESLP-SGG, Caja 753, Expediente 1.
39 Cayetano Chávez to Gobernador, Acámbaro, 1 September 1824, in AGEG-M, Caja 4, Expediente 1, Fojas 13–14.
40 "[U]no que sirve de sala consistorial, escuela y cárcel, y otro de comunidad de los indígenas." "Plan Estadistico que manifiesta la situacion de la Villa de San Martin Hac.das y Ranchos de su Comprehencion," in AHESLP-SGG, Caja 646, Expediente 3.
41 See, e.g., Francisco de Santiago Quintanilla to Gobernador, Celaya, 26 August 1824, in AGEG-M, Caja 1, Expediente 2, Fojas 20–22; and José Gervacio Días to Gobernador, Tierra Nueva, 27 August 1826, in AHESLP-SGG, Caja 55, Expediente 12.
42 For such descriptions, see, e.g., "Espediente promovido p.r el alc.e auxiliar del Pueblo de Emenquaro," 1827, in AGEG-M, Caja 43, Expediente 1. Actas de Ayuntamiento, Apaseo, 19 June 1829, in AGEG-M, Caja 78, Expediente 2.

alderman or officer in a brotherhood, through which all men were expected to rise in the course of their lifetimes.[43] The *cargo* system constituted indigenous towns as political and spiritual enterprises that were animated entirely by the participation of their inhabitants.

The preservation of corporate government structures increased the capacity of native Mexicans for legal and political action. In some municipalities, indigenous residents took advantage of their capacity for collective voice to demand freedom from service in the civic militias. Local policing was one of the functions indigenous towns filled through the *cargo* system, and they resented having to send additional men to help keep the peace in mestizo municipal seats. In 1827, the *alcalde auxiliar* of San Pedro, part of the municipality of Salamanca, wrote to Guanajuato's governor "in the name of the *común de naturales* [indigenous commoners]" of the village. He reported

that by order of that illustrious town council of Salamanca] we have begun to be listed in the civic militia of that town, without consideration that of all the people living in the said village [of San Pedro] the smaller part are wretched day workers, and the bigger part are employed in the spinning of cotton, which mechanical exercise at most earns them one *real* per day, and therefore they are always living in the utmost misery.[44]

In this petition the *alcalde auxiliar* not only represented San Pedro's indigenous inhabitants as a colonial-era corporate body but articulated assumptions about indigenous wretchedness that were themselves of colonial origin. In 1839, the *alcalde auxiliar* of Nativitas, an indigenous village in the same municipality, approached the governor with a petition that took this rhetorical strategy as far as it would go. Nativitas "is in its totality composed of miserable, stupid, and fearful indigenous people," afraid that if they entered the militia "they will not be given enough time to exercise their lowly trades as spinners and weavers of blankets by which they maintain their families."[45] Salamanca's town government in both cases

43 For a discussion of the voluminous anthropological literature on the *cargo* system and its relationship to the historical evidence, see John Chance and William Taylor, "Cofradías and cargos: An historical perspective on the Mesoamerican civil-religious hierarchy," *American Ethnologist* 12/1 (1985), 1–26. While Chance and Taylor posit an integration of civil and religious positions only during the nineteenth century, Guardino in his work on Oaxaca has found evidence for their entwinement already in the late-colonial period. Guardino, *Time of Liberty*, 51.

44 "[Q]ue por disposición de aquel Ilustre Ayuntamiento se nos ha comenzado a listar en la milicia cívica de dicha villa, sin considerar el que, cuantos habitantes existen en el referido pueblo, son unos infelices jornaleros la menor parte, y la mayor, empleados en el hilado de algodón, cuyo mecánico ejercicio solo les produce cuando más un real diario, y por tanto, siempre están constituidos en la mayor miseria." José María de la Merced Pérez to Gobernador, no place or date, in AGEG-J, Caja 9, Expediente 10.

45 "[S]e compone en su totalidad de indígenas miserables estúpidos y medrosos" ; and "[N]o se les deje el tiempo necesario para ejercer sus mezquinos oficios de hilanderos y tejedores de mantas con

denied the depictions of indigenous poverty and convinced the governor not to grant the petitions.[46]

Although sometimes portraying themselves as wretched, poor, and even stupid, in concrete resource conflicts indigenous groups acted not as helpless subjects but as assertive and combative legal players. They carried on long and costly lawsuits by collecting contributions that, according to their detractors, were not always voluntary.[47] Outside the courtroom, they sometimes took action without awaiting legal sanction. Inhabitants of the indigenous village of Tocuaro, for example, according to Acámbaro's town council in 1827 cut off the head town's water supply, as they wanted the water for their fields and tanning industry. The town council further accused the natives of regularly rustling cattle from a hacienda with which they were engaged in a boundary dispute.[48] Indigenous inhabitants of Jerécuaro in 1828 diverted a stream whose water, according to a report from the mestizo mayor, had "since immemorial times" been used by an adjacent hacienda. Upon finding their channels destroyed, the natives staged a riot that would have ended badly had the mayor not been able to reason with them. The mayor saw little he could do to prevent a repeat of the occurrence:

In a town like this, which is only made up of indigenous people little accustomed to subordination because my predecessors left them abandoned to their extravagances, who hear that they are free and [therefore] believe they are free to do whatever they please, it is very possible that these scenes and other worse ones will repeat themselves, considering that here there are no means available to contain them by force.[49]

The mayor further reported that Jerécuaro's civic militia was largely indigenous, as was the town's second *alcalde*, who had taken a leading role in the riot by ringing the church bells.

que mantienen a sus familias." Olayo González to Gobernador, no place or date, in AGEG-G, Caja 71, Expediente 11.

46 See the governor's responses in the margins of Marcelo Estrada to Gobernador, Salamanca, 11 June 1827, in AGEG-M, Caja 46, Expediente 4; and Rodrigo García de León to Gobernador, Salamanca, 31 January 1839, in AGEG-G, Caja 71, Expediente 11.

47 Actas de Ayuntamiento, San Luis de la Paz, 13 December 1827, in AGEG-M, Caja 40, Expediente 15; José Urbano Rodríguez to Secretario de Gobierno, San Miguel de Allende, 22 February 1850, and letter from José Dolores Ramírez, 18 February 1850, both in AGEG-M, Caja 177, Expediente 5.

48 "Espediente promovido p.r el Y. Ayuntam.to de Acambaro contra el alcalde auxiliar y otros vecinos del barrio de Tocuaro," 1827, in AGEG-J, Caja 8, Expediente 2.

49 "En un pueblo como en este que no mas se compone de indígenas poco acostumbrados a la subordinación porque mis antecesores los han abandonado a sus extravagancias: que oyen que son libres y que creen serlo para hacer cuanto les da la gana; es muy posible que se repitan estas escenas y otras muy peores si se considera que no hay aquí arbitrio alguno para contenerlos con la fuerza." José Almón to Gobernador, Jerécuaro, 13 February 1828, in AGEG-M, Caja 65, Expediente 2.

Collective militancy was a tactic with strong precedents in the colonial era. But demands for self-government and resource control could also be made in liberal terms. When, in 1826, a mestizo resident of Huaje attacked the towns' officials for being indigenous and therefore incapable of governing, one of them replied: "this injurious expression is very much against the system of government by which we are ruled, for that makes all citizens of whichever class equal."[50] In 1837, a group of petitioners from Coecillo, Guanajuato, made a similar argument when asking the governor to install a local justice of the peace in their town, thus making it less dependent on the court in nearby León:

How could it not be burdensome to the Indians of Coecillo to sue and be sued, for quantities of less than one hundred pesos, before the first *alcaldes* of León? Whatever somebody's role in the cases, they leave their town to go to judges who know them little or not at all; who cannot give them a quick hearing because of the occupations with which they are surrounded etc.[51]

This argument was similar to the ones we encountered from mestizo residents of Cerritos and San Pedro de los Pozos, seeking independence from the municipal administrations of Guadalcázar and San Luis de la Paz. But there was an important difference. The writers from Coecillo called attention not to the physical but to the social and cognitive distance between the "Indians" of their town and the judges of León, described as both too busy and too unknowing to effectively fulfill their duties. As an indigenous town, Coecillo had been shaped by a particular history and, in turn, merited a particular kind of consideration. It was the purpose of government, wrote the petitioners,

to give representation and stimulus (to elevate themselves) to men, families, and towns, especially and markedly to those [towns] that, like ours, because it is composed of Indians, urgently needs a higher degree of heat in order to leave behind the cold degradation in which it was and still is as a consequence of the government of the kings of Spain.[52]

---

50 "[E]sta expresión injuriosa es muy contraria al sistema de Gobierno que nos rige, pues este nos hace a todos iguales a todo ciudadano de cualquiera clase." Letter from Huaje, 10 March 1826, in AGEG-J, Caja 6, Expediente 9.

51 "¿Cómo no les ha de ser gravoso a los Indios del Coecillo, demandar y ser demandado, por cantidades de menos de cien pesos ante los primeros alcaldes de León? Cualquier papel que hagan en sus contenciones, salen de su pueblo para acudir a jueces, que los conocen muy poco o nada; que no pueden prestarles pronto oído por las ocupaciones, que los rodean etc." Undated letter, Coecillo, in AGEG-M, Caja 141, Expediente 1.

52 "[D]ar representación y estímulos (para elevarse) a los hombres, a las familias y a los pueblos, especial y señaladamente a los que como el nuestro, que por componerse de Indios, necesita urgentemente un grado más de calor para salir del frío abatimiento en que estuvo y aún está a consecuencia del gobierno de los Reyes de España." Undated letter, Coecillo, in AGEG-M, Caja 141, Expediente 1.

By acknowledging the perseverance of a distinct indigenous identity as a problematic legacy of the colonial period, the writers echoed a concern often voiced by mestizo elites. Unlike mestizo elites, they attributed this perseverance not to a deficiency in indigenous social organization but to their continued subjection to paternalistic administrative structures. Recognizing indigenous difference, they argued, should be a motive "not for enfolding us in a dependency so intimate and disadvantageous to us but for broadening our path and our capacities." Only in that way would they reach "the same [cultural] level as the other citizens, so that the notable signs of different races of men on the same soil will finally disappear."[53] According to these writers, native self-government was not a throwback to the colonial period but a necessary learning experience in a process of dynamic adjustment.

By suggesting – however politely and obliquely – that mestizo-dominated town councils were guilty of at least some discriminatory practices, the letter writers from Coecillo challenged the idea that only indigenous people remained stuck in the past. Indigenous leaders from Rioverde, San Luis Potosí, made this critique more bluntly. Petitioning the governor to annul a fraudulent municipal election, they charged that the elected government was in the pockets of a local hacendado, whom it had already favored with access to the town's water supply.[54] "Ah! Who gives away the rights of a town?" the complainants asked. "Can it be that the rights and resources of a state aren't safe?"[55] They went on to argue that by conspiring against the rights of a town the fraudulent faction, and the hacendado who paid them, had also conspired "against the entire nation, against the government, against the sweat and work of so much care taken by this Honorable Congress [of San Luis Potosí]," whose laws were "so rational as well as sacred since they were born from the divine laws for the common benefit of the republic."[56] San Luis Potosí's council of state

---

53 "[N]o para que se nos estreche por una dependencia tan íntima y desventajosa para nosotros; sino para ampliarnos el camino y facilidades"; and"[el] nivel de los otros ciudadanos hasta lograr que desaparezcan las remarcables señales de distintas razas de hombres en un mismo suelo." Undated letter, Coecillo, in AGEG-M, Caja 141, Expediente 1.

54 The conflict was probably an instance of a long history of disputes over access to water between Rioverde and the nearby Hacienda de Jabalí, as described in Claudia Serafina Berumen Félix, "La legislación decimonónica y la Media Luna (San Luis Potosí)," in *Agua y tierra en México, siglos XIX y XX*, vol. 1, eds. Antonio Escobar Ohmstede, Martín Sánchez Rodríguez, and Ana Ma. Gutiérrez Rivas, 103–123 (Zamora: El Colegio de Michoacán, 2008).

55 "¡A! ¿Quién regala los derechos de un pueblo? ¿No estarán seguros los derechos, y ramos de un estado?" Letter from Rioverde in AHESLP-SGG, Caja 29, Expediente 8, Fojas 4–6.

56 "[C]ontra entera Nación, contra el Gobierno contra el sudor y trabajo de tanto desvelo de este Honorable Congreso" ; and "[T]an racionales, como sagradas, por ser nacidas de las divinas, para el beneficio común de la República." Letter from Rioverde in AHESLP-SGG, Caja 29, Expediente 8, Fojas 4–6.

dismissed the petition out of hand as animated by a "spirit of discord."[57] But according to the complainants, Rioverde's indigenous residents were aligned with the law while the hacendado and his backers menaced the republican enterprise. They presented themselves as a collectivity, and petitioned the governor as indigenous people, not because they wanted to recover any sort of corporate privilege but because the republican system, violated by the hacendado who had rigged Rioverde's municipal elections, had been unable to protect their rights to a fair share of the town's water supply. They alleged that in response to their public-spirited concern, the hacendado had boasted "that none of the Indians of the town will [ever] govern."[58]

According to indigenous leaders from Coecillo and Rioverde, a collective indigenous identity endured because discriminatory practices against indigenous people also endured. It was mestizo politicians, and not indigenous groups, who were guilty of carrying aspects of the colonial past into the republican era. Ignoring the persistence of indigenous corporatism, theirs, too, was an involved and partial perspective. But it was a perspective that proved that the categories of liberal thought could be used to excoriate the traditionalism of the mestizo as well as the indigenous side in Mexico's post-colonial interethnic relations.

(3) **Mestizo racism**. José María Mora, often regarded as the most representative liberal thinker of Mexico's post-independence period, exemplifies the ambivalence intellectuals of his generation felt about the country's indigenous population.[59] Mora explained the existence of racial divisions in Mexican society as the effect of the oppression and segregationist policies of the colonial era. On that account, race had no enduring reality outside of social practices and institutions; if Mexico's indigenous people remained recognizably different, that was only because one could not "repair in a few days the evils caused by the abjection of many centuries."[60] But at other times Mora spoke of race as a highly determinate category:

It appears to have been confirmed by the observations of the most impartial philosophers that each known caste of men has an organization which is peculiar to itself, is in accord with its character, and has an influence not only on the color of

---

57　"[E]spíritu de discordia." Council of State, San Luis Potosí, 19 January 1826, in AHESLP-SGG, Caja 29, Expediente 8, Fojas 28–29.

58　"[Q]ue no gobernará ninguno de los Indios del pueblo." Letter from Rioverde in AHESLP-SGG, Caja 29, Expediente 8, Fojas 4–6.

59　The best treatment discussing both Mora and his contemporaries remains Charles Hale, *Mexican Liberalism in the Age of Mora, 1821–1853* (New Haven: Yale University Press, 1968), chapter 7. See also Donald Fraser, "La política de desamortización en las comunidades indígenas, 1856–1872," *Historia Mexicana* 21/4 (1972), 618–624; and Anne Staples, "José María Luis Mora," in *Historiografía Mexicana*, vol. 3, "El surgimiento de la historiografía nacional," eds. Virginia Guedea, 241–256 (Mexico City: Universidad Nacional Autónoma de México, 1997), 247–248.

60　"[R]eparar en pocos días los males causados por la abyección de muchos siglos." Mora, *México y sus revoluciones*, vol. 1, 68. On the impact of colonial oppression on the character of Mexico's indigenous people, see pp. 168–184.

its skin but, more importantly, on its physical strength and on its mental and, equally, its industrious faculties.[61]

In various places Mora argued that Mexico's indigenous people were physically and culturally inferior: "backward and degraded remains of the ancient Mexican population" who "in their present state and until they have undergone considerable changes, can never reach the degree of enlightenment, civilization, and culture of Europeans nor maintain themselves as equals in a society formed by both."[62]

Mora's attitude was widely shared not only among Mexico's intellectual classes but among the provincial politicians whose work brought them into regular contact with indigenous people. Mestizo politicians – and sometimes ordinary citizens – who had disagreements with native Mexicans frequently used racist assumptions to frame their accounts of the situation. A government official of Celaya shortly after independence expressed his alarm about the mismanagement of public affairs in indigenous settlements. The inhabitants of those settlements "necessarily find themselves subdued by the insupportable yoke of a total ignorance, even heavier than that which they suffered for the long space of three centuries."[63] In an electoral dispute in 1825, a group of residents of Rincón de Tamayo wrote that their indigenous opponents were "without the exception of a single one, vicious idiots and full of nonsense."[64] In 1843, the town council of León reported that the state of public affairs in two nearby towns would never take a turn for the better as long as those towns were allowed to govern themselves, the reason being "that the majority who compose the said towns are indigenous."[65] Such racist assumptions were widely shared by politicians and other authority figures in all parts of the country.[66]

---

61 "Parece ya averiguado por las observaciones de los filósofos mas imparciales, que cada casta de los hombres conocidos tiene una organización que le es peculiar, esta en consonancia con su carácter, e influye no solo en el color de su piel, sino lo que es mas, en sus fuerzas físicas, en sus facultades mentales, e igualmente en las industriales." José María Luis Mora, *México y sus revoluciones*, ed. Agustin Yañez (Mexico City: Porrúa, 1965), vol. 1, 63–64.

62 Quoted in Hale, *Mexican Liberalism*, 223.

63 "[E]stos pueblos necesariamente se hallan sometidos al insoportable yugo de una total ignorancia, más pesado aun que el que sufrieron por el largo espacio de tres siglos." Francisco de Santiago Quintanilla to Gobernador, Celaya, 26 August 1824, in AGEG-M, Caja 1, Expediente 2, Foja 20.

64 "[S]in excepción de ninguno son unos idiotas viciosos y lleno de nulidades." "Expediente promovido p.r el ciud.o Lazaro Martinez y otros vecins del Rincon de Tamayo," 1825, in AGEG-M, Caja 13, Expediente 2.

65 "[Q]ue la mayoría de que se componen dichos pueblos son de indígenas." Miguel de Obregón to Gobernador, León, 23 June 1843, in AGEG-M, Caja 157, Expediente 3.

66 For quotations of racist statements by officials and authorities in various parts of the country, see, e.g., Guardino, *Time of Liberty*, 239; Antonio Escobar Ohmstede, "Los condueñazgos indígenas en las Huastecas Hidalguense y Veracruzana: ¿Defensa del espacio comunal?"; and Héctor Cuauhtémoc Hernández Silva, "El Valle del Yaqui y los proyectos económicos de las élites regionales de Sonora. 1830–1857," both in *Indio, nación y comunidad*, ed. Escobar Ohmstede, 171–188, and 293–301; Escobar Ohmstede, "'Ha variado el sistema gubernativo de los pueblos,'" 173; José Antonio Serrano Ortega, *Jerarquía territorial y transición política: Guanajuato, 1790–1836* (Mexico City: El Colegio de Michoacán, Instituto Mora, 2001), 159; and O'Hara, *A Flock Divided*, 200.

Mestizos deployed racist tropes to link the petty affairs of local politics to overarching elite fears of racial violence and social revolution. Reporting a dispute with the government of the indigenous town of Xichú, an army commander described Xichú's civic militia as composed of "those natives so inclined to subversion," adding that the residents of various adjacent settlements had been officers "in the epoch of [18]10" whom "I knew to behave as lovers of the revolution."[67] For some politicians, memories of past violence were enough to suggest an eternal enmity between the races – even if the natives had been victims rather than perpetrators of atrocities. In 1831, when Mexico was ruled by its first openly reactionary government, the *jefe político* of San Miguel de Allende proposed to abolish the municipal government of Xichú on the grounds of its inhabitants' long-standing enmity to their superiors. "[A]ccording to reports," he wrote,

> the indigenous residents of the said town of Xichú are and have been so vicious that in the last century, while the Spanish Government ruled, by order of the Viceroy and on the grounds of the excesses that were there committed, it was decreed to completely destroy that population.

He added that while he didn't know why the decision had not been carried out, he did know that "the case is true."[68] Thus, for the *jefe político* a vague and questionable report of the planned eradication of a large human settlement constituted proof, not of the oppressive tendency of the colonial government but of the eternal perversity of that settlement's native inhabitants.[69] The town council of Xilitla, San Luis Potosí, also evoked a past event to draw conclusions about the character of a group of indigenous adversaries. Apparently responding to a complaint lodged against them before the governor, members of the council first alleged that the complainants – "enemies of good order, disturbers of the peace" – represented only a small number of the town's indigenous residents.[70] The council then explained that the complainants were attacking a local religious cult, and that their attack on religion was a direct continuation of

---

67 "[A]quellos naturales tan inclinados a la subversión" ; "la época de 10" ; and "yo les conocí una conducta amante de la revolución." José María Rangel to Gobernador, San Luis de la Paz, 30 June 1824, in AGEG-M, Caja 3, Expediente 9, Fojas 8, 13.

68 "[S]on y han sido tan perversos los indígenas del repetido pueblo de Xichú según noticias, que en el siglo pasado que rigió el Gobierno Español por orden del Virrey y por los excesos que allí se cometían, decretó se destruyese completamente aquella población" ; "el caso es cierto." "Espediente instruido á efecto de suprimir el Ylte. Ayuntam.to del Pueblo de Xichú," in AGEG-M, 1831, Caja 107, Expediente 13.

69 When talking of the planned destruction of Xichú, the *jefe político* may have had in mind the resettlement, rather than the massacre, of its inhabitants.

70 "[E]nemigos del buen orden, perturbadores de la paz." Letter from Xilitla, 6 February 1827, in AHESLP-SGG, Caja 81, Expediente 3, Fojas 9–10.

the destruction of the old town of Xilitla, when priests, church, and town together were sacrilegiously and inhumanly finished off more than one and a half centuries ago, which horrible attack was perpetrated by the ancestors and race of those who we infer moved this representation [against us], who are known in these parts as the Mecos Otomís.[71]

Although in this instance the natives rather than the Spaniards were remembered as perpetrators of racial violence, once again a distant memory provided an interpretive frame for understanding the nature and motives of the writers' present-day opponents.

Mestizos referencing past racial violence expressed a kind of cognitive nostalgia. Colonial Mexico was remembered as a place where social fissures had been simpler than they were now. The politics of race had also been easy: the natives must be kept in their place lest they go on a rampage. And while some politicians invoked racial tropes in order to defend anti-democratic measures, racist sentimentality could also serve openly illiberal ends, such as the reintroduction of corporal punishment. In 1825 the mayor of San José del Valle, who may himself have been indigenous, wrote of the residents of his town

that these [citizens] are carried away by evil, for when [in the colonial period] in order to subordinate them they were given lashes, some order was observed; but now it is impossible, for they don't at all respect the authority that the sovereignty of the Nation has conferred on me.[72]

The mayor of Coscatlan similarly proposed "to carry out the punishment of lashes on the rustic Indians of this town." Even though he realized that current laws "abominated" that form of correction, he argued that "for these incautious Indians it is not harmful, for to them it is the manna [*sic*] that they value most and that they prefer to being put in jail "[73] Even if we disregard the hyperbole, the mayor's statement remains an authoritarian

---

71   "[L]a destrucción del pueblo antiguo de Xilitla acabando sacrílega e inhumanamente con sacerdotes, iglesia y pueblo todo, hace un siglo y más de medio, cuyo horrible atentado se perpetró por los antepasados, y raza de los que inferimos movieron esta representación, que son conocidos por estos países por los Mecos Otomís." Letter from Xilitla, 6 February 1827, in AHESLP-SGG, Caja 81, Expediente 3, Fojas 9–10.

72   "[Q]ue éstos son llevados por mal, pues cuando para subordinarlos se les daba de cuartazos, entonces sí, se observaba algún orden; pero ahora es imposible, pues nada respectan la autoridad que la soberanía de la Nación me ha conferido." Buenaventura González to Gobernador, San José del Valle, 10 November 1825, in AHESLP-SGG, Caja 28, Expediente 10.

73   "[V]erificar el castigo de azotes a los indígenas rústicos de este pueblo"; and "[E]n estos incautos indígenas no es nocivo, pues para ellos es el maná que aprecian más, y no las demás prisiones." José Solorzano to Gobernador, Coscatlan, 27 October 1826, in AHESLP-SGG, Caja 59, Expediente 16, Foja 10.

fantasy: native Mexicans at times expressed a particular loathing, never a preference, for the indignity of corporal punishment.[74]

Politicians in hacienda-dominated areas sometimes used racist tropes to argue for the reinstatement of coercive labor regimes. In 1824, the mayor of San Miguel el Grande (later San Miguel de Allende) used fears of racial violence as a justification for arresting an indigenous man who "was seducing the Indians of [a farm or estate] not to work."[75] In 1822, the town council of Tancanhuitz, in San Luis Potosí's Huasteca region, proposed to congregate indigenous families into a stable settlement and to coerce all loafers to work on local farms. This measure was required, the council explained, because in their current state "these Indians are useful neither to themselves nor to the population of the towns," and making them work would lift them out of "the dark state in which they live."[76] Using a similar line of reasoning, an official on the town council of Aquismón in 1830 defended the practice of forcing natives to work on nearby haciendas as an "immemorial custom" without which the natives would give way to their natural laziness. He explained that if republican law had been followed in his municipality, and forced labor abolished in practice,

agriculture would, to say it like this, have been proscribed; and robbery, idleness, and drunkenness, and all vices, would have settled themselves on its rubble, for those miserable [Indians] even with the stimulus of hunger do not dedicate themselves to their fields and live in eternal misery.[77]

In spite of such protestations, by 1835 the abolition of forced labor had finally become effective in the area. In that year, the government of Ciudad del Valle, citing a report from Aquismón, wrote that local agriculture had been sunk into depression by the natives' refusal to work and by the legal impossibility of coercing them. For this state of affairs, the town council directly

74   On indigenous complaints about being whipped, often at the hands of their own authorities, see
     "Expediente Civil instruido en la congregacion de Tanchanaco en averiguacion de los ecsesos de
     que han acusado al Juez de Paz de dho. puno, los Yndigenas dela misma congregacion," 1840, in
     AHESLP-SGG, Caja 732, no expediente; Legajo 49, Expediente 16, in AHJ, Teposcolula,
     Criminal, 1810; Legajo 49, Expediente 18, in AHJ, Teposcolula, Criminal, 1810; Legajo 52,
     Expediente 9, in AHJ, Teposcolula, Criminal, 1823; Legajo 52, Expediente 11, in AHJ,
     Teposcolula, Criminal, 1823; and Legajo 59, Expediente 46, in AHJ, Teposcolula, Civil, no
     date. For a similar complaint from the state of Veracruz, see Ducey, *Nation of Villages*, 100.

75   "[Q]uien andaba seduciendo a los Indios de la nominada labor para que no trabajaran." Ignacio Cruces
     to Gobernador, San Miguel el Grande, 25 June 1824, in AGEG-M, Caja 5, Expediente 1, Foja 22.

76   "[E]stos Indios ni son útiles para sí mismos, ni para el común de los pueblos"; and "[el] estado de
     obscuridad en que viven." Report from Tancanhuitz, 28 February 1822, photocopy in possession
     of author.

77   "[S]e habría proscrito, por decirlo así, la agricultura; y el robo, y la pereza, y la embriaguez, y todos
     los vicios se habrían sentado sobre los escombros de esta, puesto que aquellos miserables ni con el
     estímulo del hambre se entregan a sus sembrados, y viven en una eterna miseria." Pedro de Acosta
     to Gobernador, Aquismón, 3 July 1830, in AHESLP-SGG, Caja 286, Expediente 6.

blamed the new republican liberty: its report quoted the natives' response to all demands for their labor as a defiant, "I am a free citizen and farmer."[78]

Not all racial thought remained as inflexible as that of self-interested landowners and their political allies, just as not all indigenous politics remained in the thrall of the village corporation. Many mestizo politicians believed in the ideal of racial equality. Many believed, too, that in order for the difference between races to disappear it was necessary first to give the natives their freedom. Thus, the complainant of Aquismón, who requested that indigenous Mexicans be made to work in the hacienda economy for their own good as well as that of the country, was unable to sway San Luis Potosí's political establishment. And the common concern among mestizo politicians to remove old-regime *caciques* or *principales* attests to a belief that indigenous society could be brought in line with republican norms by removing the tangible remnants of its subjection.

An uncompromising racism nevertheless remained at all times a powerful force in provincial life, where it gave voice, from the first years of Mexico's republican enterprise, to a reactionary politics that associated the utopia of legal equality with anarchy and racial violence. This racism shaped the context in which indigenous authorities plotted their own engagement with the post-colonial state. The defense of collective rights and spheres of autonomy – which animated indigenous support for both liberal and conservative political projects – must be seen in this light. Historians have often read that defense as an expression of the traditionalism of native society. They have assumed that indigenous political culture, with its collective landholding, emphasis on community, and putative "localocentrism," was incompatible with a principled liberalism.[79] Such arguments overlook the fact that liberalism presented itself to indigenous Mexicans not

---

78 "Yo soy ciudadano libre y agricultor." Report from Ciudad de Valles, 11 May 1835, in AHESLP-SGG, Caja 530, unnumbered Expediente.

79 Examples of scholarship assuming a strict division between indigenous culture and the liberal norms of equality and individualism are Lira, *Comunidades indígenas*; Rina Ortiz Peralta, "Inexistentes por decreto: Disposiciones legislativas sobre los pueblos de Indios en el siglo XIX. El caso de Hidalgo," in *Indio, nación y comunidad*, ed. Escobar Ohmstede, 153–169; Antonio Annino, "Pueblos, liberalismo, y nación en México," in *Inventando la nación: Iberoamérica. Siglo XIX*, eds. Antonio Annino and François-Xavier Guerra, 399–430 (Mexico City: Fondo de Cultura Económica, 2003); Falcón, *México descalzo*; Antonio Escobar Ohmstede, "Introducción. La 'modernización' de México a través del Liberalismo. Los pueblos indios durante el Juarismo," in *Los pueblos indios en los tiempos de Benito Juárez (1847–1872)*, ed. Antonio Escobar Ohmstede, 9–29 (Mexico City: Universidad Autónoma Metropolitana, 2007) and Raymond Buve, "Pueblos indígenas de Tlaxcala, las leyes liberales juaristas y la guerra de Reforma: una perspectiva desde abajo, 1855–1861," in *Los pueblos indios en los tiempos de Benito Juárez*, ed. Escobar Ohmstede, 91–121. The term "localocentric," used in Eric Wolf's classic article "Closed Corporate Peasant Communities in Mesoamerica and Central Java," *Southwestern Journal of Anthropology* 13/1 (1957), 1–18, has more recently been revived in Eric Van Young, *The Other Rebellion: Popular Violence, Ideology, and the Mexican Struggle for Independence, 1810–1821* (Stanford: Stanford University Press, 2001).

as a reality, but as a profession of intent, and as such, more often than not, was belied by the practical articulation of state power. Indigenous corporate institutions therefore could act as bulwarks against both the illiberal and the liberal tendencies of the outside world. The survival of these institutions can tell us little about the actual reception of liberal values in native society.

III Land Conflicts

Historians of colonial Mexico have long discarded the usefulness of a dichotomy that opposes a European tradition of private to a native Mexican tradition of communal landownership. Indigenous governments, according to James Lockhart, "took a more active role in [land] allocation than their contemporary European counterparts," and in particular made possession of land contingent on requirements of residence, usufruct, and civic and religious service; but subject to these requirements, cultivators could sell, rent, or bequeath their parcels as freely as their European counterparts.[80] Contrary to historical stereotypes, native land disputes were therefore as likely to occur between individuals as between towns or as between towns and surrounding haciendas. And although the number of conflicts between towns and haciendas diminished during the "agrarian decompression" of the early republican period, disputes between the residents of indigenous towns remained commonplace.[81]

In this section, I analyze eighty-one land disputes that native Mexicans brought before district courts in the southern state of Oaxaca between 1796 and 1859. Moving my discussion from the Center-North of the country to Oaxaca allows me to work with judicial records from the colonial period, which in Guanajuato and San Luis Potosí have not been preserved in significant numbers. It also allows me to explore the effect of liberal legal notions on indigenous society in a region where indigenous people were numerically dominant. For while indigenous towns in Guanajuato and San Luis Potosí existed at the margins of a social landscape that was dominated by mestizo towns and haciendas, in Oaxaca this relationship was reversed. Here, indigenous people were by far the majority of the population, and in many areas they were the only population. One reason for this was the inaccessibility of the state's cross-cutting mountain ranges. Another reason was that Spanish settlers

---

80 James Lockhart, *The Nahuas after the Conquest: A Social and Cultural History of the Indians of Central Mexico, Sixteenth through Eighteenth Centuries* (Stanford: Stanford University Press, 1992), 142–176, here 142. See also William Taylor, *Landlord and Peasant in Colonial Oaxaca* (Stanford: Stanford University Press, 1972), 72–78; Terraciano, *Mixtecs of Colonial Oaxaca*, 205–209; and Caterina Pizzigoni, *Life Within: Local Indigenous Society in Mexico's Toluca Valley, 1600–1800* (Stanford: Stanford University Press, 2013), chapter 2.

81 On agrarian decompression, see John Tutino, *From Insurrection to Revolution in Mexico: Social Bases of Agrarian Violence, 1750–1940* (Princeton: Princeton University Press, 1986), chapter 6.

in Oaxaca had encountered a dense and settled indigenous population and had consequently developed – to a much greater extent than in Guanajuato and San Luis Potosí – an economic model that depended on the integrity of native society. In the colonial period, native Oaxacans had been made not only to pay tribute but also to produce the cotton blankets and cochineal dye that had been a chief source of profit for Spanish merchants.[82] Indigenous towns in Oaxaca therefore entered the national period with intact landholdings and confident territorial identities. When their lands did come under pressure, it was most commonly from neighboring indigenous towns and not from Spanish settlers.[83]

The absence in Oaxaca of the routine hostility that characterized interethnic relations in Guanajuato and San Luis Potosí makes it easier to focus attention on the ways in which Mexico's transition to a republican system of government influenced the adjudication of land conflicts occurring within native society. As in mestizo towns, local mayors were the principal dispute adjudicators in indigenous towns. These magistrates appear to have tried most cases verbally, leaving no records for historians to work with. However, in both the colonial and the republican periods non-indigenous district judges were responsible for dealing with complaints brought before them by individuals appealing the rulings of town magistrates. Land disputes therefore generated documents only when people were unsatisfied with the workings of local institutions. No matter how varied the details of particular cases, all land conflicts aired before district courts belonged to a dimension of native legal culture that ran counter to the "localocentric" tendencies diagnosed by some scholars.

In order to bring land conflicts before district judges, indigenous litigants were obliged to keep up with new laws and legal conventions. Most claimants seeking justice outside their towns did so on the technical ground of dispossession (*despojo*). An Oaxacan law from 1825 required plaintiffs in such cases to establish (1) what had been dispossessed, including, in the case of land conflicts, the location and boundaries of the land in question; (2) when and by whom the dispossession had been carried out; and (3) how long the plaintiff had enjoyed usufruct of the disputed good before the act of dispossession.[84] For example, in a complaint from 1843 Alejo Benito Gopar of the settlement de la Olla, in the district of Ejutla, began by describing the boundaries of a plot of rain-fed land he had inherited from his mother.[85] Goptar then presented the judge with three witnesses, all farmers, who answered affirmatively to his

---

82   For details, see Brian Hamnett, *Politics and Trade in Southern Mexico 1750–1821* (Cambridge: Cambridge University Press, 1971); and Baskes, *Indians, Merchants, and Markets*.

83   Philip Dennis, *Intervillage Conflict in Oaxaca* (New Brunswick, N.J.: Rutgers University Press, 1987).

84   "Decreto. Prescribe el modo con que debe procederse en las causas de despojo," 23 September 1826, article 2, in *Colección de leyes, decretos y circulares del estado libre y soberano de Oaxaca* (Oaxaca: Imprenta del Estado en el Instituto, 1851), 300–303.

85   AHJ, Ejutla: Civil, Legajo 2, Expediente 6, 1843.

questions "whether . . . they know and it is true that for more than ten years I have quietly and pacifically, without contradiction by any person, possessed the land in question, cultivating it and receiving its fruits," and "whether they also know that on the eleventh of the current month . . . my nephews José María and Bartolo Ríos, by order of their mother María de la Soledad, went and sowed two *almudes* [or about fifteen liters] of corn in the Western part [of that land] without any kind of permission from me."[86] Based on the information received, Ejutla's district judge confirmed Goptar's right to the land and ordered his sister to pay all costs related to the litigation.

Plaintiffs in district courts needed to show not only that they had the law on their sides but also that they had exhausted local avenues of redress. Some disputants, by describing town officials as venal or inebriated, dramatized the disjuncture between the promise of republican justice and the persistence of old-regime realities in local social and political relations. Antonio Vázquez described his mayor as the puppet of a local power broker who, in turn, "only administers justice to the person who first gets him drunk."[87] Inés María of San Miguel Amatitlan alleged that her nephew, and adversary in a land conflict, "prepared a nice meal (surely in order to buy justice)" for the men of the town council.[88] And Ignacio Martín, of San George Nuchita, gave the following description of how he and his protector [*patrón*] José Justo Vargas were mistreated by the local justice of the peace. When asked by Vargas why Martín's land had been taken from him,

The señor justice of the peace responded that he had ordered it and it would be done, threatening Vargas with jail . . . Then Vargas said again that he thought it worthwhile to talk more about the matter . . ., [but] because the justice of the peace was completely drunk he didn't understand what Vargas said, nor [Vargas] what the justice [said] . . .; then irritated the justice of the peace took the staff that unfortunately he had taken into his fist, with the intention of hitting my *patrón* with it, which he didn't carry out.[89]

86 "Si . . . saben, les consta y es cierto que más de diez años continuos llevo de poseer quieta y pacíficamente, sin contradicción de persona alguna la referida tierra, cultivándola y recibiendo sus frutos"; and "Si también saben y les consta que el día once del corriente mes . . . fueron mis sobrinos José María y Bartolo Ríos de orden de su madre María de la Soledad y sembraron dos almudes de maíz por la parte del poniente sin contar conmigo para nada."

87 "[S]olo le ministra la justicia al que primero lo embriaga." Legajo 36, Expediente 19, in AHJ, Huajuapam, Civil, 1857.

88 "[L]es hizo un comelitón [*sic*] (seguramente para ganar la justicia)." Legajo 10, Expediente 2, in AHJ, Huajuapam, Civil, 1836.

89 "El señor juez de paz contestó, que él lo había mandado y eso se había de hacer, amenazando a Vargas con la cárcel . . . Entonces Vargas reprodujo que le parecía escusado hablar más sobre el particular . . . como por que estando el señor juez de paz citado sumamente briago, ni el entendía lo que Vargas le decía, ni éste lo que el juez . . .; entonces irritado el juez de paz tomó el bastón que desgraciadamente acaba de empuñar, con intención de pegarle con él a mi patrón, lo que no verificó." Legajo 11, Expediente 8, in AHJ, Huajuapam, Civil, 1837.

The justice's behavior, Martín argued, presented an affront to republican law: "I . . . see that here [in the district court of Huajuapam] the laws are respected, whereas in my unfortunate town they are not respected, nor in this day are others observed than those dictated by liquor." He finally asked, "Is it possible that after our wise legislators have tried so hard to give us the wisest possible laws, for only with those can our *patria* be happy, in my wretched town they are in the hands of a man who, if he deserves the name of man, that is only because nature distinguished his form from that of irrational beings?"[90]

Martín presented his lawsuit as a defense of freedom and property against arbitrary power in a way that strongly echoed elite liberal discourse. Most complainants, however, referenced liberal ideals implicitly, by accusing local magistrates of substantial violations of republican legal procedure: "The said functionary [justice of the peace], carried away by violence, without form or figure of judgment on the basis only of his authority . . . proceeded to put [my adversary] in possession of the mentioned land with contempt of justice and grave harm to myself"; the terrain "was taken from me on the simple order of Don Juan de los Santos and given to my sister-in-law María Sebastiana without any legal form of judgment"; "the mayor of my town Bernardo García, without [previously] having cited me, by his own authority . . . has dispossessed me of the said field"; the mayor took my house land "with no figure of judgment proceeding with violence"; "of which fields I have been dispossessed . . . by the mayor of my town without any judgment or other formed process being practiced for this act"; my adversaries "should not have been put in possession [of the land] without me being beforehand by law and right defeated in the corresponding trial, on account of whose notable omission and the informal manner of proceeding of the mayor Canseco he has inflicted on me a violent dispossession."[91] Women claimed that they found it particularly difficult to be taken seriously by local officials: María Manuela and María Magdalena of San

90 "Veo igualmente que aquí son respetadas las leyes, en lugar que en mi desgraciado pueblo, ni se respetan, ni se observan hoy otras que las que dicta el licor"; and "¿Será posible que después de que nuestros sabios legisladores se han afanado tanto en darnos las más sabias leyes, pues que solo por ellas puede ser feliz nuestra patria éstas estén en mi pueblo infeliz en manos de un hombre que si bien pudo merecer el nombre de hombre es porque la naturaleza lo distinguió de la forma de irracional?" Legajo 11, Expediente 8, in AHJ, Huajuapam, Civil, 1837.

91 "Dicho funcionario llevado de la violencia sin forma ni figura de juicio prevalido solamente de su autoridad . . . procedió a ponerla en posesión de la mencionada tierra con menosprecio de la justicia y grave perjuicio mío." Legajo 2, Expediente 31, in AHJ, Ocotlan, Civil, 1838; "[S]e . . . me quitó por el simple dicho de Don Juan de los Santos y se lo entregó a mi hermana política María Sebastiana, sin ninguna forma legal de juicio." Legajo 36, Expediente 19, in AHJ, Huajuapam, Civil, 1857; "el alcalde de mi pueblo Bernardo García sin haberme citado de autoridad propia . . . me ha despojado de dicho terreno." Legajo 5, Expediente 30, in AHJ, Ocotlan, Civil, 1858; "sin figura de justicia procediendo con violencia." Legajo 1, Expediente 12, in AHJ, Ocotlan, Civil, 1829; "de cuyos terrenos he sido despojado . . . por el alcalde de mi pueblo, sin que para este acto practicara juicio u otro auto formado." Legajo 5, Expediente 31, in AHJ, Ocotlan, Civil, 1859; "no debían haber sido metidos en posesión sin ser yo antes por fuero y derecho vencido en el juicio

Table 2: *Indigenous Land Disputes in Late Colonial and Republican Oaxaca*[95]

	Appeals to District Judges' Paternalism	Town Magistrates Accused of Ethical Misconduct	Town Magistrates Accused of Procedural Violations
Late colonial period, 1796–1806 (n = 26)	31 percent (8)	19 percent (5)	4 percent (1)
Republican period, 1820–1859 (n = 55)	7 percent (4)	36 percent (20)	27 percent (15)

George Nuchita finally brought an inheritance claim to the district judge in Huajuapam because they were "miserable women" and "perhaps by reason of that misfortune the justice of our town hasn't heard us."[92] Luisa Apolonia of Zahuatlan claimed that the town mayor had taken a plot she had been given by a now-deceased sibling and redistributed it to her half-brother, "saying to my mentioned brother that it is his for being a man."[93] Although the women did not formulate their arguments in explicitly procedural terms, they did imply that they had been deprived of a proper hearing. Local magistrates who wished to justify their decisions had no choice but to do so on the same grounds on which they had been indicted – to detail the legal steps they had, in fact, taken in their handling of land dispute cases.[94] By appealing to the procedural guarantees encoded in republican law, plaintiffs elevated a formalistic notion of equality over the variety of informal considerations – based either on the special needs or on the social prominence of one of the parties – that had previously influenced the adjudication of land conflicts in indigenous towns.

By the nineteenth century, indigenous Mexicans were not new to airing their disputes in venues away from their home towns. After all, participating in the Spanish legal system was one of the mechanisms that had first allowed Latin America's native populations to gain a stake in the colonial order. However, if we examine the rhetoric and legal reasoning by which native plaintiffs pursued their conflicts, significant differences between the late-colonial and early republican periods become evident. As shown in Table 2,

correspondiente por cuya notable omisión y por la informe manera de proceder del alcalde Canseco éste me ha inferido un violento despojo." Legajo 3, Expediente 14, in AHJ, Ocotlan, Civil, 1849.

92   "[U]nas infelices mujeres"; and "quizá por esta desgracia la justicia de nuestro pueblo no nos ha oído." Legajo 10, Expediente 27, in AHJ, Huajuapam, Civil, 1837.

93   "[D]iciendo a dicho mi hermano le corresponde por ser hombre." Legajo 36, Expediente 16, in AHJ, Huajuapam, Civil, 1857.

94   See the cases in Legajo 10, Expediente 1, in AHJ, Huajuapam, Civil, 1836; and legajo 3, Expediente 17, in AHJ, Ocotlan, Civil, 1851.

95   The 26 colonial conflicts can be found in AHJ, Teposcolula: Criminal, Legajo 47, Expediente 30. 1805; Civil, Legajo 51, Expediente 17, 1796; Legajo 52, Expediente 14, 1797; Legajo 52, Expediente

in twenty-six disputes from the late colonial period, 19 percent of plaintiffs accused their magistrates of ethical misconduct, such as corruption, inebriation in office, or violent and arbitrary behavior, and 4 percent – just one plaintiff – accused a magistrate of having committed a procedural violation. In fifty-five cases from the republican period, the figures, at 36 and 27 percent, were nearly twice as high in the first and almost seven times higher in the second category. By contrast, the percentage of plaintiffs who described themselves as poor wretches and appealed to the district judges' paternal protection was more than four times higher in the colonial than in the republican sample of cases.

All in all, while claimants in the early republican cases were 8.6 times more likely to invoke professional or procedural than paternalistic criteria, the preponderance in the late-colonial cases was, by a factor of 1.3, on the opposite side.[96] These numbers show that among Oaxaca's indigenous population a process of transition, from a legal culture based on deference and the expectation of charity to one based on rights and the demand for

15, 1797; Legajo 52, Expediente 30, 1798; Legajo 52, Expediente 31, 1798; Legajo 52, Expediente 39, 1799; Legajo 52, Expediente 56, 1799; Legajo 53, Expediente 1, 1800; Legajo 53, Expediente 3, 1800; Legajo 53, Expediente 10, 1800; Legajo 53, Expediente 13, 1800; Legajo 53, Expediente 14, 1800; Legajo 53, Expediente 26, 1801; Legajo 53, Expediente 31, 1801; Legajo 53, Expediente 39, no date; Legajo 53, Expediente 40, 1801; Legajo 53, Expediente 43, 1801; Legajo 53, Expediente 44, no date. AHJ, Villa Alta, Civil; Legajo 35, Expediente 16, 1803; Legajo 35, Expediente 24, 1805; Legajo 35, Expediente 26, 1805; Legajo 36, Expediente 10, 1805; Legajo 36, Expediente 18, 1806; Legajo 37, Expediente 1, 1806; Legajo 37, Expediente 17, 1806. The 56 republican conflicts can be found in AHJ, Ejutla: Civil, Legajo 1, Expediente 6, 1827; Legajo 2, Expediente 6, 1843; Legajo 2, Expediente 9, 1843; and Legajo 2, Expediente 20, 1852. AHJ, Huajuapam: Civil, Legajo 4, Expediente 17, 1820; Legajo 6, Expediente 7, 1832; Legajo 7, Expediente 13, 1833; Legajo 8, Expediente 15, 1834; Legajo 9, Expediente 15, 1835; Legajo 9, Expediente 17, 1835; Legajo 10, Expediente 1, 1836; Legajo 10, Expediente 2, 1836; Legajo 10, Expediente 13, 1837; Legajo 10, Expediente 27, 1837; Legajo 11, Expediente 8, 1837; Legajo 15, Expediente 2, 1842; Legajo 25, Expediente 5, 1851; Legajo 35, Expediente 15, 1856; Legajo 36, Expediente 16, 1857; Legajo 36, Expediente 19, 1857; Legajo 37, Expediente 11, 1860; Legajo 37, Expediente 29, 1859; Legajo 37, Expediente 30, 1859; and Legajo 37, Expediente 32, 1859. AHJ, Juxtlahuaca: Civil, Legajo 1838–1888, Expediente 1844. AHJ, Ocotlan: Civil, Legajo 1, Expediente 1, 1826; Legajo 1, Expediente 12, 1829; Legajo 1, Expediente 15, no date; Legajo 1, Expediente 16, 1830; Legajo 2, Expediente 3, 1833; Legajo 2, Expediente 4, 1833; Legajo 2, Expediente 12, 1833; Legajo 2, Expediente 16, 1834; Legajo 2, Expediente 21, 1834; Legajo 2, Expediente 27, 1836; Legajo 2, Expediente 31, 1838; Legajo 3, Expediente 14, 1849; Legajo 3, Expediente 17, 1851; Legajo 5, Expediente 2, 1857; Legajo 5, Expediente 22, 1859; Legajo 5, Expediente 30, 1858; Legajo 5, Expediente 31, 1859; and Legajo 5, Expediente 33, 1859. AHJ, Teposcolula: Civil, Legajo 59, Expediente 46, no date; Legajo 60, Expediente 16, 1822; Legajo 63, Expediente 35, no date; Legajo 66, Expediente 8, 1836; Legajo 66, Expediente 22, 1837; Legajo 67, Expediente 6, no date; Legajo 67, Expediente 11, 1839; Legajo 67, Expediente 12, no date; Legajo 67, Expediente 41, 1840; Legajo 68, Expediente 9, 1841; Legajo 68, Expediente 30, 1841; and Legajo 69, Expediente 20, 1847.

96 The findings for the late-colonial period are supported by Deborah Kanter's analysis of land conflicts in the Toluca Valley at that time. Deborah Kanter, *Hijos del Pueblo: Gender, Family, and Community in Rural Mexico, 1730–1850* (Austin: University of Texas Press, 2008), 29–35.

procedural guarantees, dramatically took off in the early republican period. Plaintiffs denouncing the failure of local magistrates to abide by liberal standards of justice were active agents in this process of transition.

Nowhere in Mexico has the relationship between territorial sovereignty and insular localism seemed stronger than in Oaxaca, where even today society remains divided into a larger number of municipalities than anywhere else in the country and where land conflicts between neighboring towns have provoked cycles of retaliatory violence that sometimes can be traced over centuries.[97] Evidence from indigenous land disputes nevertheless shows that such territorial militancy could coexist with a strong commitment to liberal legal standards and individual property rights. The fact that town residents felt the need to take their disputes to regional district courts of course indicates that these rights were not always respected. But it also indicates that residents were confident enough in the authority of the legal state to expect district-court judgments, and the principles on which they rested, to have some practical force.

Indigenous men and women pressing their claims in district courts rarely framed their demands in openly ideological terms. They did not talk about "liberty," "equality," or "citizenship." In that regard, Ignacio Martín was the exception rather than the rule. Most claimants instead talked about rights: what was rightfully theirs, what had been wrongfully taken. Yet while claimants were not concerned with abstract liberal notions but with gaining or recovering land, they still appealed to such notions, tacitly and by way of contrast, when detailing the abuses of which they thought themselves victims. In the context of local land disputes, liberty and equality meant holding magistrates accountable to certain professional standards and preventing official displays of violence and favoritism. Liberal values, while seldom explicitly invoked, animated the denunciation of specific abuses. They were powerful because they were taken for granted.

What explains the receptiveness of native society to liberal values and procedural standards? Nineteenth-century Mexican elites perceived corporate bodies like indigenous towns strictly as obstacles to the creation of republican institutions. But not all elements of corporate culture worked against the transition to a republican system of justice. Indigenous society had long valued the virtue of hard work that Spanish society disdained and that in the nineteenth century became the ethical foundation for challenges to old-regime entitlement structures. Indeed, in the Spanish imperial world useful work had been the particular function of America's native peoples, as political and spiritual rule had been the role of the colonizers. Spanish authorities had been aware that indigenous labor carried the weight of the imperial enterprise. "Because the Indians are useful to all

97   Guardino, *Time of Liberty*, 229–231; Dennis, *Intervillage Conflict in Oaxaca*.

and for all," reads a royal decree from 1601, "all must watch out for them, and for their conservation, since everything would cease without them."[98] Indigenous subjects engaged in litigation had often contrasted the egotism of their adversaries with the usefulness of their own occupations.[99]

Pride in one's work and its usefulness, sometimes mobilized for political or personal gain, in indigenous towns carried easily into the post-independence era. In the land disputes of the early republican period, plaintiffs often found it important to stress the labor they had invested in the land for whose possession they were fighting. For example, José María Torres of Miltepec wrote of the effort it had taken him to make a disputed terrain productive. "At the cost of indescribable industry and labor I cleared it, freed it from stones, and made it bigger, using stakes to force the river to change direction, and ... I enjoyed it quietly and pacifically until this date."[100] Evocations of work also served a more concrete purpose. In indigenous towns, to own land meant to actively possess it – to clear it, sow it, or, in rare cases, rent it to others.[101] Thus, Alejo Benito Gopar called on witnesses to testify "that for more than ten continuous years I have possessed the said land quietly and peacefully without the contradiction of anybody, cultivating it and receiving its fruits."[102] Without proof of actual usufruct, legal claims of possession were weakened. In 1859, when Pablo Espinosa claimed ownership of a field he had inherited from his father, he lost the lawsuit because he could not prove that he had really been working the land; in fact, one of his own witnesses admitted that Espinosa "did not sow [the land]" at the time it was taken from him.[103] In 1837, in a case for which no outcome is recorded, the justice of the peace of San José Ayuquilla opposed Isidoro de Santiago's ownership rights to a field in part by pointing to de Santiago's neglect of the land in question: "if he was given the land in the year [18]33, why has he only now begun to clear and prepare it?"[104]

Landownership in indigenous towns was tied not only to active usufruct but also to participation in a town's civil-religious hierarchy. In 1856, Francisco Vidal, a resident of the native quarter (*barrio*) of

---

98 Quoted in Owensby, *Empire of Law*, 69.   99   Owensby, *Empire of Law*, 72–73.

100 "A fuerzas de industria y trabajo indecible, lo desmonté, limpié de piedras, y lo hice más grande obligando con estacas a que el rio cambiase su dirección, y ... lo disfruté quieta y pacíficamente hasta esta fecha." Legajo 35, Expediente 15, in AHJ, Huajuapam, Civil, 1856.

101 On this point, see also Margarita Menegus Bornemann, *La Mixteca Baja entre la Revolución y la Reforma: Cacicazgo, territorialidad y gobierno siglos XVIII–XIX* (Oaxaca City: Universidad Autónoma "Benito Juárez" de Oaxaca, 2009), 100, 140.

102 "[Q]ue más de diez años continuos llevo de poseer quieta y pacíficamente, sin contradicción de persona alguna la referida tierra, cultivándola y recibiendo sus frutos." Legajo 2, Expediente 6, in AHJ, Ejutla, Civil, 1843.

103 "[N]o lo sembraba." Legajo 37, Expediente 30, in AHJ, Huajuapam, Civil, 1859.

104 "[S]i desde el año de 33 se le dio aquella tierra ¿porque hasta ahora viene saliendo con el desmonte y limpia de ella?" Legajo 66, Expediente 8, in AHJ, Teposcolula, Civil, 1837.

Huajuapam, was given possession of a field to reward his service in the community. But the land was also claimed by Nazario Rosas, who paid rent to its previous owner – a man whose father, like Vidal, had been given the land in exchange for public services rendered. Vidal responded by arguing that a son had a right to his father's possession only as long as he, too, served in civil or religious community posts. In the present instance, Rosas "doesn't render any service in the *barrio* where he doesn't even have a house, for he spends his time elsewhere and is a vagabond and of bad conduct."[105] In the same *barrio*, Hipolito Casiano Vidal – perhaps a relative of Francisco – went to court to defend his right to a plot that "belongs to him in adjudication for the services he lends."[106] The land had been taken from him by Gervacio Mendoza "for no other motive than that of [Mendoza] being the greatest *principal* [elder or dignitary] of the *barrio*, and those always commit scandals."[107] Confronted with evidence of Vidal's willingness to render community service, Mendoza ceded his own claim to the land.

These examples show that native litigants in land disputes in early-republican Oaxaca shared colonial-era understandings of the relationship between landownership and service obligations. They repudiated particular practices associated with the old regime – favoritism, informal decision-making, arbitrary violence – and appealed to new, liberal notions of procedural justice and professional conduct. But they did not, as did the inhabitants of some haciendas, repudiate an entire value system linked to old-regime forms of territorial control; their challenges to colonial habits emerged from within indigenous towns' corporate structures and not against them. Our examination of native land disputes thus refutes the idea – invented by eighteenth- and nineteenth-century ideologues and too often repeated by later historians – that corporate traditions were inevitably opposed to individual rights in post-colonial Mexico. The two could also be mutually sustaining.

105   "[N]o presta ningunos servicios al barrio en donde no tiene ni casa, pues anda ausente y es un hombre vagamundo y de mala conducta." Legajo 37, Expediente 11, in AHJ, Huajuapam, Civil, 1860.

106   "[L]e pertenece en adjudicación por los servicios que presta." Legajo 37, Expediente 29, in AHJ, Huajuapam, Civil, 1859.

107   "[S]in más motivo que el de ser el primero principal del barrio y éstos cometen a cada pasa arbitrariedades." Legajo 37, Expediente 29, in AHJ, Huajuapam, Civil, 1859.

5

Dictatorship

I Mythologies

In the late 1840s, Mexico's civic militias, which for more than two decades had kept their towns safe and pulled tens of thousands of lower- and middle-class men into a participatory relationship to the post-colonial legal state, were either replaced by National Guard companies or abandoned. During the years of civil war that followed, legal institutions were further weakened by the effects of warfare and by widespread social and agrarian violence. While municipal governments continued to function, de facto power often passed from civilian to military authorities. At the highest level of government, President Benito Juárez used the civil wars to justify restricting the rights of citizens, passing legislation by decree and, in 1865, against the letter of the Constitution and to the consternation of some of his closest collaborators, extending his presidency for a second term.[1] A reconstruction of the sudden shifts and constant adjustments that characterized local power structures during the civil-war era lies outside the scope of this study. Rather, this chapter picks up our analysis of Mexican legal culture at a time when the civil wars were over and - following another decade of political instability - a new regime was being consolidated by the dictator Porfirio Díaz.

Díaz first became president in 1876 by means of a military revolt. While still on the outside of political power, he had demanded an end to the practice of presidential re-election, and he consequently arranged for Manuel González to succeed him four years later. In 1884 Díaz in turn succeeded González and once more occupied the presidency. In 1888 Díaz was re-elected, Congress having allowed for consecutive re-elections by amending the Constitution. In 1890, Congress again amended the Constitution, this time to authorize the possibility of perpetual re-elections. It was in the 1890s, writes Claudio Lomnitz, after Díaz's third

---

1 Daniel Cosío Villegas, *Historia Moderna de México: La República Restaurada: La Vida Política* (Mexico City: Editorial Hermes, 1955), 68; Paul Garner, *Porfirio Díaz* (London: Pearson Education Limited, 2001), 36–43; Richard N. Sinkin, *The Mexican Reform, 1855–1876* (Austin: University of Texas Press, 1979), 80–85.

re-election, that "the idea was formed that Porfirio Díaz was 'The Prince of Peace' and 'The Necessary Man,'" the nation's only hope for preventing a descent into chaos. An "elaborate theater of state," focused on the person of the dictator, became central to the regime's strategy of legitimization.[2] When, in 1911, Díaz was forced into exile by the Mexican Revolution, he was eighty years old, had been seven times re-elected, and, for a majority of Mexicans, represented the mystical center of power of the only form of government they had known since their childhoods.[3]

The personality cult that developed around the figure of Porfirio Díaz in the 1890s has had a major influence on the historiography of his regime, which has taken many of its cues from pro- and anti-Díaz polemics first formulated during the dictator's lifetime.[4] Díaz opponents, and most decisively the militants of the Mexican Liberal Party and their journalistic allies, explored topics and established interpretations that would guide the research of generations of historians. For example, the Yaqui deportations, labor unrest and repression, debt peonage, the usurpation of native lands, the curtailment of civic and political rights, and the unchecked power of department chiefs, or *jefes políticos*, are topics already explored in John Kenneth Turner's classic work of reportage, *Barbarous Mexico*, parts of which began appearing in 1909.[5] Turner and other Díaz opponents forged these elements into a comprehensive story of an all-powerful dictator presiding over a lawless empire. "The President of Mexico is cruel and vindictive," Turner wrote, "and his country has suffered bitterly." Major elements of the anti-Díaz position would reappear in foundational works of the country's professional historiography, which interpreted the Díaz regime as a radical break with Mexico's nineteenth-century liberal tradition.[6] They would also be influential in the work of

2   Claudio Lomnitz, "Preguntas sobre el porfiriato," *Nexos* 451 (July 2015), 18.

3   According to Enrique Krauze, one of the first and most astute analysts of the Díaz cult, Porfirio Díaz believed in the cult himself. Díaz, Krauze writes, "incarnated before himself – and without a shadow of cynicism – a Father of the Patria and, for moments, perhaps, the Patria itself." Enrique Krauze, *Místico de la autoridad: Porfirio Díaz* (Mexico City: Fondo de Cultura Económica, 1987), 82, and more broadly on the Díaz cult 52–87.

4   Useful historiographical essays on the Porfiriato include Thomas Benjamin and Marcial Ocasio-Meléndez, "Organizing the Memory of Modern Mexico: Porfirian Historiography in Perspective, 1880s–1980s," *Hispanic American Historical Review* 64/2 (1984); Garner, *Porfirio Díaz*, chapter 1; and Mauricio Tenorio Trillo and Aurora Gómez Galvarriato, *El Porfiriato* (Mexico City: Centro de Investigación y Docencia Económicas, 2006).

5   John Kenneth Turner, *Barbarous Mexico* (Austin: University of Texas Press, 1969). On Turner's research and political commitments, see Claudio Lomnitz, *The Return of Comrade Ricardo Flores Magón* (New York: Zone Books, 2014), especially chapters 8–10.

6   Leopoldo Zea, *Positivism in Mexico*, trans. Josephine Schulte (Austin: University of Texas Press, 1974); Jesús Reyes Heroles, *El liberalismo mexicano*, 2nd ed., vol. 3, *La integración de las ideas* (Mexico City: Fondo de Cultura Económico, 1974), xv–xviii and 640–644.

social historians who identified the Díaz regime with a process of popular immiseration issuing in major episodes of industrial and agrarian strife and, eventually, in the first of the twentieth century's great social revolutions.[7]

A second historiographical trend views the Porfiriato from the perspective not of its eventual overthrow but, on the contrary, of its astonishing longevity. Elements of this approach go back to the writings of politician-intellectuals who penned apologias for the Díaz regime either during or shortly after his rule. Admitting that the dictator had infringed on freedoms and democratic processes, these writers held that such methods had been the price for creating order in a backward society. As Francisco Bulnes put it with characteristic hyperbole, "To smear and condemn General Díaz for not having done the impossible: being a democratic president in a country of slaves, goes beyond the permissible in stupidity."[8] Justo Sierra more soberly wrote that the Porfirian regime was paradoxically "a personal government that defends and reinforces legality, springing as it does from the national resolution to banish anarchy once and for all."[9] Similar assumptions about the anarchy of Mexico's early national history have guided some recent attempts to interpret the Porfiriato as a species of "authoritarian liberalism," deploying autocratic methods to bring order and even, according to Paul Garner, "legal equality" to a conflict-wracked

---

7 On these points, see Garner, *Porfirio Díaz*, 6–7; and Benjamin and Ocasio-Meléndez, "Organizing the Memory," 344–352, 360–361. Important studies on – broadly speaking – the repressive and anti-popular nature of the Díaz regime include Rodney Anderson, *Outcasts in their Own Land: Mexican Industrial Workers, 1906–1911* (DeKalb: Northern Illinois University Press, 1976); Allen Wells, *Yucatán's Gilded Age: Haciendas, Henequen, and International Harvester, 1860–1915* (Albuquerque: University of New Mexico Press, 1985); John Tutino, *From Insurrection to Revolution in Mexico: Social Bases of Agrarian Violence, 1750–1940* (Princeton: Princeton University Press, 1986), chapter 7; Daniel Nugent, *Spent Cartridges of Revolution: An Anthropological History of Namiquipa, Chihuahua* (Chicago: University of Chicago Press, 1993), chapter 3; Romana Falcón, "Force and the Search for Consent: The Role of the Jefaturas Políticas of Coahuila in National State Formation"; Gilbert Joseph, "Rethinking Mexican Revolutionary Mobilization: Yucatán's Seasons of Upheaval, 1909–1915"; and Daniel Nugent and Ana María Alonso, "Multiple Selective Traditions in Agrarian Reform and Agrarian Struggle: Popular Culture and State Formation in the *Ejido* of Maniquipa, Chihuahua," in *Everyday Forms of State Formation: Revolution and the Negotiation of Rule in Modern Mexico*, eds. Gilbert Joseph and Daniel Nugent, 107–134, 135–169, 209–246 (Durham: Duke University Press, 1994). The classic revindication of the Mexican Revolution as a popular event is Alan Knight, *The Mexican Revolution*, 2 vols. (Cambridge: Cambridge University Press, 1986).

8 "Deturpar y condenar al general Díaz por no haber ejecutado lo imposible: ser Presidente demócrata en país de esclavos, sobrepasa a lo permitido en estupidez." Francisco Bulnes, *El verdadero Díaz y la Revolución* (Mexico City: Editora Nacional, 1967), 24.

9 Justo Sierra, *The Political Evolution of the Mexican People*, trans. Charles Ramsdell (Austin: University of Texas Press, 1969), 366. The most theoretically rigorous formulation by a member of the Porfirian elite of the paradoxical relationship between dictatorship on the one hand and constitutionalism on the other was Emilio Rabasa, *La constitución y la dictadura: Estudio sobre la organización política de México* (Mexico City: Cien de México, 2002 [1912]).

nation.[10] Less controversially, historians have described the Porfiriato as an epoch of unprecedented cultural vitality and material transformation: more than thirty years of stability in which the arts and learning flourished, architectural projects remade the experience of public life, and the construction of railroads pulled local economies out of more than half a century of torpor, allowing the appearance of Mexico's first industrial enterprises and the introduction of modern machinery in many branches of agriculture.[11]

For all their differences, both interpretive trends describe the Díaz regime as a radical point of inflection in Mexico's post-independence history. Díaz appears in one trend as a kind of constitutional outlaw and in the other as the architect of whatever rule of law was compatible with the social reality of his country. But both trends see the Porfiriato as radically different from earlier nineteenth-century regimes; at most, they acknowledge some continuities with the extra-constitutional methods of rule pioneered by the governments of Benito Juárez and Sebastián Lerdo de Tejada during the Restored Republic (1867–1876). This perspective is shared by scholars who stress the interdependence of the illiberal and the constructive dimensions of the Porfirian dictatorship – scholars who show how the emergence of a modern industrial sector relied on the rent-seeking behavior of oligopolistic entrepreneurs, or how a working-class culture of self-improvement drew on the moralizing discourse of mine owners and other elites.[12] As a historical figure who gave his name to an era, Díaz has

---

10 Garner, *Porfirio Díaz*, 31–33, and *British Lions and Mexican Eagles*, 14; Mauricio Tenorio-Trillo, *Mexico at the World's Fairs: Crafting a Modern Nation* (Berkeley: University of California Press, 1996), 29–30, also attributes a belief in the principle of legal equality to Porfirian elites.

11 Studies stressing the cultural vitality – including a fair share of cultural hubris and subversive irony – of the Porfiriato include William Beezley, *Judas at the Jockey Club and Other Episodes of Porfirian Mexico* (Lincoln: University of Nebraska Press, 1987); Tenorio-Trillo, *Mexico at the World's Fairs*; and Steven Bunker, *Creating Mexican Consumer Culture in the Age of Porfirio Díaz* (Albuquerque: University of New Mexico Press, 2012). Studies stressing the transformation of the Porfirian economy – private and public – include Mario Cerutti, *Burguesía, capitales e industria en el norte de México: Monterrey y su ámbito regional (1850–1910)* (Mexico City: Alianza Editorial, 1992); Marcello Carmagnani, *Estado y mercado: La economía pública del liberalismo mexicano, 1850–1911* (Mexico City: Fideicomiso Historia de las Américas, 1994); María Cecilia Zuleta, *De cultivos y contribuciones: Agricultura y Hacienda Estatal en México en la "Época de la Prosperidad". Morelos y Yucatán 1870–1910* (Mexico City: Universidad Autónoma Metropolitana, 2006); Paul Garner, *British Lions and Mexican Eagles: Business, Politics, and Empire in the Career of Weetman Pearson in Mexico, 1889–1919* (Stanford: Stanford University Press, 2011). For an overview of the relevant economic history, see Paolo Rigguzi, "From Globalization to Revolution? The Porfirian Political Economy: An Essay on Issues and Interpretations," *Journal of Latin American Studies* 41/2 (2009).

12 Stephen Haber, *Industry and Underdevelopment: The Industrialization of Mexico, 1890–1940* (Stanford: Stanford University Press, 1989); William French, *A Peaceful and Working People: Manners, Morals, and Class Formation in Northern Mexico* (Albuquerque: University of New Mexico Press, 1996).

come to be associated with a will to progress that – whatever one's judgment of the results – finally brought his country under the sway of modern desires, ironies, and transgressions.

That Mexicans lived through profound transformations during the Porfiriato is surely right. Yet a focus only on the experience of rupture perpetuates an understanding of the period, and of its place in Mexican history, that remains uncomfortably close to the stuff of Porfirian legend. In examining the legal culture of the Díaz regime, this chapter will be attentive to the regime's dependence on existing routines and institutions as well as its innovations; for in order to understand what was new during the Porfiriato, it is necessary to examine the use the regime made of what was old and habitual. The states of Guanajuato and San Luis Potosí, largely unaffected by extreme abuses like forced labor or the wholesale destruction of villages, are ideal settings for exploring the Porfirian legal order in its most unassuming presentation.

Most of this chapter will be concerned with legal culture as it was being practiced in Mexico in the 1890s. I thus pass over the civil-war period, the Restored Republic, and the consolidation of the dictatorship in the 1880s – all periods when local institutions were fluid and caught in the interplay between competing political forces. I also stop short of an analysis of Díaz's final ten years in power, when the dictator grew old and stubborn and his regime, in the minds of even sympathetic observers, lost its political bearings.[13] The 1890s, and in particular the period after 1893, when the last popular challenges to the re-election principle had been put down, were the time when Díaz was at the height of his popularity and his administration at its most commanding. In the 1890s "Díaz's personal dictatorship was not only established but was clearly seen to be established."[14] The image of the Porfiriato as a break with the past was made in those years. Once we situate Porfirian legal culture within the larger context of Mexico's post-colonial history, what remains of that image?

II *Jefes Políticos*

The idea of a rupture between the legal cultures of the Porfiriato and that of the early republic is no doubt most convincingly embodied by the figure of the *jefe político* or political chief. Porfirian *jefes políticos* took on an intermediary function between local and regional administrations that to some extent had earlier been filled by variously named officials – police chiefs, district chiefs,

---

13 The best analysis of the final decade of the Porfiriato is still Alan Knight, *The Mexican Revolution:* vol. 1, *Porfirians, Liberals, and Peasants* (Cambridge: Cambridge University Press, 1986), chapters 1–3.

14 Knight, *Mexican Revolution*, vol. 1, 21.

prefects, subprefects (*jefes de policía, jefes de departamento, prefectos, subprefectos*) –
who had resided in district capitals and who had been tasked with overseeing
the work of municipal governments.[15] The process by which *jefes políticos* rose
from an essentially supervisory function to the political clout for which they
became famous would no doubt repay closer examination. Broadly speaking,
it appears to have been related to the reconfiguration of local power structures, and in particular to municipal governments' loss of control over local
armed forces, during the mid-century civil wars. In the course of the Reform
era and Restored Republic, *jefes políticos* became agents of a muscular inter-
ventionism, on behalf of elite-dominated levels of government, into local
political life.[16]

Whatever the details of their rise to prominence, by the 1890s *jefes
políticos* had acquired notoriety for their corruption and abusive behavior.[17]
In Guanajuato and San Luis Potosí, no less than in other parts of the
country, *jefes políticos* elicited a constant stream of complaints. They were
accused of putting convicts to work in their homes or their businesses; of
usurping the functions of local governments; of privatizing public lands for
their own benefit or that of their allies; of lending support to landowners
who abused workers and tenants; and of using arbitrary imprisonment, and
sometimes deportation, as forms of social control.[18] A distinct category of
complaint concerned the meddling of *jefes políticos* in judicial affairs, explicitly excluded from their otherwise broad realm of competencies. Residents
of Mineral de Peregrina complained that their auxiliary *jefe político* not only
pocketed the fines he imposed for various misdemeanors, or that he made

15 Falcón, "Force and the Search for Consent," 109, 113; José Antonio Serrano Ortega, *Jerarquía
    territorial y transición política: Guanajuato, 1790–1836* (Zamora: El Colegio de Michoacán, 2001),
    197–199.
16 François-Xavier Guerra, *México: Del Antiguo Régimen a la Revolución*, trans. Sergio Fernández Bravo,
    vol. 1 (Mexico City: Fondo de Cultural Económica, 1988), 122–125.
17 Knight, *Mexican Revolution*, vol. 1, 28, and 25–32 for a broader discussion of *jefes políticos*.
18 Heliodoro Galindo et al. to Gobernador, San Diego de la Unión, 17 September 1895, in AGEG-M,
    Caja 242, Expediente 15; Andrés Rivera to Gobernador, Guanajuato, 27 July 1895, in AGEG-M,
    Caja 242, Expediente 1; Romualdo Sánchez to Gobernador, Ocampo, 22 June 1896, in AGEG-M,
    Caja 243, Expediente 12; Report from Guanajuato, 20 September 1900, in AGEG-J, Caja 107,
    Expediente 13; J. Trinidad Gutiérrez and Domingo Prieto to Gobernador, Guanajuato,
    15 March 1899, in AGEG-J, Caja 107, Expediente 14; Martina Leija to Juez de Distrito, in CCJ-
    SLP, Expediente 10/1893; María Gerónima Laredo de Esparza to Juez de Distrito, in CCJ-SLP,
    Expediente 11/1893; Arcadio Alvarez to Juez de Distrito, Venado, 1 November 1893, in CCJ-
    SLP, Expediente 178/1893; and Petition from Apolonio Mireles, San Luis Potosí,
    21 November 1895, in CCJ-SLP, Expediente 196/1895. On discussions of similar abuses perpe-
    trated by *jefes políticos* in other parts of the country, see Falcón, "Force and the Search for Consent";
    Jaime Salazar Adame, "Movimientos populares durante el Porfiriato en el estado de Guerrero
    (1885–1891)," in *Porfirio Díaz frente al descontento popular regional*, eds. Katz and Lloyd, 107–108,
    111, 113–114; and Mark Saad Saka, *For God and Revolution: Priest, Peasant, and Agrarian Socialism
    in the Mexican Huasteca* (Albuquerque: University of New Mexico Press, 2013), 67–69.

unmotivated arrests "of people who are not being scandalous," but also that he personally held court over criminals rather than sending them before the competent judges.[19] The auxiliary chief of the town of Ocampo was accused of "exercising purely judicial functions" and of carrying out the "violation of our individual guarantees."[20] The auxiliary chief of Eménguaro, appointed by the *jefe político* of Salvatierra, was said in his turn to have appointed men "with the character of auxiliary judges and chiefs." In this case the complainants emphasized not the illegality of those appointments but rather their falling on persons "of bad backgrounds and immoderate behavior, motives on account of which the commission of crimes, as a necessary consequence of the diminution of [legal] guarantees, has notoriously risen."[21]

Jefes políticos derived their power from two sources. First, public law in Guanajuato permitted *jefes políticos* to impose fines of up to 100 pesos or prison terms of up to eight days for "the simple offences that some functionary or private person commits against the superior authority, which, by commission, [the *jefes políticos*] exercise in the district."[22] In San Luis Potosí, a similar regulation made *jefes políticos* responsible for imposing fines of up to 50 pesos or prison terms of up to 15 days "for disorderly conduct [*faltas de policía*], or offences committed against [the *jefes políticos'*] authority."[23] Such competencies were ultimately anchored in Mexico's 1857 Constitution, which in its Article 21 permitted public authorities to impose "a fine of up to 500 pesos or reclusion of up to one month" on any citizen.[24] As Francisco Bulnes would point out, this provision, imposing no burden of proof on authorities and granting no right of appeal to their victims, in effect made it possible to imprison Mexican citizens in perpetuity simply by having them freed and immediately rearrested.[25]

Although administrative arrests in Guanajuato and San Luis Potosí were not in practice used in quite so drastic a fashion, *jefes políticos* did on occasion

19 "[A] personas que no dan ningún escándalo." Copy of the report of a visita to Mineral de Peregrina, Guanajuato, 24 October 1896, in AGEG-M, Caja 243, Expediente 7.

20 Roninaldo Sánchez and Demetrio Díaz de León to Gobernador, Ocampo, 22 June 1896, in AGEG-M, Caja 243, Expediente 12.

21 "[D]e malos antecedentes, y de inmoderada conducta, motivos por los cuales han venido en notorio aumento la comisión de delitos como una forzosa consecuencia de la diminución de garantías." Juan Hernández and Ricardo de Aguila to Gobernador, 9 February 1896, in AGEG-M, Caja 243, Expediente 16.

22 "Ley orgánica, para el gobierno y administración interior de las jefaturas políticas del estado," Guanajuato, 15 December 1891, article 19, paragraphs 3 and 4, in AGEG-Leyes y Decretos.

23 "Ley orgánica reglamentaria de la sección IX del título 2.0 de la Constitución del Estado sobre jefes políticos," San Luis Potosí, 2 November 1872, article 11, paragraph 18, in AHESLP-Leyes y Decretos.

24 "[H]asta quinientos pesos de multa, o hasta un mes de reclusión." *Constitución Política de la República Mexicana de 1857*, article 21.

25 Bulnes, *El verdadero Díaz*, 53–54.

make use of their powers to impose limited fines or prison terms.[26] For example, when a woman accused a *jefe político* from the city of San Luis Potosí of jailing her husband, Román Puente, without giving a motive, the *jefe político* explained that "a fine of 25 pesos was imposed on Puente for disorderly conduct, and not having paid it I imposed an arrest of 15 days on him."[27] And when Pudenciano Mendoza of Venado, San Luis Potosí, accused the town's *jefe político* of fining him in a matter that had already gone to trial – and that therefore lay outside the *jefe político*'s competencies – the *jefe político* countered that he had fined Mendoza because "first disregarding my directive, he then comes at me with arrogant words, challenging my authority."[28]

As important as their ability to fine and imprison was the de facto power *jefes políticos* derived from their control of local police forces. After the Three Year War and War of the French Intervention, town governments in Guanajuato had reconstituted their police forces using small contingents of the National Guard and – a new development in all but the biggest towns – paid gendarmes, often recruited from among demobilized soldiers. As in the 1820s, neighborhood watches of respectable citizens also patrolled the towns at night.[29] By the 1890s, most National Guard companies had been disbanded, and corps of professional gendarmes had become the main providers of urban policing.[30] Commanding these forces

26 Jefe Político to Juez de Distrito, Venado, in CCJ-SLP, Expediente 41/1890; Jefe Político to Juez de Distrito, San Luis Potosí, [11?] January 1893, in CCJ-SLP, Expediente 4/1893; Jefe Político to Juez de Distrito, San Luis Potosí, 6 September 1895, in CCJ-SLP, Expediente 158/1895; and Jefe Político to Juez de Letras, Guadalcázar, 24 February 1898, in CCJ-SLP, Expediente 41/1898.

27 "[A] Puente le fue impuesto una multa de $25 por faltas a la policía y no habiéndola satisfecho se le impuso un arresto de quince días." Jefe Político to Juez de Distrito, San Luis Potosí, 6 September 1895, in CCJ-SLP, Expediente 158/1895. For another case in which a *jefe político* invoked his power to fine or arrest, see Jefe Político to Juez de Distrito, Venado, in CCJ-SLP, Expediente 41/1890. For a discussion of contemporary understandings of the term "policía," see Ariel Rodríguez Kuri, *La experiencia olvidada: El Ayuntamiento de México: política y gobierno, 1876–1912* (Mexico City: El Colegio de México, 1996), 33–37.

28 "[D]esoyendo primero mi llamado viene después con términos altaneros y faltando a mi autoridad." Jefe Político to Juez de Distrito, Venado, in CCJ-SLP, Expediente 41/1890.

29 Memorias de administración, Acámbaro, 1868, and Tarandacuao, December 1868, in AGEG-M, Caja 218, Expediente 2; Apaseo, 1868, in AGEG-M, Caja 218, Expediente 3; Moroleón, 29 December 1868, in AGEG-M, Caja 219, Expediente 1; and Pénjamo, 15 March 1869, in AGEG-M, Caja 219, Expediente 9. The conversion of soldiers into local police forces followed a national directive: "Manda poner en asamblea una parte del ejército y que otra se emplee en formar los cuerpos de policía de los Estados," 30 July 1867, in Dublán and Lozano, *Legislación Mexicana*, vol. 10, 31–32.

30 On the disbanding of the National Guard, see Garner, *Porfirio Díaz*, 111–112. On the new, professional gendarmes, see Corte de caja, Santa María del Río, 28 February 1893, in AHESLP-SGG, Caja 1893.1, Expediente 10; Presupuesto Municipal, San Ciro, 14 April 1893, in AHESLP-SGG, Caja 1893.11, Expediente 5; Corte de Caja, Salinas, 30 September 1893, in AHESLP-SGG, Caja 1893.18, Expediente 1; Estado de administración pública, San Felipe, 28 February 1895, in

were the *jefes políticos*, whose duties, according to Guanajuato's state regulations, included the arrest of criminals and vagabonds; the suppression of "any scandalous meetings that take place in the cafés, taverns, or other public houses"; the search of private residences and private documents anytime that a "summary and administrative inquiry or some other proof" convinced them of "the necessity, urgency, or convenience of the procedure"; and the taking of whichever other measures were needed for "[m]aking sure that in general public order and tranquility will not be disturbed."[31] *Jefes políticos* thus commanded most local armed forces and held broad discretionary powers about how to employ them – a dramatic departure from the early republican period, when civic militias had been commanded by elected officers and town governments.

Perhaps the best way to appreciate the magnitude of the powers that came to be concentrated in the office of the *jefe político* is to consider what people could do to protect themselves against these officials' abuses. A relatively new but, by the 1890s, already routinely used means of protection was the legal recourse of the *amparo*. A kind of protective judicial intervention, the *amparo* had its origins in the colonial period, at which time it was rooted in the authority of the viceroy and his representatives to protect petitioners against legal transgressions committed by public officials and powerful private actors.[32] Most commonly, indigenous subjects would bring *amparo* petitions against landowners or local magistrates before the General Indian Court in Mexico City, whose judges often responded by ordering a halt to the offensive action until a judicial authority could decide on its legality.[33] In the national period, liberal jurists and politicians resurrected the *amparo* as an instrument for protecting Mexican citizens against violations of their constitutional rights. Following years of debate and aborted experimentation, the *amparo* was enshrined in the 1857 Constitution and, after the French

---

AGEG-M, Caja 240, Expediente 17; "Noticia que manifiesta el número de fuerza," Romita, 23 April 1894, in AGEG-M, Caja 241, Expediente 10; Estado de administración pública, Dolores Hidalgo, 6 June 1895, in AGEG-M, Caja 242, Expediente 6.

31 "[U]na averiguación sumaria y administrativa u otra prueba"; "la necesidad, urgencia o conveniencia del procedimiento"; and "Cuidar de que en lo general no se perturben la tranquilidad y orden públicos." "Ley orgánica, para el gobierno y administración interior de las jefaturas políticas del estado," Guanajuato, 15 December 1891, article 12, article 14 paragraphs 6, 7, article 17 paragraphs 3, 6, 13, and article 19 paragraph 9, in AGEG-Leyes y Decretos. While the regulations governing *jefaturas políticas* in San Luis Potosí were slightly less specific, they also put the command of all local police forces in the hands of the *jefes políticos*. "Ley orgánica reglamentaria de la sección IX del título 2.0 de la Constitución del Estado sobre jefes políticos," San Luis Potosí, 2 November 1872, articles 10 and 11 paragraph 16, in AHESLP-Leyes y Decretos.

32 Andrés Lira González, *El amparo colonial y el juicio de amparo mexicano: Antecedentes novohispanos del juicio de amparo* (Mexico City: Fondo de Cultura Económica, 1972).

33 Brian Owensby, *Empire of Law and Indian Justice in Colonial Mexico* (Stanford: Stanford University Press, 2008), chapter 3.

Intervention (1862–1867), made into an effective legal instrument by a succession of regulatory laws. By the 1890s, it had become a common mechanism of defense against all manner of official abuses.[34]

Amparo trials had a simple format: the aggrieved party would petition a district judge, describing the nature of the grievance and specifying which constitutional articles had been violated; the judge would forward the complaint to the offending authority and request a formal position statement; finally, based on these accounts as well as any other evidence he felt it necessary to collect, the judge would decide to either support or reject the petition of *amparo*. At this point, successful petitioners could expect relief from whichever rights violation they had petitioned against – for example, to be set free if they had been wrongfully jailed – since the judge's decision had the form of a binding order and non-compliance on the part of local officials was rare. All *amparo* cases were eventually reviewed by the Supreme Court in Mexico City, which sometimes overturned the lower judges' decisions.

For those with the means to pursue it, an *amparo* suit could be an effective means for gaining judicial protection. It was surely a costly means: while I have found no information about the price legal experts charged for writing *amparo* petitions, there can be little doubt that for most Mexicans it would have represented a substantial investment. Just as important, it was a means with a limited scope of action. *Amparo* judges could stop particular abuses but not remove abusive officials or award damages to victims. The *amparo* could therefore not curb *jefes políticos'* transgressive behavior except on a case-by-case basis. Nor did it curb their ability, even within particular cases, to harm and intimidate citizens. That many *jefes políticos* were unbothered by unfriendly *amparo* decisions is shown by the high number of cases in which, once their victims had filed the initial petition, they simply ignored the judge's request to justify their actions. For example, in 1892 a *jefe político* in the city of San Luis Potosí ordered that Petra Badillo remain in jail – she had been arrested by a policeman who she claimed was a former lover – without giving any motive; in 1893, a *jefe político* exiled Zeferino Esparza to Tampico because he suspected him of having committed a robbery; and in the same year, a *jefe político* had Arcadio Álvarez arrested in Mineral de Charcas, according to Álvarez without telling him why.[35] In all of these

---

34 Raúl Pérez Johnston, "Juicio de amparo," in *Diccionario histórico judicial de México*, ed. Suprema Corte de Justicia, 901–910 (Mexico City: Dirección General de Casas de la Cultura Jurídica y Estudios Históricos, 2010), 901–907; Timothy James, *Mexico's Supreme Court: Between Liberal Individual and Revolutionary Social Rights, 1867–1934* (Albuquerque: University of New Mexico Press, 2013), chapter 1.

35 Petra Badillo to Juez de Distrito, San Luis Potosí, 1 August 1892, in CCJ-SLP, Expediente 180/1892; María Gerónima Laredo de Esparza to Juez de Distrito, no place or date, in CCJ-SLP, Expediente 11/1893; and Arcadio Álvarez to Juez de Letras, Venado, 1 November 1893, in CCJ-SLP, Expediente 178/1893.

cases, the prisoners petitioned for judicial protection, and in all of them the *jefes políticos* failed to respond to the petitioners' complaints when ordered to do so by district judges. The petitioners thus won their *amparo* suits, and were allowed to return to their ordinary lives, while bearing the expense for their legal petitions and whatever loss in work, well-being, and reputation their days in jail or exile had cost them.

Mexican citizens who wished to gain relief not just from particular administrative transgressions but from the routine abusiveness of *jefes políticos* also had the option to file complaints with their governors. The governments of Guanajuato and San Luis Potosí would investigate such complaints by demanding a response from the offending *jefe político*. If they judged that a *jefe político* had committed an offence, they would decide whether the offence was a light one, in which case they would "ordain whatever seems to [them] just and convenient," or whether it constituted a significant breach of common or administrative law, in which case they would suspend the *jefe político* from his office and remit him to the appropriate judge.[36] The corrections that governments could impose on *jefes políticos* by executive order consisted, in Guanajuato, of a fine of up to 500 pesos and the payment of damages to any injured party, and, in San Luis Potosí, of a fine of up to 500 pesos and a work suspension of up to three months.[37] The major implication of these rules was that citizens could not by themselves file judicial charges against *jefes políticos*; it was up to their governors to decide whether a complaint would be examined in court.

Lodging a complaint about a *jefe político* was a risky step: having appointed the *jefes* in the first place, governors might be bound to them not only by feelings of class and professional solidarity but also by ties of friendship or patronage. Once cleared of their charges, *jefes políticos* could easily exact revenge on maligners. It was nevertheless a step that residents of Guanajuato – though not, it seems, of San Luis Potosí – were sometimes willing to take. Let us examine the details, and the handling by Guanajuato's governor, of four such complaints.

(1) On 7 November 1894 María Jesús Martínez and her brother, Antonio Morales, were arrested by a group of gendarmes while descending to Valle

---

36 "[P]rovidenciará lo que le parezca justo y conveniente." "Ley orgánica, para el gobierno y administración interior de las jefaturas políticas del estado," Guanajuato, 15 December 1891, articles 32 and 33, in AGEG-Leyes y Decretos; and "Ley orgánica reglamentaria de la sección IX del título 2.o de la Constitución del Estado sobre jefes políticos," San Luis Potosí, 2 November 1872, articles 15 and 16, in AHESLP-Leyes y Decretos.

37 "Ley orgánica, para el gobierno y administración interior de las jefaturas políticas del estado," Guanajuato, 15 December 1891, article 35, in AGEG-Leyes y Decretos; and "Ley orgánica reglamentaria de la sección IX del título 2.o de la Constitución del Estado sobre jefes políticos," San Luis Potosí, 2 November 1872, article 18, in AHESLP-Leyes y Decretos.

de Santiago from a hillside suburb. Having spent a night in the woman's prison, Martínez was brought before *jefe político* Francisco Franco, who told her "that my brother had been apprehended because his name was not Antonio but Jesús, whom the law was pursuing as a bandit." Martínez could only answer "that my brother did not have that name [of Jesús] but that of Antonio, as could be confirmed by persons who knew him, as it could be confirmed that the Jesús for whom they were looking was a different person than my brother." The *jefe político* ordered Martínez returned to her cell, where she was kept for the next seventeen days "without knowing for which offence."[38]

In the evening of the day that Martínez was interviewed by the *jefe político*, her brother was taken from his prison, led by an escort in the direction of Puruándiro, "and in between Ranchos de los Reyes and los Magueyes they shot him dead, without it being known where they buried him, only that his hat is kept in the court of Puruándiro."[39] Martínez believed that her brother had been killed for having entertained "illicit relations" with the wife of one of the gendarmes. Her demand, however, concerned not the punishment of the *jefe político* or the murderous policemen but the clearing of her brother's name and persecution of the bandit for whom he had been mistaken:

Our family having been hurt by such a terrible proceeding, and desiring to justify ourselves, I denounce the event which I have related so that in the inquiry that will be made in this regard it may be clarified who is the person of Jesús Morales; with the understanding that if I receive an order for his apprehension, within three days the true Jesús Morales who was being pursued will be brought before the law.[40]

She and her family, she wrote, were "satisfied about the moral respectability" of her brother. They decided to file a complaint in order to rescue his reputation.[41]

38 "[Q]ue ese nombre no tenía mi hermano, sino el de Antonio, como se lo acreditaría con personas que lo conocían, lo mismo que le acreditaría que el Jesús a quien buscaban era otra persona distinta de mi hermano"; and "sin saber por qué delito." María Jesús Martínez to Gobernador, Valle de Santiago, 30 October 1895, in AGEG-J, Caja 104, Expediente 20.

39 "[Y] en medio de los Ranchos de los Reyes y los Magueyes, lo fusilaron, sin saber el punto donde lo sepultaron, y solo sí, que su sombrero se halla en el juzgado de Puruándiro." María Jesús Martínez to Gobernador, Valle de Santiago, 30 October 1895, in AGEG-J, Caja 104, Expediente 20.

40 "Lastimada nuestra familia por procedimiento tan terrible, y deseando justificarnos, denuncio el hecho que he referido para que en la averiguación que al efecto se haga, se esclarezca quien es la persona de Jesús Morales; bajo el concepto de que si se me da una orden para su aprehensión, al tercer día al más tardar, será presentado ante la justicia al verdadero Jesús Morales que perseguía." María Jesús Martínez to Gobernador, Valle de Santiago, 30 October 1895, in AGEG-J, Caja 104, Expediente 20.

41 "[S]atisfecha de su hombría de bien"; María Jesús Martínez to Gobernador, Valle de Santiago, 30 October 1895, in AGEG-J, Caja 104, Expediente 20.

Asked to respond to Martínez's accusation, the *jefe político* reported that Martínez had been registered as an inmate in the woman's prison not in the period she had mentioned but about two weeks later, and then not for seventeen but for eighteen days. The cause of her imprisonment had been her behavior as a "scandalous drunk."[42] This meant, the *jefe político* pointed out, that Martínez had lied about both the cause and the length of her internment. About Martínez's brother, Antonio Morales, the *jefe político* interviewed the police commandant and his subalterns, who all "declared that they had not participated in the apprehension of an individual carrying that name and surname."[43] Martínez had also claimed that her brother had been interned not in the town jail but in the cavalry barracks, yet in none of the daily reports from the chief cavalry officer was there any mention of a prisoner brought to or taken from that building. The *jefe político* deduced that Martínez had lied a second time. Guanajuato's governor agreed. Tasked with deciding how to proceed with the complaint, he simply wrote in the margin of the *jefe político*'s report, "Noted: be it told to the complainant that, as from the report given by the district administration of Valle [de Santiago] the charges she makes against the same administration [*sic*] are shown to be baseless, her petition is dismissed."[44]

(2) In April 1894 six female workers from two houses of prostitution entered Salvatierra's hospital "for having found themselves ill." Prostitution was not illegal, and the brothels' owners, Nieves Sandoval and María Gómez, pointed out that they always tried "to comply with the legal requisites [of owning houses of prostitution], and making sure that the women show up at the check-up every week."[45] For Salvatierra, like many other towns in Porfirian Mexico, had passed regulations that required sex workers to be registered with the town government and submit to weekly health checks.[46] Sandoval

---

42 "[E]bria escandalosa"; and "De esa falsedad se desprenden las demás en que incurre en su escrito de queja"; Francisco Franco to Secretario de Gobierno, Valle de Santiago, 25 November 1895, in AGEG-J, Caja 104, Expediente 20.

43 "[T]odos manifestaron no haber intervenido en la aprehensión de ningún individuo que lleve ese nombre y apellido"; Francisco Franco to Secretario de Gobierno, Valle de Santiago, 25 November 1895, in AGEG-J, Caja 104, Expediente 20.

44 "Enterado: Dígase a la quejosa que como del informe rendido por la jefatura del Valle aparecen desvanecidos los cargos que hace a la propia jefatura, no ha lugar a su solicitud." Marginal note by Gobernador, Francisco Franco to Secretario de Gobierno, Valle de Santiago, 25 November 1895, in AGEG-J, Caja 104, Expediente 20.

45 "[P]or haberse encontrado enfermas"; and "procurando cumplir con los requisitos legales y teniendo el cuidado de que las mujeres ocurran semanariamente al registro." Nieves Sandoval and María Gómez to Gobernador, Salvatierra, 30 April 1894, in AGEG-M, Caja 241, Expediente 13.

46 See "Reglamento formado por el H. Ayuntamiento para reglamentar a las mujeres públicas que viven de la prostitución en esta ciudad," Salvatierra, 14 March 1893, in AGEG-M, Caja 240, Expediente 15.

and Gómez at first sent daily rations of food to their hospitalized workers but were eventually prohibited from doing so, perhaps because hospital staff were unwilling to countenance the comings and goings of people associated with a brothel. When the patients requested to be allowed once more to receive food from the outside, they met with a harsh response: "The señor *jefe político*," wrote Sandoval and Gómez, "qualified the complaint as an act of insubordination, and noting the names of the complainers, ordered that they be taken from the hospital [and] put them incommunicado in the woman's jail."[47] He then had them banished from town. Such acts, according to Sandoval and Gómez, were "prohibited by the Constitution and qualified by the penal code as abuse of authority and illegal detention." They wrote to the governor demanding "that he do strict justice and that he protect us from the irregular acts" of the *jefe político*.[48]

The *jefe político* did not dispute the details of the complaint against him. Rather, he responded with a reference to the women's insolence and an evocation of the general moral hazard posed by prostitution. He had banished the women because the staff of the hospital "could no longer bear the presence [of the prostitutes], on account of the frequent scandals they committed." He claimed that the women had themselves declared a preference for being exiled to Celaya, and so he sent them there "keeping in mind also the good that would result for this population [of Salvatierra] if this class of women no longer lived in it."[49] Upon reviewing the case, the governor did not reverse or punish the actions of the *jefe político*, though he did "commend to him," for the future, "the greatest attention to the legitimacy of all his acts in order to avoid motives or pretexts for complaints."[50]

(3) On 1 July 1895, Andrés Rivera, a "native and resident of Silao," was arrested "for the reason that a mule, which I possessed and had legally acquired in exchange for a different one, was *conocido* [i.e., recognized and

47　"El señor jefe político calificó la queja como acto de insubordinación y tomando nota de las nombres de las quejosas, las mandó sacar del Hospital, las puso incomunicadas en las recogidas." Nieves Sandoval and María Gómez to Gobernador, Salvatierra, 30 April 1894, in AGEG-M, Caja 241, Expediente 13.

48　"[P]rohibidos por la Constitución y calificados por el Código Penal de abuso de autoridad y detención ilegal"; and "se haga estricta justicia y que se nos ponga a cubierto de las arbitrariedades." Nieves Sandoval and María Gómez to Gobernador, Salvatierra, 30 April 1894, in AGEG-M, Caja 241, Expediente 13.

49　"[Y]a los empleados no podían soportarlas, por los frecuentes escándalos que cometían"; and "[E]n atención también del bien que resultaría a esta población con la no permanencia de esa clase de mujeres en élla." Jefe político to Gobernador, in AGEG-M, Caja 241, Expediente 13.

50　Marginal note by gobernador from 3 May 1894, Jefe Político to Gobernador, in AGEG-M, Caja 241, Expediente 13.

reported as being stolen]."[51] The *jefe político* went on to order the arrest of Rivera's father and the confiscation of three more of the family's mules as well as their pack gear – "for our profession is that of muleteers, conveyers of feed and grain to this market [of Guanajuato]."[52] The two Riveras, thinking that they were the victims of a mistake, were eager to clear their names:

we expected that the next day we would be placed, as would have been natural, at the disposition of a judge, before whom the question of the demand for the mule that had been reported [as stolen] would be aired, and before whom we would have proven our honesty, as well as our property in the animals that had been ordered confiscated from our home.[53]

But the Riveras were disappointed, for instead of being handed over to a judge, father and son found themselves sent to León as army recruits. Only after pursuing a successful *amparo* suit were they again put in liberty, more than three weeks after their initial arrest.

Andrés Rivera sent his complaint to the governor in order to demand not that the *jefe político* be punished but that his animals – which, according to informants, the *jefe político* had sold as strays – be returned to him.

[A]nd as it is notorious and publicly known in Silao how badly the señor *jefe político*, who is of a violent temper, treats the poor, this has prevented us from presenting ourselves to that señor to reclaim what is ours by right and has been taken from us in a violent, illegal, and unjust manner.[54]

Rivera concluded his plea by noting "that my three animals with all their gear are worth thirty pesos, [representing] the only patrimony we possessed for providing for our numerous family, who today lack what is necessary, because that is how the señor *jefe político* of Silao ordered it."[55] In this case,

---

51 "[O]riginario y vecino de Silao"; and "por el motivo de habérseme conocido un burro que yo poseía y había adquirido legalmente a cambio de otro." Andrés Rivera to Gobernador, Silao, 27 July 1895, in AGEG-M, Caja 242, Expediente 17.

52 "[P]ues nuestra ocupación es la de arrieros, conductores de pasturas y semillas a ésta plaza." Andrés Rivera to Gobernador, Silao, 27 July 1895, in AGEG-M, Caja 242, Expediente 17.

53 "[E]sperábamos que al día siguiente se nos consignara como era natural a disposición de un juez, ante quien se ventilara la cuestión del reclamo de la burra que se me conoció, y ante quien habríamos probado nuestra honradez, así como la propiedad de los animales que se nos mandaron sacar de la casa." Andrés Rivera to Gobernador, Silao, 27 July 1895, in AGEG-M, Caja 242, Expediente 17.

54 "[Y] como es público y notorio en Silao lo mal que trata a la gente pobre el señor jefe político, que es de genio violento, esto nos ha impedido presentarnos a dicho señor a reclamar lo que tan justamente nos corresponde, y que nos ha sido quitado de una manera violenta, ilegal e injusta." Andrés Rivera to Gobernador, Silao, 27 July 1895, in AGEG-M, Caja 242, Expediente 17.

55 "[P]ues debo hacer presente que mis tres animales con todo y sus avíos son de un valor de treinta pesos, único patrimonio que teníamos para el sostén de nuestra numerosa familia, que hoy carece de

we have no version of events challenging Rivera's story, as the *jefe político* went personally to Guanajuato in order to justify his actions. Based on his verbal report, the governor ruled that "by virtue of the facts received [Rivera's] petition is dismissed."[56]

(4) On 14 February 1896 Leandro Toscano, a storeowner from Mineral de Pozos, was arrested by order of the town's auxiliary *jefe político*, who accused Toscano of having insulted his authority. The prisoner was kept in jail for the duration of his trial. After the first hearing at the municipal court, Toscano reported that "the citizen *jefe* [*político*] in my presence ordered the señor jailer 'to keep me rigorously separated without allowing me any contact to my family, nor to talk to anybody.'"[57] Toscano remained in jail for a month before finally being set free by order of a judge from San Luis de la Paz, probably by means of a writ of *amparo*. But Toscano's tribulations were not over. On 22 April he wrote that the *jefe político* "lately persecutes me in such a tenacious or irrational manner that it is impossible for me to stay in this place, which is my home."[58] A day earlier, the *jefe político* had sent a policeman to escort Toscano to his office, where he accused him of being a *tinterillo* – someone practicing law without proper qualification – and told Toscano that if he did not stop giving legal counsel to "scoundrels [*personas bribón*]," he would be arrested as a *vago* – an idler or vagabond.

The *jefe político*'s accusation that Toscano was a *tinterillo*, and therefore liable for persecution for vagrancy, rested on growing state efforts to police the provision of legal services, making it harder for the poor to gain legal advice and assistance.[59] In Guanajuato, a law from 1891 ordered *jefes políticos* to "persecute and arrest *vagos*, dispatching them without delay to a competent judge," and specifically listed *tinterillos* (also known as *huizacheros*) under that category.[60] But Toscano did not believe himself guilty,

---

lo necesario porque así lo dispuso el señor jefe político de Silao." Andrés Rivera to Gobernador, Silao, 27 July 1895, in AGEG-M, Caja 242, Expediente 17.

56　"[E]n virtud de los datos recibidos no ha lugar a atender su solicitud." Marginal note by the governor in José Aranda to Secretario de Gobierno, Silao, 3 August 1895, in AGEG-M, Caja 242, Expediente 17.

57　"[E]l ciudadano jefe ordenó en mi presencia al señor alcaide 'se me pusiera separado rigurosamente sin permitirme ningún conducto a mi familia, ni hablar con nadie ...." Leandro Toscano to Gobernador, Mineral de Pozos, 22 April 1896, in AGEG-J, Caja 105, Expediente 16.

58　"[U]ltimamente me persigue de una manera tan tenaz o irracional que no es posible permanecer en aquel lugar, que es mi residencia." Leandro Toscano to Gobernador, Mineral de Pozos, 22 April 1896, in AGEG-J, Caja 105, Expediente 16.

59　On *tinterillos*, see Andrés Lira, "Abogados, tinterillos y huizacheros en el México del siglo XIX," at http://biblio.juridicas.unam.mx/libros/2/700/25.pdf, accessed 27 December 2015.

60　"Perseguir, aprehender y consignar sin demoras a los vagos, a su Juez competente"; and "las personas que se ocupan ... en promover y seguir pleitos como apoderados, como defensores de reos, o como cesionarios de cobranza, sin tener título de abogado, de agente de negocios o de

for he had never appeared "in any court at any time to defend the rights of others."[61] All he had done was to help Paula Núñez to obtain an *amparo* and to compose, on behalf of an unnamed person who had asked for it, a legal complaint against an abusive official. The *jefe político* responded that Toscano, by admitting to such activities, had incriminated himself, for it was just the rendering of such legal assistance that marked him as a *tinterillo*. To this the *jefe* added testimonial evidence that Toscano had in the past attempted to pass himself off as a titled lawyer in Mineral de Pozo's auxiliary court.[62]

The *jefe político* also used testimonial evidence to defend himself against the charges made against him. At his urging, a number of witnesses produced short dispositions confirming that Toscano, in the words of one, "had the audacity of having profaned your [the *jefe político*'s] person and authority in my presence."[63] Against the accusation that he had ordered Toscano to be isolated in jail, the *jefe político* provided a statement from Toscano's jailer. "While it is true that Toscano was not kept with the other prisoners," this man wrote, "that was because I received an order from the judge [and not the *jefe político*] to put him apart because he was known as a *'tinterillo'* and it was feared he would cause an uprising in the jail population."[64] The jailer, whose professional future depended on the goodwill of the *jefe político*, had been left in no doubt as to what kind of statement was expected of him: in asking him to report on the veracity of Toscano's accusation, the *jefe político* had added the words "Since I did not order you such a thing [placing Toscano in solitary confinement]" to his written request.[65] In this as in all previous cases, Guanajuato's governor took the side of the *jefe político*, whom he further admonished to initiate legal action against Toscano in case that, after prior warning, he should continue to work as a *tinterillo*.[66]

It is clear from these cases that the option of reporting abusive *jefes políticos* did not, in Guanajuato, serve as a serious mechanism of accountability. In all

procurador." "Ley orgánica, para el gobierno y administración interior de las jefaturas políticas del estado," Guanajuato, 15 December 1891, article 17 paragraph 13, in AGEG-Leyes y Decretos.

61 "[A] ningún juzgado en ningún tiempo a defender derechos ajenos." Leandro Toscano to Gobernador, Mineral de Pozos, 22 April 1896, in AGEG-J, Caja 105, Expediente 16.

62 Y. Barrera to Secretario del Gobierno, Pozos, 21 May 1896, Documento 7, and Documento 11, all in AGEG-J, Caja 105, Expediente 16.

63 "[T]uvo el atrevimiento, de haber profanado de su persona y autoridad en mi presencia." Documento 9; see also Documento 7 and Documento 11, all in AGEG-J, Caja 105, Expediente 16.

64 "Si bien no estuvo en común de presos fue a que recibí orden del mismo juez el que lo pusiera separado por razón de ser conocido como 'tinterillo' temiendo fuera a sublevar la prisión." Documento 5, in AGEG-J, Caja 105, Expediente 16.

65 "Como yo no ordené a Usted tal cosa." Documento 3, in AGEG-J, Caja 105, Expediente 16.

66 Marginal note by Gobernador in document dated Guanajuato, 6 June 1896, in AGEG-J, Caja 105, Expediente 16.

four cases, as well as in three other complaints preserved with their outcomes, the governor sided with the *jefes políticos* against their detractors.[67] That a formal complaint mechanism existed at all, and thus an appearance of accountability was kept, probably had to do with the rootedness of Mexico's nineteenth-century liberal tradition. Yet the workings of that mechanism verged on the parodic: *jefes políticos* requested underlings to write testimonies in terms they all but dictated, or cited administrative correspondence to prove the non-existence of illegal acts – like murder – that would have hardly left traces in official records. The complaint process thus had the form of a kind of administrative theater: it showed the state to take an interest in official abuses, and yet as long as *jefes políticos* acted their part, the outcome would almost certainly be in their favor.

III Privatization

Jefes políticos played havoc with the lives of Mexicans of all social classes and political affiliations. For example, in 1895 some of the principal residents of the patrician stronghold San Miguel de Allende denounced their *jefe político* for damaging private residences in an attempt to rectify one of the city's thoroughfares about which neither they nor the town council had been consulted.[68] That they were rich did not make them immune. A great majority of victims of *jefe político* abuses nevertheless belonged to the middle and lower classes.[69] Even Leandro Toscano, the merchant and alleged *tinterillo* from Mineral de Pozos, was contemptuously described as the operator of only "a small shop or tavern whose capital does not reach thirty pesos" by the auxiliary *jefe político* whom he had accused of arbitrary proceedings.[70]

That *jefes políticos* were by and large nasty to the poor and deferential to the rich reflected a growing process of social polarization. During the Díaz regime, the Mexican economy went through a period of sustained growth and modernization. Mexican railway lines measured 400 miles at the beginning of the Porfiriato and 19,000 miles at its end.[71] In the same period, "industrial production rose by an annual rate of 6.5 per cent, mining by 7 percent, exports

---

67 For complaints not described in the text, see Julio Vázquez et al. to Gobernador, San Miguel de Allende, 10 September 1895, in AGEG-M, Caja 242, Expediente 18; Romualdo Sánchez to Gobernador, Ocampo, 22 June 1896, in AGEG-M, Caja 243, Expediente 12; Felipe Cortes to Gobernador of Guanajuato, Puruándiro, 8 April 1897, in AGEG-G, Caja 199, Expediente 1.

68 Julio Vázquez et al. to Gobernador, San Miguel de Allende, 10 September 1895, in AGEG-M, Caja 242, Expediente 18.

69 Knight, *Mexican Revolution*, vol. 1, 29–30.

70 "[U]n tendejón o cantina cuyo capital no llega a treinta pesos." Y. Barrera to Secretaría de Gobierno, Pozos, 21 May 1896, in AGEG-J, Caja 105, Expediente 16.

71 Joseph and Buchenau, *Mexico's Once and Future Revolution*, 21.

by 6 per cent, and imports by 5 per cent."[72] However, most gains from this growth accrued to the rich or well-off. By studying the average body height of Mexican military recruits – a reliable proxy for nutritional well being during childhood and adolescence – Moramay López-Alonso has shown that during the second half of the century Mexico's poor majorities experienced an objective process of immiseration. This process was not turned around during even the most prosperous years of the Díaz regime.[73] For a majority of laborers, peasants, and artisans, living conditions in the final decades of the nineteenth century were worse, and opportunities for advancement more restricted, than they had been in the early republican period.

The growing disparity between the rich and the poor was in one sense a sign of the times: it was animated by processes that, independently of political context, were either global in scale or had strong parallels in other parts of the world. Thus, population growth put increasing pressure on the resource base of Mexico's agrarian economy while the diffusion of new technologies, revolution in transportation, and growth of global markets favored capital-intensive methods of production. These trends harmed artisans and small-scale farmers and increased the economic power of those with money and access to credit.

But class polarization was also helped along by specific legislative choices. The 1856 Lerdo Law famously mandated the privatization of all corporate-owned land, excepting only pastures and woodlands (*ejidos*). While many states had already passed similar laws, and while indigenous land in some ethnically mixed towns had already been privatized, the 1856 disentailment law was the first to be backed by a national government.[74] The Ley Lerdo was followed by various colonization laws – the most important from 1883 – that promoted the survey and sale of public lands, including lands that were being exploited by rural folks without formal titles.[75] By making it easier for land to be traded, and thus for landownership to become concentrated, the abolition of corporate land tenure sharpened the process of class formation that had been put in motion by extra-political forces.

---

72 Garner, *Porfirio Díaz*, 165.

73 Moramay López-Alonso, *Measuring Up: A History of Living Standards in Mexico, 1850–1950* (Stanford: Stanford University Press, 2012), section 2 and especially pages 110–114.

74 On earlier, state-specific disentailment laws, see Fraser, "La política de desamortización," 622–624.

75 On the survey and colonization laws and their implementation, see Robert Holden, *Mexico and the Survey of Public Lands: The Management of Modernization 1876–1911* (DeKalb: Northern Illinois University Press, 1994); and Inocencio Noyola, "Los juicios de apeos y deslindes en San Luis Potosí, 1883–1893," and Antonio Escobar Ohmstede, "El fraccionamiento privado y comunal en el oriente potosino durante la segunda mitad del siglo XIX. Una aproximación," both in *Agua y tierra en México, siglos XIX y XX*, vol. 1, ed. Antonio Escobar Ohmstede, Martín Sánchez Rodríguez, and Ana Ma. Gutiérrez Rivas, 331–357, 209–244 (Zamora: El Colegio de Michoacán, 2008).

The privatization laws were among the most massive legislative interventions into social life carried out by the post-colonial state – only army recruitment had a comparable impact – and the way they were executed can tell us a lot about the relationship between legal culture and class formation in nineteenth-century Mexico. Historians used to assume that the privatization of indigenous land was fundamentally violent and extralegal: a massive act of dispossession, the rapine perpetrated by a rising mestizo nation on the body of Mexico's native population.[76] In recent decades, scholarship has done much to complicate this story. The 1856 disentailment law strengthened a concept of private property that, as we saw in the previous chapter, had by no means been alien to native landholding practices. Furthermore, the law was drafted to benefit, not hurt, inhabitants of the towns to which it applied. When its author, Miguel Lerdo de Tejada, received complaints that the law was being used to deprive indigenous landholders of their plots and fields, he passed further decrees to clarify its intent, emphasizing that it was meant "to favor the most humble classes" and ordering that terrains worth less than two hundred pesos should be adjudicated for free.[77]

Indigenous towns, and sometimes inhabitants of the same town, varied in how they responded to the privatization laws.[78] Many towns took advantage of the opportunity to regularize their landholding regimes through the acquisition of individual property titles.[79] In the municipality of Ocoyoacac in Mexico State, studied by Margarita Menegus Bornemann, lands formerly used for covering the cost of religious practices (*propios* or

76 The American scholar Eyler Simpson referred to land disentailment as "the cold rape of the pueblos" while the conception of disentailment as a conflict between modernity and tradition is implicit in, among others, Richard Sinkin, *The Mexican Reform: A Study in Liberal Nation Building* (Austin: University of Texas Press, 1979). For a dissection of the historiography, see Emilio Kourí, "Interpreting the Expropriation of Indian Pueblo Lands in Porfirian Mexico: The Unexamined Legacies of Andrés Molina Enríquez," *Hispanic American Historical Review* 82/1 (2002), 69–74, 110–116; Simpson quoted on p. 116; and Daniela Marino, "La desamortización de las tierras de los pueblos (Centro de México, siglo XIX). Balance historiográfico y fuentes para su estudio," *América Latina en la Historia Económica* 16 (2001), 33–43.

77 "[F]avorecer a las clases más desvalidas." Fraser, "La política de desamortización," 635–636; Florencia Mallon, *Peasant and Nation: The Making of Postcolonial Mexico and Peru* (Berkeley: University of California Press, 1995), 98–99; Jennie Purnell, "With All Due Respect: Popular Resistance to the Privatization of Communal Lands in Nineteenth-Century Michoacan," *Latin American Research Review* 34/1 (1999), 89–91.

78 For a range of responses from indigenous towns in the Purépecha highlands, in Michoacán, see Fernando Pérez Montesinos, "Poised to Break: Liberalism, Land Reform, and Communities in the Purépecha Highlands of Michoacán, Mexico, 1800–1915," PhD Dissertation, Georgetown University (2014), 174–179.

79 Mallon, *Peasant and Nation*, 105–106, 121–123; Purnell, "With All Due Respect," 92–93; Frans Schryer, *The Rancheros of Pisaflores: The History of a Peasant Bourgeoisie in Twentieth-Century Mexico* (Toronto: University of Toronto Press, 1980), 27–28; Ian Jacobs, *Ranchero Revolt: The Mexican Revolution in Guerrero* (Austin: University of Texas Press, 1982), 47–48.

tierras de comunidad) were privatized under the terms of the disentailment laws in the 1860s, lands already held in private usufruct (*tierras de común repartimiento*) between 1867 and 1875, and large parts of the town's *ejido*, or commons, after 1887.[80] Here, the implementation of the disentailment laws appears to have been fair and impartial. Although pressure to proceed with disentailment stemmed in part from outsiders' attempts to lay claim to town properties, all land was awarded to its former indigenous users. Nearby haciendas did not benefit from privatization, and Ocoyoacac remained dominated by small property holders.[81] In other regions, including the Mixteca Baja, towns achieved similar effects by forming agricultural societies whose shareholders were able to own land in common under liberal property law.[82]

Although it has become clear that privatization in nineteenth-century Mexico cannot be simply equated to an attack on native communities, there were also many instances in which the process really did play out in the way the black legend has always assumed, as a massive and violent land grab by local elites and mestizo outsiders.[83] Not surprisingly, whether the privatization process respected or violated the rights of indigenous landowners depended in part on the suitability of their lands for commercial agriculture. Edgar Mendoza García shows that most communal lands in the district of Coixtlahuaca, Oaxaca – where indigenous peasants grew traditional crops such as corn and beans – were privatized to local users without much fuss or conflict. There, the reform laws contributed to a process of class differentiation only to the extent that it made it easier for the rich or resourceful to accumulate land through purchase.[84] By contrast, in the district of Cuicatlán, where land was well suited to coffee cultivation, the privatization process became violent after

---

80 Margarita Menegus Bornemann, "Ocoyoacac: Una comunidad agraria en el siglo xix," *Historia Mexicana* 30/1 (1980), 43–51.

81 Menegus Bornemann, "Ocoyoacac," 55–56.

82 Smith, *Roots of Conservatism*, 169–175, 308–313; Frans Schryer, *Ethnicity and Class Conflict in Rural Mexico* (Princeton: Princeton University Press, 1990), 88–101; Michael Ducey, "Liberal Theory and Peasant Practice: Land and Power in Northern Veracruz, Mexico, 1826–1900," in *Liberals, the Church, and Indian Peasants: Corporate Lands and the Challenge of Reform in Nineteenth-Century Spanish America*, ed. Robert Jackson, 65–90 (Albuquerque: University of New Mexico Press, 1997).

83 See, e.g., Purnell, "With All Due Respect," 93–96, 101–111; Jacobs, *Ranchero Revolt*, 49; Saad Saka, *For God and Revolution*, chapter 5; Paul Friedrich, *Agrarian Revolt in a Mexican Village* (Chicago: University of Chicago Press, 1970), 43–44; and Antonio Escobar Ohmstede, "Los condueñazgos indígenas en las Huastecas Hidalguense y Veracruzana: ¿Defensa del espacio comunal?," in *Indio, nación, y comunidad en el México del siglo XIX*, ed. Antonio Escobar Ohmstede, 171–188 (Mexico City: Centro de Estudios Mexicanos y Centroamericanos, 1993), 174–178.

84 Edgar Mendoza García, "Distrito político y desamortización: Resistencia y reparto de la propiedad comunal en los pueblos de Cuicatlán y Coixtlahuaca, 1856–1910," in *Culturas de pobreza y resistencia: Estudios de marginados, proscritos, y descontentos. México, 1804–1910*, ed. Romana Falcón, 209–236 (Mexico City: Colegio de México, 2005), 212–218, 221–226; and Edgar Mendoza García, *Los bienes de comunidad y la defensa de las tierras en la Mixteca oaxaqueña: cohesión y autonomía del municipio de Santo Domingo Tepenene, 1856–1912* (Mexico City: Senado de la República, 2004).

1892, when a railway line linked the region to global commodity markets. Here, domestic and foreign businessmen, with the help of the district's *jefe político*, were able to manipulate the privatization process and deprive towns of almost all of their landholdings.[85] Peasants who had worked their land to produce for local and regional markets now had few choices but to seek work on the plantations whose owners had dispossessed them.

In places like Cuicatlán, where acts of violence paved the way for the establishment of commercial plantations, privatization can be understood as a form of "primitive accumulation," turning peasants into proletarians and dividing society into hostile classes defined by their relationship to the means of production.[86] However, unlike in Karl Marx's account of primitive accumulation in Europe, privatization in Mexico did not take place in a pre-liberal context. The disentailment laws were respectful of existing land rights and – as the examples of Ocoyoacac, the Mixteca Baja, and Coixtlahuaca attest – were often implemented according to liberal understandings of fairness and equity. "Primitive accumulation," when and where it was carried out, existed in tension with the liberal state much more than it signified its fulfillment.

Emilio Kourí's study of disentailment in the Totonac town of Papantla, Veracruz, gives a particularly rich account of the tension between norm and practice in the local politics of privatization.[87] The disentailment of Papantla's Totonac lands began in 1875, when a booming vanilla market created new incentives for implementing a disentailment policy that regional lawmakers had vainly attempted to impose since independence. The break-up of communal landholdings proceeded in two stages. Between 1875 and 1878, Papantla's indigenous lands were divided into twenty-three large lots and signed over to collective shareholding companies called *condueñazgos*.[88] Then, between 1889 and 1900, the various *condueñazgos* were subdivided into individual parcels, each one titled to a particular owner.[89] Throughout the process, the driving force behind disentailment was a coalition of mestizo merchants, who resided in the town center and linked Papantla's vanilla production to international markets, and prosperous Totonac farmers: respected community leaders who held commanding positions in the local militia and could count on the support of sizeable parts of the population.

85 Mendoza García, "Distrito político y desamortización."
86 Karl Marx, *Capital*, vol. 1, trans. Ben Fowkes (New York: Vintage Books, 1977), chapters 26–27. The best discussion of the role that the dispossession of indigenous communities played in the formation of new class categories in a Latin American context is Jeffrey Gould, *To Die in This Way: Nicaraguan Indians and the Myth of Mestizaje, 1880–1965* (Durham: Duke University Press, 1998), chapter 7.
87 Emilio Kourí, *A Pueblo Divided: Business, Property, and Community in Papantla, Mexico* (Stanford: Stanford University Press, 2004).
88 Kourí, *A Pueblo Divided*, 138–156.   89 Kourí, *A Pueblo Divided*, 205–280.

Both stages of privatization were carried out in a manner that allowed some farmers to acquire large holdings while leaving others landless. During the first stage of disentailment, some *condueñazgo* shares were awarded to town merchants and recent immigrants who had not belonged to the landholding indigenous group. By contrast, no provision was made for the children of shareholders: while under previous land-use regimes new generations of Totonac farmers had been able to stake out farms on uncultivated terrain, under the new arrangement they could gain land only by inheriting the shares of their parents.[90] Opportunities for abuse multiplied during the second stage of the land division. Subdividing the lots into individual parcels was unavoidably contentious since on each lot some parcels were better, or better located, than others. The idea of assigning parcels by lottery was nevertheless discarded because it was inconvenient to those who owned multiple shares and wanted to consolidate their parcels into unitary holdings. As a result, Kourí writes, "parcel assignation would be the product ... of prior claims, hurried negotiations, and backroom deals."[91] In some cases, poor shareholders were effectively robbed or swindled out of their land by local politicians. In order to silence opponents, who threatened legal action against the division, Papantla's merchants and Totonac leaders called in the army and mobilized local militias, which eventually carried out a ruthless campaign of terror, killing or deporting unknown numbers of dissidents.

Kourí's study highlights both the violence and the sheer fraud used by native and mestizo elites to make the privatization process work in their favor. It is unlikely that beneficiaries of land reform in Papantla thought of themselves as acting outside the law: they merely did what was necessary, they surely believed, to implement the reform laws against reactionaries and other political troublemakers. This interpretation drew substance from the nature of the opposition, which was animated by a desire to turn back the clock on privatization, at one point coalescing around the figure of a wandering religious healer, or *curandero*, who lamented the moral degeneration of society and urged a return to a lost age of virtue and social harmony.[92] Against such enemies, Papantla's elites saw themselves as embodying the forces not only of progress but of legality. Nevertheless, even the beneficiaries of Papantla's land privatization cannot have been easy about the manner in which they achieved their purpose. The length and intensity of the battle over privatization, and the recourse to extreme violence and intimidation to snuff out even strictly legal challenges to partition, weakened norms and institutions on whose protection the rights of the new property owners would also come to depend.

---

90   Kourí, *A Pueblo Divided*, 169–171.   91   Kourí, *A Pueblo Divided*, 210.
92   Kourí, *A Pueblo Divided*, 175–179.

Guanajuato, where agriculture was not linked to global commodity markets and the stakes of privatization were lower, offers an interesting contrast to
the violent privatization process in Papantla. Here, disentailment, while not
free from political manipulation, remained much closer to legal forms. Three
cases may serve to illustrate this point. In May 1898, twenty-four native
citizens of the town of Eménguaro approached the *jefe político* of Yuriria with
a complaint about the illegal manner in which an auxiliary *jefe político* had
handled the division of their lands.[93] The complainants never specified why
they thought the division was illegal nor who its beneficiaries were, referring
for that purpose to a previous letter that I have not been able to locate. They
made it clear, however, that they thought the partition had been carried out in
violation of "the spirit of the Reform laws, which were passed to benefit and
not to exploit our indigenous race." They also emphasized that they were not
against the idea of a land division per se. If Yuriria's *jefe político* were to declare
"the nullity and invalidity of the expressed partition, returning things to how
they were before," he might go on to adjudicate Eménguaro's community
lands according to the terms of the law.[94] They added that anyone who
considered himself harmed by a reversal of the partition would "have his rights
reserved to approach the competent tribunals for contentious matters."[95]

Why did the petitioners press for an administrative reversal of the
division effected by the *jefe político*, rather than address themselves to
a judge? The problem with going to court was that it was the responsibility
of the plaintiffs of a case to prove they were in the right – a process that,
even if successful, could take years and even decades. Meanwhile, all use
rights would belong to the party occupying the land at the trial's beginning. Residents of the town of Valtierra, also facing a situation in which
their lands had been awarded to an outsider without their knowledge,
explained the rationale for avoiding a legal confrontation: "it is not just,"
they wrote, "to oblige us to play the role of plaintiffs, when that role
corresponds to those who believe they have grazing rights to land that
is in our possession."[96] Complainants who requested an administrative

---

93 "[L]a ilegalidad de los procedimientos del auxiliar Pablo Hernández"; and "el repartimiento
    y adjudicación de terrenos de la comunidad de Eménguaro." Trinidad Ramírez et al. to Jefe
    político, Yuriria, 24 May 1898, in AGEG-M, Caja 244, Expediente 33.

94 "[El] espíritu de las leyes de Reforma, que fueron expedidos para beneficiar y no para explotar
    a nuestra raza indígena"; and "la nulidad e insubsistencia de la expresada partición y adjudicación,
    volviendo a poner las cosas como estaban antes." Trinidad Ramírez et al. to Jefe político, Yuriria,
    24 May 1898, in AGEG-M, Caja 244, Expediente 33. Trinidad Ramírez et al. to Jefe político,
    Yuriria, 24 May 1898, in AGEG-M, Caja 244, Expediente 33.

95 "[S]e le dejarán a salvo sus derechos para que ocurra a los tribunales que serán competentes en caso
    de contienda."

96 "[N]o es justo que se nos obligue a hacer el papel de actores, cuando le corresponde a los que se
    crean con derecho al pasto en terrenos de que estamos en posesión." Rafael R. Ceballos et al. to
    Gobernador, Valtierra, 13 October 1900, in AGEG-J, Caja 107, Expediente 21.

nullification of a partition thus acknowledged the power of the privatization process to determine the point of departure for any subsequent legal contest. However, the requests from Eménguaro and Valtierra were both denied: once a land division had been carried out, wrote the *jefe político* of Yuriria, it could not be undone except by a competent judge, for the lands in question were now "in the power of a third person" whose constitutional rights would be violated by an administrative act reversing the earlier adjudication.[97]

I have found only one case in which a *jefe político* responded positively to a complaint about a land adjudication that had already been settled. In the village of Monte de San Nicolás, Antonia Moran and her siblings in 1895 successfully registered their titles to a piece of land, which earlier "like many [terrains] in the sierra of this city [Guanajuato] had been transmitted between members of my family from fathers to son without any interruption."[98] The siblings went to the auxiliary *jefe político* of the settlement, and

[o]n the basis of what is foreseen in the federal laws passed by señor [Benito] Juárez from 9 and 21 October as well as 7 November of 1856, we requested the adjudication of the mentioned land that we were already possessing, in lots valued at less than 200 pesos, to me and each one of my six siblings.[99]

The Morans were successful in their mission:

As the expressed laws were passed to favor us inhabitants of the Sierra, and as they gave the *jefes políticos* the authority to adjudicate these small lots to their possessors, the said political authority . . . issued a property title, dated 30 April 1895, to all of us, adjudicating each one a lot whose value is less than 200 pesos.[100]

That none of the lots exceeded 200 pesos in value was important because it meant that the Morans would not have to pay a titling fee.

---

97 "[E]n poder de tercera persona." Marginal note, Yuriria, 30 July 1898, in AGEG-M, Caja 244, Expediente 33.

98 "[C]omo muchos en la Sierra de esta Ciudad, se vino trasmitiendo entre los de mi familia de padres a hijos sin interrupción ninguna." Antonia Moran to Gobernador, Guanajuato, 13 March 1896, in AGEG-M, Caja 243, Expediente 7.

99 "Fundándonos en lo prevenido por las leyes federales expedidas por el Señor Juárez el 9 y el 21 de octubre así como el 7 de noviembre de 1856, solicitamos la adjudicación del mencionado terreno que ya poseíamos, en lotes de valor de menos de doscientos pesos, para mí y para cada uno de mis seis hermanos." Antonia Moran to Gobernador, Guanajuato, 13 March 1896, in AGEG-M, Caja 243, Expediente 7.

100 "Como las referidas leyes fueron expedidas en favor de nosotros los serranos, y como por ellas se facultó a los jefes políticos para que adjudicasen esos pequeños lotes en favor de los poseedores, la referida autoridad política . . ., nos expidió con fecha 30 de abril de 1895 un título de propiedad para todos nosotros, adjudicándonos a cada uno un lote cuyo valor no llega a doscientos pesos." Antonia Moran to Gobernador, Guanajuato, 13 March 1896, in AGEG-M, Caja 243, Expediente 7.

Less than a year after the adjudication, the family ran into trouble. "Lately, destructions carried out by some robbers of wood, sent by the señores de la Garma in order to harm us, have begun to appear on the said farm."[101] The de la Garmas, landowners with a large number of dependents, were notorious for taking the law in their own hands. In the same year as Moran's complaint, they invaded land owned by other residents of the sierra, carrying off two mules and eight donkeys.[102] Authorities, both in Monte de San Nicolás and in the city of Guanajuato, were reluctant to confront such powerful figures. When Moran and her siblings attempted to register a complaint, the *jefe político* auxiliar of Monte de San Nicolás sent them to the municipal justice of Guanajuato. The municipal justice also refused to hear them, claiming the issue lay outside his competence. They then went to the criminal judge, "and this authority referred us to the señor *jefe político* [of the district of Guanajuato], who told us to go back to the criminal judge."[103]

When Moran elevated her complaint to the state governor, the situation became more complicated. The de la Garma family, the auxiliary *jefe político* of Monte de San Nicolás now reported, was also claiming possession of the land in question:

It is true that the señoras Moran, after the formation of the respective documents, were issued the title of adjudication of the said farm by the authority I represent, but that title . . . is conditional, that is to say, it does not confer rights to them except in the case that there is nobody else with better ones.[104]

Based on this report, the government assessor opined – and the governor almost certainly agreed – that no action could be taken until a court had decided to whom the land really belonged.[105] Unlike the natives of Eménguaro or Valtierra, the de la Garma family, as powerful and, presumably,

---

101   "Últimamente comenzaron a aparecer en el referido rancho destrozos que clandestinamente ejecuta-ban algunos ladrones de leña enviados por los señores de la Garma para que nos perjudicaran." Antonia Moran to Gobernador, Guanajuato, 13 March 1896, in AGEG-M, Caja 243, Expediente 7.

102   Pedro Mayorga et al. to Gobernador, Guanajuato, 15 September 1896, in AGEG-G, Caja 105, Expediente 4. See also J. Vallejo to Gobernador, Guanajuato, 1 January 1892, in AGEG-M, Caja 239, Expediente 3, for a similar, earlier case.

103   "[Y] esta autoridad nos remitió al señor jefe político, quien manifestó que volviéramos al juez de lo criminal." Antonia Moran to Gobernador, Guanajuato, 13 March 1896, in AGEG-M, Caja 243, Expediente 7.

104   "Es cierto que a las señoras Moran, previa la formación del expediente respectivo, se les expidió por la autoridad que represento el título de adjudicación de dicho rancho, pero este título . . . es condicional, es decir, no les confiere derechos, sino en el caso de que no haya otra persona que los tenga mejores." Cecilio Estrada to Secretario de Gobierno, Guanajuato 17 March 1896, in AGEG-M, Caja 243, Expediente 7.

105   Carlos Robles to Gobernador, Guanajuato, 6 April 1896, in AGEG-M, Caja 243, Expediente 7. I have come upon no case in which Guanajuato's governor did not follow the recommendation of his assessor.

well connected landowners, were thus able to effect an administrative reversal of a previous adjudication.

By manipulating the process of land privatization, *jefes políticos* benefited wealthy allies and harmed vulnerable sectors of society. Their actions intensified the social polarization Mexicans were experiencing in the second half of the nineteenth century and established a clear linkage between political privilege and economic success. It is nevertheless noteworthy how quick Guanajuato's *jefes políticos* were to lead land conflicts in which they had taken a hand back into a judicial framework. Rather than invalidate the law, they suspended it briefly to change the relative positions of legal disputants. Guanajuatan elites were thus modest in their use of fraud and, perhaps as a result, avoided a descent into violence when applying the reform laws in their own favor. Unlike their counterparts in Papantla, they were able to accumulate land, and create a pool of disposable labor, almost without abandoning the rule of law or even the pretense of its equal application.

IV Labor

Jefes políticos' lack of accountability, coupled with their prominence in the local administration of justice, seems to confirm interpretations of the Porfiriato as a decisive break with the early republican period. Against the egalitarianism of early republican legal culture, *jefes políticos* represented an anti-popular model of public administration often associated with the ideology of positivism, imported by Europhile intellectuals in the final decades of the century and giving an explicitly hierarchical cast to the regime's ideological foundation.[106] But Porfirian elites did not build their legal regime from scratch. By studying the experience of soldiers and of hacienda residents during the dictatorship, we can gain perspectives on cultural sources of Porfirian anti-populism that had their roots not in cosmopolitan intellectual fads but in local social and political histories.

The taming of Mexico's army – its subjection to civilian control – was one of the great achievements of the Porfirian dictatorship. The regime demobilized most of the 70,000 soldiers belonging to National Guard units and other irregular forces of the civil-war period and, after 1880, reduced the size

---

106 For two classic discussions of positivism in Porfirian Mexico – one describing it as an anti-liberal class ideology, the other as an anti-popular current within Mexican Liberalism – see Zea, *Positivism in Mexico,* and Charles Hale, *The Transformation of Liberalism in Late Nineteenth-Century Mexico* (Princeton: Princeton University Press, 1989). For discussions of the influence of positivism on Porfirian legal and criminological thought, see Robert Buffington, *Criminal and Citizen in Modern Mexico* (Lincoln: University of Nebraska Press, 2000); and Elisa Speckman Guerra, *Crimen y castigo: Legislación penal, interpretaciones de la criminalidad y administración de justicia: Ciudad de México, 1872–1910* (Mexico City: El Colegio de México, 2002).

of the regular army by more than a quarter.[107] It also reduced the number of officers and moved military strongmen to posts far from their home base. As a result of these policies, the government was able to banish the scourge of barracks revolts – a major factor in the instability that had plagued previous national administrations – from Mexican politics.[108] The military's subordination to the central government also meant that the abolition of its special legal jurisdiction, the *fuero militar*, first declared in the 1857 Constitution, could finally be achieved in practical terms.

While the domestication of the military was a significant event in the political culture of nineteenth-century Mexico, it is far from clear whether it had an effect on civilian-military relations outside the sphere of high politics. Stephen Neufeld has shown that soldiers during the Porfiriato preserved their reputation for alcoholism, aggression, and vice. Attempts by officers to confine soldiers to their barracks did not keep soldiers from frequenting bars on the sly or from participating in drunken brawls, often involving the use of knives and resulting in death or injury. And although soldiers were now subject to civilian justice, when police came to arrest them they often fought back.[109]

But, most pervasively and routinely, the army continued to have an impact on the lives of civilians through the practice of military recruitment. In theory, recruitment during the Porfiriato was entirely based on a *sorteo*, or lottery, system, in which recruits would be selected from among all able-bodied men of a locality through a blind draw. In practice, the most common method of recruitment remained the *leva* or forced impressment, now often – though not exclusively – carried out by *jefes políticos* with the help of special army detachments.[110] The leading role *jefes políticos* took in army recruitment contributed to the mixture of fear and contempt many Mexicans felt toward them and, increasingly, toward the state they represented.

Unlike the recruitment committees of an earlier era, *jefes políticos* neither investigated the morality of the men they impressed nor offered them an opportunity to prove their good character. Sometimes they impressed men they found politically troubling, and in one case discovered by Neufeld a *jefe político* impressed a man whose land he wished to possess.[111] More often, *jefes políticos* recruited lower-class men they found suspect or ill-behaved. For example, Mariano Barrera, from the city of San Luis Potosí, was consigned to the military "for supposedly stealing a mirror"; Felipe Catañon of Ojuelos, in Jalisco, for "behaving badly in this town"; and Francisco Rangel of Salinas del Peñon Blanco, for "being ... truly pernicious on account of his loose

107 Knight, *Mexican Revolution*, vol. 1, 17–19; Garner, *Porfirio Díaz*, 111–114.
108 Garner, *Porfirio Díaz*, 115.
109 Stephen Neufeld, *The Blood Contingent: The Military and the Making of Modern Mexico, 1876–1911* (Albuquerque: University of New Mexico Press, 2017), chapter 6.
110 Neufeld, *Blood Contingent*, chapter 1.   111 Neufeld, *Blood Contingent*, chapter 1.

conduct."[112] The specificity of the behaviors recruitment juntas had attributed to earlier generations of recruits, from gambling and idleness to drinking, violence, and domestic neglect, were largely missing from the reports that *jefes políticos*, when challenged, submitted in support of their recruitment choices.

Recruitment had always deprived men of the due-process guarantees that the Mexican justice system afforded to ordinary criminal suspects. But recruitment during the Porfiriato was qualitatively different from what it had earlier been; now even the pretense of legality was abandoned. While recruits were often able to regain their freedom by filing for *amparo* protection, *jefes políticos* and army commanders attempted to prevent that possibility by keeping recruits in the dark about their destiny and concealing their whereabouts from their families. For example, the recruits Francisco Ramirez, Agustín Carranza, and Juan Santolla reported being put in prison without having been informed "of the cause of that procedure."[113] Felipe Castañon was kept ignorant about not only the cause of his arrest but also his intended destiny: while his wife correctly feared that he would be "consigned to the service in arms," she did not know that, at the time of her writing, he was already on his way to a regiment in Tampico, rather than in the prison in San Luis Potosí where she supposed him to be.[114] More than mere symptoms of the arrogance of power, the use of misinformation and the feigned loss of bureaucratic knowledge were tactics designed to make it harder for recruits and their families to file timely suits for *amparo* protection.[115] The abandonment of even the flawed legal procedures of the early republican period, and the suspension of any kind of specificity in the accusations made against recruits, ruptured the association between recruitment and bad conduct that had played so large a role in creating a shared republican ethos among the Mexican citizenry. It no longer mattered whether a man worked hard or spent most of his days in taverns, or whether he fed his children or wasted his money on card games or sexual conquests. Recruitment had become a punishment for being poor rather than for being wicked.

Haciendas, no less than the army, had long resisted the spread of liberal norms and practices in post-colonial Mexico. As long as landlords were economically weak, the absence of robust public institutions gave hacienda

---

112 "[P]or un supuesto robo de un espejo"; "observando en esta villa mala conducta"; and "siendo dicho individuo verdaderamente pernicioso por la conducta relajada que observa." Donaciana Meléndez to Juez de distrito, San Luis Potosí, 4 April 1892, in CCJ-SLP, Expediente 27/1892; José Refugio Gutiérrez to *Jefe político* de Tampico, Ojuelos de Jalisco, 3 November 1895, in CCJ-SLP, Expediente 186/1895; Letter from Rafael de Castillo, Salinas, 19 October 1892, in CCJ-SLP, Expediente 233/1892.

113 "[S]in darnos a conocer la causa de tal procedimiento." Petition from Francisco Ramirez, Agustín Carranza, and Juan Santolla, San Luis Potosí, 11 March 1896, in CCJ-SLP, Expediente 23/1896.

114 Petition from Inocencia Ramos de Castañon, San Luis Potosí, 8 November 1895, and letter from jefe político, San Luis Potosí, 8 November 1895, both in CCJ-SLP, Expediente 186/1895.

115 Neufeld, *Blood Contingent*, chapter 1.

tenants unprecedented freedom to live and work according to their own devices, out of reach of the legal state and its enforcers. But in the 1840s landlords began to recover many of their former powers. After the civil wars of the 1850s and 1860s, the hacienda economy continued to grow, and during the Porfiriato it picked up added momentum.[116] Under the Díaz regime, hacienda profits soared while the position of tenants, workers, and smallholders deteriorated, often drastically. Just south of Mexico City, in the sugarcane fields of Morelos, haciendas swallowed up whole peasant villages. "Hidden darkly in the fields of high, green cane," John Womack has written, "the ruins of places like Acatlipa, Cuauchichinola, Sayula, and Ahuehuepan rotted into the earth."[117] In parts of southern and southeastern Mexico, expanding plantations bound laborers to their operations through a form of debt peonage that bore a close resemblance to slavery.[118] And in north-central Mexico, including Guanajuato and San Luis Potosí, haciendas continued to rely on either free labor or on tenantry and, increasingly, sharecropping arrangements to keep their lands in production, but paid less wages, and charged more rent or higher harvest shares, than they had done earlier in the century.[119]

While rural social relations changed less dramatically in Guanajuato and San Luis Potosí than they did in other parts of the country, in these states, too,

116 With this periodization, I am following Tutino, *From Insurrection to Revolution*, chapters 7–9. On the dynamism of hacienda agriculture during the Porfiriato even outside areas producing for a global market, see María Vargas-Lobsinger, *La hacienda de "La Concha": Una empresa algodonera de La Laguna 1883–1917* (Mexico City: Universidad Nacional Autónoma de México, 1984); Hans-Günther Mertens, *Atlixco y las haciendas durante el Porfiriato*, trans. Hermilo Boeta Saldierna (Puebla: Universidad Autónoma de Puebla, 1988); and Simon Miller, *Landlords and Haciendas in Modernizing Mexico: Essays in Radical Reappraisal* (Amsterdam: CEDLA, 1995). Although the chronology of productive innovation in Mexico's hacienda economy appears to have been highly variable, a number of historians have detected a trend in that direction beginning in or shortly after the 1840s. See Miller, *Landlords and Haciendas in Modernizing Mexico*, chapters 2 and 5; Margaret Chowning, "Reassessing the Prospects for Profit in Nineteenth-Century Mexican Agriculture from a Regional Perspective: Michoacán, 1810–1860," in *How Latin America Fell Behind: Essays on the Economic Histories of Brazil and Mexico, 1800–1914*, ed. Stephen Haber, 179–215 (Stanford: Stanford University Press, 1997); and Ricardo Rendón Garcini, *Dos haciendas pulqueras en Tlaxcala, 1857–1884* (Mexico City: Universidad Iberoamericana, 1990), especially 148–150.

117 Womack, *Zapata and the Mexican Revolution*, 46.

118 Turner, *Barbarous Mexico* wrote the most famous but by no means the only contemporary description of debt peonage as a form of slavery. Historical scholars who have found the analogy plausible include Friedrich Katz, "Labor Conditions on Haciendas in Porfirian Mexico: Some Trends and Tendencies," *Hispanic American Historical Review* 54/1 (1974), 14–23; and Alan Knight, "Mexican Peonage: What Was It and Why Was It?" *Journal of Latin American Studies* 18/1 (1986).

119 Katz, "Labor Conditions," 24–26; Tutino, *From Insurrection to Revolution*, 307–312; Knight, *Mexican Revolution*, vol. 1, 91–92; Miller, *Landlords and Haciendas in Modernizing Mexico*, chapter 3.

landlords looked for methods to exert greater control over people living on or nearby their estates. One such method was the use of brute force. In 1895, the owners of the Hacienda de la Sauceda, having previously agreed to a compromise in a longstanding conflict with neighboring smallholders, not only failed to fulfill their part of the agreement, but, the peasants' lawyer wrote, "it rather appears they have taken special care to destroy and have others destroy the orchards, maguey fields, and houses of the inhabitants [of the contested land]."[120] In 1881, the administrator of the Hacienda de Gogorrón, encountering the youth Luis Sánchez in a place he considered off-limits, "on his own authority, and although there was no fight, beat him with a stick, and after that furiously whipped him."[121] And in 1882, the overseer of the same hacienda, in the company of other men, attacked Ruperto and Andrés Orta, whom he found gleaning in a field after harvest. After hitting the Ortas with sticks, the men restrained Andrés – the son – while the overseer gave him a whipping. The overseer later testified that he had beaten the gleaners because they had refused to walk off the field at his order. But witnesses contradicted that story, saying that the Ortas were already leaving when they were attacked.[122]

Hacendados also asserted their power by evicting troublesome workers and tenants. A rare occurrence in the early republican period, hacienda evictions in the second half of the century became common and, for affected tenants, traumatic occurences against which they protested fiercely, albeit mostly in vain. For example, in April 1869 six residents of the Hacienda del Pozo de Carmen petitioned the district court for an *amparo* in support of their relatives, who had been driven from homes and fields and to whom they were now giving shelter. "[O]n the 5th, 6th, and 8th of the previous [month] their doors have been forced open, twenty-six houses or huts razed to the ground, their houseware and the workshop tools they had for the manufacture of wool taken from them without any form of judgement."[123] This was a violation of the constitutional rights of the evictees, who had built their homes "with their personal money, with their labor and sacrifice."[124] In 1892, Segundino, Epigenio, Sabino, and Calixto Saucedo,

---

120 "[S]ino que antes bien parece que han puesto especial cuidado en destruir y dejar destruir las huertas, magueyeras y casas de los moradores." Manuel Díaz Barriga to Juez de letras de lo civil, Guanajuato, 20 February 1895, in AGEG-STJ, Caja 309, Expediente 6.

121 "[D]e propia autoridad, y fuera de riña, lo golpeó con una vara, y después lo cintareó a todo un encono"; Antonia Longoria to Pablo Capetillo, Villa de Reyes, 12 May 1881, in AHESLP-STJ, Caja 997, Expediente 25.

122 All documents in AHESLP-STJ, Caja 1026, Expediente 1.

123 "[C]on fecha 5, 6, y 8 del pasado han sido descerrajadas las puertas, arrasadas veintiséis casas o jacales, secuestrados sus trastos y útiles de oficina que tenían para manufacturas de lana sin forma alguna de juicio." Eusebio Vera et al. to juez de distrito, Hacienda del Pozo, 16 April 1869, in CCJ-SLP, Expediente 137/1869.

124 "[C]on su peculio, con su trabajo y sacrificio." Eusebio Vera et al. to juez de distrito, Hacienda del Pozo, 16 April 1869, in CCJ-SLP, Expediente 137/1869.

on being evicted from the Rancho de Bocas estate, protested in similar terms. They noted that their houses had been "constructed with our labor" and that "as renters of the soil we had paid our tenantry fee or rent."[125] Nevertheless, "since we are poor [the auxiliary justice] thought it was licit for him to do what he pleased," ordering "that our families leave their rooms and that our houseware and the small objects that constitute our property be thrown in the middle of a road."[126] In both cases, authorities sided with the landlords and against the tenants.

Some evictions occurred because tenants were unwilling or unable to pay their rent punctually.[127] But there were other motives. The estate administrator of the Rancho de Bocas hacienda wrote that he wished to evict the Saucedo clan because of their "bad conduct, vices, laziness ... and the grave circumstance of their having built some cellars, in the patio of the house in which they lived, where they gambled and it was suspected they hid the things whose robbery was attributed to them."[128] In another case, Ramón Ceballos explained his decision to evict Encarnación Mata and his family from the hacienda Ceballos administered by referring to "some grave offences" that Mata had committed against him.[129] The testimony of a day worker helps throw some light on the "offences" that got Mata in trouble. The worker had witnessed Ceballos enter the seasonal work camp where Mata was living. When Ceballos reproached Mata for earlier insults and for not sending his son to work on the estate, Mata began hurling invective at the administrator and "even made as if to throw himself on [Ceballos]."[130] In this and the Saucedo case, estate managers used eviction as a disciplinary measure to punish idleness, shady dealings, and acts of insubordination.

125   "[C]onstruidos con nuestro trabajo"; and "como inquilinos del suelo teníamos pagada nuestra pensión o renta." Segundino Saucedo et al. to Juez de distrito, San Luis Potosí, 28 July 1892, in CCJ-SLP, Expediente 169/1892.

126   "[S]iendo unos pobres creyó le sería lícito hacer cuanto le placiera"; and "que nuestras familias salieran de sus habitaciones y nuestros trastos y pequeños objetos que constituyen nuestra propiedad quedaran tirados en medio de un camino." Segundino Saucedo et al. to Juez de distrito, San Luis Potosí, 28 July 1892, in CCJ-SLP, Expediente 169/1892.

127   This is the reason given for an eviction in Juan José Ortiz to Juez de distrito, Hacienda del Pozo de Carmen, 25 April 1869, in CCJ-SLP, Expediente 138/1869.

128   "[M]ala conducta, vicios, ociosidad de los Saucedo y la grave circunstancia de haber hecho unas cuevas dentro del patio de la casa que habitaban, donde jugaban y se sospechaba ocultaban las cosas que les atribuían robaban." Letter from Paulino Zamarrón, Rancho de Bocas, 3 August 1892, in CCJ-SLP, Expediente 169/1892.

129   "[L]e cometió algunas faltas graves." Testimony of Ramón Ceballos, 13 May 1881, in AHESLP-STJ, Caja 996, Expediente 22.

130   "[H]asta hizo impulsos de echársele encima." Testimony of Macario Loredo, 23 June 1881, in AHESLP-STJ, Caja 996, Expediente 22.

Landlords intent on brutalizing or evicting their tenants were often able to rely on their closeness to local agents of the state.[131] For example, peasants living on land they contested with the Hacienda de la Sauceda complained in 1899 that

we are victims of all manner of abuses and harassments not only from the señores who call themselves owners of la Sauceda but also from the local authorities of the same place, who at the same time that they fulfill public functions are private employees, intimate friends, or godfathers of the señor Ygnacio Jaime, who administers the Sauceda.

They went on to describe how the administrator, with the backing of the auxiliary justice, "destroys our orchards, banishes us, and even prohibits us from keeping animals in the interior of our homes."[132] The auxiliary *jefe político* and captain of the local police, when asked to report on the matter, came down on the side of their colleagues. They denied that any orchards had been damaged, and further wrote that while it was true that the local justice was godfather to the estate administrator, and the substitute auxiliary *jefe* an estate employee, "that does not mean that both functionaries have not always fulfilled their duty."[133]

The eviction of the Saucedo clan on the Rancho de Bocas hacienda provides a further example of the entanglement of public and private authority in many estate settlements. Here, the family were first notified of their eviction by a man called Doroteo Salas, whom the administrator had put in charge of "the vigilance and order of the farm."[134] When the Saucedos refused to follow Salas's orders, the estate's substitute auxiliary justice, at the request of the administrator, became involved in the matter. "In light of that request," he related,

---

131 This was true also in the Atlixco Valley in Puebla, studied by Hans-Günther Mertens. Here, "the mayors of the pueblos [from which seasonal hacienda labor was recruited] and the justices of the peace of the same constantly received cash payments from Emilio Maurer," who was the largest landowner in the valley. Mertens, *Atlixco y las haciendas*, 189.

132 "[S]omos víctimas de todo género de abusos y vejaciones por parte no solo de los señores que se dicen dueños de la Sauceda sino además por parte de las autoridades del mismo punto, las cuales al mismo tiempo que desempeñan cargos públicos son empleados particulares, amigos íntimos o compadres del señor Ignacio Jaime, quien administra la Sauceda"; and "destruye nuestras huertas, nos destierra, y aun nos prohíbe que tengamos animales en el interior de nuestras casas." J. Trinidad Gutiérrez and Domingo Prieto to Gobernador, Guanajuato, 15 March 1899, in AGEG-G, Caja 107, Expediente 14.

133 "[E]sto no obsta para que ambos funcionarios hayan cumplido siempre con su deber." Jefe auxiliar de la Sauceda and Capitán de la Policía Montada to Gobernador, Guanajuato, 22 March 1899, in AGEG-G, Caja 107, Expediente 14.

134 "[D]e la vigilancia y del orden de la finca." Letter from Paulino Zamarrón, Rancho de Bocas, 3 August 1892, in CCJ-SLP, Expediente 169/1892.

I gave a written order to [Salas] to inform the present complainants that they had to leave and exit the farm, with the understanding that he would proceed in whichever way necessary if they didn't obey, but privately asking [Salas] not to use weapons against them in case they resisted but to report what happened, in order to proceed as the case demanded.[135] The justice wrote vaguely that the eviction had not actually been handled in the manner suggested. But while he denied having played a direct role in the eviction, the document he gave to Salas was clearly designed to intimidate the Saucedo family and convince them that resistance was futile. That the Saucedos held the justice responsible for their misfortune suggests that they were either shown his order or, at the least, were aware that he had promised to put his weight behind the administrator's eviction plan.

Besides their connection to state officials, estate owners and administrators also benefited from a growing police presence in the countryside. Some police forces were under their immediate control. We saw in the third chapter that already in the 1830s, state governments had made hacendados responsible for organizing a rural police. Hacendados, however, had only sporadically put together armed bands, usually in response to specific threats like bandit incursions. During the Porfiriato, landowners were again encouraged to take an active role in rural policing. In San Luis Potosí, two 1894 laws mandated the establishment of a rural police force in order "to guard the security of the countryside and pursue robbers."[136] Town governments would propose, and the state governor confirm, men to lead the new force, "preferably from among the owners of haciendas and *ranchos*, and otherwise from among their administrators and dependents."[137] The commanders, in turn, would choose their subalterns "from among the residents or servants of good conduct and honesty."[138] Except during campaigns of more than three days, service in the police would be unremunerated.[139] While I have found no information about the

---

135   "En vista de tal petición, di una orden escrita a [Salas] para que previniese la desocupación y salida de la finca a los hoy quejosos, bajo el concepto de proceder a lo que hubiere lugar si no obedecían, encargando en lo privado al mismo [Salas] que no hiciese armas contra ellos si se resistían, sino que diese cuenta de lo que ocurriese para proceder, según el caso." Letter from Paulino Zamarrón, Rancho de Bocas, 3 August 1892, in CCJ-SLP, Expediente 169/1892.

136   "[C]uidar de la seguridad de los campos y perseguir a los ladrones." Ley Número 28, 31 May 1894, article 7, in AHESLP-Leyes y Decretos.

137   "[S]erán escogidos de toda preferencia entre los propietarios de haciendas o ranchos, y en su defecto entre sus administradores o dependientes." Ley Número 28, 31 May 1894, article 9, in AHESLP-Leyes y Decretos.

138   "[E]ntre los vecinos o sirvientes de buena conducta y honradez." "Reglamento de la Policía Rural del Estado," 23 July 1894, article 3, in AHESLP-Leyes y Decretos.

139   "Reglamento de la Policía Rural del Estado," 23 July 1894, article 11, in AHESLP-Leyes y Decretos.

police's regular modus operandi, commanders and ordinary policemen frequently petitioned the government to be relieved from their service, suggesting that they saw it as a real commitment.[140]

In Guanajuato, privately raised forces played an important but subsidiary role in rural police work. An 1884 government report praised "the participation in this point [of rural policing] of some owners of rural farms and various private persons, who have helped the political authorities to maintain an active vigilance and to undertake the persecution of evil-doers with good success."[141] And in the 1890s, town governments sometimes listed private posses – called *acordadas* – as the rural arm of the municipal police.[142] However, for the most part the countryside was secured by contingents of soldiers paid by the state treasury and stationed in small towns and settlements, many of them on haciendas.[143] In at least one instance, an estate manager specifically requested the presence of an armed contingent on the hacienda under his care.[144]

Army contingents in Guanajuato probably played a similar role in keeping the peace in the countryside as Díaz's famous national police force – the *rurales* – did in Central Mexico. The *rurales* constituted a mobile political police that was employed to settle social conflicts in favor of the rich and well connected. According to Paul Vanderwood, the *rurales* "protected payrolls in transit, hustled factory hands to their machines, kept campesinos slashing cane, drove natives from productive land wanted for commercial

---

140 See the petitions from Leandro Rodríguez, Melitón Rodríguez, Jesús Aguilar, Leandro Morales, Ezequiel Enriquez, Agustín Ugarte, Bonifacio Herrera, Ricardo Ortiz, Pedro Cornejo, Paz Berrones, and Epitacio Salinas, all in AHESLP-SGG, Caja 1895.1, Expediente 5.

141 "[L]a participación que han tomado algunos propietarios de fincas rústicas y varios particulares, que han ayudado a las autoridades políticas a mantener una activa vigilancia y a emprender con buen éxito la persecución de malhechores." "Memoria leída por el C. Gobernador interino del Estado Libre y Soberano de Guanajuato, General Pablo Rocha y Portú, en la solemne instalación del 11.o congreso constitucional, verificado el 15 de septiembre de 1884" (Guanajuato: Imprenta del Estado, 1885), 18.

142 Reports from Dolores Hidalgo, 6 June, 6 August, 6 September, and 6 October 1895, in AGEG-M, Caja 242, Expediente 6. Report from Acámbaro, 4 January 1896, in AGEG-M, Caja 243, Expediente 2.

143 "Memoria leída por el C. Gobernador Constitucional del Estado Libre y Soberano de Guanajuato General de División Manuel González en la solemne instalación del 12.o Congreso Constitucional verificada el 15 de setiembre de 1886" (Mexico City: Imprenta de 'El Gran Libro', 1887), 5–6; "Memoria presentada por el C. Gobernador Constitucional del Estado Libre y Soberano de Guanajuato, General de División Manuel González en cumplimiento de la fracción 8.a, artículo 61, de la Constitución del mismo, en la solemne instalación del 14.o Congreso Constitucional, verificada el 15 de Septiembre de 1890" (Mexico City: Imprenta de Ignacio Escalante, 1890), 5–6; and "Memoria sobre la administración pública del Estado de Guanajuato presentada al Congreso del mismo por el C. Gobernador Constitucional Lic. Joaquín Obregón González el 1.o de Abril de 1895 (Morelia: Imprenta y Litografía de la Escuela I. M. Porfirio Díaz, 1895), 19.

144 Ignacio Jaime et al. to Secretaría de Gobierno, de la Sauceda, 12 May 1894, in AGEG-M, Caja 241, Expediente 4.

development, and escorted dignitaries anywhere on request."[145] Like army soldiers, the *rurales* were notorious for loose morals and abusive behavior. Some forced merchants to sell them goods on credit only to either leave town for another post or desert from service. Enjoying immunity from civilian prosecution, the *rurales* had "permission to carouse, bully, and show off their machismo where they worked."[146] In one of the clearest examples of the degradation of Porfirian public life, the country's premier federal police force came to embody precisely that strand of anti-social masculinity that, in an earlier and more aspirational era in the history of Mexican legal culture, the civic militias had been created to combat.

The presence of armed forces in the countryside may well have brought a perception of security to some estate residents, though it surely appeared as an unwelcome intrusion of state power to others. Above all, rural police forces shored up the power of landowners relative to their workers and tenants. During the Porfiriato landlords were able to treat the rural poor with a brutality – beatings, evictions, the destruction of orchards – for which I have found no parallels in the early republican period. Tales about the abuses committed by hacendados and their minions became legendary. One such tale, put into writing decades later by the radical agrarian Antonio Díaz Soto y Gama, tells of an event that had occurred in Soto y Gama's home state of San Luis Potosí. On the Hacienda de Pastoriza, close to the town of Matehuala,

> the administrator of the said hacienda . . . by pure force tied a miserable worker to a yoke, substituting him for one of the oxen . . ., and not satisfied with such a disgrace proceeded to pierce or jab the worker with the "gorguz" (that is to say with the rod used for goading the oxen), giving him in that way various wounds from which blood flowed.[147]

Hacendados' ascendancy over their tenants and workers was a decades-long process whose beginning, in the late 1840s, preceded not only the Porfirian dictatorship but also the civil-war period and the Restored Republic. It was nevertheless in the Porfirian era that these changes coalesced into a deep cultural fissure, noticed and commentated by contemporaries.[148]

---

145 Paul Vanderwood, *Disorder and Progress: Bandits, Police, and Mexican Development* (Lincoln: University of Nebraska Press, 1981), 119.

146 Vanderwood, *Disorder and Progress*, 125.

147 "[E]l administrador de dicha hacienda . . ., unció a viva fuerza a un infeliz peón a una yunta, sustituyéndolo a uno de los bueyes . . ., y no conforme con semejante infamia, se dedicó a herir o pinchar al mismo peón con el 'gorguz' (o sea con el asta que se usa para aguijonear a los bueyes), haciéndole así varias heridas de las que manaba sangre." Antonio Díaz Soto y Gama, *Historia del agrarismo en México* (Mexico City: Ediciones Era, 2002), 527.

148 For a larger discussion of this cultural fissure, see Ana María Alonso, *Thread of Blood: Colonialism, Revolution, and Gender on Mexico's Northern Frontier* (Tucson: University of Arizona Press, 1995), chapter 7.

Not all hacienda residents were mistreated during the Porfiriato, and some no doubt continued to take advantage of the opportunities for relaxed behavior offered by the crudity of rural instruments of social control. But for those who did not, the possibility of tying estates into a legal regime built on a valorization of labor no longer existed: whether true or apocryphal, Soto y Gama's story illustrates a reality in which labor, instead of a source of social power, had become a symbol of subjection.

V Local Courts

Examples of abuses committed by hacendados, *jefes políticos*, and, sometimes, other public officials could be almost infinitely extended. During the last decade of the Porfiriato the correspondence pages of the radical journal *Regeneración* – published by the Flores Magón brothers and other dissident journalists, at first from Mexico and then from exile in the United States – were full of denunciations of government transgressions sent in by correspondents from all parts of the country. This correspondence, Claudio Lomnitz has recently argued, distorted the Flores Magón brothers' perception of the country's political mood and led them and their Liberal Party into strategic blunders, including two disastrous attempts to foment revlution in 1906 and 1908. The brothers wrongly imagined that "[e]ach town was ready to boil over into revolution, and the only thing that was needed to effect this revolt was coordination, communication, and intellectual leadership."[149] Historians, in turn, have sometimes presented reports like those published in *Regeneración* as evidence about the overall character of the Porfirian justice system.

That people were moved to report official transgressions to newspapers, courts, or regional governments nevertheless suggests that they lived in a cultural context in which such acts were still regarded as abusive and illegal. While outrages such as random detentions and extralegal executions became increasingly common, they were not – except perhaps in some regions during the final years of the regime – common enough to appear normal. Even *jefes políticos* were not universally despised.[150] In the indigenous Mixteca Baja, Porfirian *jefes políticos* did not interfere in the work of town governments and generated little in the way of popular opposition.[151] In Guanajuato, town residents, when confronted with plans for the removal

---

149 Lomnitz, *Return of Comrade Ricardo Flores Magón*, 83–85 and 233, here 233.

150 Some *jefes políticos* interceded on behalf of the poor in local social conflicts. For examples, see Kourí, *A Pueblo Divided*, 240–275; and Paul Vanderwood, *The Power of God against the Guns of Government: Religious Upheaval in Mexico at the Turn of the Nineteenth Century* (Stanford: Stanford University Press, 1998), 75, 123.

151 Benjamin Smith, *The Roots of Conservatism in Mexico: Catholicism, Society, and Politics in the Mixteca Baja, 1750–1862* (Albuquerque: University of New Mexico Press, 2012), 162–163, 167–168.

of a popular *jefe político*, sometimes pressured the government to keep him in office.[152] Whether citizens perceived a *jefe político* as fair or abusive might depend on their position in local factional struggles. The signatories of a letter from Ciudad Victoria, for example, wrote that "the tranquility and harmony that we enjoy depends on the integrity, rectitude, and discretion with which [our *jefe político*] proceeds" and warned the government not to believe calumnies that a different faction, consisting of " alien personalities who . . . do not belong to our soil," had invented against that official.[153]

Jefes políticos as a group were prone to committing abuses because they were not accountable to the people they governed. But *jefes políticos* were only a part of the state's institutional ensemble; nowhere were they all-powerful. In Guanajuato and San Luis Potosí, popularly elected *ayuntamientos*, or town councils, continued to be in charge of the "interior government of the towns" under the states' new, Reform-era Constitutions.[154] Unfortunately, we do not know to what extent municipal elections were affected by the kind of fraud that was widely practiced in national elections during the Restored Republic and Porfiriato.[155] Ariel Rodríguez Kuri argues that the *ayuntamiento* of Mexico City, while selected through competitive elections in the 1880s, became "colonized" by the Porfirian political machine in the following decade, and Alan Knight writes that at the end of the Díaz period "local elections became a sham, conducted amidst apathy and indifference, and municipal authorities became the supine servants of the executive, irremovable, unresponsive to local opinion, and starved of funds."[156] However, as Rodríguez himself emphasizes, Mexico City's position as the seat of the national government made its municipal politics highly anomalous, and Knight, as a historian of the Mexican Revolution, is concerned above all with identifying sources of tension in the final decade of the regime. It would be unwise to take these historians' findings as indicative of the general state of local politics in 1890s Mexico.

---

152   Two letters to Governor, Tarimoro, 22 September 1894, in AGEG-M, Caja 241, Expediente 20; Cesario Pérez to Gobernador, Victoria, 5 July 1894, in AGEG-J, Caja 102, Expediente 18; Dionicio García et al. to Gobernador, Victoria, 7 March 1896, in AGEG-M, Caja 243, Expediente 22.

153   "[L]a tranquilidad y armonía que gozamos, depende de la integridad, rectitud y mesura con que procede dicho Señor"; and "exóticas personalidades, que . . . no pertenecen a nuestro suelo"; Dionicio García et al. to Gobernador, Victoria, 7 March 1896, in AGEG-M, Caja 243, Expediente 22.

154   "El gobierno interior de los pueblos." *Constitución política del estado de Guanajuato con sus adiciones y reformas* (Guanajuato: Goerne, Patiño y Cía, 1912), articles 69 and 70; *Constitución política del estado libre y soberano de San Luis Potosí decretada el 13 de julio de 1861* (San Luis Potosí: Tip. de la Escuela Industrial Militar, 1913), article 65.

155   Laurens Ballard Perry, *Juárez and Díaz: Machine Politics in Mexico* (DeKalb: Northern Illinois University Press, 1978), chapter 3.

156   Rodríguez Kuri, *La experiencia olvidada*, 51–72; Knight, *Mexican Revolution*, vol. 1, 25.

Most likely, fraud and corruption in local politics were common in areas characterized by rapid development and its attendant social contradictions. For example, the municipal council of Papantla, Veracruz, was consistently controlled by mestizo merchants with a strong interest in the privatization of Totonac lands.[157] The municipal government of the copper town of Cananea was little more than an arm of the Cananea Consolidated Copper Company, and things in other mining towns were not much different.[158] But in most towns the stakes of municipal office-holding were considerably lower. And while the town of Cananea was incorporated only in 1901, and Papantla had long been a bastion of mestizo power in a majoritarian indigenous region, many more towns had robust democratic traditions and strong reputations as upholders of popular sovereignty. In the sierras and the largely indigenous South, Knight argues that municipalities "retained some of their old freedom and autonomy" into the 1900s.[159] In less remote areas, like much of Guanajuato and San Luis Potosí, there is no reason to suppose that Porfirian development led only to social conflict and political corruption. Indeed, the ubiquity of the demand for municipal liberties in the revolution of 1910 suggests that in the popular imagination local governments remained strongly associated with the nineteenth-century liberal tradition.

In the 1890s, in a context of economic growth and improved public finances, municipal governments had more money than previously to spend on education, public hygiene, and material improvements.[160] They built new public structures – markets, schools, fountains, railway stations – and improved the ones that already existed. In regions where *jefes políticos* were far and between, *ayuntamientos* also continued to be in charge of local policing. It is probably for this reason that people in San Luis Potosí, unlike those in Guanajuato, did not, or not often, petition their government for the correction or removal of abusive *jefes políticos*. Guanajuato in 1892 had thirty-one departments, each one the responsibility of a *jefe político* who, in turn, appointed auxiliary officials in smaller towns and settlements. In San Luis Potosí, by contrast, the position of auxiliary *jefe político* did not exist, and in 1894 there were just twelve *jefes políticos* in the state, each stationed in one of the district capitals of the state.[161] The smaller number

157 Kourí, *A Pueblo Divided.*

158 Christine Mathias, "At the Edges of Empire: Race and Revolution in the Mexican Border Town of Cananea, 1899–1917," B.A. thesis, Yale University, 2007, 16–18, 23–27; Knight, *Mexican Revolution*, vol. 1, 143–144.

159 Knight, *Mexican Revolution*, vol. 1, 25.

160 On the improved public finances of the Porfiriato, see Carmagnani, *Estado y mercado*; and Zuleta, *De cultivos y contribuciones.*

161 Ley orgánica, para el gobierno y administración interior de las jefaturas políticas del estado," Guanajuato, 15 December 1891, articles 1, 43, and 45 in AGEG-Leyes y Decretos.

meant a reduction of competencies, including in the crucial area of law enforcement: the command of local police forces, while ultimately under the *jefes políticos'* oversight, as a day-to-day operation remained in the hands of the town councils governing the state's more than forty municipalities.[162] In San Luis Potosí, *jefes políticos* thus had a smaller scope for committing abuses than did their counterparts in Guanajuato, and town councils remained the institutions most directly responsible for upholding the law and preserving public security.

But the most important counterbalance to the power exercised by *jefes políticos* consisted not of town councils, over which *jefes políticos* had a formal supervisory function, but of local courts, in whose affairs they were expressly forbidden to meddle.[163] Unlike in earlier times, most courts in the 1890s operated independently of town councils. According to an 1893 law, municipal justices in Guanajuato would be elected in indirect elections from among registered lawyers, though the law allowed for the election of unsalaried lay justices in towns lacking the money to employ professionals. Wherever they deemed them necessary, town councils could appoint auxiliary justices, responsible for keeping the peace, apprehending delinquents, taking first steps to establish the facts in criminal investigations, and resolving civil cases concerning values of up to twenty-five pesos.[164] An 1903 law from San Luis Potosí allowed less room for the exercise of democratic choice, ordering both auxiliary and municipal justices – the latter called *jueces menores* – to be appointed by the state's Supreme Court.[165] The *jueces menores*, however, would work alongside popularly elected *alcaldes*, who were not required to be legal professionals but were endowed with identical functions. The creation of parallel legal positions was probably intended to allow for situations in which the Supreme Court was

162 While I have found no exact count of municipalities for 1895, in 1899 the state governor gave the number as forty-four. *Memoria presentada al H. Congreso del estado de San Luis Potosí por el Gobernador Constitucional Ingeniero Blas Escontría, relativa a los actos administrativos correspondiente al período de Agosto de 1898 a igual mes de 1899* (San Luis Potosí: Tipografía de la Escuela I. Militar, 1899). On the number of departments and jefes políticos in 1894, see "Ley de Egresos para el año de 1895," 10 December 1894, section 12, in AHESLP-Leyes y Decretos.

163 "Ley orgánica, para el gobierno y administración interior de las jefaturas políticas del estado," Guanajuato, 15 December 1891, article 24 paragraphs 8 and 9, in AGEG-Leyes y Decretos; and "Ley orgánica reglamentaria de la sección IX del título 2.o de la Constitución del Estado sobre jefes políticos," San Luis Potosí, 2 November 1872, article 13 paragraphs 3 and 9, in AHESLP-Leyes y Decretos.

164 "Ley orgánica de los tribunales del estado," Guanajuato, 14 December 1893, articles 2–3, 7–9, in AGEG-Leyes y Decretos.

165 "Ley orgánica de los tribunales del estado," San Luis Potosí, 6 June 1903, articles 7, 31, in AHESLP-Leyes y Decretos. In judicial circles, the relative merits of filling judgeships through appointment or popular election were eagerly debated throughout the Porfiriato. See Speckman Guerra, *Crimen y castigo*, 267–272.

unable to fill the position of *juez menor*, either because a town lacked funds or because no trained lawyers could be found for the post.

After 1871, the functions of municipal justices were largely defined in a series of legal codes passed at the national level and adopted, with little or no modification, by the majority of Mexican states, including Guanajuato and San Luis Potosí.[166] According to those codes, municipal or "minor" justices were responsible for trying civil disputes concerning values of up to one hundred pesos – and after 1880, five hundred pesos – as well as for carrying out "the investigation of crimes, the collection of their evidences, and the discovery of their authors, accomplices, and accessories."[167] These functions were almost identical to the ones municipal mayors had been given during the first federalist period and considerably more involved than those carried out by justices of the peace under the centralist administrations of the 1830s and 1840s.

During the Díaz dictatorship auxiliary and municipal justices remained the authorities people most often approached with their fights and their grievances. Women who suffered domestic abuse still took their partners to court to gain a modicum of protection.[168] In the district of Tenango in the Toluca Valley, the wife of José Prisciliano in 1910 accused her husband of having caused her serious injuries: acting at the instigation of his sister, José "threw a jar against her breast and then picked up a cord with a hook at the end, and with that he hit her."[169] In the same district, María Petra in 1890 told a judge that her husband had kicked her until she fell to the ground and then thrashed her with a stick, injuring her right arm.[170] While Soledad

166 Helen Clagett, *A Guide to the Law and Legal Literature of the Mexican States* (Washington: Library of Congress, 1947), 53–54, 124.

167 "[L]a investigación de los delitos, la reunión de sus pruebas y el descubrimiento de sus autores, cómplices y encubridores." "Código de procedimientos penales," 15 September 1880, article 11, in Manuel Dublán and José María Lozano (eds.), *Legislación Mexicana, ó, Colección completa de las disposiciones legislativas expedidas desde la independencia de la República*, vol. 15 (Mexico City: Imprenta y Litografía de Eduardo Dublan y Comp., 1886), 4. For civil cases, see "Código de procedimientos civiles," 13 August 1872, article 1094, in Dublán and Lozano (eds.), *Legislación Mexicana*, vol. 12 (Mexico City: Imprenta del Comercio de E. Dublan y Comp., 1882), 307; and "Código de procedimientos civiles," 15 September 1880, article 1049, in Dublán y Lozano (eds.), *Legislación Mexicana*, vol. 15, 149.

168 Ana Lidia García Peña shows that laws protecting women from "excessive" domestic violence were weakened during the Reform era, but also shows that women continued to use all legal means at their disposal against violent spouses. Ana Lidia García Peña, *El fracaso del amor: Género e individualismo en el siglo XIX mexicano* (Mexico City: El Colegio de México, 2006), chapters 2 and 3.

169 "[L]e aventó un jarro en el pecho y luego agarró un lazo que tenía en la punta un garabato y con ese le pegó." Quoted in Soledad González and Pilar Iracheta, "La violencia en la vida de las mujeres campesinas: El distrito de Tenango, 1880–1920," in *Presencia y transparencia: La mujer en la historia de México*, eds. Carmen Ramos Escandón et al., 111–161 (Mexico City: El Colegio de México, 1987), 128.

170 González and Iracheta, "La violencia en la vida de las mujeres campesinas," 130.

González Montes and Pilar Iracheta, who report these two cases, do not record the punishment meted out to the offending husbands, Ana María Alonso has found that Porfirian judges in Chihuahua usually condemned abusive husbands to periods of between eight and thirty days in jail.[171]

Victims of theft or hurtful gossip also continued to make use of the local justice system, frequently taking their neighbors to court to defend their goods and reputations. For example, on 5 September 1893 mine worker Magdaleno Pérez and his wife, Juliana Velázquez, traveled from their home in Cerro de San Pedro to nearby Villa de Juárez, where they filed a complaint against María Patricia [Seiva?] "for the injuries that without any motive she causes Velázquez." María Patricia was a neighbor who "for any small reason insults [Juliana Velázquez] and now has lately yelled at her that she is a whore in front of her husband Pérez."[172] Implicating Velázquez's sexual honor, María Patricia had, perhaps deliberately, endangered the couple's domestic peace by exciting the mistrust of the husband. When brought before justice Cristobal Nava, María Patricia denied having insulted her neighbor but nevertheless

offers, although she hasn't done so, not to insult [Velázquez and Pérez] again in word or deed, submitting herself to the punishment the authority will impose if she commits the same offence, for which she offers señor Don Mariano Pardo as her guarantor for her better behavior.[173]

A few weeks later, justice Nava dealt with a case of larceny concerning "a fattened black hog with the identifying mark of having its right ear slashed, and having smooth hair."[174] In this case, Nava was no more able to prove the guilt of the suspects than the auxiliary justice of the *rancho* where the theft had occurred, as the suspects were able to give a sound explanation for how they had come into possession of the fresh pork discovered in the house of one of their sisters.

Porfirian justices like Cristobal Nava played a far more frequent and intimate role in the lives of Mexican citizens than did the newly empowered

---

171 Alonso, *Thread of Blood*, 226.

172 "[P]or las injurias que le infiere a la Velázquez sin motivo cual ninguno"; and "[P]or cualesquiera leve motivo le ofende y ahora últimamente le ha gritado que es una puta delante de su marido Pérez." Alcaldía Constitucional de Villa de Juárez, 5 September 1893, in AHESLP-SGG, Caja 1893.18, Expediente 2.

173 "[O]frece aunque no lo ha hecho, no volver a ofenderlos de palabras ni de obras, sometiéndose al castigo que la autoridad le impusiere si reincidiere en este mismo delito, para lo cual ofrece como su fiador para su mejor manejo en lo sucesivo al señor Don Mariano Pardo" Alcaldía Constitucional de Villa de Juárez, 5 September 1893, in AHESLP-SGG, Caja 1893.18, Expediente 2.

174 "[U]na marrana gorda prieta con la señal de tener rajada una oreja del lado derecho siendo el pelo liso." Alcaldía Constitucional de Villa de Juárez, 23 September 1893, in AHESLP-SGG, Caja 1893.18, Expediente 2.

jefes políticos. Most Mexicans continued to live in a world where conflicts over pigs or reputations could make or break efforts to live good lives and, perhaps, to enjoy a measure of worldly success. Local justices attended to that world: in both Guanajuato and San Luis Potosí, they were required to keep their offices open for at least six hours a day if they were drawing a salary, and two hours a day if they were not.[175] Justices were thus the local faces of a system of law in which *jefes políticos* only sporadically interfered. It was largely due to their work, and the legal culture they represented, that the actions of *jefes políticos* could come to be perceived as abusive and out of the ordinary.

The central role that local courts played in the administration of justice challenges the claim – made by Díaz opponents at the time and informing a significant part of the subsequent historiography – that the legal culture of the Díaz regime was uniformly illiberal and repressive. An understanding of the Porfiriato as a period only of rupture misses both the continuities between the dictatorship and previous Mexican governments and the nature of the changes that did occur – or, at least, that became consolidated – during the long *pax porfiriana.* If we want to understand the Porfirian system of rule, we must find a way of conceptualizing the ability of some social actors to act violently and extra-legally within a larger institutional frame-work that, however imperfectly, continued to represent the egalitarian aspirations of Mexico's revolutionary-liberal tradition. That is a task to which we will turn in the Conclusion.

Nevertheless, the evidence here presented also shows that approaches highlighting the repressive character of the Porfiriato still tell us more about the Díaz regime than those attempting to read a concern with legality, let alone legal equality, into the regime's policies and aspirations. On the level of local administration, the regime vested vast and barely accountable powers in the office of the *jefe político,* thus ruining any chances of managing liberal modernization schemes – and most notably the policy of land privatization – in an equitable or disinterested manner. Furthermore, the regime's greatest triumph, the steady growth of the economy, to a large extent took place in spaces – plantations, company towns, haciendas – in which the functions of the legal state were partly or wholly absorbed by private interests. The Porfirian legal system cannot be reduced to its abuses. But what was new and original about it all tended toward the abusive.

---

175 "Ley orgánica de los tribunales del estado," Guanajuato, 14 December 1893, article 29, in AGEG-Leyes y Decretos; and "Ley orgánica de los tribunales del estado," San Luis Potosí, 6 June 1903, articles 24 and 38, in AHESLP-Leyes y Decretos.

Conclusion: Law and Exception in the Making of Modern Mexico

The nineteenth-century state is often associated with the triumph of the rule of law over alternative sources of public and private authority. It is imagined as a legal state. Certainly, a progressive deepening of the rule of law has never been thought of as the only available trajectory for countries in the nineteenth-century West or even nineteenth-century Europe; scholars have long acknowledged the existence of multiple pathways to post-revolutionary state formation. A progressive deepening of the rule of law has nevertheless been thought of as a universal model, or ideal type, for such a pathway. In places where the model seems ill-fitting, like Germany or much of Latin America, the nineteenth-century state has been described either as trapped in old-regime habits or as simply non-functional.[1] In the case of Mexico, it has been described as both.[2]

Such descriptions are hard to square with the evidence presented in this book. No analysis that concentrates on colonial residues or anarchic social forces can account for the vitality and egalitarianism of Mexico's legal culture in the immediate post-independent decades. Nor can it explain

1 For Germany, see the discussion of the literature in David Blackbourn and Geoff Eley, *The Peculiarities of German History: Bourgeois Society and Politics in Nineteenth-Century Germany* (New York: Oxford University Press, 1984). For examples of such views about Latin America, see, e.g., Stanley and Barbara Stein, *The Colonial Heritage of Latin America: Essays on Economic Dependence in Perspective* (New York: Oxford University Press, 1970); François-Xavier Guerra, *Modernidad e Independencias: Ensayos sobre las revoluciones hispánicas* (Madrid: Editorial MAPFRE, 1992); and Lester Langley, *The Americas in the Age of Revolution 1750–1850* (New Haven: Yale University Press, 1996). Unfortunately, the notion of a still-born republicanism in post-independence Latin America appears to have become hegemonic among both global (but non-Latin Americanist) historians and Latin Americanists in non-historical disciplines (cultural studies, political science, sociology) who lack familiarity with nineteenth-century archives. See the discussion in James Sanders, *The Vanguard of the Atlantic World: Creating Modernity, Nation, and Democracy in Nineteenth-Century Latin America* (Durham, NC: Duke University Press, 2014), 9–13.
2 E.g., François-Xavier Guerra, *México: Del Antiguo Régimen a la Revolución*, vol. 1, trans. Sergio Fernández Bravo (Mexico City: Fondo de Cultural Económica, 1988); Antonio Annino, "The Two-Faced Janus: The Pueblos and the Origins of Mexican Liberalism," in *Cycles of Conflict, Centuries of Change: Crisis, Reform, and Revolution in Mexico*, eds. Elisa Servín, Leticia Reina, and John Tutino, 60–90 (Durham, NC: Duke University Press, 2007).

the particular kind of illiberalism that emerged in the country at the end of the century. For the Porfirian legal order was parasitic on cultural and institutional parameters first established in the earlier period: within a context of legal equality, it depended on the creation of zones in which the rule of law was deliberately weakened or even suspended. But suspending the law could help the few only as long as the law remained in force for the many. In that regard, the structure of privilege that characterized the Díaz regime evolved from the innovations of the post-independence decades rather than representing a return to a pre-liberal era.

While the consolidation of an illiberal autocracy in nineteenth-century Mexico was not a foregone conclusion – the early republican decades held the possibility of other viable futures – it was, nonetheless, how the post-colonial struggle between different cultural and political projects temporarily came to rest. It was also a legacy that the nineteenth century bequeathed on the twentieth. How, then, should we understand the peculiar mixture of rule and exception that characterized the Porfirian legal regime? In this book, we have come across three kinds of policies and administrative practices that served to suspend or, at least, interfere with the rule of law. Each had early roots in elite opposition to the egalitarian paradigm of Mexico's post-independence legal culture, and each became commonplace in the period of reconstruction following the civil wars of the 1850s and 1860s.

(1) Beginning in the 1820s, elites engaged in constant efforts to keep substantial settlements free from the institutional manifestations of the legal state. In mestizo towns like Cerritos or San Pedro de los Pozos, patrician elites opposed residents' attempts to break their dependence on distant municipal seats; on agricultural estates, landowners opposed tenants' attempts to convert their settlements into formal townships; and in indigenous towns, elites mobilized colonial-era corporate structures to encroach on individual property rights. In each of these settings, there were people who labored for the creation of republican legal institutions or, in indigenous towns, for the reformation of those institutions that already existed. And in each setting, such labors prompted the mobilization of counter-efforts that sought to exclude these populations from the full exercise of legal rights guaranteed by successive Mexican constitutions.

(2) Mexico's elites also weakened the legal state by vesting public functions in private individuals. Landowners who took censuses, organized elections, and, eventually, mobilized rural police forces were not simply – and inevitably – the bearers of private interests they might more or less conscientiously put aside while fulfilling their public duties. Rather, they acquired formal administrative functions precisely on account of the informal powers encompassed in their wealth and social standing. During the Porfiriato, when personal connections were a major factor in the appointment of powerful district chiefs, or *jefes*

políticos, the boundary between public and private domains became uncertain even in regions where haciendas did not predominate. This privatization of public institutions created anomalous legal zones in a topical as well as a territorial sense. Apart from affecting particular geographic jurisdictions it had a special impact on those areas of law, mostly related to property owner-ship, tenancy arrangements, and labor relations, that touched directly on the interests of the new judicial agents and their backers and supporters. At least in part, it was this creeping privatization of law that in many indigenous towns, during the disentailment of corporate landholdings in the second half of the century, allowed both mestizo and native elites to enter into alliances with local *jefes políticos* and – in direct contravention of the laws – gain legal title to town lands at the expense of their previous owners.

(3) A final policy that undermined the law in nineteenth-century Mexico was the creation of armed forces whose members were not bound by the rules of the ordinary legal order. It is true that both the army and the rural police were governed by regulations that remained part of the total corpus of Mexican public law: formally speaking, the relation between soldiers or *rurales* on the one hand and civilians on the other was contained in a larger unity. But the idea of a formal unity was not reflected in concrete institutional arrangements. Nor was it believed by most Mexican citizens. From the perspective of civilians, exposed to abuses for which they had no effective remedies, soldiers and rural policemen belonged to a sphere of power in which not only the republican legal order but also its cultural presuppositions had been put on hold – a sphere in which daring and belligerence, and not labor and constancy, held pride of place among masculine values. In the army and rural police, behavioral norms commonly associated with crime or vagrancy, against which the post-colonial legal regime had been explicitly erected, colonized the exercise of state-sanctioned violence.

Although each of these policies sometimes stood on its own, their greatest impact was cumulative. Privatizing key positions in the judicial adminis-tration worked best in places that had earlier been deprived of public institutions; delegating the use of violence to organizations whose mem-bers were unrestrained by prevailing legal and cultural codes worked best in places whose judicial institutions had earlier been privatized. Taken together, these practices created a patchwork of more or less anomalous legal zones that confronts us with a formidable theoretical puzzle: how do we understand a legal regime that was partly defined by the possibilities it provided for its own suspension? Addressing this question is important not only for understanding the post-colonial societies of Mexico or even Latin America. Rather, the appearance of zones of exception appears to have been a common feature of nineteenth-century legal cultures in many parts of the world. For example, in Europe groups with clear stakes in the era's social conflicts often controlled important legal institutions. Aristocrats continued to furnish most rural judges in Britain and Prussia until the end of the century, and manufacturers dominated the industrial councils that, in France and Rhineland Germany, became responsible for settling disputes between workers and factory owners.[3] In Europe's colonial possessions, Hannah Arendt has argued that a permanent suspension of legality, supported by a racist ideology, was implied in the creation of an administrative system whose agents were accountable neither to a European public nor to the people over whose destinies they ruled.[4]

Legal regimes with parallels to the one that in Mexico became consolidated under the Porfirian dictatorship also remain a prominent feature of the world today, especially – but by no means exclusively – in the global South.[5] In Latin America, including Mexico, the "transition to democracy" that began in the 1980s has nowhere issued in the universal accessibility of legal rights and protections, and political scientists now debate whether regimes holding periodic competitive elections may be called "democratic" in spite of the absence of a basic respect for the rule of law on the part of public officials.[6] Many people in Latin America live, precariously, in informal settlements that lack access to basic state services.[7] It also remains common for the military to enjoy special jurisdictions, for the police to

---

3 On the judicial powers of the aristocracy, see Dominic Lieven, *The Aristocracy in Europe, 1815–1914* (New York: Columbia University Press, 1993), 206, 214. On industrial courts, see William Reddy, *The Rise of Market Culture: The Textile Trade and French Society, 1750–1900* (Cambridge: Cambridge University Press, 1984), 72, 98, 103–104; and Jonathan Sperber, *Rhineland Radicals: The Democratic Movement and the Revolution of 1848–1849* (Princeton: Princeton University Press, 1991), 54–57.

4 Hannah Arendt, *The Origins of Totalitarianism* (New York: Harcourt, Brace, 1951), chapters 5, 7. To give a concrete example, in the mining compounds of the British protectorate of Southern Rhodesia, the legal functions of the state were handed over to mining companies, just as they were handed over to plantation and hacienda owners on plantations and haciendas in Porfirian Mexico. The whipping of workers by company officials was common, and even extreme physical abuses, leading to the death of workers, went unpunished by the settler-controlled court system. See Charles van Onselen, *Chibaro: African Mine Labour in Southern Rhodesia 1900–1933* (Johannesburg: Ravan Press, 2001), 136–150.

5 For sophisticated discussions of the relationship between law and disorder in the post-colonial world, see the essays in Jean and John Comaroff (eds.), *Law and Disorder in the Postcolony* (Chicago: University of Chicago Press, 2006).

6 E.g., Phillippe Schmitter, "Dangers and Dilemmas of Democracy," in *The Global Resurgence of Democracy*, 2nd ed., eds. Larry Diamond and Marc Plattner, 76–93 (Baltimore: John Hopkins University Press, 1996); Joe Foweraker and Roman Krznaric, "The Uneven Performance of Third Wave Democracies: Electoral Politics and the Imperfect Rule of Law in Latin America," *Latin American Politics and Society* 44/3 (2002); Larry Diamond, "Elections without Democracy: Thinking about Hybrid Regimes," *Journal of Democracy* 13/2 (2002); and Peter Smith, *Democracy in Latin America: Political Change in Comparative Perspective*, 2nd ed. (New York: Oxford University Press, 2012).

7 Guillermo O'Donnell, *Democracy, Agency, and the State: Theory with Comparative Intent* (New York: Oxford University Press, 2010), 152–154. For a historical case study, see Brodwyn Fischer, *A Poverty of Rights: Citizenship and Inequality in Twentieth-Century Rio de Janeiro* (Stanford: Stanford University Press, 2008).

torture suspects, and for police and paramilitary forces to intimidate, detain, or assassinate civil-society leaders opposing the interests of political and economic elites.[8] In this context, efforts by Latin American citizens to transcend the limits of formal political channels through mass mobilizations, the creation of autonomous communal spaces, or the support of populist strongmen, which scholars sometimes describe as examples of a "post-liberal" mode of politics, might at least partly be read as attempts to achieve the very traditional liberal ideal of meaningful legal rule.[9]

Carl Schmitt and Giorgio Agamben's discussions of the relationship between sovereignty and law, as revealed in the juridical figure of the state of exception, offer an important conceptual aid for understanding the appearance of anomalous legal zones in modern systems of power. Equating sovereignty with the authority to suspend the legal order – "[s]overeign is he who decides on the exception" – Schmitt argued that the power to suspend legal protections in times of perceived emergency entailed a further power to define the conditions of the law's ordinary application.[10] "The exception," he wrote, "appears in its absolute form when a situation in which legal prescriptions can be valid must first be brought about."[11] Sovereignty would then be about ordering society in a manner that makes it receptive to the rule of law. As Agamben stresses in his reading of Schmitt's work, such a conception of sovereignty makes it impossible to think of the sovereign as standing altogether outside the realm of law.[12] Rather, "the telos of [Schmitt's] theory is the inscription of

8   See the essays in Juan Méndez, Guillermo O'Donnell, and Paulo Sérgio Pinheiro, eds., *The (Un) Rule of Law and the Underprivileged in Latin America* (Notre Dame: University of Notre Dame Press, 1999), and especially the chapters by Nigel Rodley, "Torture and Conditions of Detention in Latin America," 25–41; Paul Chevigny, "Defining the Role of the Police in Latin America," 49–70; and Roger Plant, "The Rule of Law and the Underprivileged in Latin America: A Rural Perspective," 87–108. See also Nancy Scheper-Hughes, "Death Squads and Democracy in Northeastern Brazil," in *Law and Disorder in the Postcolony*, eds. Comaroff and Comaroff, 150–187; as well as the various Latin American country reports issued by Amnesty International, for example "Mexico 2015/16," available at https://www.amnesty.org/en/coun tries/americas/mexico/report-mexico, accessed 21 March 2016.

9   On "post-liberalism," see Benjamin Arditi, *Politics on the Edges of Liberalism: Difference, Populism, Revolution, Agitation* (Edinburgh: Edinburgh University Press, 2007), and "Arguments about the Left Turns in Latin America: A Post-Liberal Politics?" *Latin American Research Review* 43/3 (2008); and Maxwell Cameron, "Toward Postliberal Democracy in Latin America?" paper presented at the REMLAM conference *What's Left? The Left Turn in Latin America, 15 Years After*, Montreal, 23–24 March 2016.

10 Carl Schmitt, *Political Theology: Four Chapters on the Concept of Sovereignty*, trans. George Schwab (Cambridge: MIT Press, 1985), 5.

11 Schmitt, *Political Theology*, 13.

12 Giorgio Agamben, *Homo Sacer: Sovereign Power and Bare Life*, trans. Daniel Heller-Roazen (Stanford: Stanford University Press, 1998), 15–20, 25–28, 36–38; and *State of Exception*, trans. Kevin Attell (Chicago: University of Chicago Press, 2005), 32–36.

the state of exception within a juridical context." Agamben stresses the paradox contained in this effort, since "what must be inscribed within the law is something that is essentially exterior to it, that is, nothing less than the suspension of the juridical order itself."[13]

Pitched at the level of formal juridical logic, Schmitt and Agamben's analyses leave no room for examining the relationship between the law and non-state, societal sources of normativity.[14] Lauren Benton has shown that in five hundred years of European overseas expansion, imperial agents, who rarely spread the rule of law in an even and homogeneous fashion, ended up producing "[p]eculiar forms of attenuated and partial sovereignty" and "[m]ultiple anomalous legal spaces" – legal spaces, then, that appear to confirm Schmitt and Agamben's insight into the reliance of modern state-craft on the state of exception.[15] However, Benton argues that the "lumpy juridical order" of the European colonial world was not premised on an opposition between law on one side and exception on the other. Rather, it was premised on the existence of multiple layers of often competing authorities, all of which strove to justify their positions within the total context of imperial law. In such a system, there was no space for the kind of "juridical void" posited by Agamben, since "exceptional moments of apparent legal rupture" would only be "[converted] into experiments in other kinds of law."[16] In nineteenth-century Mexico, as well, the existence of spaces that were legally anomalous did not open the door to moral chaos. Rather, in zones where the rule of law was suspended, social relations were structured by alternative ethical codes associated with the principles of property, social precedence, or communal tradition.

In spite of these caveats, Schmitt and Agamben's conception of sover-eignty as a decision about the law – and hence a decision bound to the law but not by the law – captures a dimension of legal politics that mostly gets lost in Benton's grand historical sweep. Benton describes European imper-ial states between 1400 and 1900 as frameworks for the administration of conflict endowed with an immense absorptive capacity: settlers and natives, merchants and pirates, priests and soldiers all brought their claims before

---

13 Agamben, *State of Exception*, 32–33. This paradox, situating the state of exception in a "no-man's land between public law and political fact, and between the juridical order and life" (Agamben, *State of Exception*, 1), is the source of Schmitt and Agamben's disagreement over whether the state of exception connects the law to an ultimate fullness of power (Schmitt) or an ultimate state of anomie (Agamben).

14 For a helpful discussion of Schmitt and Agamben's marginalization of "the political nature of the societal," see Jef Huysmans, "The Jargon of Exception – On Schmitt, Agamben and the Absence of Political Society," *International Political Sociology* 2 (2008), here 167.

15 Lauren Benton, *A Search for Sovereignty: Law and Geography in European Empires, 1400–1900* (New York: Cambridge University Press, 2010), 279–280.

16 Benton, *Search for Sovereignty*, 290.

imperial tribunals, thus acknowledging their status as imperial subjects.[17] Benton does not claim that the imperial state was neutral with regard to the conflicts it arbitrated. Nevertheless, her emphasis on the state as legal arbiter leaves her little room for exploring its role in such conflicts as an involved and interested actor, nor for exploring the extent to which the form of the state itself may have been at issue in conflicts between competing social groups. In the case of the Spanish Empire and its successor states, such considerations become crucial for understanding the popular uprisings of the late eighteenth century – such as, most notably, the 1780–1782 Andean rebellion – as well as the independence wars and subsequent civil conflicts of the nineteenth.[18]

In this book we have seen that the emergence of anomalous legal zones in nineteenth-century Mexico cannot be understood apart from a history of struggle about the nature and social foundations of the post-colonial state. Let us recall the principal features of that struggle. On one side stood proponents of what I have called revolutionary liberalism – the idea that all adult male citizens, no matter their social position, were legal equals. The struggle for revolutionary liberalism was able to define Mexico's nineteenth-century history to the extent it did because it was a deeply popular project. It would be misleading, albeit not entirely anachronistic, to speak of support for the project as an alliance between the working and peasant classes on the one hand and a stratum of local elites, including shopkeepers, professionals, and medium-size farm owners, on the other. Mexicans did think about the world in terms of classes and social groups but they did not only, and perhaps not primarily, think about it in those terms. The independence and immediate post-independence period in particular

17 See *A Search for Sovereignty* as well as Benton's previous book, *Law and Colonial Cultures: Legal Regimes in World History, 1400–1900* (New York: Cambridge University Press, 2002).

18 For studies placing the Andean insurgency of the early 1780s within a global context of revolution, incipient nationalisms, and anti-colonial state formation, see Charles Walker, *Smoldering Ashes: Cuzco and the Creation of Republican Peru, 1780–1840* (Durham, NC: Duke University Press, 1999), chapter 2; and Sinclair Thomson, *We Alone Will Rule: Native Andean Politics in the Age of Insurgency* (Madison: University of Wisconsin Press, 2002). Benton herself describes the creation of areas of judicial "indeterminacy" in nineteenth-century India as a deliberate British policy. The colonial government, she writes, "insisted on the importance of not specifying legal arrangements in treaties or other agreements with [quasi-sovereign] native states" so as to keep open a margin for pure (that is, legally unrestrained) political decision-making. While recognizing that it would be "tempting to adopt the conceptual aid of exception to talk about this project," Benton goes on to argue that the government attempted to lead even this deliberate zone of indeterminacy back to the legal order by announcing the creation of a new, imperial law that incorporated the category of indeterminacy. But in talking about the creation of a kind of law that, even in its ordinary application, was defined by its deliberate indeterminacy, it seems to me that Benton describes precisely "this no-man's-land between public law and political fact" that Agamben seeks to analyze in his study of the state of exception. Benton, *A Search for Sovereignty*, 257–260, 294. Agamben, *State of Exception*, 1.

was a time when social categories were fluid and their significance contested and uncertain. The rich lost some of their wealth, and the poor gained a chance of asserting themselves. In this context, revolutionary liberalism emerged as a project that mobilized people who shared a commitment to certain moral and behavioral norms, irrespective of their relative social positions.

Moral and behavioral norms did much to determine the practical articulation of Mexico's post-colonial legal order. The realization of legal equality depended on the strength of a social vision that could tie republican institutions to the ethical imperatives of concrete life practices. Revolutionary liberalism in nineteenth-century Mexico was a viable proposition when and where people were willing to commit to the values of labor and domesticity – and hence also, at least implicitly, to the model of social discipline entailed by those values – in their personal lives. The relationship between behavioral norms and the rule of law was most visible in mestizo towns, where hard-working patriarchs, by participating in the police force of the civic militia, stood guard over a citizen ideal they themselves embodied. This labor-based legal culture was egalitarian in a restricted sense: it treated adults differently from children and men differently from women, and it drew a line – firm in principle but indistinct in reality – between virtuous workers, to whom it gave rights and protections, and profligate idlers, whom it expelled into the alternate world of the military.

The relationship between a valorization of labor and the appearance of liberal legal institutions was equally pronounced in estate settlements. Hacienda tenants opposing the private authority exercised by their landlords argued that labor, and not property, was the only productive foundation on which a republican legal system could be realistically constructed; giving in to the authority of property was, in effect, to reproduce a form of colonial tyranny and thus to collude in the atrophy of the republican enterprise. In indigenous towns, where local politics were inflected with ethnic as well as ideological motives, and larger allegiances were constrained by the racism of mestizo society, the relationship between the rule of law and the values of labor and domesticity was more tenuous. But even here such a relationship was not absent. It was central to the efforts of indigenous commoners to hold their governments accountable in the distribution and, in the second half of the century, the formal privatization of town lands. In indigenous towns, too, the patriarchal family became the exemplary subject of the liberal state even as it remained embedded in colonial-era corporate structures.

In post-colonial Mexico a commitment to an egalitarian legal regime was common but not automatic: it was refused as often as it was undertaken. On the other side of the struggle about the shape of the new legal

regime stood a diverse coalition of actors. Most unambiguously, the army
rejected the ideal of equality as a matter of institutional policy. Apart from
the army, we can distinguish five groups of people who opposed the
ascendency of revolutionary liberalism: among popular sectors, (1) many,
and perhaps most, hacienda residents and (2) many indigenous commoners;
among elite sectors, (3) urban patricians, (4) owners of agricultural estates,
and (5) some native elites and *principales*. Each of these groups had different
reasons for opposing the idea that labor constituted the productive and
ethical foundation of republican law. Hacienda residents and indigenous
commoners opposed the liberal system in favor of structures of legitimacy
that hearkened back to the colonial period. For the first, haciendas served as
"regions of refuge" in a similar way that, according to James Scott, the
mountain area of Zomia was for centuries a region of refuge for peasants in
Southeast Asia: a territory that was buffered against the severity of the fiscal
and military burdens as well as the disciplinary strictures imposed by the
state. Indigenous commoners who rejected the privatization of land and
dismantling of corporate institutions similarly invoked an older, pre-liberal
legal modus. By staging riots, raiding cattle from encroaching haciendas, or
filing lawsuits in the name of a town's colonial-era *común*, native citizens
practiced a narrow and exclusive kind of solidarity that helped them cope
with the abiding racism of mestizo society but deprived them of the
opportunity to contribute to the construction of new state institutions.

In contrast to hacienda tenants and indigenous commoners, patricians,
landowners, and indigenous elites dealt with the challenge of liberalism not
by clinging to the corporate distinctions of the colonial period but by
exploring ways to build structures of privilege into the institutions of
a formally egalitarian legal system. They did so at different times and with
different intensities. Patrician politicians argued already in the early post-
independence years that not labor but the interlocked phenomena of education, wealth, and social precedence were necessary to support the constitutional order; and they questioned whether people who lacked these attributes
were capable of even passively enjoying the same liberties as those who
possessed them. Landowners, by contrast, were prodded into combining
their emphasis on property rights with a practice of state-backed law enforcement little by little, and sometimes against their will. Finally, some
indigenous elites found ways of converting their ethnic attributes into
legal rights and powers only late in the century when, taking advantage of
the policy of land disentailment, they were able to convert formerly communal town lands into large private holdings. These groups attacked not the
idea of legal equality itself but the more foundational idea that a legal order
could be based on the productive principle of labor. In the conditions of
nineteenth-century Mexico, they argued, only the authority attached to
wealth or social precedence could guarantee the rule of law. These were

forward-looking ideas. They took advantage of the disciplinarian possibilities of a unitary, nominally egalitarian, legal state while organizing judicial institutions in a way that created new positions of privilege.

For zones of weakened legality were, of course, also zones of privilege. The privilege they conferred was different from the one that colonial elites had, as a matter of course, commanded due to their caste and group ascriptions. Indeed, the formation of anomalous legal zones within a system that continued to define itself by its legal egalitarianism placed the Díaz regime at a considerable distance from colonial instruments of rule, notwithstanding its "neo-colonial" reputation. The celebration of republican values, including the republican legal system enshrined in the 1857 Constitution, formed an indispensable part of the dictatorship's modus operandi; it provided that horizon of normalcy without which the creation of conditions of exceptionality, or legal suspension, would not have been meaningful. Change in nineteenth-century Mexico was thus dialectical: elites reacting against the egalitarianism of the early republican years incorporated elements of that egalitarianism into their own system of law. They did this, not because they had reflected on the matter, but because for most the formal hierarchies of the colonial era were no longer a part of their cognitive universe.

From the perspective of Porfirian elites, the hidden and de facto nature of legal privilege carried substantial rewards. In at least two ways, it allowed for the exercise of a peculiarly efficient – and, perhaps, peculiarly modern – kind of power. First, by declaring its loyalty to the historic principles of Mexican liberalism, for which the dictator and many high-ranking officials had risked their lives fighting, the Díaz regime created a considerable problem of legitimacy for potential opponents. The point is perhaps not entirely obvious: why, after all, should it have been difficult to challenge a legal system that consistently disregarded its own ideological premises? Part of the answer has to do with a kind of innocence that had characterized Mexico's previous political history. In none of the confrontations of the early republican period had Mexicans had occasion to distinguish between a regime's governing practice and its declarations of principle. Before 1835, national factional divisions had been associated with substantive policy issues: for or against the expulsion of Spaniards, for or against the expansion of the civic militias, for or against the taxation of landed property. After 1835, the major civil conflicts had been about the country's constitutional foundations, and thus about such vital questions as whether municipal councils should be elected or appointed and whether adult male suffrage should be universal or restricted to property holders. In both periods, political divisions had been clear and substantive. During the Porfiriato this ideological clarity disappeared from the practice of politics. Opposing the existence of anomalous legal zones – which existed against rather than in harmony with official declarations of principle – required the development of new critical faculties, capable of looking beyond particular instances of abuse, which the regime might always blame on individual agents or officials, and at the systematic character of the regime's cultivation of illegality.

Challenging the legitimacy of the Porfirian legal system was difficult also because that system produced a patchy and fragmented experience of the law. Violence and illegality have been persistent themes in scholarship about the Porfiriato because they occurred in the country's most socially and economically dynamic areas, because they issued in a major social revolution, and because, until recently, most historians were uncynical enough to assume that the systemic presence of such phenomena, when it comes to the overall evaluation of a historical period, deserves a more than ordinary share of attention. These are compelling reasons. Nevertheless, I have argued that the emergence of zones of exception in late nineteenth-century Mexico also implied the preservation of other areas of law that remained as functional as they had ever been. For significant sectors of the population, it was possible to perceive the dictator as Díaz wanted to be perceived: as a beacon of peace and legal rule. Even zones of exception were not created equal. While discussions of legal deprivation often take their cue from the situation of people who have been altogether stripped of legal rights and attributes – for example, refugees, concentration-camp inmates, or, in certain historical contexts, national minorities – the deprivation suffered in most of those zones was of a less total kind.[19] Their inhabitants were seldom completely abandoned by public institutions: whether the rule of law was blocked, privatized, or vested in the extra-legal bodies of the army and rural police, there were always other courts to which people could take legal business, other authorities before whom they could denounce abuses. The peculiarity of their situation was only that in order to do so they confronted institutional hurdles many of them had no way of surmounting. In the matter of legal deprivation, the Porfirian regime produced a host of individual frustrations rather than a strong, shared sense of grievance.

A second way in which the informal nature of Porfirian privilege helped advance a new system of rule was by leaving people at the bottom of the legal hierarchy with no instruments to oppose the injustices to which they were exposed. In this regard, it is particularly instructive to compare the Díaz regime with the governments of the colonial era. Colonial inequality had

---

19 For influential discussions of legal abandonment, see Agamben, *Homo Sacer* and *State of Exception*; and Arendt, *Origins of Totalitarianism*, chapter 9. For exemplary recent studies of historical instances of – often less than total – forms of legal deprivation, see Mae Ngai, *Impossible Subjects: Illegal Aliens and the Making of Modern America* (Princeton: Princeton University Press, 2004); Fischer, *A Poverty of Rights*; and Miranda Spieler, *Empire and Underworld: Captivity in French Guiana* (Harvard: Harvard University Press, 2012).

been formal in kind, with society divided into different classes defined by their legal attributes. While some of these classes were subordinate to others, even subordinate groups had rights that allowed them to contest, and put limits on, the way dominant groups exercised their power. Indigenous people, for example, regularly took their complaints to the General Indian Court in Mexico City, designed to offer protection against abuses committed by local state agents such as the *corregidores* or *alcaldes mayores*. After independence, such protective institutions disappeared together with legalized forms of social difference. Residents of anomalous legal zones thus experienced a kind of emptying, or thinning out, of their legal personae; in varying degrees they approached the state of "bare life" that Agamben has placed at the center of his discussion of modern regimes of exception.[20]

In contrast to the legal inequality of the colonial period, that of the Porfiriato was based on a privative state. Formally the equals of their superiors, residents of zones of legal exception were divested of powers that offered them protection against those superiors' abuses. This divestment was related to the replacement of labor with property as the value on which state sovereignty came to rest and for the sake of which the rule of law would routinely be suspended. Certainly, as foreign investment poured into the country and the economy experienced its first sustained growth in the national era, the enforcement of ideals of work and domesticity did not cease to be a priority for Porfirian political and economic elites. But work discipline was now an establishment concern in its own right, while its association with civic morality and the joint creation of a legalized public sphere lost most of its force. Labor was no longer a foundation for sovereign power but a subject on which that power would be exercised.

While I have drawn on Schmitt and Agamben's discussions of the state of exception to describe the illiberal legal order that emerged in Mexico at the end of the nineteenth century, I have departed from Schmitt and Agamben by treating exceptional legal states as institutional rather than juridical phenomena. The formal declaration of a state of exception always exposes the limited self-sufficiency of the law. It invokes a realm of necessity in which the rules of the legal state are temporarily unviable. The creation of institutional zones of exception, by contrast, hides behind the rules of the legal state. It is characterized by its invisibility. While further study would be needed to gain a global perspective on the relationship between law and exception in the modern world, it seems to me likely that it is in this second sense that, in the last two centuries, states of exception have had the more pervasive – and, from a liberal perspective, the more corrosive – effects on the exercise of power in ostensibly law-governed nations.

---

20   Agamben, *Homo Sacer.*

Bibliography

Archives

Mexico City

Archivo General de la Nación (AGN)
  Gobernación

Guanajuato

Archivo General del Estado de Guanajuato (AGEG)
  Guerra (G)
  Justicia (J)
  Leyes y Decretos
  Municipios (M)
  Supremo Tribunal de Justicia (STJ)
Archivo Histórico Municipal de León (AHML)
  Jefatura Política
  Justicia
Archivo Municipal de Guanjuato (AMG)
  Ayuntamiento de Guanjuato – Militar (AG-M)

San Luis Potosí

Archivo Histórico del Estado de San Luis Potosí (AHESLP)
  Leyes y Decretos
  Provincia de San Luis Potosí (PSLP)
  Secretaría General de Gobierno (SGG)
  Supremo Tribunal de Justicia (STJ)
Archivo Municipal de Ciudad Fernández (AMCF)
Archivo Municipal de Rioverde (AMRV)
Casa de Cultura Jurídica de San Luis Potosí (CCJ-SLP)

Oaxaca

Archivo Histórico Judicial (AHJ)
Archivo Histórico Municipal de Teposcolula (AHMT)

Querétaro

Archivo Histórico del Poder Judicial de Querétaro (AHPJQ)
Documentos Judiciales (DJ)

Published Primary Sources

Amnesty International. "Mexico 2015/16." https://www.amnesty.org/en/countries/ameri cas/mexico/report-mexico. Accessed 21 March 2016.

Bulnes, Francisco. *El verdadero Díaz y la Revolución.* Mexico City: Editora Nacional, 1967.

Colección de las leyes y decretos expedidos por el Congreso General de los Estados-Unidos Mejicanos, Tomo III, que comprende los del Segundo Constituyente, second edition. Mexico City: Imprenta de Galvan á cargo de Mariano Arévalo, 1829.

Colección de leyes, decretos y circulares del estado libre y soberano de Oaxaca. Oaxaca: Imprenta del Estado en el Instituto, 1851.

Constitución política del Estado libre de Guanajuato, sancionada en 14 de abril de 1826; decretos en que se han hecho reformas a la misma, y reglamento interior del h. congreso del mismo Estado. Tipografia de Oñate: 1826.

Constitución política del Estado libre de S. Luis Potosí. Mexico City: Imprenta del águila, 1826.

Constitución Política de la Monarquía Española. Promulgada en Cádiz a 19 Marzo de 1812. Cádiz: Imprenta Real, 1812.

Constitución Política de la República Mexicana de. 1857.

Dublán, Manuel, and José María Lozano, eds. *Legislación Mexicana, ó, Colección completa de las disposiciones legislativas expedidas desde la independencia de la República.* 32 vols. Mexico City: Various publishers, 1876–1902.

Leyes Constitucionales. [1836].

"Memoria de la administracion publica del Estado de Guanajuato, correspondiente al año de 1831, que el Vice-Gobernador Constitucional, en ejercicio del poder ejecutivo, presenta en cumplimiento del articulo 82 de la Constitucion del mismo Estado." Mexico City: Imprenta del Aguila, 1832.

"Memoria del Secretario de Estado y del despacho de la Guerra presentada a las Camaras en enero de 1825." Mexico City: Imprenta del Supremo Gobierno de los Estados-unidos mexicanos, en Palacio, 1825.

"Memoria instructiva, que en cumplimiento de la parte 4.a del articulo 109 de la Constitucion del estado de Guanajuato, presenta al Superior Gobierno del mismo su primer Vice-Gobernador Constitucional, Año de 1830." Guanajuato: Imprenta del Supremo Gobierno administrada por el C. Ruperto Rocha, 1831.

"Memoria leída por el C. Gobernador Constitucional del Estado Libre y Soberano de Guanajuato General de División Manuel González en la solemne instalación del 12.o Congreso Constitucional verificada el 15 de setiembre de 1886." Mexico City: Imprenta de "El Gran Libro", 1887.

"Memoria leída por el C. Gobernador interino del Estado Libre y Soberano de Guanajuato, General Pablo Rocha y Portú, en la solemne instalación del 11.o congreso constitucional, verificado el 15 de septiembre de 1884." Guanajuato: Imprenta del Estado, 1885.

"Memoria presentada al H. Congreso del estado de San Luis Potosí por el Gobernador Constitucional Ingeniero Blas Escontría, relativa a los actos administrativos correspondiente al período de Agosto de 1898 a igual mes de 1899." San Luis Potosí: Tipografía de la Escuela I. Militar, 1899.

"Memoria presentada por el C. Gobernador Constitucional del Estado Libre y Soberano de Guanajuato, General de División Manuel González en cumplimiento de la fracción 8.a, artículo 61, de la Constitución del mismo, en la solemne instalación del 14.o Congreso Constitucional, verificada el 15 de Septiembre de 1890." Mexico City: Imprenta de Ignacio Escalante, 1890.

"Memoria que el Gobernador del Estado de Guanajuato formo para dar cumplimiento a la parte 8.a del articulo 161 de la Constitucion Federal, ampliandola en otros ramos para conocimiento del Congreso del mismo Estado, todo por lo respectivo al año de 1826." Mexico City: Imprenta y librería a cargo de Martin Rivera, 1827.

"Memoria que presenta el Gobernador de Guanajuato al Congreso Constituyente del estado de los negocios públicos que han estado á su cuidado, desde 10 de Mayo de 1824 hasta 31 de Diciembre de 1825." Guanajuato: Imprenta del supremo Gobierno en Palacio, 1826.

"Memoria que presenta el Gobernador del estado de Guanajuato, de su administracion publica correspondiente al año de 1829, para cumplir con lo dispuesto en el artículo 161 fraccion 8.a de la constitucion federal, y en el 82 de la particular del mismo Estado." Guanajuato: Imprenta del Supremo Gobierno a cargo del C. Jose Maria Carranco, 1830.

"Memoria sobre la administración pública del Estado de Guanajuato presentada al Congreso del mismo por el C. Gobernador Constitucional Lic. Joaquín Obregón González el 1.o de Abril de 1895." Morelia: Imprenta y Litografía de la Escuela I. M. Porfirio Díaz, 1895.

Mora, José María Luis. *México y sus revoluciones*, vol. 1, ed. Agustin Yañez. Mexico City: Porrúa, 1965.

Planes en la nación Mexicana. Mexico City: Cámara de senadores de la República Mexicana, 1987.

Rabasa, Emilio. *La constitución y la dictadura: Estudio sobre la organización política de México*. Mexico City: Cien de México, 2002 [1912].

Ramírez y Sesma, Joaquín, ed. *Colección de decretos, ordenes y circulares: espedidas por los gobiernos nacionales de la Federación Mexicana desde el año de 1821 hasta el de 1826 para el arreglo del ejército de los Estados-Unidos Mexicanos*. Mexico City: Imprenta a cargo de Martin Rivera, 1827.

"Real Declaración sobre puntos esenciales de la ordenanza de Milicias Provinciales de España, que interin se regla la formal, que corresponde á estos Cuerpos, se debe observar como tal en todas sus partes." Mexico City: D.Felipe de Zúñiga y Ontiveros, calle de la Palma, 1781 [1767].

Recopilación de leyes de los Reynos de las Indias. Madrid: Vda. de J. Ibarra, 1791.

Sierra, Justo. *The Political Evolution of the Mexican People*. Trans. Charles Ramsdell. Austin: University of Texas Press, 1969.

Turner, John Kenneth. *Barbarous Mexico*. Austin: University of Texas Press, 1969.

Zarco, Francisco. *Historia del Congreso Extraordinario Constituyente {1856–1857}*. Mexico City: El Colegio de México, 1956.

Secondary Sources

Acemoglu, Daron, and James Robinson. *Why National Fail: The Origins of Power, Prosperity, and Poverty*. New York: Crown Publishing Group, 2012.

Adelman, Jeremy, ed. *Colonial Legacies: The Problem of Persistence in Latin American History*. New York: Routledge, 1999.

Adelman, Jeremy. "Introduction: The Problem of Persistence in Latin American History." In *Colonial Legacies: The Problem of Persistence in Latin American History*. Edited by Jeremy Adelman, 1–14 New York: Routledge, 1999.

Agamben, Giorgio. *Homo Sacer: Sovereign Power and Bare Life*. Trans. Daniel Heller-Roazen. Stanford: Stanford University Press, 1998.

State of Exception. Trans. Kevin Attell. Chicago: University of Chicago Press, 2005.

Aguirre, Carlos, and Robert Buffington, eds. *Reconstructing Criminality in Latin America*. Wilmington, DE: Scholarly Resources, 2000.

Aguirre Beltrán, Gonzalo. *Regiones de Refugio: El desarrollo de la comunidad y el proceso dominical en Mestizo América*. Mexico City: Instituto Indigenista Interamericano, 1967.

Alonso, Ana María. *Thread of Blood: Colonialism, Revolution, and Gender on Mexico's Northern Frontier*. Tucson: University of Arizona Press, 1995.

Amis, Martin. *The War against Cliché: Essays and Reviews, 1971–2000*. London: Jonathan Cape, 2001.

Anderson, Rodney. *Outcasts in Their Own Land: Mexican Industrial Workers, 1906–1911*. DeKalb: Northern Illinois University Press, 1976.

Anna, Timothy. *Forging Mexico: 1821–1835*. Lincoln: University of Nebraska Press, 1998.

Annino, Antonio. "Soberanías en lucha." In *Inventando la nación: Iberoamérica. Siglo XIX*. Edited by Antonio Annino and François-Xavier Guerra, 152–184. Mexico City: Fondo de Cultura Económica, 2003.

"Pueblos, liberalismo, y nación en México." In *Inventando la nación: Iberoamérica. Siglo XIX*. Edited by Antonio Annino and François-Xavier Guerra, 399–430. Mexico City: Fondo de Cultura Económica, 2003.

"The Two-Faced Janus: The Pueblos and the Origins of Mexican Liberalism." In *Cycles of Conflict, Centuries of Change: Crisis, Reform, and Revolution in Mexico*. Edited by Elisa Servín, Leticia Reina, and John Tutino, 60–90. Durham, NC: Duke University Press, 2007.

Annino, Antonio and François-Xavier Guerra, eds. *Inventando la nación: Iberoamérica. Siglo XIX*. Mexico City: Fondo de Cultura Económica, 2003.

Archer, Christon. *The Army in Bourbon Mexico, 1760 – 1810*. Albuquerque: University of New Mexico Press, 1977.

Arditi, Benjamin. *Politics on the Edges of Liberalism: Difference, Populism, Revolution, Agitation*. Edinburgh: Edinburgh University Press, 2007.

"Arguments about the Left Turns in Latin America: A Post-Liberal Politics?" *Latin American Research Review* 43/3 (2008): 59–81.

Arendt, Hannah. *The Origins of Totalitarianism*. New York: Harcourt, Brace, 1951.

Armstrong, Nancy. *Desire and Domestic Fiction: A Political History of the Novel*. New York: Oxford University Press, 1987.

Arnold, Linda. "Privileged Justice? The Fuero Militar in Early National Mexico." In *Judicial Institutions in Nineteenth-Century Latin America*. Edited by Eduardo Zimmermann, 49–64. London: Institute of Latin American Studies, 1999.

Arrom, Silvia. "Popular Politics in Mexico City: The Parian Riot, 1828." *Hispanic American Historical Review* 68/2 (1988): 245–268.

Austin, John. *The Province of Jurisprudence Determined*. New York: B. Franklin, 1970.

Ballard Perry, Laurens. *Juárez and Díaz: Machine Politics in Mexico*. DeKalb: Northern Illinois University Press, 1978.

Baskes, Jeremy. *Indians, Merchants, and Markets: A Reinterpretation of the Repartimiento and Spanish Indian Economic Relations in Late Colonial Oaxaca, Mexico, 1750–1821*. Stanford: Stanford University Press, 2000.

Bauer, Arnold. *Chilean Rural Society from the Spanish Conquest to 1930*. New York: Cambridge University Press, 1975.

Bayly, C. A. *The Birth of the Modern World 1780–1914: Global Connections and Comparisons.* Malden, MA: Blackwell Publishing, 2004.

Bazant, Jan. *Cinco haciendas Mexicanas: Tres siglos de vida rural en San Luis Potosí (1600–1910).* 3rd ed. Mexico City: El Colegio de México, 1995.

Beattie, Peter. *The Tribute of Blood: Army, Honor, Race, and Nation in Brazil, 1864–1945.* Durham, NC: Duke University Press, 2001.

Beezley, William. *Judas at the Jockey Club and Other Episodes of Porfirian Mexico.* Lincoln: University of Nebraska Press, 1987.

Benjamin, Thomas and Marcial Ocasio-Meléndez. "Organizing the Memory of Modern Mexico: Porfirian Historiography in Perspective, 1880s–1980s." *Hispanic American Historical Review* 64/2 (1984): 323–364.

Benjamin, Walter. "Critique of Violence." In *Reflections: Essays, Aphorisms, Autobiographical Writings.* Edited by Peter Demetz, 277–300. Trans. Edmund Jephcott. New York: Harcourt Brace Jovanovich, 1978.

Benson, Nettie Lee. *The Provincial Deputation in Mexico: Harbinger of Provincial Autonomy, Independence, and Federalism.* Austin: University of Texas Press, 1992.

Benton, Lauren. *Law and Colonial Cultures: Legal Regimes in World History, 1400–1900.* Cambridge: Cambridge University Press, 2002.

A Search for Sovereignty: Law and Geography in European Empires, 1400–1900. New York: Cambridge University Press, 2010.

Berman, Harold. *Law and Revolution: The Formation of the Western Legal Tradition.* Cambridge: Harvard University Press, 1983.

Berumen Félix, Claudia Serafina. "La legislación decimonónica y la Media Luna (San Luis Potosí)." In *Agua y tierra en México, siglos XIX y XX.* Vol. 1. Edited by Antonio Escobar Ohmstede, Martín Sánchez Rodríguez, and Ana Ma. Gutiérrez Rivas, 103–123. Zamora: El Colegio de Michoacán, 2008.

Bethell, Leslie, ed. *The Cambridge History of Latin America.* 6 vols. Cambridge: Cambridge University Press, 1986.

Blackbourn, David, and Geoff Eley. *The Peculiarities of German History: Bourgeois Society and Politics in Nineteenth-Century Germany.* New York: Oxford University Press, 1984.

Borah, Woodrow. *Justice by Insurance: The General Indian Court of Colonial Mexico and the Legal Aides of the Half-Real.* Berkeley: University of California Press, 1983.

Boyer, Richard. "Women, *La Mala Vida*, and the Politics of Marriage." In *Sexuality and Marriage in Colonial Latin America.* Edited by Asunción Lavrin, 252–286. Lincoln: University of Nebraska Press, 1989.

Brading, David. *Miners and Merchants in Bourbon Mexico, 1763–1810.* New York: Cambridge University Press, 1971.

Haciendas and Ranchos in the Mexican Bajío: León 1700–1860. New York: Cambridge University Press, 1978.

Breña, Roberto. *El primer liberalismo español y los procesos de emancipación de América, 1808–1824.* Mexico City: El Colegio de México, 2006.

Brittsan, Zachary. "In Faith or Fear: Fighting with Lozada." PhD dissertation. University of California San Diego, 2010.

Buffington, Robert. *Criminal and Citizen in Modern Mexico.* Lincoln: University of Nebraska Press, 2000.

Bunker, Steven. *Creating Mexican Consumer Culture in the Age of Porfirio Díaz.* Albuquerque: University of New Mexico Press, 2012.

Buve, Raymond. "Un paisaje lunar habitado por bribones y sus víctimas. Mirada retrospectiva al debate sobre las haciendas y los pueblos durante el Porfiriato (1876–1911)." In *Don Porfirio presidente . . ., nunca omnipotente: Hallazgos, reflexiones y debates. 1876–1911.*

Edited by Romana Falcón and Raymond Buve, 121–152. Mexico City: Universidad Iberoamericana, 1998.

"Pueblos indígenas de Tlaxcala, las leyes liberales juaristas y la guerra de Reforma: una perspectiva desde abajo, 1855–1861." In *Los pueblos indios en los tiempos de Benito Juárez (1847–1872)*. Edited by Antonio Escobar Ohmstede, 91–121. Mexico City: Universidad Autónoma Metropolitana, 2007.

Cameron, Maxwell. "Toward Postliberal Democracy in Latin America?" Paper presented at the REMLAM conference *What's Left? The Left Turn in Latin America, 15 Years After.* Montreal, 23–24 March 2016.

Cañedo Gamboa, Sergio. "Merchants and Family Business in San Luis Potosí, Mexico: The Signs of an Economic Upsurge, 1820–1846." PhD dissertation. University of California San Diego, 2011.

Cañedo Gamboa, Sergio, and María Isabel Monroy Castillo. *Ponciano Arriaga: La formación de un liberal 1811–1847.* San Luis Potosí: Gobierno del Estado de San Luis Potosí and Archivo Histórico del Estado, 2008.

Cañeque, Alejandro. *The King's Living Image: The Culture and Politics of Viceregal Power in Mexico.* New York: Routledge, 2004.

Caplan, Karen. *Indigenous Citizens: Local Liberalism in Early National Oaxaca and Yucatán.* Stanford: Stanford University Press, 2010.

Carmagnani, Marcello. *El regreso de los dioses: El proceso de reconstitución de la identidad étnica en Oaxaca. Siglos XVII y XVIII.* Mexico City: Fondo de Cultura Económica, 1988.

Estado y mercado: La economía pública del liberalismo mexicano, 1850–1911. Mexico City: Fideicomiso Historia de las Américas, 1994.

Castañedea, Jorge. *Mañana Forever? Mexico and the Mexicans.* New York: Alfred A. Knopf, 2011.

Castillo, Norma Angélica. "Cambios y continuidades entre las repúblicas indias y los ayuntamientos constitucionales de Cholula, 1768–1865." In *Poder y legitimidad en México en el siglo XIX: Instituciones y cultura política.* Edited by Brian Connaughton, 137–179. Mexico City: Universidad Autónoma Metropolitana, 2003.

Centeno, Miguel Angel. *Blood and Debt: War and the Nation-State in Latin America.* University Park: Pennsylvania State University Press, 2002.

Cerutti, Mario. *Burguesía, capitales e industria en el norte de México: Monterrey y su ámbito regional (1850–1910).* Mexico City: Alianza Editorial, 1992.

Cervantes, Fernando. *The Devil in the New World: The Impact of Diabolism in New Spain.* New Haven: Yale University Press, 1994.

Chambers, Sarah. *From Subjects to Citizens: Honor, Gender, and Politics in Arequipa, Peru, 1780–1854.* University Park: The Pennsylvania State University Press, 1999.

"Crime and Citizenship: Judicial Practice in Arequipa, Peru, during the Transition from Colony to Republic." In *Reconstructing Criminality in Latin America.* Edited by Carlos A. Aguirre and Robert Buffington, 19–40. Wilmington, Del.: Scholarly Resources, 2000.

Families in War and Peace: Chile from Colony to Nation. Durham, NC: Duke University Press, 2015.

Chance, John, and William Taylor. "Cofradías and Cargos: An Historical Perspective on the Mesoamerican Civil-Religious Hierarchy." *American Ethnologist* 12/1 (1985): 1–26.

Chance, John. *Conquest of the Sierra: Spaniards and Indians in Colonial Oaxaca.* Norman: University of Oklahoma Press, 1989.

Chatterjee, Partha. *Nationalist Thought and the Colonial World: A Derivative Discourse.* London: Zed Books, 1993.

The Nation and Its Fragments: Colonial and Postcolonial Histories. Princeton: Princeton University Press, 1993.

Chevalier, François. *Land and Society in Colonial Mexico: The Great Hacienda*. Trans. Alvin Eustis. Berkeley: University of California Press, 1963.

"Acerca de los orígenes de la pequeña propiedad en el occidente de México. Historia comparada." In *Despues de los latifundios: La desintegración de la gran propiedad agraria en México*. Edited by Heriberto Moreno García, 3–12. El Colegio de Michoacán, Fondo para Actividades Sociales y Culturales de Michoacán, 1981.

Chevigny, Paul. "Defining the Role of the Police in Latin America." In *The (Un)Rule of Law and the Underprivileged in Latin America*. Edited by Juan Méndez, Guillermo O'Donnell, and Paulo Sérgio Pinheiro, 49–70. Notre Dame: University of Notre Dame Press, 1999.

Chowning, Margaret. "The Contours of the Post-1810 Depression in Mexico: A Reappraisal from a Regional Perspective." *Latin American Research Review* 27/2 (1992): 119–150.

"Reassessing the Prospects for Profit in Nineteenth-Century Mexican Agriculture from a Regional Perspective: Michoacán, 1810–1860." In *How Latin America Fell Behind: Essays on the Economic Histories of Brazil and Mexico, 1800–1914*. Edited by Stephen Haber, 179–215. Stanford: Stanford University Press, 1997.

Wealth and Power in Provincial Mexico: Michoacán from the Late Colony to the Revolution. Stanford: Stanford University Press, 1999.

Clagett, Helen. *A Guide to the Law and Legal Literature of the Mexican States*. Washington: Library of Congress, 1947.

Coatsworth, John. "Obstacles to Economic Development in Nineteenth Century Mexico." *American Historical Review* 83/1 (1978): 80–100.

Comaroff, Jean, and John Comaroff, eds. *Law and Disorder in the Postcolony*. Chicago: University of Chicago Press, 2006.

Connaughton, Brian, ed. *Poder y legitimidad en México en el siglo XIX: Instituciones y cultural política*. Mexico City: Biblioteca de Signos, 2003.

Prácticas populares, cultura política y poder en México, siglo XIX. Mexico City: Universidad Autónoma Metropolitana, Unidad Iztapalapa / Casa Juan Pablos, 2008.

Cook, Sherburne, and Woodrow Borah. *Essays in Population History: Mexico and the Caribbean*. Vol. 1. Berkeley: University of California Press, 1971.

Cosío Villegas, Daniel. *Historia Moderna de México: La República Restaurada: La Vida Política*. Mexico City: Editorial Hermes, 1955.

Costeloe, Michael. *The Central Republic in Mexico, 1835–1846: Hombres de Bien in the Age of Santa Anna*. Cambridge: Cambridge University Press, 1993.

Craiutu, Aurelian. *Liberalism under Siege: The Political Thought of the French Doctrinaires*. New York: Lexington Books, 2003.

Cypher, James. "Reconstituting Community: Local Religion, Political Culture, and Rebellion in Mexico's Sierra Gorda, 1846–1880." PhD dissertation. Indiana University Bloomington, 2007.

Deas, Malcolm. "The Man on Foot: Conscription and the Nation-State in Nineteenth-Century Latin America." In *Studies in the Formation of the Nation-State in Latin America*. Edited by James Dunkerley, 77–93. London: Institute of Latin American Studies, 2002.

Dennis, Philip. *Intervillage Conflict in Oaxaca*. New Brunswick, NJ: Rutgers University Press, 1987.

Derrida, Jacques. "Force of Law: The 'Mystical Foundation of Authority.'" Trans. Mary Quaintance and Gil Andijar. In Jacques Derrida, *Acts of Religion*, 228–298. New York: Routledge, 2002.

De Vega, Mercedes. "La opción federalista en Zacatecas, 1820–1835." In *Cincuenta años de historia en México*. 2 vols. Edited by Alicia Hernández Chavez and Manuel Miño Grijalva, vol. 2: 243–259. Mexico City: El Colegio de México, 1991.

Diamond, Larry. "Elections without Democracy: Thinking about Hybrid Regimes." *Journal of Democracy* 13/2 (2002): 21–35.

Diamond, Larry, and Marc Plattner, eds. *The Global Resurgence of Democracy*. 2nd ed. Baltimore: John Hopkins University Press, 1996.

Díaz, Arlene. *Female Citizens, Patriarchs, and the Law in Venezuela, 1786–1904*. Lincoln: University of Nebraska Press, 2004.

Díaz Soto y Gama, Antonio. *Historia del agrarismo en México*. Mexico City: Ediciones Era, 2002.

Douglas, Lawrence, Austin Sarat, and Martha Merrill Umphrey, eds. *Law and the Utopian Imagination*. Stanford: Stanford University Press, 2014.

Douglas, Lawrence, Austin Sarat, and Martha Merrill Umphrey. "Law and the Utopian Imagination: An Introduction." In *Law and the Utopian Imagination*. Edited by Lawrence Douglas, Austin Sarat, and Martha Merrill Umphrey, 1–22. Stanford: Stanford University Press, 2014.

Drake, Paul. *Between Tyranny and Anarchy: A History of Democracy in Latin America, 1800–2006*. Stanford: Stanford University Press, 2009.

Ducey, Michael. "Liberal Theory and Peasant Practice: Land and Power in Northern Veracruz, Mexico, 1826–1900." In *Liberals, the Church, and Indian Peasants: Corporate Lands and the Challenge of Reform in Nineteenth-Century Spanish America*. Edited by Robert Jackson, 65–90. Albuquerque: University of New Mexico Press, 1997.

A Nation of Villages: Riot and Rebellion in the Mexican Huasteca, 1750–1850. Tucson: University of Arizona Press, 2004.

Duncan, Kenneth, and Ian Rutledge, eds. *Land and Labour in Latin America: Essays on the Development of Agrarian Capitalism in the Nineteenth and Twentieth Centuries*. New York: Cambridge University Press, 1977.

Dunkerley, James, ed. *Studies in the Formation of the Nation-State in Latin America*. London: Institute of Latin American Studies, 2002.

Dworkin, Ronald. *Law's Empire*. Cambridge: Harvard University Press, 1986.

Earle, Rebecca, ed. *Rumours of Wars: Civil Conflict in Nineteenth-Century Latin America*. London: Institute of Latin American Studies, 2000.

Echeverri, Marcela. "Popular Royalists, Empire, and Politics in Southwestern New Granada, 1809–1819." *Hispanic American Historical Review* 91/2 (2011): 237–269.

Eley, Geoff. *Forging Democracy: The History of the Left in Europe, 1850–2000*. New York: Oxford University Press, 2002.

Eley, Geoff, and Ronald Grigor Suny, eds. *Becoming National: A Reader*. New York: Oxford University Press, 1996.

Escalante Gonzalbo, Fernando. *Ciudadanos imaginarios: memorial de los afanes y desventuras de la virtud y apología del vicio triunfante en la República Mexicana: tratado de moral pública*. Mexico City: Centro de Estudios Sociologicos and Colegio de México, 1992.

Escobar Ohmstede, Antonio, ed. *Indio, nación, y comunidad en el México del siglo XIX*. Mexico City: Centro de Estudios Mexicanos y Centroamericanos, 1993.

Los pueblos indios en los tiempos de Benito Juárez (1847–1872). Mexico City: Universidad Autónoma Metropolitana, 2007.

Escobar Ohmstede, Antonio. "Los condueñazgos indígenas en las Huastecas Hidalguense y Veracruzana: ¿Defensa del espacio comunal?" In *Indio, nación, y comunidad en el México del siglo XIX*. Edited by Antonio Escobar Ohmstede, 171–188. Mexico City: Centro de Estudios Mexicanos y Centroamericanos, 1993.

"Los ayuntamientos y los pueblos indios en la Sierra Huasteca: Conflictos entre nuevos y viejos actores, 1812–1840." In *La Reindianización de América, siglo XIX*. Edited by Leticia Reina, 294–316. Mexico City: Siglo Veintiuno, 1997.

"Introducción. La 'modernización' de México a través del Liberalismo. Los pueblos indios durante el Juarismo." In *Los pueblos indios en los tiempos de Benito Juárez (1847–1872)*. Edited by Antonio Escobar Ohmstede, 9–29. Mexico City: Universidad Autónoma Metropolitana, 2007.

"El fraccionamiento privado y comunal en el oriente potosino durante la segunda mitad del siglo XIX. Una aproximación." In *Agua y tierra en México, siglos XIX y XX*. Vol. 1. Edited by Antonio Escobar Ohmstede, Martín Sánchez Rodríguez, and Ana Ma. Gutiérrez Rivas, 209–244. Zamora: El Colegio de Michoacán, 2008.

"'Ha variado el sistema gubernativo de los pueblos'. La ciudadanía gaditana y republicana fue ¿imaginaria? para los indígenas. Una visión desde las Huastecas." In *Poder y gobierno local en México, 1808–1857*. Edited by María del Carmen Salinas Sandoval, Diana Birrichaga Gardida, and Antonio Escobar Ohmstede, 151–192. Mexico City: El Colegio Mexiquense, 2011.

Escobar Ohmstede, Antonio, Martín Sánchez Rodríguez, and Ana Ma. Gutiérrez Rivas, eds. *Agua y tierra en México, siglos XIX y XX*. Vol. 1. Zamora: El Colegio de Michoacán, 2008.

Esherick, Joseph, Hasan Kayali, and Eric Van Young, eds. *Empire to Nation: Historical Perspectives on the Making of the Modern World*. Lanham, MD: Rowman & Littlefield Publishers, Inc., 2006.

Falcón, Romana. "Force and the Search for Consent: The Role of the *Jefaturas Políticas* of Coahuila in National State Formation." In *Everyday Forms of State Formation: Revolution and the Negotiation of Rule in Modern Mexico*. Edited by Gilbert Joseph and Daniel Nugent, 107–134. Durham, NC: Duke University Press, 1994.

México descalzo: Estrategias de sobrevivencia frente a la modernidad liberal. Mexico City: Plaza Janés, 2002.

Falcón, Romana, ed. *Culturas de pobreza y resistencia: Estudios de marginados, proscritos, y - descontentos. México, 1804–1910*. Mexico City: Colegio de México, 2005.

Falcón, Romana, and Raymond Buve, eds. *Don Porfirio presidente ..., nunca omnipotente: Hallazgos, reflexiones y debates. 1876–1911*. Mexico City: Universidad Iberoamericana, 1998.

Fallaw, Ben, and Terry Rugeley, eds. *Forced Marches: Soldiers and Military Caciques in Modern Mexico*. Tucson: University of Arizona Press, 2012.

Fischer, Brodwyn. *A Poverty of Rights: Citizenship and Inequality in Twentieth-Century Rio de Janeiro*. Stanford: Stanford University Press, 2008.

Florescano, Enrique. *Etnia, estado y nación: Ensayo sobre las identidades colectivas en México*. Mexico City: Nuevo Siglo Aguilar, 1997.

Foucault, Michel. *The History of Sexuality*. Vol. 1. Trans. Robert Hurley. New York: Vintage Books, 1990.

Discipline and Punish: The Birth of the Prison. Trans. Alan Sheridan. New York: Vintage Books, 1995.

Foweraker, Joe, and Roman Krznaric. "The Uneven Performance of Third Wave Democracies: Electoral Politics and the Imperfect Rule of Law in Latin America." *Latin American Politics and Society* 44/3 (2002): 29–60.

Fowler, Will. *Military Political Identity and Reformism in Independent Mexico. An Analysis of the Memorias de Guerra (1821–1855)*, Research Paper No. 47. London: Institute for Latin American Studies, 1996.

Mexico in the Age of Proposals, 1821–1853. London: Greenwood Press, 1998.

"Civil Conflict in Independent Mexico, 1821–1857: An Overview." In *Rumours of Wars: Civil Conflict in Nineteenth-Century Latin America*. Edited by Rebecca Earle, 49–86. London: Institute of Latin American Studies, 2000.

Santa Anna of Mexico. Lincoln: University of Nebraska Press, 2007.

Fowler, Will and Humberto Morales Moreno. "Introducción: Una (Re)definición del conservadurismo Mexicano del siglo diecinueve." In *El conservadurismo mexicano en el siglo XIX*, 11–36. Puebla: Benemérita Universidad Autónoma de Puebla, 1999.

Fowler, Will, and Humberto Morales Moreno, eds. *El conservadurismo mexicano en el siglo XIX*. Puebla: Benemérita Universidad Autónoma de Puebla, 1999.

Fraser, Donald. "La política de desamortización en las comunidades indígenas, 1856–1872." *Historia Mexicana* 21/4 (1972): 615–652.

French, William. *A Peaceful and Working People: Manners, Morals, and Class Formation in Northern Mexico.* Albuquerque: University of New Mexico Press, 1996.

———. *The Heart in the Glass Jar: Love Letters, Bodies, and the Law in Mexico.* Lincoln: University of Nebraska Press, 2015.

Friedrich, Paul. *Agrarian Revolt in a Mexican Village.* Chicago: University of Chicago Press, 1970.

Frye, David. *Indians into Mexicans: History and Identity in a Mexican Towns.* Austin: University of Texas Press, 1996.

Frye, Northrop. "Crime and Sin in the Bible." In *Northrop Frye on Religion: Excluding the Great Code and Words with Power*, 133–146. Toronto: University of Toronto Press, 1996.

Galeano, Eduardo. *Open Veins of Latin America: Five Centuries of the Pillage of a Continent.* Trans. Cedric Belfrage. New York: Monthly Review Press, 1973.

García Martínez, Bernardo. "Los poblados de hacienda: Personajes olvidados en la historia del México rural." In *Cincuenta años de historia en México: En el Cincuentenario del Centro de Estudios Históricos.* Vol. 1. Edited by Alicia Hernández Chávez and Manuel Miño Grijalva, 331–370. Mexico City: El Colegio de México, 1991.

García Peña, Ana Lidia. *El fracaso del amor: Género e individualismo en el siglo XIX mexicano.* Mexico City: El Colegio de México, 2006.

García Ugarte, Marta Eugenia. *Hacendados y rancheros queretanos (1780–1920).* Mexico City: Consejo Nacional para la Cultura y las Artes, 1992.

Garner, Paul. *Porfirio Díaz.* New York: Pearson Education, 2001.

———. *British Lions and Mexican Eagles: Business, Politics, and Empire in the Career of Weetman Pearson in Mexico, 1889–1919.* Stanford: Stanford University Press, 2011.

Gibson, Charles. *The Aztecs under Spanish Rule: A History of the Indians of the Valley of Mexico 1519–1810.* Stanford: Stanford University Press, 1964.

Gillingham, Paul. *Cuauhtémoc's Bones: Forging National Identity in Modern Mexico.* Albuquerque: University of New Mexico Press, 2011.

Gonzalbo Aizpuro, Pilar. "La familia en México colonial: Una historia de conflictos cotidianos." *Mexican Studies/Estudios Mexicanos* 14/2 (1998): 389–406.

González, Soledad, and Pilar Iracheta. "La violencia en la vida de las mujeres campesinas: El distrito de Tenango, 1880–1920." In *Presencia y transparencia: La mujer en la historia de México.* Edited by Carmen Ramos Escandón et al., 111–161. Mexico City: El Colegio de México, 1987.

González y González, Luis. *Pueblo en vilo: Microhistoria de San José de Gracia.* Mexico City: El Colegio de México, 1968.

Gootenberg, Paul. "Fishing for Leviathans? Shifting Views on the Liberal State and Development in Peruvian History." *Journal of Latin American Studies* 45/1 (2013): 121–141.

Gould, Jeffrey. *To Die in This Way: Nicaraguan Indians and the Myth of Mestizaje, 1880–1965.* Durham, NC: Duke University Press, 1998.

Grandin, Greg. *The Blood of Guatemala: A History of Race and Nation.* Durham, NC: Duke University Press, 2000.

Griffin, Charles. *Los temas sociales y económicos en la época de la Independencia.* Caracas: Fundación John Boulton, 1962.

Guardino, Peter. *Peasants, Politics, and the Formation of Mexico's National State: Guerrero, 1800–1857.* Stanford: Stanford University Press, 1996.

———. *The Time of Liberty: Popular Political Culture in Oaxaca, 1750–1850.* Durham, NC: Duke University Press, 2005.

"La identidad nacional y los afromexicanos en el siglo XIX." In *Prácticas populares, cultura política y poder en México, siglo XIX.* Edited by Brian Connaughton, 259–301. Mexico City: Universidad Autónoma Metropolitana, Unidad Iztapalapa / Casa Juan Pablos, 2008.

"Gender, Soldiering, and Citizenship in the Mexican-American War of 1846–1848." *American Historical Review* 119/1 (2014): 23–46.

Guarisco, Claudia. *Los indios del valle de México y la construcción de una nueva sociabilidad política, 1770–1835.* Zincantepec: El Colegio Mexiquense, 2003.

La reconstitución del espacio político indígena: Lima y el Valle de México durante la crisis de la monarquía española. Castelló de la Plana: Universitat Jaume I, 2011.

Guedea, Virginia, ed. *Historiografía Mexicana.* Vol. 3. "El surgimiento de la historiografía nacional." Mexico City: Universidad Nacional Autónoma de México, 1997.

Guedea, Virginia. "The Process of Mexican Independence." *American Historical Review* 105/1 (2000): 116–130.

Güémez Pineda, Arturo. "El establecimiento de corporaciones municipales en Yucatán y los mayas: de la Constitución de Cádiz a la guerra de castas." In *Poder y gobierno local en México, 1808–1857.* Edited by María del Carmen Salinas Sandoval, Diana Birrichaga Gardida, and Antonio Excobar Ohmstede, 261–301. Mexico City: El Colegio Mexiquense, 2011.

Guerra, François-Xavier. *México: Del Antiguo Régimen a la Revolución.* 2 vols. Trans. Sergio Fernández Bravo. Mexico City: Fondo de Cultura Económica, 1988.

Modernidad e Independencias: Ensayos sobre las revoluciones hispánicas. Madrid: Editorial MAPFRE, 1992.

Guzmán López, José Elías. "Ciudadanía y educación en el mundo hispánico. Guanajuato durante la primera república federal." PhD dissertation. San Nicolás de Hidalgo: Universidad Michoacana, 2011.

Guzmán Pérez, Moisés, ed. *Cabildos, Repúblicas y Ayuntamientos Constitucionales en la Independencia de México.* Morelia: Comisión institucional para la conmemoración del bicentenario de la independencia y el centenario de la revolución mexicana, Instituto de investigaciones históricas Universidad Michoacana de San Nicolás de Hidalgo, and H. Congreso del estado de Michoacán de Ocampo, 2009.

Haber, Stephen. *Industry and Underdevelopment: The Industrialization of Mexico, 1890–1940.* Stanford: Stanford University Press, 1989.

Haber, Stephen, ed. *How Latin America Fell Behind: Essays on the Economic Histories of Brazil and Mexico, 1800–1914.* Stanford: Stanford University Press, 1997.

Hale, Charles. *Mexican Liberalism in the Age of Mora, 1821–1853.* New Haven: Yale University Press, 1968.

"Political and Social Ideas in Latin America, 1870–1930." In *The Cambridge History of Latin America.* Vol. 4. Edited by Leslie Bethell, 367–441. Cambridge: Cambridge University Press, 1986.

The Transformation of Liberalism in Late Nineteenth-Century Mexico. Princeton: Princeton University Press, 1989.

Hall, Robert. *Voices of the People: Democracy and Chartist Political Identity, 1830–1870.* Monmouth: Merlin Press, 2007.

Hamnett, Brian. *Politics and Trade in Southern Mexico 1750–1821.* Cambridge: Cambridge University Press, 1971.

"Royalist Counterinsurgency and the Continuity of Rebellion: Guanajuato and Michoacán, 1813–20." *Hispanic American Historical Review* 51/3 (1982): 19–48.

"Mexican Conservatives, Clericals, and Soldiers: The 'Traitor' Tomas Mejía through Reform and Empire, 1855–1867." *Bulletin of Latin American Research* 20/2 (2001): 187–209.

Harris III, Charles. *A Mexican Family Empire: The Latifundio of the Sánchez Navarros, 1765–1867*. Austin: University of Texas Press, 1975.

Hart, H. L. A. *The Concept of Law*. London: Oxford University Press, 1961.

Haworth, Daniel. "The Mobile National Guard of Guanajuato, 1855–1858: Military Hybridization and Statecraft in *Reforma Mexico*." In *Forced Marches: Soldiers and Military Caciques in Modern Mexico*. Edited by Ben Fallaw and Terry Rugeley, 49–80. Tucson: University of Arizona Press, 2012.

Hernández Chávez, Alicia. *Anenecuilco: Memoria y vida de un pueblo*. 2nd ed. Mexico City: El Colegio de México, Fondo de Cultura Económica, 1993.

——. *Las fuerzas armadas mexicanas: Su función en el montaje de la República*. Mexico City: El Colegio de México, 2012.

Hernández Chavez, Alicia, and Manuel Miño Grijalva, eds. *Cincuenta años de historia en México*. 2 vols. Mexico City: El Colegio de México, 1991.

Hérnandez Silva, Héctor Cuauhtémoc. "El Valle del Yaqui y los proyectos económicos de las élites regionales de Sonora. 1830–1857." In *Indio, nación, y comunidad en el México del siglo XIX*. Edited by Antonio Escobar Ohmstede, 293–301. Mexico City: Centro de Estudios Mexicanos y Centroamericanos, 1993.

Herzog, Tamar. *Upholding Justice: Society, State, and the Penal System in Quito (1650–1750)*. Ann Arbor: University of Michigan Press, 2004.

Hobbes, Thomas. *Leviathan*. Edited by C.B. MacPherson. New York: Penguin Books, 1985.

Hobsbawm, Eric. *The Age of Revolutions, 1789–1848*. Cleveland: World Pub. Co., 1962.

Holden, Robert. *Mexico and the Survey of Public Lands: The Management of Modernization 1876–1911*. DeKalb: Northern Illinois University Press, 1994.

Holt, Thomas. *The Problem of Freedom: Race, Labor, and Politics in Jamaica and Britain, 1832–1938*. Baltimore: John Hopkins University Press, 1992.

Huber, Evelyne. "Introduction." In *Agrarian Structure and Political Power: Landlord and Peasant in the Making of Latin America*. Edited by Evelyne Huber and Frank Safford, 3–20. Pittsburgh: University of Pittsburgh Press, 1995.

Huber, Evelyne, and Frank Safford, eds. *Agrarian Structure and Political Power: Landlord and Peasant in the Making of Latin America*. Pittsburgh: University of Pittsburgh Press, 1995.

Hunefeldt, Christine. *Liberalism in the Bedroom: Quarreling Spouses in Nineteenth-Century Lima*. University Park: Pennsylvania State University Press, 2000.

Huysmans, Jef. "The Jargon of Exception – On Schmitt, Agamben and the Absence of Political Society." *International Political Sociology* 2/2 (2008): 165–183.

Jackson, Robert, ed. *Liberals, the Church, and Indian Peasants: Corporate Lands and the Challenge of Reform in Nineteenth-Century Spanish America*. Albuquerque: University of New Mexico Press, 1997.

Jacobs, Ian. *Ranchero Revolt: The Mexican Revolution in Guerrero*. Austen: University of Texas Press, 1982.

James, Timothy. *Mexico's Supreme Court: Between Liberal Individual and Revolutionary Social Rights, 1867–1934*. Albuquerque: University of New Mexico Press, 2013.

Jones, Greta. *Social Darwinism and English Thought: The Interaction between Biological and Social Theory*. Atlantic Highlands, NJ: Humanities Press, 1980.

Joseph, Gilbert. "Rethinking Mexican Revolutionary Mobilization: Yucatán's Seasons of Upheaval, 1909–1915." In *Everyday Forms of State Formation: Revolution and the Negotiation of Rule in Modern Mexico*. Edited by Gilbert Joseph and Daniel Nugent, 135–169. Durham, NC: Duke University Press, 1994.

Joseph, Gilbert, and Jürgen Buchenau. *Mexico's Once and Future Revolution: Social Upheaval and the Challenge of Rule since the Late Nineteenth-Century*. Durham, NC: Duke University Press, 2013.

Joseph, Gilbert, and Daniel Nugent, eds. *Everyday Forms of State Formation: Revolution and the Negotiation of Rule in Modern Mexico*. Durham, NC: Duke University Press, 1994.

Kanter, Deborah. *Hijos del Pueblo: Gender, Family, and Community in Rural Mexico, 1730–1850*. Austin: University of Texas Press, 2008.

Katz, Friedrich. "Labor Conditions on Porfirian Haciendas: Some Trends and Tendencies." *Hispanic American Historical Review* 54/1 (1974): 1–47.

"Mexico: Restored Republic and Porfiriato." In *The Cambridge History of Latin America*, vol. 5. Edited by Leslie Bethell, 3–78. Cambridge: Cambridge University Press, 1986.

Katz, Friedrich, ed. *Riot, Rebellion, and Revolution: Rural Social Conflict in Mexico*. Princeton: Princeton University Press, 1988.

Katz, Friedrich, and Jane-Dale Lloyd, eds. *Porfirio Díaz frente al descontento popular regional (1891–1893): Antología documental*. Mexico City: Universidad Iberoamericana, 1986.

Keith, Robert. "Encomienda, Hacienda and Corregimiento in Spanish America: A Structural Analysis." *Hispanic American Historical Review* 51/3 (1971): 431–446.

Kellogg, Susan. *Law and the Transformation of Aztec Culture, 1500–1700*. Norman: University of Oklahoma Press, 1995.

Knight, Alan. "El liberalismo mexicano desde la Reforma hasta la Revolución (una interpretación)." *Historia Mexicana* 35/1 (1985): 59–91.

The Mexican Revolution. 2 vols. Cambridge: Cambridge University Press, 1986.

"Mexican Peonage: What Was It and Why Was It?" *Journal of Latin American Studies* 18/1 (1986): 41–74.

"Subalterns, Signifiers, and Statistics: Perspectives on Mexican Historiography." *Latin American Research Review* 37/2 (2002): 136–158.

Kourí, Emilio. "Interpreting the Expropriation of Indian Pueblo Lands in Porfirian Mexico: The Unexamined Legacies of Andrés Molina Enríquez." *Hispanic American Historical Review* 82/1 (2002): 69–118.

A Pueblo Divided: Business, Property, and Community in Papantla, Mexico. Stanford: Stanford University Press, 2004.

Krauze, Enrique. *Místico de la autoridad: Porfirio Díaz*. Mexico City: Fondo de Cultura Económica, 1987.

Siglo de caudillos: Biografía política de México (1810–1910). Barcelona: Tusquets Editores, 1994.

Laclau, Ernesto. *On Populist Reason*. New York: Verso, 2005.

Langley, Lester. *The Americas in the Age of Revolution 1750–1850*. New Haven: Yale University Press, 1996.

Lara Nieto, María del Carmen. *Ilustración española y pensamiento inglés: Jovellanos*. Granada: Editorial Universidad de Granada, 2008.

Larson, Brooke. *Trials of Nation Making: Liberalism, Race, and Ethnicity in the Andes, 1810–1910*. New York: Cambridge University Press, 2004.

Lasso, Marixa. *Myths of Harmony: Race and Republicanism during the Age of Revolution, Colombia, 1795–1831*. Pittsburgh: University of Pittsburgh Press, 2007.

Lauderdale Graham, Sandra. *House and Street: The Domestic World of Servants and Masters in Nineteenth-Century Rio de Janeiro*. Austin: University of Texas Press, 1992.

Lavrin, Asunción, ed. *Sexuality and Marriage in Colonial Latin America*. Lincoln: University of Nebraska Press, 1989.

Lieven, Dominic. *The Aristocracy in Europe, 1815–1914*. New York: Columbia University Press, 1993.

Lipsett-Rivera, Sonya. *Gender and the Negotiation of Daily Life in Mexico, 1750–1856*. Lincoln: University of Nebraska Press, 2010.

Lira González, Andrés. *El amparo colonial y el juicio de amparo mexicano: Antecedentes novohis-panos del juicio de amparo.* Mexico City: Fondo de Cultura Económica, 1972.

Comunidades indígenas frente a la ciudad de México: Tenochtitlan y Tlatelolco, sus pueblos y barrios, 1812–1919.* Zamora: El Colegio de Michoacán, 1983.

"Abogados, tinterillos y huizacheros en el México del siglo XIX." At http://biblio .juridicas.unam.mx/libros/2/700/25.pdf. Accessed 27 December 2015.

Lockhart, James. "Encomienda and Hacienda: The Evolution of the Great Estate in the Spanish Indies." *Hispanic American Historical Review* 49/3 (1969): 411–429.

The Nahuas after the Conquest: A Social and Cultural History of the Indians of Central Mexico, Sixteenth through Eighteenth Centuries. Stanford: Stanford University Press, 1992.

Lomnitz, Claudio. *The Return of Comrade Ricardo Flores Magón.* New York: Zone Books, 2014.

"Preguntas sobre el porfiriato." *Nexos* 451 (July 2015): 17–21.

López-Alonso, Moramay. *Measuring Up: A History of Living Standards in Mexico, 1850–1950.* Stanford: Stanford University Press, 2012.

Lynch, John. *The Spanish American Revolutions 1808–1826.* London: Weidenfeld and Nicolson, 1973.

MacIntyre, Alasdair. *After Virtue.* Notre Dame: University of Notre Dame Press, 1981.

MacLachlan, Colin. *Criminal Justice in Eighteenth-Century Mexico: A Study of the Tribunal of the Acordada.* Berkeley: University of California Perss, 1974.

Mallon, Florencia. "Peasants and State Formation in Nineteenth Century Mexico: Morelos, 1848–1858." *Political Power and Social Theory* 7 (1988): 1–54.

Peasant and Nation: The Making of Postcolonial Mexico and Peru. Berkeley: University of California Press, 1995.

Margadant, Ted. *French Peasants in Revolt: The Insurrection of 1851.* Princeton: Princeton University Press, 1979.

Marino, Daniela. "La desamortización de las tierras de los pueblos (Centro de México, siglo XIX). Balance historiográfico y fuentes para su estudio." *América Latina en la Historia Económica* 16 (2001): 33–43.

Martínez Alier, Juan. "Relations of Production in Andean Haciendas: Peru." In *Land and Labour in Latin America: Essays on the Development of Agrarian Capitalism in the Nineteenth and Twentieth Centuries.* Edited by Kenneth Duncan and Ian Rutledge, 141–164. New York: Cambridge University Press, 1977.

Marx, Karl. *Capital.* Vol. 1. Trans. Ben Fowkes. New York: Vintage Books, 1977.

Mathias, Christine. "At the Edges of Empire: Race and Revolution in the Mexican Border Town of Cananea, 1899–1917." B.A. thesis: Yale University, 2007.

Mayer, Arno. *The Persistence of the Old Regime: Europe to the Great War.* New York: Pantheon Books, 1981.

McAlister, Lyle. *The 'Fuero Militar' in New Spain 1764–1800.* Gainesville: University of Florida Press, 1957.

McEnroe, Sean. *From Colony to Nationhood in Mexico: Laying the Foundations, 1560–1840.* New York: Cambridge University Press, 2012.

McGraw, Jason. *The Work of Recognition: Caribbean Colombia and the Postemancipation Struggle for Citizenship.* Chapel Hill: University of North Carolina Press, 2014.

McNamara, Patrick. *Sons of the Sierra: Juárez, Díaz, and the People of Ixtlán, Oaxaca, 1855–1920.* Chapel Hill: University of North Carolina Press, 2007.

McPhee, Peter. *The Politics of Rural Life: Political Mobilization in the French Countryside, 1846–1852.* New York: Oxford University Press, 1992.

Medina Bustos, José Marcos. "El gobierno indígena en una zona de frontera durante la transición del Antiguo Régimen al liberalismo. El caso de la provincia de Sonora (1763–1831)." In *Poder y gobierno local en México, 1808–1857.* Edited by María del

Carmen Salinas Sandoval, Diana Birrichaga Gardida, and Antonio Escobar Ohmstede, 225–260. Mexico City: El Colegio Mexiquense, 2011.

Méndez, Cecilia. *The Plebeian Republic: The Huanta Rebellion and the Making of the Peruvian State, 1820–1850*. Durham, NC: Duke University Press, 2005.

Méndez, Juan, Guillermo O'Donnell, and Paulo Sérgio Pinheiro, eds. *The (Un)Rule of Law and the Underprivileged in Latin America*. Notre Dame: University of Notre Dame Press, 1999.

Mendoza García, Edgar. *Los bienes de comunidad y la defensa de las tierras en la Mixteca oaxaqueña: cohesión y autonomía del municipio de Santo Domingo Tepenene, 1856–1912*. Mexico City: Senado de la República, 2004.

"Distrito político y desamortización: Resistencia y reparto de la propiedad comunal en los pueblos de Cuicatlán y Coixtlahuaca, 1856–1910." In *Culturas de pobreza y resistencia: Estudios de marginados, proscritos, y descontentos. México, 1804–1910*. Edited by Romana Falcón, 209–236. Mexico City: Colegio de México, 2005.

Menegus Bornemann, Margarita. "Ocoyoacac: Una comunidad agraria en el siglo xix." *Historia Mexicana* 30/1 (1980): 33–78.

La Mixteca Baja entre la Revolución y la Reforma: Cacicazgo, territorialidad y gobierno siglos XVIII-XIX. Oaxaca City: Universidad Autónoma "Benito Juárez" de Oaxaca, 2009.

Mertens, Hans-Günther. *Atlixco y las haciendas durante el Porfiriato*. Trans. Hermilo Boeta Saldierna. Puebla: Universidad Autónoma de Puebla, 1988.

Meyer, Jean. *Esperando a Lozada*. Mexico City: CONACYT, 1984.

Miller, Simon. *Landlords and Haciendas in Modernizing Mexico: Essays in Radical Reappraisal*. Amsterdam: CEDLA, 1995.

Moore, Barrington. *Social Origins of Dictatorship and Democracy: Lord and Peasant in the Making of the Modern World*. Boston: Beacon Press, 1967.

Mörner, Magnus. "The Spanish American Hacienda: A Review of Recent Research and Debate." *Hispanic American Historical Review* 53/2 (1973): 183–216.

Moore, Jr., Barrington. *Social Origins of Dictatorship and Democracy: Lord and Peasant in the Making of the Modern World*. Boston: Beacon Press, 1966.

Moreno García, Heriberto, ed. *Despues de los latifundios: La desintegración de la gran propiedad agraria en México*. Zamora: El Colegio de Michoacán, 1981.

Muro, Manuel. *Historia de San Luis Potosí*. Vol. 2. San Luis Potosí: Sociedad Potosina de Estudios Históricos, 1973.

Neufeld, Stephen. *The Blood Contingent: The Military and the Making of Modern Mexico, 1876–1911*. Albuquerque: University of New Mexico Press, 2017.

Newman, Elizabeth Terese. "From Prison to Home: Labor Relations and Social Control in Nineteenth-Century Mexico." *Ethnohistory* 60/4 (2013): 663–692.

Ngai, Mae. *Impossible Subjects: Illegal Aliens and the Making of Modern America*. Princeton: Princeton University Press, 2004.

Nickel, Herbert. *Morfología social de la hacienda mexicana*. Trans. Angélica Scherp and Alberto Luis Gómez. 2nd ed. Mexico City: Fondo de Cultura Económica, 1996.

North, Douglass, and Barry Weingast. "Constitutions and Commitment: The Evolution of Institutions Governing Public Choice in Seventeenth-Century England." *Journal of Economic History* 49/4 (1989): 803–832.

Noyola, Inocencio. "Los juicios de apeos y deslindes en San Luis Potosí, 1883–1893." In *Agua y tierra en México, siglos XIX y XX*. Vol. 1. Edited by Antonio Escobar Ohmstede, Martín Sánchez Rodríguez, and Ana Ma. Gutiérrez Rivas, 331–357. Zamora: El Colegio de Michoacán, 2008.

Nugent, Daniel. *Spent Cartridges of Revolution: An Anthropological History of Namiquipa, Chihuahua*. Chicago: University of Chicago Press, 1993.

Nugent, Daniel, and Ana María Alonso. "Multiple Selective Traditions in Agrarian Reform and Agrarian Struggle: Popular Culture and State Formation in the Ejido of

Maniquipa, Chihuahua." In *Everyday Forms of State Formation: Revolution and the Negotiation of Rule in Modern Mexico*. Edited by Gilbert Joseph and Daniel Nugent, 209–246. Durham, NC: Duke University Press, 1994.

O'Donnell, Guillermo. *Democracy, Agency, and the State: Theory with Comparative Intent*. New York: Oxford University Press, 2010.

O'Hara, Matthew. *A Flock Divided: Race, Religion, and Politics in Mexico, 1749–1857*. Durham, NC: Duke University Press, 2010.

Ortiz Escamilla, Juan. "Las fuerzas militares y el proyecto de estado en México, 1767–1835." In *Cincuenta años de historia en México*. 2 vols. Edited by Alicia Hernández Chavez and Manuel Miño Grijalva, vol. 2: 261–282. Mexico City: El Colegio de México, 1991.

Guerra y gobierno: Los pueblos y la independencia de México. Seville, Spain: Instituto Mora, El Colegio de México, Universidad Internacional de Andalucia, and Universidad de Sevilla, 1997.

and José Antonio Serrano Ortega. "Introducción." In *Ayuntamientos y liberalismo gaditano en México*. Edited by Juan Ortiz Escamilla and José Antonio Serrano Ortega, 9–18. Zamora and Xalapa: El Colegio de Michoacán and Universidad Veracruzana, 2007.

Ortiz Escamilla, Juan, and José Antonio Serrano Ortega, eds. *Ayuntamientos y liberalismo gaditano en México*. Zamora and Xalapa: El Colegio de Michoacán and Universidad Veracruzana, 2007.

Ortiz Peralta, Rina. "Inexistentes por decreto: Disposiciones legislativas sobre los pueblos de Indios en el siglo XIX. El caso de Hidalgo." In *Indio, nación, y comunidad en el México del siglo XIX*. Edited by Antonio Escobar Ohmstede, 153–169. Mexico City: Centro de Estudios Mexicanos y Centroamericanos, 1993.

Osterhammel, Jürgen. *The Transformation of the World: A Global History of the Nineteenth Century*. Trans. Patrick Camiller. Princeton: Princeton University Press.

Overmyer-Velazquez, Mark. *Visions of the Emerald City: Modernity, Tradition, and the Formation of Porfirian Oaxaca, Mexico*. Durham, NC: Duke University Press, 2006.

Owensby, Brian. *Empire of Law and Indian Justice in Colonial Mexico*. Stanford: Stanford California Press, 2008.

Pani, Erika. "La 'innombrable': monarquismo y cultura política en el México decimonónico." In *Prácticas populares, cultural política y poder en México, siglo XIX*. Edited by Brian Connaughton, 369–394. Mexico City: Universidad Autónoma Metropolitana and Casa Juan Pablos, 2008.

Pastor, Rodolfo. *Campesinos y reforma. La mixteca, 1700–1856*. Mexico City: El Colegio de México, 1989.

Payne, Howard. *The Police State of Louis Napoleon Bonaparte 1851–1860*. Seattle: University of Washington Press, 1966.

Peloso, Vincent. *Peasants on Plantations: Subaltern Strategies of Labor and Resistance in the Pisco Valley, Peru*. Durham, NC: Duke University Press, 1999.

Pérez Johnston, Raúl. "Juicio de amparo." In *Diccionario histórico judicial de México*. Edited by Suprema Corte de Justicia, 901–910. Mexico City: Dirección General de Casas de la Cultura Jurídica y Estudios Históricos, 2010.

Perez Montesinos, Fernando. "Poised to Break: Liberalism, Land Reform, and Communities in the Purépecha Highlands of Michoacán, Mexico, 1800–1915." PhD Dissertation, Georgetown University, 2014.

Pérez Toledo, Sonia. *Trabajadores, espacio urbano y sociabilidad en la Ciudad de México, 1790–1867*. Mexico City: Universidad Autónoma Metropolitana – Unidad Iztapalapa, 2011.

Piccato, Pablo. *City of Suspects: Crime in Mexico City, 1900–1931*. Durham, NC: Duke University Press, 2001.

Pietschmann, Horst. *Las reformas borbónicas y el sistema de intendencias en Nueva España: Un estudio político administrativo.* Trans. Rolf Roland Meyer Misteli. Mexico City: Fondo de Cultura Económica, 1996.

Pizzigoni, Caterina. *Life Within: Local Indigenous Society in Mexico's Toluca Valley, 1600–1800.* Stanford: Stanford University Press, 2013.

Plant, Roger. "The Rule of Law and the Underprivileged in Latin America: A Rural Perspective." In *The (Un)Rule of Law and the Underprivileged in Latin America.* Edited by Juan Méndez, Guillermo O'Donnell, and Paulo Sérgio Pinheiro, 87–108. Notre Dame: University of Notre Dame Press, 1999.

Price, Richard. *British Society 1680–1880: Dynamism, Containment, Change.* New York: Cambridge University Press, 1999.

Purnell, Jennie. "With All Due Respect: Popular Resistance to the Privatization of Communal Lands in Nineteenth-Century Michoacan." *Latin American Research Review* 34/1 (1999): 85–121.

Racine, Karen. "'This England and This Now': British Cultural and Intellectual Influence in the Spanish American Independence Era." *Hispanic American Historical Review* 90/3 (2010): 423–454.

Ramírez Vega, María Dolores. "Indios, poblamiento y fundación de la congregación de Nuestra Señora de los Dolores, 1646–1720." B.A. Thesis. Universidad de Guanajuato, 2012.

Ramos Escandón, Carmen, et al. *Presencia y transparencia: La mujer en la historia de México.* Mexico City: El Colegio de México, 1987.

Rangel Silva, José Alfredo. "Las voces del pueblo. La cultura política desde los ayuntamientos: San Luis Potosí (1820–1823)." In *Poder y gobierno local en México, 1808–1857.* Edited by María del Carmen Salinas Sandoval, Diana Birrichaga Gardida, and Antonio Escobar Ohmstede, 123–149. Mexico City: El Colegio Mexiquense, 2011.

Razo, Armando. *Social Foundations of Limited Dictatorship: Networks and Private Protection during Mexico's Early Industrialization.* Stanford: Stanford University Press, 2008.

Reddy, William. *The Rise of Market Culture: The Textile Trade and French Society, 1750–1900.* Cambridge: Cambridge University Press, 1984.

Reina, Leticia, ed. *La Reindianización de América, siglo XIX.* Mexico City: Siglo Veintiuno, 1997.

Reina, Leticia. "The Sierra Gorda Peasant Rebellion, 1847–50." In *Riot, Rebellion, and Revolution: Rural Social Conflict in Mexico.* Edited by Friedrich Katz, 269–294. Princeton: Princeton University Press, 1988.

"Local Elections and Regime Crises: The Political Culture of Indigenous People." In *Cycles of Conflict, Centuries of Change: Crisis, Reform, and Revolution in Mexico.* Edited by Elisa Servín, Leticia Reina, and John Tutino, 91–126. Durham, NC: Duke University Press, 2007.

Renan, Ernest. "What Is a Nation?." In *Becoming National: A Reader.* Edited by Geoff Eley and Ronald Grigor Suny, 41–55. New York: Oxford University Press, 1996.

Rendón Garcini, Ricardo. *Dos haciendas pulqueras en Tlaxcala, 1857–1884.* Mexico City: Universidad Iberoaméricana, 1990.

Reyes Heroles, Jesús. *El liberalism mexicano.* 2nd ed. 3 vols. Mexico City: Fondo de Cultura Económica, 1974.

Rigguzi, Paolo. "From Globalization to Revolution? The Porfirian Political Economy: An Essay on Issues and Interpretations," *Journal of Latin American Studies* 41/2 (2009): 347–368.

Ríos Zúñiga: Rosalina. *Formar ciudadanos: Sociedad civil y movilización popular en Zacatecas, 1821–1853.* Mexico City: ESU, Universidad Nacional Autónoma de México, 2005.

"Popular Uprising and Political Culture in Zacatecas: The Sombrerete Uprisings (1829)." *Hispanic American Historical Review* 87/3 (2007): 499–536.

Rodley, Nigel. "Torture and Conditions of Detention in Latin America." In *The (Un)Rule of Law and the Underprivileged in Latin America*. Edited by Juan Méndez, Guillermo O'Donnell, and Paulo Sérgio Pinheiro, 25–41. Notre Dame: University of Notre Dame Press, 1999.

Rodríguez Kuri, Ariel. *La experiencia olvidada: El Ayuntamiento de México: política y gobierno, 1876–1912.* Mexico City: El Colegio de México, 1996.

Rodríguez O., Jaime. *The Independence of Spanish America.* Cambridge: Cambridge University Press, 1998.

Roseberry, William. "Hegemony and the Language of Contention." In *Everyday Forms of State Formation: Revolution and the Negotiation of Rule in Modern Mexico*. Edited by Gilbert Joseph and Daniel Nugent, 355–366. Durham, NC: Duke University Press, 1994.

Rueschemeyer, Dietrich, Evelyne Huber Stephens, and John Stephens. *Capitalist Development and Democracy.* Chicago: University of Chicago Press, 1992.

Rugeley, Terry. *Yucatán's Maya Peasantry and the Origins of the Caste War.* Austin: University of Texas Press, 1996.

Saad Saka, Mark. *For God and Revolution: Priest, Peasant, and Agrarian Socialism in the Mexican Huasteca.* Albuquerque: University of New Mexico Press, 2013.

Salazar Adame, Jaime. "Movimientos populares durante el Porfiriato en el estado de Guerrero (1885–1891)." In *Porfirio Díaz frente al descontento popular regional (1891–1893): Antología documental*. Edited by Friedrich Katz and Jane-Dale Lloyd, 97–184. Mexico City: Universidad Iberoamericana, 1986.

Salinas Sandoval, María del Carmen, Diana Birrichaga Gardida, and Antonio Escobar Ohmstede, eds. *Poder y gobierno local en México, 1808–1857.* Mexico City: El Colegio Mexiquense, 2011.

Salvatore, Ricardo. *Wandering Paysanos: State Order and Subaltern Experience in Buenos Aires during the Rosas Era.* Durham, NC: Duke University Press, 2003.

Salvucci, Richard. "Mexican National Income in the Era of Independence, 1800–40." In *How Latin America Fell Behind: Essays on the Economic Histories of Brazil and Mexico, 1800–1914.* Edited by Stephen Haber, 216–242. Stanford: Stanford University Press, 1997.

Samponaro, Frank. "The Political Role of the Army in Mexico." PhD dissertation. State University of New York at Stony Brook, 1974.

Sánchez Montiel, Juan Carlos. "De poblados de hacienda a municipios en el altiplano de San Luis Potosí." In *Estudios de Historia Moderna y Contemporánea de México* 31 (2006): 57–81.

——— "Nuevos ayuntamientos y reformulación de la representación política: San Luis Potosí, 1812–1835." PhD dissertation. Instituto de Investigaciones Doctor José María Luis Mora, 2007.

——— *De poblados de hacienda a municipios en San Luis Potosí.* San Luis Potosí: Comisión del Bicentenario de la Independencia Nacional y Centenario de la Revolución Mexicana, 2011.

Sánchez Silva, Carlos. *Indios, comerciantes y burocracia en la Oaxaca poscolonial, 1786–1860.* Oaxaca City: Instituto Oaxaqueño de las Culturas and Universidad Autónoma Benito Juárez de Oaxaca, 1998.

Sánchez Silva, Carlos, ed. *Historia, Sociedad y Literatura de Oaxaca: Nuevos enfoques.* Oaxaca City: Universidad Autónoma Benito Juárez de Oaxaca, 2004.

Sanders, James. *Contentious Republicans: Popular Politics, Race, and Class in Nineteenth-Century Colombia.* Durham, NC: Duke University Press, 2004.

The Vanguard of the Atlantic World: Creating Modernity, Nation, and Democracy in Nineteenth-Century Latin America. Durham, NC: Duke University Press, 2014.

Santoni, Pedro. "The Failure of Mobilization: The Civic Militia of Mexico in 1846." *Mexican Studies/Estudios Mexicanos* 12/2 (1996): 169–194.

Scardaville, Michael. "(Hapsburg) Law and (Bourbon) Order: State Authority, Popular Unrest, and the Criminal Justice System in Bourbon Mexico City." In *Reconstructing Criminality in Latin America.* Edited by Carlos Aguirre and Robert Buffington, 1–18. Wilmington: Scholarly Resources Inc., 2000.

"Los procesos judiciales y la autoridad del estado: Reflexiones en torno a la administración de la justicia criminal y la legitimidad en la ciudad de México, desde finales de la Colonia, hasta principios del México independiente." In *Poder y legitimidad en México en el siglo XIX: Instituciones y cultural política.* Edited by Brian Connaughton, 379–428. Mexico City: Biblioteca de Signos, 2003.

Schaefer, Timo. "Citizen-Breadwinners and Vagabond-Soldiers: Military Recruitment in Early Republican Southern Mexico." *Journal of Social History* 46/4 (2013): 953–970.

"Law of the Land? Hacienda Power and the Challenge of Republicanism in Postindependence Mexico." *Hispanic American Historical Review* 94/2 (2014): 207–236.

Scheper-Hughes, Nancy. "Death Squads and Democracy in Northeastern Brazil." In *Law and Disorder in the Postcolony.* Edited by Jean and John Comaroff, 150–187. Chicago: University of Chicago Press, 2006.

Schiavone, Aldo. *The Invention of Law in the West.* Trans. Jeremy Carden and Antony Shugaar. Cambridge: Harvard University Press, 2012.

Schmitt, Carl. *Political Theology: Four Chapters on the Concept of Sovereignty.* Trans. George Schwab. Cambridge: MIT Press, 1985.

Schmitter, Phillippe. "Dangers and Dilemmas of Democracy." In *The Global Resurgence of Democracy.* 2nd ed. Edited by Larry Diamond and Marc Plattner, 76–93. Baltimore: John Hopkins University Press, 1996.

Schryer, Frans. *The Rancheros of Pisaflores: The History of a Peasant Bourgeoisie in Twentieth-Century Mexico.* Toronto: University of Toronto Press, 1980.

Ethnicity and Class Conflict in Rural Mexico. Princeton: Princeton University Press, 1990.

Scott, James. *The Art of Not Being Governed: An Anarchist History of Upland Southeast Asia.* New Haven: Yale University Press, 2009.

Serrano Ortega, José Antonio. "El ascenso de un caudillo en Guanajuato: Luis de Cortázar, 1827–1832." *Historia Mexicana* 43/1 (1992): 49–80.

El contingente de sangre: los gobiernos estatales y departamentales y los métodos de reclutamiento del ejército permanente mexicano, 1824–1844. Mexico City: Instituto Nacional de Antropología e Historia, 1993.

Jerarquía territorial y transición política: Guanajuato, 1790–1836. Zamora: El Colegio de Michoacán; Mexico City: Instituto Mora, 2001.

Servín, Elisa, Leticia Reina, and John Tutino, eds. *Cycles of Conflict, Centuries of Change: Crisis, Reform, and Revolution in Mexico.* Durham, NC: Duke University Press, 2007.

Sewell, William. *Work and Revolution in France: The Language of Labor from the Old Regime to 1848.* Cambridge and New York: Cambridge University Press, 1980.

A Rhetoric of Bourgeois Revolution: The Abbé Sieyes and What Is the Third Estate? Durham, NC: Duke University Press, 1994.

Shelton, Laura. *For Tranquility and Order: Family and Community on Mexico's Northern Frontier, 1800–1850.* Tucson: University of Arizona Press, 2011.

Silva Prada, Natalia. "Las manifestaciones políticas indígenas ante el proceso de control y privatización de tierras: México, 1786–1856." In *Poder y legitimidad en México en el siglo XIX: Instituciones y cultural política.* Edited by Brian Connaughton, 75–135. Mexico City: Biblioteca de Signos, 2003.

Sims, Harold Dana. *The Expulsion of Mexico's Spaniards, 1821–1836.* Pittsburgh: University of Pittsburgh Press, 1990.

Sinkin, Richard. *The Mexican Reform, 1855–1876.* Austin: University of Texas Press, 1979.

Skocpol, Theda. "A Critical Review of Barrington Moore's Social Origins of Dictatorship and Democracy." *Politics and Society* 4/1 (1973): 1–34.

Smith, Benjamin. *The Roots of Conservatism in Mexico: Catholicism, Society, and Politics in the Mixteca Baja, 1750–1962.* Albuquerque: University of New Mexico Press, 2012.

Smith, Peter. *Democracy in Latin America: Political Change in Comparative Perspective.* 2nd ed. New York: Oxford University Press, 2012.

Socolow, Susan Migden. *The Women of Colonial Latin America.* New York: Cambridge University Press, 2000.

Soifer, Hillel David. *State Building in Latin America.* New York: Cambridge University Press, 2015.

Sordo Cedeño, Reynaldo. *El Congreso en la primera República Centralista.* Mexico City: El Colegio de México, Instituto Tecnológico Autónomo de México, 1993.

Sotelo Inclán, Jesús. *Raíz y razón de Zapata.* 2nd ed. Mexico City: Fondo de Cultura Económica, 1970.

Speckman Guerra, Elisa. *Crimen y castigo: Legislación penal, interpretaciones de la criminalidad y administración de justicia (Ciudad de México, 1872–1910).* Mexico City: El Colegio de México, 2002.

Sperber, Jonathan. *Rhineland Radicals: The Democratic Movement and the Revolution of 1848–1849.* Princeton: Princeton University Press, 1991.

The European Revolutions, 1848–1851. Cambridge: Cambridge University Press, 1994.

Spieler, Miranda. "The Legal Structure of Colonial Rule during the French Revolution." *William and Mary Quarterly* 66/2 (2009): 365–408.

Empire and Underworld: Captivity in French Guiana. Cambridge: Harvard University Press, 2012.

Staples, Anne. "José María Luis Mora." In *Historiografía Mexicana,* Vol. 3: *El surgimiento de la historiografía nacional.* Edited by Virginia Guedea, 241–256. Mexico City: Universidad Nacional Autónoma de México, 1997.

Stedman Jones, Gareth. *Languages of Class: Studies in English Working Class History 1832–1982.* Cambridge: Cambridge University Press, 1983.

Stein, Stanley and Barbara Stein. *The Colonial Heritage of Latin America: Essays on Economic Dependence in Perspective.* New York: Oxford University Press, 1970.

Stern, Steve. *Peru's Indian Peoples and the Challenge of Spanish Conquest: Huamanga to 1640.* Madison: University of Wisconsin Press, 1982.

The Secret History of Gender: Women, Men, and Power in Late Colonial Mexico. Chapel Hill: University of North Carolina Press, 1995.

Stevens, Donald Fithian. *Origins of Instability in Early Republican Mexico.* Durham, NC: Duke University Press, 1991.

Storch, Robert. "The Policeman as Domestic Missionary: Urban Discipline and Popular Culture in Northern England, 1850–1880." *Journal of Social History* 9/4 (1976): 481–509.

Suprema Corte de Justicia, ed. *Diccionario histórico judicial de México.* Mexico City: Dirección General de Casas de la Cultura Jurídica y Estudios Históricos, 2010.

Tamanaha, Brian. *On the Rule of Law: History, Politics, Theory.* Cambridge: Cambridge University Press, 2004.

Taylor, William. *Landlord and Peasant in Colonial Oaxaca.* Stanford: Stanford University Press, 1972.

Drinking, Homicide, and Rebellion in Colonial Mexican Villages. Stanford: Stanford University Press, 1979.

Tenenbaum, Barbara. *The Politics of Penury: Debts and Taxes in Mexico, 1821–1855.* Albuquerque: University of New Mexico Press, 1986.

Tenorio-Trillo, Mauricio. *Mexico at the World's Fairs: Crafting a Modern Nation.* Berkeley: University of California Press, 1996.

Tenorio-Trillo, Mauricio, and Aurora Gómez Galvarriato. *El Porfiriato.* Mexico City: Centro de Investigación y Docencia Económicas, 2006.

Terraciano, Kevin. *The Mixtecs of Colonial Oaxaca: Ñudzahui History, Sixteenth through Eighteenth Centuries.* Stanford: Stanford University Press, 2001.

Therborn, Göran. "The Rule of Capital and the Rise of Democracy." *New Left Review* 103 (1977): 3–41.

Thompson, E.P. *Whigs and Hunters: The Origin of the Black Act.* London: Allen Lane, 1975.

Thomson, Guy. "Bulwarks of Patriotic Liberalism: The National Guard, Philharmonic Corps, and Patriotic Juntas in Mexico, 1847–1888." *Journal of Latin American Studies* 22/1 (1990): 31–68.

with David LaFrance. *Patriotism, Politics, and Popular Liberalism in Nineteenth-Century Mexico: Juan Francisco Lucas and the Puebla Sierra.* Wilmington: Scholarly Resources Inc., 1999.

Thomson, Sinclair. *We Alone Will Rule: Native Andean Politics in the Age of Insurgency.* Madison: University of Wisconsin Press, 2002.

Thurner, Mark. *From Two Republics to One Divided: Contradictions of Postcolonial Nationmaking in Andean Peru.* Durham, NC: Duke University Press, 1997.

Tombs, Robert. *France 1814–1914.* New York: Longman, 1996.

Tucker Thompson, Angela. *Las otras guerras de México.* Guanajuato City: Ediciones La Rana, 1998.

Tutino, John. *From Insurrection to Revolution in Mexico: Social Bases of Agrarian Violence, 1750–1940.* Princeton: Princeton University Press, 1986.

"The Revolution in Mexican Independence: Insurgency and the Renegotiation of Property, Production, and Patriarchy in the Bajío, 1800–1855." *Hispanic American Historical Review* 78/3 (1998): 367–418.

"El desarrollo liberal, el patriarcado y la involución de la violencia social en el México porfirista: El crimen y la muerte infantil en el altiplano central." In *Don Porfirio presidente . . ., nunca omnipotente: Hallazgos, reflexiones y debates. 1876–1911.* Edited by Romana Falcón and Raymond Buve, 231–272. Mexico City: Universidad Iberoamericana, 1998.

Making a New World: Founding Capitalism in the Bajío and Spanish North America. Durham, NC: Duke University Press, 2011.

Tyler, Tom. *Why People Obey the Law.* Princeton: Princeton University Press, 2006.

Uribe-Uran, Victor. "The Great Transformation of Law and Legal Culture: 'The Public' and 'the Private' in the Transition from Empire to Nation in Mexico, Colombia, and Brazil, 1750–1850." In *Empire to Nation: Historical Perspectives on the Making of the Modern World.* Edited by Joseph W. Esherick, Hasan Kayali, and Eric Van Young, 95–148. Lanham, MD: Rowman & Littlefield Publishers, Inc., 2006.

Vanderwood, Paul. *Disorder and Progress: Bandits, Police, and Mexican Development.* Lincoln: University of Nebraska Press, 1981.

The Power of God against the Guns of Government: Religious Upheaval in Mexico at the Turn of the Nineteenth Century. Stanford: Stanford University Press, 1998.

Van Onselen, Charles. *Chibaro: African Mine Labour in Southern Rhodesia 1900–1933.* Johannesburg: Ravan Press, 2001.

Van Oosterhout, K. Aaron. "Confraternities and Popular Conservatism on the Frontier: Mexico's Sierra del Nayarit in the Nineteenth Century." *The Americas* 71/1 (2014): 101–130.

Van Young, Eric. *Hacienda and Market in Eighteenth-Century Mexico: The Rural Economy of the Guadalajara Region, 1675–1820*. Berkeley: University of California Press, 1982.

——. "Mexican Rural History since Chevalier: The Historiography of the Colonial Hacienda." *Latin American Research Review* 18/3 (1983): 5–61.

——. "Agrarian Rebellion and Defense of Community: Meaning and Collective Violence in Late-Colonial and Independence-Era Mexico," *Journal of Social History* 27/2 (1993): 245–269.

——. "The New Cultural History Comes to Old Mexico." *Hispanic American Historical Review* 79/2 (1999): 211–247.

——. *The Other Rebellion: Popular Violence, Ideology, and the Mexican Struggle for Independence, 1810–1821*. Stanford: Stanford University Press, 2001.

Vargas-Lobsinger, María. *La hacienda de "La Concha": Una empresa algodonera de La Laguna 1883–1917*. Mexico City: Universidad Nacional Autónoma de México, 1984.

Vázquez, Josefina Zoraida. "Centralistas, conservadores y monarquistas 1830–1853." In *El conservadurismo mexicano en el siglo XIX*. Edited by Will Fowler and Humberto Morales Moreno, 115–133. Puebla: Benemérita Universidad Autónoma de Puebla, 1999.

——. *Dos décadas de desilusiones: En busca de una fórmula adecuada de gobierno (1832–1854)*. Mexico City: El Colegio de México, 2009.

Viotti da Costa, Emilia. *Crowns of Glory, Tears of Blood: The Demerara Slave Rebellion of 1823*. New York: Oxford University Press, 1994.

——. *The Brazilian Empire: Myths and Histories*. Rev. ed. Chapel Hill: University of North Carolina Press, 2000.

Voekel, Pamela. *Alone Before God: The Religious Origins of Modernity in Mexico*. Durham, NC: Duke University Press, 2002.

Wahrman, Dror. *Imagining the Middle Class: The Political Representation of Class in Britain, c. 1780–1840*. Cambridge: Cambridge University Press, 1995.

Waldron, Jeremy. *The Law*. New York: Routledge, 1990.

Walker, Charles. *Smoldering Ashes: Cuzco and the Creation of Republican Peru, 1780–1840*. Durham, NC: Duke University Press, 1999.

Warren, Richard. *Vagrants and Citizens: Politics and the Masses in Mexico City from Colony to Republic*. Wilmington: SR Books, 2001.

Weber, Max. *Politics as a Vocation*. Trans. H.H. Gerth and C. Wright Mills. Philadelphia: Fortress Press, 1964.

Wells, Allen. *Yucatán's Gilded Age: Haciendas, Henequen, and International Harvester, 1860–1915*. Albuquerque: University of New Mexico Press, 1985.

Wiarda, Howard. *The Soul of Latin America: The Cultural and Political Tradition*. New Haven: Yale University Press, 2001.

Wolf, Eric. "Types of Latin American Peasantry: A Preliminary Discussion." *American Ethnologist* 57/3 (1955): 452–471.

——. "Closed Corporate Peasant Communities in Mesoamerica and Central Java." *Southwestern Journal of Anthropology* 13/1 (1957): 1–18.

Womack, Jr., John. *Zapata and the Mexican Revolution*. New York: Vintage Books, 1968.

Wood, Andy. *The Memory of the People: Custom and Popular Senses of the Past in Early Modern England*. Cambridge: Cambridge University Press, 2013.

Yannakakis, Yanna. *The Art of Being In-Between: Native Intermediaries, Indian Identity, and Local Rule in Colonial Oaxaca*. Duke University Press, 2008.

Zahler, Reuben. *Ambitious Rebels: Remaking Honor, Law, and Liberalism in Venezuela, 1780–1850.* Tucson: University of Arizona Press, 2013.

Zavala, Silvio. *Las instituciones jurídicas en la conquista de América.* 3rd ed. Mexico City: Editorial Porrua, 1988.

La encomienda indiana. 3rd ed. Mexico City: Editorial Porrúa, 1992.

Zea, Leopoldo. *Positivism in Mexico.* Trans. Josephine Schulte. Austin: University of Texas Press, 1974.

Zimmermann, Eduardo, ed. *Judicial Institutions in Nineteenth-Century Latin America.* London: Institute of Latin American Studies, 1999.

Zuleta, María Cecilia. *De cultivos y contribuciones: Agricultura y Hacienda Estatal en México en la 'Época de la Prosperidad'. Morelos y Yucatán 1870–1910.* Mexico City: Universidad Autónoma Metropolitana, 2006.

Index

Other Books in The Series

Lightning Source UK Ltd.
Milton Keynes UK
UKHW041643220219

337738UK00001B/37/P

9 781316 640784